Matthew's Gospel

BOOKS BY JAMES D. QUIGGLE

DOCTRINAL SERIES

Biblical History
Adam and Eve, a Biography and Theology
Angelology, a True History of Angels

Essays
Biblical Essays
Biblical Essays II
Biblical Essays III
Biblical Essays IV

Marriage and Family
Marriage and Family: A Biblical Perspective
Biblical Homosexuality
A Biblical Response to Same-gender Marriage

Doctrinal and Practical Christianity
First Steps, Becoming a Follower of Jesus Christ
A Christian Catechism (with Christopher McCuin)
Why and How to do Bible Study
Thirty-Six Essentials of the Christian Faith
The Literal Hermeneutic, Explained and Illustrated
The Old Ten In the New Covenant
Christian Doctrine, The Theology of Christianity
Christian Living, A Practical Theology of the Christian Life
Spiritual Gifts
Also Known As Tongues
Why Christians Should Not Tithe

Dispensational Theology
A Primer On Dispensationalism
Understanding Dispensational Theology
Covenants and Dispensations in the Scripture
Dispensational Soteriology
Dispensational Eschatology, An Explanation and Defense of the Doctrine
Rapture: A Bible Study on the Rapture of the New Testament Church

Antichrist, His Genealogy, Kingdom, and Religion

God and Man
God's Choices, Doctrines of Foreordination, Election, Predestination
God Became Incarnate
Life, Death, Eternity
Did Jesus Go To Hell?
Against Physicalism, Annihilationism, and Conditionalism
Ordo Salutis: The Way of Salvation

Small Group Bible Studies
Elementary Bible Principles (with Linda M. Quiggle)
Counted Worthy (with Linda M. Quiggle)

COMMENTARY SERIES

The Old Testament
A Private Commentary on the Bible: Judges
A Private Commentary on the Book of Ruth
A Private Commentary on the Bible: Esther
A Private Commentary on the Bible: Song of Solomon
A Private Commentary on the Bible: Daniel
A Private Commentary on the Bible: Jonah
A Private Commentary on the Bible: Habakkuk
A Private Commentary on the Bible: Haggai

The New Testament
James Quiggle Translation New Testament (JQTNT)

The Gospels and Acts
A Private Commentary on the Bible: Matthew's Gospel
A Private Commentary on the Bible: Mark's Gospel
A Private Commentary on the Bible: Luke 1–12
A Private Commentary on the Bible: Luke 13–24
A Private Commentary on the Bible: John 1–12
A Private Commentary on the Bible: John 13–21
A Private Commentary on the Bible: Acts 1–14
A Private Commentary on the Bible: Acts 15–28

Other Works On the Gospels
Four Voices, One Testimony (a Gospel Harmony)
Jesus Said "I Am"

The Parables and Miracles of Jesus Christ
The Passion and Resurrection of Jesus the Christ
The Christmas Story, As Told By God
Christmas Card Theology and the Bible

Pauline Letters
A Private Commentary on the Bible: 1 Corinthians
A Private Commentary on the Bible: 2 Corinthians (in 2025)
A Private Commentary on the Bible: Galatians
A Private Commentary on the Bible: Ephesians
A Private Commentary on the Bible: Philippians
A Private Commentary on the Bible: Colossians
A Private Commentary on the Bible: Thessalonians
A Private Commentary on the Bible: Pastoral Letters
A Private Commentary on the Bible: Philemon

General Letters
A Private Commentary on the Book of Hebrews
A Private Commentary on the Bible: James
A Private Commentary on the Bible: 1 Peter
A Private Commentary on the Bible: 2 Peter
A Private Commentary on the Bible: John's Epistles
A Private Commentary on the Bible: Jude

Revelation
A Private Commentary on the Bible: Revelation 1–7
A Private Commentary on the Bible: Revelation 8–16
A Private Commentary on the Bible: Revelation 17–22

REFERENCE SERIES
James Quiggle Translation New Testament (JQTNT)
Dictionary of Doctrinal Words
Old and New Testament Chronology (With David Hollingsworth)
(Also in individual volumes: Old Testament Chronology; New Testament Chronology)

Exposition of
Matthew's Gospel

James D. Quiggle

Copyright Page

Exposition of Matthew's Gospel

Copyright 2016 James D. Quiggle. All rights reserved.

Christicommunity edition 2025.

ISBN: 979-8-9877278-3-6

Originally published 2016 as *A Private Commentary on the Bible: Matthew's Gospel*

Translation of the New Testament is from *James Quiggle Translation New Testament.* Copyright 2024, James D. Quiggle

Bible versions that may be cited or quoted are listed below, sourced from PC Study Bible®, version 5, release 5.2. Copyright© 1988–2008, by BibleSoft, Inc.

Holman Christian Standard Bible (HCSB), Copyright 1999, 2000, 2002, 2003, by Holman Bible Publishers. Scripture quotations marked HCSB are from the Holman Christian Standard Bible®, Copyright © 1999, 2000, 2002, 2003 by Holman Bible Publishers. Used by permission. Holman Christian Standard Bible®, Holman CSB®, and HCSB® are federally registered trademarks of Holman Bible Publishers.

New King James Version® (NKJV). Copyright © 1982, 1983 by Thomas Nelson Inc. Used by permission. All rights reserved.

The Holy Bible: New International Version (NIV), Copyright 1973, 1978, 1984 by International Bible Society. Used by permission of Zondervan Publishing House. All rights reserved.

Contents

Preface ii
Introduction 1
Matthew One 13
Matthew Two 27
Matthew Three 41
Matthew Four 57
Matthew Five 83
Matthew Six 113
Matthew Seven 129
Matthew Eight 143
Matthew Nine 161
Matthew Ten 175
Matthew Eleven 189
Matthew Twelve 199
Matthew Thirteen 213
Matthew Fourteen 227
Matthew Fifteen 237
Matthew Sixteen 247
Matthew Seventeen 261
Matthew Eighteen 271
Matthew Nineteen 285
Matthew Twenty 299
Matthew Twenty-One 307
Matthew Twenty-Two 321
Matthew Twenty-Three 335
Matthew Twenty-Four 347
Matthew Twenty-Five 371
Matthew Twenty-Six 381
Matthew Twenty-Seven 407
Matthew Twenty-Eight 433
Appendix: Who Knew Jesus Was Deity? 447
Sources 471

Preface

The *Private Commentary* on the Old and New Testaments is my interpretation of the Bible, neither more nor less. I am responsible for the use made of all quoted and cited material.

The scope of the *Private Commentary* series is to bring the reader to a practical understanding of the scriptures. I explain and discuss each verse, idea, theme, and biblical truth as discovered in turn during the course of the exposition. My target audience is the Bible college/seminary student, Bible study/small group leader, Sunday School teacher, and local church Pastor. My point of view is a conservative theology. Other opinions concerning the Scripture are presented and discussed as I believe will profit the target audience. Bible students who desire to understand and apply the scriptures are invited to study the book with me and come to their own conclusions.

Introduction

The Author And His Text

The ancients believed Matthew was the author of the gospel bearing his name. According to the testimony of Papias (AD 70–155), as quoted by Eusebius (AD 260–340): "So then Matthew wrote the oracles in the Hebrew Language, and everyone interpreted them as he was able."[1]

A Greek gospel of Matthew was in existence at the time Papias wrote, because it is quoted in the Epistle of Barnabas, which was written ca. 70–131. Thus, it is reasonable to assume Papias knew the same gospel in the same Greek text that we know today. However, this does not explain the "oracles" written in the "Hebrew language" language.

The word "oracles," *logia*, could mean a collection of words, a collection of Christ's discourses, or even the collection of Old Testament sayings (*testimonia*) found in the gospel. However, the word *logia* was also used in ancient writings to indicate a work containing a narrative of events. The most likely sense of Papias is, "So then Matthew wrote the narrative [of Christ's life]."

This brings us to "in the Hebrew Language, and everyone interpreted them as he was able." The word "interpreted" has a basic meaning of "explain." Thus, "everyone explained Matthew's narrative as he was able." If this was the intended meaning, then Papias was not saying Matthew wrote in Hebrew and everyone translated from the Hebrew into Greek as he was able, but that Matthew wrote a narrative of Christ's life and everyone explained the narrative as he was able. How then to understand Papias? There are three options:

> Papias was speaking of a collection of Christ's sayings, written in Hebrew by Matthew, which others interpreted to develop Greek gospels from Matthew's Hebrew text.
>
> Papias had not seen a Hebrew Gospel of Matthew but was depending on tradition that this gospel was written in Hebrew.
>
> Papias substituted the purpose of Matthew's *logia*, "for the Hebrews" for the language of the people for whom it was

---

[1] Schaff, *NPNF*, 1:173.

Introduction

intended. "Interpreted" is to be understood in its basic meaning of "explained."

As to option one, the existing Greek texts of Matthew's Gospel do not show signs of having been translated from a Hebrew original, nor as having been written by more than one person (as would be the case if "everyone interpreted" a Hebrew original by translating it into Greek). The second option is likely, but doesn't explain what Papias wrote about the gospel. The third option seems best. When we consider that Matthew's Gospel was written *for* the Hebrews, Papias' statement may be understood so as to fit the historical facts. "So then Matthew wrote the narrative of Christ's life for the Hebrews, and everyone explained them as he was able." Matthew wrote his Gospel in Greek, with a view to proving to the Jews that Jesus was the Messiah.

Why would Matthew write his Gospel in the Greek language if the primary audience spoke Hebrew? Most Jews lived outside Palestine in countries where Latin and Greek were the primary languages; the Greek language (the *Koine* dialect) was the *lingua franca* of the day which almost everyone spoke; the Holy Spirit guided Matthew to write his Gospel in a language easily accessible to generations to come, gentiles as well as Hebrews.

Those who treat New Testament Scripture more as ancient literature and less as divinely inspired always try to relate the date of writing to the destruction of Jerusalem, AD 70. If the destruction of Jerusalem is mentioned, then, according to this view, it must have been written after AD 70. If Temple practices and worship are viewed as ongoing, then it must have been written prior to AD 70. Matthew gives opportunity for both views. Many modern scholars, believing that Matthew is redacting Mark's gospel, propose a late date for Matthew.

All of these views are highly imaginative and speculative. The testimony of the ancients is that Matthew was written about 30 years after the Ascension, However, David Alan Black (*Why Four Gospels?*) has proposed Matthew was written ca. AD 42, as the first evangelistic document for the New Testament church, and was used by Paul on his missionary journeys. His arguments are worth investigating.

As to provenance (where it was written) the answer is "unknown." All imaginative speculations assume historical circumstances based on the gospel's subject matter. Most who ponder this question assume a predominantly Jewish community in

Introduction

an urban environment, possibly in upper Galilee or Syria, perhaps at Antioch in Syria. The truth is, no one knows. The larger truth is that it does not matter. Matthew is writing about historical events, not current events. What does it matter, for example, where any of the several biographies of US president Harry Truman were written? Such biographies are historical accounts of Truman's life, not a reflection of the biographer's circumstances as he was writing. So, common sense tells us, should we view the historical accounts (Matthew, Mark, Luke, John) of the life of Christ.

The Four Gospels

The Four Gospels we have today were accepted as genuine accounts of the life of Christ early in the second century, as has been established through quotations and allusions in the writings of early church fathers and heretics. The authority of the Four Gospels was intrinsic, not imposed from without; therefore their authenticity was accepted without dispute (whereas other so-called gospels were rejected). The Four Gospels were first identified by the same names in use today by Irenaeus, AD 202, and Tertullian, AD 208. Testimony from the first and second centuries indicate Matthew was regarded as first written and John as last written. Matthew was the most quoted gospel in early Christianity.

There will always be a question concerning the sources of Matthew's gospel, re: the so-called "synoptic problem." Did Matthew depend on another gospel writer, such as Mark? Mark agrees with Matthew about 90 percent of the time. However 92 percent of that agreement is in the words of Christ.

A number of hypotheses have been proposed to resolve the synoptic problem. Two of the most popular are: a lost source document called "Q" (abbreviating the German *quelle* for "source"), assumed to be a reproduction of oral tradition; that Mark was first and both Luke and Matthew copied from Mark. No source document, whether the fabled "Q" or another, has ever been produced, and there is little agreement on what parts of Matthew came from a hypothetical source document or documents.

Oral tradition accounts for the differences between the Synoptics, but not the similarities. As to Matthew redacting Mark, it is not easy to see what object Matthew or any other of the evangelists could have had in mind by compiling a new gospel out of one or more of the others, which were acknowledged to be the works of apostles or their companions. The redaction theory does not account for either differences or similarities. If one used another

Introduction

as a source document, why aren't they (the Synoptics) more alike, and why are there glaring differences?

The better solution is that the Synoptics are three personal accounts written by three individuals, accounts that are based on living memory of the life of Christ—their own memories and those of others who were present during Jesus' public ministry—brought together through the promise of Christ concerning the Holy Spirit, "He will teach you all things, and bring to your remembrance all things that I said to you," John 14:26.

In an illustration, suppose three persons visit the same national park, take pictures, and keep a journal. When they each put together a narration and photos of their visit, some are of places they visited in common, some unique to them. The narration and photos of places visited in common are similar, but each person took the photos from his particular point of view, and narrated the scene according to what he found most interesting.

The similarities in the Synoptics indicate an eyewitness source: Matthew as a disciple of Jesus; Mark using Peter's preaching and reminiscences (according to Papias); Luke interviewing eyewitness and using some previously written accounts (according to Luke 1:2). John, writing about thirty years after Matthew, Mark, and Luke, focused on the Jerusalem ministry, but shows familiarity with the Synoptics. The differences indicate each wrote independent accounts; the similarities that they are writing about the same events. Thus, we have an accurate account of the life of Christ in four narratives, each written from its author's particular point of view, interests, and purposes. Nor should we forget the Holy Spirit who inspired the words the writers wrote, and through them fulfilled God's purpose in leaving his people these narratives of Christ's life.

The Four Gospels were not written so much for those who had known Christ, but for the generations to come, to accurately inform their faith. Saving knowledge of Christ as Savior comes from testimony, most often the testimony of those who are saved. An oral tradition of "Christ died to save me and you from our sins" would have—and does—proclaim the Gospel of Salvation worldwide. But the Christian's faith is more than salvation. The Four Gospels provide the basis for an informed faith, and the basis for the further testimony of the Acts and epistles (e.g., John 16:12–15).

Some of the similarities among the Synoptic witnesses are due

Introduction

to the ancient scribes who copied the original texts in the four centuries following AD 33. Some scribes amended the texts, so that similar events or discourses read the same. Often these changes appear only in the Byzantine texts (the texts used by the KJV/NKJV) versus the Western (Alexandrian, Egyptian, Vaticanus) texts. In my translation work, I have considered the opinions of textual scholars concerning these texts. When the scholar's views seemed justified for contextual reasons, I adopted those views. I have explained my choices in "translation notes."

The Gospels are in a genre known by the Greeks as *bíoi*, or biography.[1] The ancient Greco-Roman biographies were not the same as modern biographies. In substance they ranged from fictional accounts of persons about who little was known, but were held to deserve a biography, to historically accurate narratives reflecting the ideals and methods of ancient historiography.

The Four Gospels, especially John's Gospel, reflect the best characteristics of ancient historiography:

An accurate topography and chronology

Judicious selectivity in the materials presented

Explanatory narrative asides

Eyewitness testimony

Discourses and dialogues

The Greco-Roman biographies focused more on individuals than the political or military events that are the subject of most ancient and modern historiography. The best *bíoi*—and the Four Gospels are in that category—used historiographic methods to recount the real past of a real person.

The most significant difference between modern histories and biographies, and ancient histories and *bíoi*, is the narrative form (story-telling) the ancients used to hold the reader's attention while instructing them. The best histories and *bíoi* were developed from living eyewitness testimony.

In the view of the ancients, history could really only be written within the period in which the author could, if not himself an eyewitness, at least interview still living eyewitnesses. Similarly, it was biographies that also fulfilled this condition that tended to approximate historiography

---

[1] Bauckham, *Testimony*, 16–21, 93–112; and *Eyewitnesses*, 276–277.

Introduction

and would be expected to have the kind of accuracy that properly researched historiography would have.[1]

It was only when a long period of time separated the biographer from his subject that the biography could not be truly historical, and fictive elements crept in.

The Synoptic Gospels were written within thirty to forty years after Christ's death, thus within the lifetime of living witnesses. Internal evidence and ancient testimony suggest Mark's Gospel was written circa AD 50–55, Matthew's Gospel circa AD 58–60, Luke's Gospel circa AD 58–62, and John's Gospel circa AD 95–96.[2] Each was created by the Holy Spirit for the purpose of preaching and teaching Christ to subsequent generations, until he comes again.

(Black suggests, and I think it worth considering, that Paul, after using Matthew's gospel [written ca. AD 42], had Luke write a gospel for gentiles, ca. AD 58–62. Paul then had Peter, in Rome [Paul was in Rome as a prisoner of Rome], review what Luke had written, prior to its publication. Peter's review resulted in a series of lectures [reported by Papias in *Fragments*] which resulted in the gospel we know as Mark, AD 66/67. I consider Black's arguments compelling.)

Because I accept the Four Gospels as historically accurate *bíoi*, I will interpret the Gospel According to Matthew as an independent account by the disciple and apostle Matthew, aka "Levi," a former tax-collector, recruited by Jesus at Matthew 9:9.

Structure Of Matthew's Gospel

Although an outline of Matthew is easily accomplished, an analysis of the structure is not so easily determined because of the large variety of structural elements.[3] Moreover, the narrative is not consistently chronological. The best idea concerning Matthew's structure is that he has collected, arranged and presented the material topically, in a series of alternating words and works, without imposing some type of unifying structural scheme.

The following is notable.[4] The infancy narratives seem to be structured to reflect the experience of Israel. The nation attained redemption through a sojourn in Egypt and a call out of Egypt.

---

[1] Bauckham, *Testimony*, 19, 20.
[2] Hollingsworth, *Chronology*, 198, 200, 205.
[3] Hagner, *Matthew 1–13*, li.
[4] Bock, *According to Scripture*, 64.

Introduction

Matthew also uses five Old Testament citations in the infancy narratives that point to Jesus as the promised messiah.

Matthew 1:22 (Isaiah 7:14)
Matthew 2:5 (Micah 5:2)
Matthew 2:15 (Hosea 11:1)
Matthew 2:17 (Jeremiah 31:15)
Matthew 2:23 (no specific Old Testament text; see comments at 2:23)

In the infancy narratives Matthew also explains who Jesus is in terms of genealogy and geography. He is a descendant of Abraham and David, who is the promised Emmanuel, "God with us." He is connected with important locations: Bethlehem in Judea, Egypt, Ramah, and Nazareth.

In the body of his gospel, Matthew uses five discourses of Jesus words alternating with narrative blocks of Jesus' works.[1] In Matthew (unlike John) the discourses are not specifically related to the works narratives. These five narratives are:

The Sermon on the Mount, chapters 5–7
Mission directives to the twelve, chapter 10
Parables of the kingdom, chapter 13
Discipleship and discipline, chapter 18
Eschatology, chapters 24–25

Matthew's Gospel is divided into three parts (1:1–4:16; 4:17–16:20; 16:21–28:20) by the phrase, *apó tóte ērxato ho Iēsoús*, "from that time Jesus began," at 4:17 and 16:21.[2] Chapters 1:1–4:16 might be termed the preparation for ministry, beginning with Jesus' birth, through his baptism, temptation in the wilderness, and start of the first Galilean ministry. Chapters 4:17–16:20 are Jesus' announcement to Israel the messianic kingdom is at hand and the character of the Kingdom. Chapters 16:21–28:20 are Jesus preparing of his apostles to carry on his mission after his ascension. Of course, this is a broad outline, not hard delimiters confining his ministry to one thing or another. For example, Jesus does not stop offering the messianic kingdom to the Jews until their final rejection through his arrest, trials, and crucifixion. *Apó tóte ērxato ho Iēsoús* tells the reader when the focus of his ministry changes. (This does

---

[1] Hagner, *Matthew 1–13*, li.
[2] Ibid., i–liii.

Introduction

not mean Israel has permanently lost the Davidic-Messianic kingdom, or that the Davidic-Messianic kingdom has been given to the New Testament church. National ethnic Israel will receive the kingdom at Christ's second advent, as prophesied, e.g., Zechariah 14:9.)

Some find a chiastic structure of alternating narrative and discourse: the narratives in chapters 1–4 relate to the narratives in 26–28; the discourses in chapters 5–7 relate to the discourses in chapters 23–25; and so on. The chiastic structure, however, is very arbitrary, and likely unreliable for interpretive purposes.

The Character Of Matthew's Gospel

Matthew uses over sixty explicit quotations from the Old Testament, and many more allusions. A distinctive feature is the "fulfillment quotations," which is Matthew's interpretive use of the Old Testament to show that the words and works of Jesus prove he is the messiah. Old Testament quotes in Matthew are from Genesis, Exodus, Leviticus, Deuteronomy, Psalms, Hosea, Micah, and Zechariah, with allusions to Daniel and possibly Ezekiel and Haggai.

Matthew uses the words "fulfill," "fulfilled," "spoken," and "it is written" to indicate these Old Testament quotations. Through these quotations Matthew develops the prophetic sense certain Old Testament scriptures have in reference to the coming messiah. (The New Testament letters writers did the same.)

The original readers were probably part of a predominantly Hebrew Christian community. This conclusion is based upon the subject matter of the gospel, not on speculation about date and place written. Matthew deliberately makes use of the Old Testament, which would have been important to the earliest believers, who for about 20 years after the crucifixion were predominantly those converted from Judaism (Hebrews or gentile proselytes). Matthew's themes reflect this view.

Matthew is interested in the kingdom of heaven, or as the Greek text expresses the concept, the kingdom of the heavens. The kingdom of the heavens is the reign of God through Jesus Christ. In relation to the gospel proclamation, Christ's reign on earth will be the fulfillment of the kingdom promised to Israel through King David's heir, 2 Samuel 7:12. Matthew's Gospel presents the reality of that doctrine.

A decidedly christological approach, explaining in detail the person and works of Jesus the Christ, the Son of God.

Introduction

Matthew prefers the titles "Lord," "Son of David," and "Christ."

The importance of righteousness and discipleship is emphasized.

Jesus' faithfulness to the Law of Moses is presented.

Grace in the proclamation of the "good news" is emphasized.

The word "church" appears in the gospels only in Matthew.

Matthew has a special interest in eschatology as applied to the Jews (not the New Testament church).

At the time Matthew's Gospel was written, evangelization through the "good news" was being taken throughout the gentile world, as commanded, Matthew 28:19; Acts 1:8. However, in the period of time Matthew is writing about, AD 30–33, the gospel restricts the offer of the gospel message to Hebrews living within the land of Israel.

Matthew 10:5–6, These twelve Jesus sent out and commanded them, saying: "Do not go into the way of the gentiles, and do not enter a city of the Samaritans. But go rather to the lost sheep of the house of Israel."

Matthew 15:24, Jesus said, "I was not sent except to the lost sheep of the house of Israel."

A close examination of the places Jesus visited (reviewing each of the Four Gospels) indicates he went to every ancient tribal territory with the possibly exception Simeon, which was located within the territory of Judah.[1] In the first century some of these ancient tribal territories were now gentile territories, thus contact with gentiles was unavoidable. But Jesus went to those places (e.g., Samaria, Gadara, the Decapolis, Tyre, others) because there were Israelis living in these long-ago tribal lands, and he was sent to the lost sheep of the house of Israel.

Some scholars make an issue of this seeming conflict between particularism and universalism in the gospel offer. They describe the church and Israel as "in obviously painful tension" in Matthew.[2] The point of this debate by skeptics is to establish a historical setting in which the gospel was written in the second century,

---

[1] *Holman Quick Source Bible Atlas*, 144.
[2] Hagner, *Matthew 1–13*, lxvii.

Introduction

wherein Jewish believers are supposed to feel disfranchised by the increasingly gentile Church.

Does Matthew's limitation on the gospel proclamation reflect the "relics of the historical tradition" (i.e., the oral tradition of the gospel story)? Or perhaps the limitation "indicates a contemporary limitation upon the mission of Matthew's community" (i.e., the people Matthew was writing for were mainly Jewish and thus Matthew's main objective is to evangelize Jews)? In these views, Matthew addressed this supposed second century tension in his gospel.

However, these and similar questions suggest a conflict where none is present in the gospel itself. As noted above, Matthew is writing about a particular period of history, AD 30–33. He is accurately recording Jesus' instructions to his disciples within that period of history, giving his gospel authenticity and credibility, thus affirming its accuracy.

The Old Testament messianic message always included sending the good news of salvation to the gentiles. However, the timing of that proclamation was always presented in terms of after the appearance of messiah. The Old Testament message was, messiah would come, bring salvation to the Jews, establish his kingdom, and then salvation would be preached to the gentiles. Peter notes this prophetic program in his Pentecost message, Acts 2:16–39. In Acts 15:7–11, fifteen years after Pentecost, James appeals to Peter's Pentecost message and the same prophetic tradition, Acts 15:13–21.

This particular understanding of the Old Testament accounts for the delay of about ten years between the resurrection/ascension and the salvation of the gentile Cornelius. What was not specifically revealed in the Old Testament messianic prophesies was Messiah's two advents and the church age between the advents, Ephesians 3:3–6. Direct action by Christ and the Holy Spirit was required to overcome this misunderstanding, re: Christ sent Peter to the gentiles, and then appointed an apostle, Paul, to preach salvation to the gentiles. (Paul's ministry gradually shifted from Jew to gentile over the approximately 15 years from Acts 13–28.)

Matthew's gospel reflects the Old Testament prophetic understanding of the messianic salvation message, because it accurately reports the historical context of the time period of Jesus' public ministry, AD 30–33. The messiah came first to Israel, then to the gentiles. Matthew's gospel recognizes the salvation message

Introduction

was for the gentiles also, e.g., Jesus heals the gentile woman's daughter, 15:21–28. After Jesus earthly mission to the Jews was completed, i.e., after his death/resurrection and just before his ascension, Matthew records Jesus' commission to his disciples to take the salvation message to Jerusalem, Samaria, and the gentiles, Acts 1:8; Matthew 28:19.

In writing his gospel, Matthew is not responding to some then-current tension between Jews and gentiles in his church community. He is faithfully recording the biblical message as prophesied in the Old Testament: messiah comes first to the Jews, then to the gentiles. All the gospels reflect this prophetic tradition. Matthew is simply more explicit, because at the time of his writing the Christian community was still predominantly Hebrew.

If Matthew was writing in Palestine prior to the destruction of the Temple and dispersion of the Jews (i.e., prior to AD 70), then his audience was primarily Hebrew. Compare with John's Gospel at a time, about AD 95, when the church's population was predominantly gentile. The same limitation is seen, but not stated, in John's Gospel, e.g., Jesus never did speak to the Greeks seeking an audience at John 12:20–21.

Matthew is not anti-Semitic, as some would suppose. The harshness of Jesus' language toward the religious leaders is an accurate account of the words Jesus spoke, and the religious tensions then-present in Judaism. Matthew was relating what happened, not creating an anti-Jewish polemic.

The Translation

The reader will notice my translation views many events and conversations in what might charitably be described as awkward English. For example, Matthew 8:18, "Now Jesus, having seen a great crowd around him" or 8:23, "And having entered the boat," or 9:14, "Then came to him John's disciples." Matthew used certain Greek verb tenses to give the reader an I-am-there-in-the-moment feeling as he and others experienced the moment. My translation attempts to communicate that in-the-moment feeling. I also tend to a more literal translation that other versions. My desire was for the reader to hear the words the way I think the original listeners, and later readers, would have heard the words. Translation notes explain why I made some choices instead of others.

Matthew One

Translation Matthew 1:1-6

1 Book of the genealogy of Jesus Christ, Son of David, Son of Abraham.

2 Abraham begot Isaac; and Isaac begot Jacob; and Jacob begot Judah and his brothers; 3 and Judah begot Perez and Zerah of Tamar; and Perez begot Hezron; and Hezron begot Ram; 4 and Ram begot Amminadab; and Amminadab begot Nahshon; and Nahshon begot Salmon; 5 and Salmon begot Boaz of Rahab; and Boaz begot Obed of Ruth; and Obed begot Jesse; 6 and Jesse begot David the king [v. 6 continued below]

EXPOSITION

Matthew begins his "good news" (gospel) with the word *bíblos*, book. By *bíblos* he doesn't mean the entire Gospel of Matthew, but the genealogy section that begins his Gospel. The first twenty-five verses are the "book of the genealogy of Jesus Christ, Son of David, Son of Abraham."

The term "son of" throughout the Bible is used in three ways: literally as by birth; figuratively, meaning a person possesses the moral characteristics of the person or thing he/she is a "son of"; as a title. In v. 1 Son of David and Son of Abraham are titles. Son of David is an application of 2 Samuel 7:12-13, 16. Son of Abraham is an application of Genesis 15:4; 17:19; cf. Galatians 3:16.

The purpose of the genealogy is to present Jesus's claim as messianic heir to the covenants God made with Abraham and David. The Abrahamic Covenant established messiah's claim to the land, Genesis 17:8, as an everlasting possession, and prophesied the messiah would be of Abraham's lineage, from whom "kings shall come." The Davidic Covenant promised an everlasting throne and king from King David's lineage.

Genealogies, as the Old Testament shows (e.g., 1 Chronicles 1-9), were important to the Jews. Matthew's purpose is to connect Jesus of Nazareth, "the one named Christ" (v. 16), with the Abrahamic and Davidic promises of the messiah. He creates three sections of fourteen generations each, showing the descent of the promise, first through Abraham's descendants, then through the royal line of King David.

Matthew One

The reason for three groups of fourteen generations is not clear. Some suggest Matthew was using the ancient discipline of *Gematria:* assigning numerical values to Hebrew letters to form some sort of code or interpretation. For example, the sum of the numeric values assigned to the consonants of David's name is fourteen, a symbolic number (Hebrew was originally a language of consonants; in its later history vowels in the form of "points" were added above or below the consonants to aid pronunciation).

Wholly apart from *Gematria*, which is a non-biblical game of numbers, there is legitimate symbolic meaning in the Bible's use of numbers. The number fourteen is composed of 7X2. Seven reflects completeness and two reflects witness, thus a complete witness. Based on this interpretation of fourteen, the literal meaning would be the time of preparation for messiah is completed.[1]

Of course, some perspective is required, lest the interpretation wander away from biblical realities. There are three groups of fourteen, resulting in 14X3=42. Forty-two is 7x6. The number six indicates something short of completion (one less than seven), the number three means perfection. Three generations of fourteen could mean a complete witness of man's imperfection; not, one supposes, the message Matthew intended to communicate. One must exercise a great deal of caution when using numerology, even Scripture-based numerology, as an interpretive tool.

Matthew 1:1–6 lists fourteen generations (cf. 1 Chronicles 1, 2) between Abraham and David. The count is fourteen names in each of the other divisions, vv. 6–11; 12–17, but each of those divisions leaves out one or more generations. Culturally this was not abnormal. Matthew uses the Greek word *gennáō*, "begot, to be begotten,"[2] as a reflection of the Hebrew cultural reference to any descendant in a person's lineage, whether the father, grandfather, or some more distant relative in the genealogical line. Neither Hebrew nor Greek has words specifically for grandfather, great-grandfather, etc. Thus, Abraham was the literal father of Isaac, who was the father of Jacob, who was renamed Israel, and through his twelve sons was the father of Israel. In the Hebrew language (Greek also) Abraham could be described as the father of Jacob, or Jacob as the son of Abraham. All those physically descended from Jacob/Israel are the children of Israel. At Deuteronomy 1:8, Moses

---

[1] Bullinger, *Number in Scripture*; Davis, *Biblical Numerology.*
[2] Zodhiates, *WSDNT*, s. v. "1080."

says to the children of Jacob/Israel, "take possession of the land the Lord swore to give to your fathers Abraham, Isaac, and Jacob and their descendants after them" (HCSB). Abraham and Isaac, though Jacob's father and grandfather, are named fathers of Israel, as well as the proper father Jacob.

In v. 8, Joram is said to have begotten Uzziah, but 1 Chronicles 3:11–12 says Joram begot Ahaziah, and Ahaziah begot Amaziah, and Amaziah begot Azariah (another Old Testament name for Uzziah). Today we would say Joram was the great-great grandfather of Uzziah, but from the Hebrew (and biblical) point of view, because Joram begat Uzziah's ancestors he was the one who had begotten Uzziah.

David is counted in both section one and two, and the generation during the seventy years of the Babylonian Captivity is counted as a generation. Matthew's purpose is theological, not statistical, so he adjust the generations to fit his purpose, and in keeping with the conventions of the language and culture.

Together, the three genealogy sections show the rise of the house of David to power, its fall from power, and its reappearance in the person of Jesus.[1] This is the line of inheritance from Abraham to David, establishing Jesus' right to the Davidic throne. Jesus' physical and royal lineage establishes him as the rightful heir of Abraham and David, thereby proclaiming him to be the promised messiah.

Including a woman in a genealogy was unusual, but God has always elevated women to their rightful place as spiritually equal to males. There are four women in Matthew's genealogy. In the first section there are three: Tamar, Rahab, and Ruth. Tamar pretended to be a prostitute to achieve her goals. Rahab and Ruth were gentiles, the first an innkeeper in Jericho, the second a Moabite; both believed in the God of Israel. God's plan of salvation was more than national and Davidic. His plan included people from all sorts of backgrounds and races, as promised in his covenant with Abraham, Genesis 17:5, "I [YHWH] have made you a father of many nations," and "count the stars if you are able to number them . . . so shall your descendants be."

Translation Matthew 1:6–11

6 [continued] and David the king begot Solomon of her of Uriah;

---

[1] Bock, *According to Scripture*, 56.

7 and Solomon begot Rehoboam; and Rehoboam begot Abijah; and Abijah begot Asa; 8 and Asa begot Jehoshaphat; and Jehoshaphat begot Joram; and Joram begot Uzziah; 9 and Uzziah begot Jotham; and Jotham begot Ahaz; and Ahaz begot Hezekiah; 10 and Hezekiah begot Manasseh; and Manasseh begot Amon; and Amon begot Josiah. 11 and Josiah begot Jeconiah and his brothers at the time of the relocation to Babylon.

EXPOSITION

By counting David in this second set, Matthew achieves fourteen generations, David to Josiah (Jeconiah properly belongs to the third section). In the second set, the names of Ahaziah, Amaziah, Joash, Jehoaha, and Jehoikim are left out. Matthew's decision to construct three genealogies of fourteen generations each required some names be left out. The fourth woman is mentioned, "her of Uriah" (Bathsheba), a woman who had committed adultery. One need not be perfect to be of use to the Lord.

Translation Matthew 1:12–17

12 And after the relocation to Babylon Jeconiah begot Shealtiel; and Shealtiel begot Zerubbabel; 13 and Zerubbabel begot Abiud; and Abiud begot Eliakim, and Eliakim begot Azor; 14 and Azor begot Zadok; and Zadok begot Achim; and Achim begot Eliud; 15 and Eliud begot Eleazar; and Eleazar begot Matthan; and Matthan begot Jacob; 16 and Jacob begot Joseph the husband of Mary, of whom was born Jesus, the one named Christ. 17 Therefore all the generations from Abraham to David were fourteen generations; and from David until the relocation to Babylon fourteen generations; and from the relocation to Babylon to the Christ fourteen generations.

EXPOSITION

The third section properly begins with the "relocation to Babylon," a literal rendering of what is generally known as the seventy year captivity of Israel during the time of the Babylonian Empire. Many Hebrews were taken to Babylon city. Daniel chapters 1–6 reveal something of conditions during that captivity.

Jeconiah to Joseph is thirteen names, thus the two generations in the captivity (70 years/35 years to a generation) are counted as one. If Jesus is counted as one generation, then the list of fourteen is Jeconiah to Jesus.

This last fourteen generations, from the Babylonian Captivity to Jesus approximates the 69 sevens in Daniel's prophecy, 9:25–26, "Know therefore and understand, that from the going forth of the command to restore and build Jerusalem until Messiah the Prince, there shall be seven sevens and sixty-two sevens" (thus 69 sevens), "the market place will be built again, and the wall, even in times of distress" (the seven sevens) and "after sixty-two sevens Messiahs will be cut off" (the crucifixion).

The full explanation of a "seven" in Daniel's prophecy is complicated, but the essence of the matter is that for this particular prophecy the Bible uses a 360 day year, and one group of sevens equals 2,520 sunset to sunset days. The sum of sixty-nine sevens is 173,880 days, which when divided by the number of days in a sidereal year, 365.264 days, gives the value 476 years, a value that fulfills Daniel's prophecy (from 444 BC to AD 33; there is no year zero between BC and AD). A more detailed explanation may be found in either of my books, *A Private Commentary on the Bible: Daniel*, or *Antichrist, His Genealogy, Kingdom, and Religion*.

Matthew carefully distinguishes Joseph as Mary's husband ("Joseph the husband of Mary") but not Jesus' father: "of whom [i.e., of Mary] was born Jesus, the one named Christ." Jesus' royal and legal inheritance comes through Joseph's descent from David through David's son Solomon (1:16),

Jesus' royal and legal inheritance also comes through Mary's descent from David through David's son Nathan, 2 Samuel 5:14; 1 Chronicles 14:4. If one compares Matthew 1:15–16 with Luke 3:23, 24, 31 it is apparent Luke gives Mary's descent. Joseph's descent in Matthew is from Matthan through his son Jacob. But Luke says Joseph descended from Matthat through his son Heli; thus Heli was Mary's father.

Jesus' biological physical connection with humanity comes through Mary alone, Luke 1:31–35. Jesus Christ the God-man is fully qualified to inherit the Abrahamic Covenant and the Davidic Covenant, and be the representative of humanity before God.

The lack of the definite article at the mention of "Christ" in v. 16 indicates it is being used as a name rather than a title, but in v. 17 the definite article is used, showing Matthew understood its meaning as a title. "Christ" is the Greek form of the Hebrew "messiah" or "anointed," the one God has appointed to be King and Savior, cf. Psalm 2:2.

Translation Matthew 1:18

18 Now of Jesus Christ the genealogy was in this manner. Mary his mother was betrothed to Joseph. Before they came together, she was pregnant from the Holy Spirit.

TRANSLATION NOTE

In v. 18 the Byzantine manuscripts have *génnēsis*, birth.[1] The Western manuscripts have *génesis*, origin.[2] The word *génnēsis* has to do with birth, whereas *génesis* has to do with genealogy. Because Matthew is explaining the genealogy of Jesus, *génesis* seems the better choice, and it is the word used at 1:1 in both Byzantine and Western manuscripts: "Book of the genealogy of" etc. The word *génnēsis*, birth, came to be used in early Christian literature to describe the nativity of Christ. The similarity of the words in sound and letters led to the one being substituted for the other by the scribes copying Matthew's Gospel.[3]

EXPOSITION

In his twenty-five verse book of genealogy, Matthew is telling the story of the origin of the messiah. The specific story of Joseph and Mary continues the genealogy of Jesus the Christ from v. 1. Matthew understands the incarnation through virgin birth, but he addresses that only briefly, at vv. 17, 18, and 23.

Mary was betrothed to Joseph. A betrothal in Hebrew culture was as binding as marriage. The same fidelity was required, and the same dissolution. The Mishnah, (compiled between 200 BC and AD 200), m. *Ketuboth* 5:2 and m. *Nedarim* 10:5, states the marriage was to be consummated within a year of the betrothal. If there was infidelity within that year a divorce was required to dissolve the betrothal. A father could legally betroth his daughter while she was still a girl (Hebrew: *nà ărâ*) at the age of twelve years and a day old, m. *Kiddushin* 2:1. At the age of twelve years, six months, and one day a *nà ărâ* became a woman (Hebrew: *bogereth*). Mary could have been as young as thirteen when Jesus was born; older than fifteen would have been unusual.

(Luke's Gospel was written AD 58–62. Assuming AD 60 for its publication, and assuming Mary was one of Luke's eyewitnesses—

---

[1] Zodhiates, *WSDNT*, s. v. "1083."

[2] Ibid., s. v. "1078."

[3] Metzger, *Textual*, 7.

likely, for much of what Luke reports of the conception and birth could come only from Mary—then if Mary was fourteen years old when Jesus was born (assuming 5 BC) she was 79 when Luke published his gospel, a very old age for the times; but the church had cared for her from AD 33, Acts 1:14.)

A betrothal agreement between parents and the prospective husband usually took place when the girl was between twelve and thirteen years of age, and was expected to be consummated about a year from the betrothal date.[1] The betrothed possessed the rights of husband and wife,[2] cohabitation and sexual activity excepted, so the only way to break a betrothal was a divorce.

Matthew says that during the betrothal period, but before the marriage celebration and subsequent sexual consummation, Joseph discovered Mary was pregnant. How and when the pregnancy took place is not explained by Matthew, but is explained by Luke 1:26–38.

Joseph naturally assumed the pregnancy was the result of Mary having sex with another man, so he decided to divorce her. When Mary told Joseph him he did not believe her pregnancy was God's work. Matthew protects the sanctity of the virgin birth, telling us what Mary would have said, but could not prove: her pregnancy was a result of the power of the Holy Spirit, "Before they came together, she was pregnant from the Holy Spirit."

Excursus: When Did Mary Tell Joseph She Was Pregnant

Based on secular history and Luke 3:1–3, Elizabeth and Mary became pregnant in 6 BC, and the births of John Baptist and Jesus took place in 5 BC. (Based on the same secular history, it is also reasonable these events took place 7 or 6 BC.) The discussion below assumes John and Jesus were conceived in 6 BC and born in 5 BC. The discussion below is a slightly edited extract from chapter two of my book, *God Became Incarnate*.

Luke says John Baptist's father Zecharias was a priest in the division of Abijah, known as the eighth division. The priests served in the temple in a rotation known as courses or divisions. David the king, with Zadok and Ahimelech the priests, divided the sons of Aaron into twenty-four divisions, 1 Chronicles 24:1–19. Each priest served in their division two times during the year, for one week

---

[1] Hagner, *Matthew 1–13*, 17.
[2] So Alexander, *Matthew*, 12, referencing Philo and Maimonides.

Matthew One

each time, from one Sabbath to the next. But during the Feasts all the divisions served together.

The divisions began their rotation at the start of the religious year, Nisan 1 (Nisan corresponds to the modern March-April). Let us assume Elizabeth became pregnant with John Baptist in June 6 BC. Zecharias' normal rotation in 6 BC was May 22–29. He would have served during Pentecost with all the priests (May 15–22) and then served his regular course.[1] The scriptures relating to the eighth division served by Zecharias in 6 BC are Luke 1:5; 1 Chronicles 24:3–5, 10.

According to Luke, Elizabeth became pregnant after Zecharias finished his temple service. It would have taken Zecharias some time to explain what had happened: he had to write it out. Then Elizabeth had to believe; then they had to have one or more times of sexual relations; then conception. The pregnancy occurred sometime in June, 6 BC.

The newly-pregnant Mary visited Elizabeth in the sixth month of Elizabeth's pregnancy, December, 6 BC. Now, women in that time were not allowed to travel alone, prevented by both custom and rabbinical law. How did Mary get from Nazareth, in the north, to Jerusalem, in the south—a trip of about 85–100 miles (depending on route taken), three to four days walking—without travelling alone? The Feast of Dedication (also called "Hanukkah" and "Lights") is held in mid-December. Mary could have travelled to Jerusalem with relatives attending this Feast, met with her relative Zecharias, and from there went with Zecharias as he returned home, in the hill country, to a city of Judah (Luke 1:39).

Let us suppose Mary conceived a day or two before she left for the Feast of Dedication, which in 6 BC was December 6–13. She made the trip to Jerusalem with her male relatives in three days, so she left December 2 or 3. She spent the next eight days celebrating the Feast. Then she traveled with Zecharias one or two days to his house, arriving December 15. Using these assumptions, Mary was about two weeks pregnant when she arrived at Elizabeth's house, Luke 1:41–45. Mary probably arrived at Elizabeth's house the fifteenth of December.

Luke 1:56 says Mary stayed about three months then returned to her house. The Feast of Dedication in 6 BC ended December 13,

---

[1] Hollingsworth, *Chronology*, Appendix 18.

Matthew One

Passover was March 20, 5 BC: about three months.

The normal gestation period for a baby boy is 270–271 days. If Elizabeth conceived in June, 6 BC, then John Baptist was born about 270 days later, in March, 5 BC. If Elizabeth conceived between June 8–30, 6 BC, John would have been born at the earliest on March 5 or 6, 5 BC, and at the latest on March 26 or 27, 5 BC, Luke 1:57–58. The Passover was Nisan 14, i.e., March 20 in 5 BC. John was probably born on March 5 or 6 because Zecharias was present. Mary, then, was present when John was born. Mary and Zecharias would have left for Jerusalem for the Passover not later than March 18 or 19.

Returning to the exposition.

When Mary arrived in late March 5 BC she was three to four months pregnant. Although her clothes could have hidden the pregnancy from all others, it would have been easy to reveal her pregnancy to Joseph. Here, then, in late March or early April, 5 BC, is when Matthew 1:18–24 took place. Mary married Joseph upon her return from visiting Elizabeth, in late March or April, 5 BC, and gave birth in late August or early September.

To complete the story of the pregnancy: if Mary conceived between December 1–3, 6 BC then a normal 270–271 day pregnancy means her gestation period would have ended at the earliest about August 30, 5 BC. Normal variations in the gestation period would allow for a late August to early September, 5 BC birth. The biblical and secular data supports the 5 BC date.

Translation Matthew 1:19–21

19 But Joseph her husband, being righteous, and not willing to expose her publicly, desired to secretly divorce her. 20 But these things he having thought (his spirit was agitated), behold, a messenger of the Lord in a dream appeared to him, saying, "Joseph, son of David, do not fear to receive Mary as your wife, for that conceived in her is from the Holy Spirit. 21 "She will bear a son, and you will call his name Jesus. For he will save his people from their sins.

TRANSLATION NOTES

In v. 20 I have translated the first clause, "But these things he having thought (his spirit was agitated)." The word translated "having thought" is *enthuméomai*. This is a compound word from *en*, "in," and *thumós*, which means "will, desire, emotion, passion, indignation, anger, wrath"; a wide range of meaning.[1] Put together, *en + thumós* means "the mind, thought, but also anger, wrath, indignation, a spirit that is aroused."[2] In the grammatical form used in v. 20, an aorist passive participle, *enthuméomai* means "to think upon." I wanted to also communicate the implication of "a spirit that is aroused," so I included in parenthesis the phrase, "his spirit was agitated." Not necessarily agitated in a negative sense, but I think Joseph was, to use a common phrase, full of conflicting emotions.

In v. 20 I have translated the Greek *ággelos*, "messenger," rather than transliterate it, "angel."

EXPOSITION

Matthew names Joseph as Mary's husband before the consummation, based on the cultural rules regarding betrothal. Did Joseph privately consider (think within himself) of divorcing her, or did he want to divorce her in a private (not public) manner? The text, a "verb adverb verb" construction, might bear either meaning. The most likely meaning is that Joseph was thinking of Deuteronomy 24:1. He wanted to write out a certificate of divorce in private so as to avoid a public trial for infidelity.

The cause of a divorce would become apparent soon enough. Joseph knew he was protected from scandal, because Mary had been gone three months. As to Mary, some might assume she had been raped before her visit to Elizabeth, which would account for her absence. She only returned, they would say (we can imagine "them" saying), to relieve Joseph of the scandal.

Joseph is noted as being righteous. The meaning is that he followed the Law of Moses. Not perfectly, of course, but his intent was to conduct himself according to the requirements of the Law. Joseph, being a righteous man, did not assume Mary had committed adultery. Her story, see Luke 1:26–38, would have seemed incredible, but also have given him pause. Mary and Joseph had known about each other for many years. He was about thirty years of age, she about thirteen (these ages were norms for marriage stretching back over many centuries in many cultures). He had seen and admired her character and probably spoken to her. That he wanted to marry her (or had agreed to an arranged

---

[1] Zodhiates, *WSDNT*, s. v. 2372."
[2] Ibid., s. v. "1760."

marriage; both are equally probable), indicated she had a similar attitude toward righteousness as he (as witnessed in Luke's Gospel). Joseph could not imagine why Mary would fabricate such a story, yet her story was difficult to believe. His heart was willing, but his faith was weak. He needed more than Mary's testimony.

Joseph didn't act in haste, and while he pondered his course of action God sent a "messenger," the Greek *ággelos*, to advise him, in a dream during sleep, v. 24. This particular messenger was one of the spirit beings known as angels. Joseph was addressed as the son of David, which would have guided him to make the mental connection to Mary's narrative of Gabriel's announcement, and connect what Mary and the angel were saying to the Old Testament messianic promises of salvation, which the angel clearly stated in v. 21 as the name *Iēsoús*, and its meaning.

The Greek *Iēsoús* is transliterated from the Hebrew *Yēshūa*, "Joshua," which means "YHWH is my help." The English pronunciation is of *Iēsoús* is "Jesus," a transliteration of the Greek word. The messenger of YHWH explained the meaning of *Iēsoús*: he will save his people from their sins. Matthew is writing in Greek, but Joseph, Mary, their family, and friends spoke Hebrew, or the similar Aramaic, in their homes and village. They all may have called Jesus by his Hebrew name Joshua. Because the New Testament writings, including Matthew, were written in Greek, the name has been handed down as *Iēsoús*, Jesus.

Translation Matthew 1:22–25

22 So all this was done that it might be fulfilled which was spoken by the Lord through the prophet, saying: 23 "Behold, the virgin shall be with child, and bear a son, and they shall call his name Immanuel," which is translated, "God with us." 24 Then Joseph, being aroused from sleep, did as the messenger of the Lord commanded him and took to him his wife, 25 and did not know her until she had brought forth her firstborn son. And he called his name Jesus.

EXPOSITION

Most commentators recognize vv. 22–23 as from Matthew, not a continuation of the angel's message. Whether or not Joseph made the connection between "that conceived in her is from the Holy Spirit," and Isaiah 7:14 is moot. Matthew makes the connection for his readers.

Matthew One

Apologetically (apology: a defense) we can say that it was Jesus' conception by the Holy Spirit in Mary that called for the Isaiah prophecy, not vice versa. That is, the virgin birth was not created by Matthew or others on the basis of the Isaiah prophecy, but rather the historical event was believed by them (Luke also, 1:26–56; 2:5) to fulfill the Isaiah prophecy. Whether or not Isaiah so understood the prophecy is also moot, because Matthew and Luke were led by the Holy Spirit to so understand Isaiah.

The incarnate God-man has two names. His first name is Immanuel, Isaiah 7:14; Matthew 1:23, which means "God with us." His second name is Jesus, Matthew 1:21, "You will name him Jesus," which translated is "savior," because "he will save his people from their sins." Compare Luke 1:31, "you will conceive . . . and bear a son . . . and call his name Jesus." His name is Immanuel Jesus, which translated is, "God with us Savior."[1]

His name "Immanuel" tells us who he was: God incarnate. His name "Jesus" tells us why he came: to save his people from their sins.[2]

Isaiah used the Hebrew ʽalmâ, "a young woman, one of whose characteristics is virginity."[3] The prophecies following Isaiah 7:14, in 8:8, 10 (introducing Immanuel) and 9:6–7 and 11:1 ff., indicate 7:14 should be seen as preparing the way for the messianic theme in this section of Isaiah.[4] The LXX translators certainly understood ʽalmâ in Isaiah 7:14 as indicating a virgin woman, translating it by the Greek *parthénos*, virgin.[5]

The name Immanuel informs our understanding of Jesus Christ. If Jesus was literally "God with us," then the incarnation of deity in humanity is a fact, the two natures of the God-man a fact. The incarnation supports the virgin birth, which is the origin of the sinless person and character of the Christ, cf. Luke 1:35, "the holy one being born will be named son of God."

Joseph's obedience mirrors Mary's. Matthew again protects the sanctity of the virgin birth; the marriage in March was not

---

[1] Quiggle, *Incarnate*, 1.
[2] Ibid, 3.
[3] Harris et al., *TWOT*, s. v. "1630b."
[4] France, *Matthew*, TNTC, 79.
[5] Zodhiates, *WSDNT*, s. v. "3933."

consummated until after Jesus was born in September. Joseph did not know Mary sexually "until" Jesus was born, indicating that after Jesus was born the marriage was sexually consummated. This fact negates the "perpetual virginity of Mary" doctrine.

Matthew Two

Translation Matthew 2:1-2

1 Now Jesus, having been born in Bethlehem of Judea in the days of Herod the king, behold, wise men from the east arrived at Jerusalem, 2 saying, "Where is the one who was born King of the Jews? For we saw his star in the east and have come to do homage to him."

TRANSLATION NOTE

The word translated "to do homage to" in v. 2, 8, is *proskunéō*, "to worship, do obeisance, show respect, fall or prostrate before . . . literally to throw a kiss in token of respect or homage."[1] Literally the wise men (*mágos*) said "we have come to bow to him," but culturally they had come to recognize him as a king. They had had not come to worship in the sense Christians think of worship toward Jesus Christ, which is why I have translated the word "to do homage to." *Proskunéō* is used several times in Matthew and I will translate the word "knelt before" or something similar, unless the context requires an act of worship.

EXPOSITION

Matthew relates the where of Jesus' birth to the Micah 5:2 prophecy, and gives his readers a time marker as to when Jesus was born: in the days of Herod the king. We know, then, that Christ was born before Herod died. Herod took possession of Israel as the Roman appointed king of the Jews in 37 BC and he died in 4 BC. Josephus reports that shortly before Herod's death there was an eclipse of the moon. It is the only eclipse mentioned by Josephus and occurred March 12/13, 4 BC. The Passover was celebrated after Herod's death on April 11, 4 BC. Therefore, Herod died between March 12 and April 11, 4 BC.

We can further delimit the date. Herod reigned for 34 years. The 34th year of his reign began March 29, 4 BC, so his death occurred sometime between March 29 and April 11, 4 BC. The meeting with the wise men had to occur early enough before his death for subsequent events to take place.

Certain "wise men" from the East met with Herod in their

---

[1] Ibid., s. v. "4352."

Matthew Two

search for one born "King of the Jews," a search based on an astronomical sighting while they were still in their own country. Considering the travel realities of the day—everyone travelled by foot, and important people with a large caravan—the wise men could not have made a trip from their homeland (discussed below) with less than two or three months preparation and travel time. Christ must have been born no later than one to three months prior to their meeting with Herod and their meeting must have been a minimum of one week before Herod ordered the death of the Bethlehem children.

These *mágos*, wise men, have been described as astrologers or astronomers (or magicians, an unlikely designation). These terms, however, indicated the same profession in ancient times: those who watched the skies, interpreted the signs, and maintained the scientific knowledge of the day. They interpreted astronomical signs and the dreams of kings with a view to political and religious events, e.g., Daniel 2:1–2.

Because this was a prophecy from a pagan prophet, Balaam, who had once lived in their region of the world, it is not unlikely the prophecy was filed in their library under "Israel, star." Why would an ancient prophecy be maintained for (circa) 1500 years? It foretold the destruction of certain nations: Moab, Sheth, Edom, and Seir. These nations were descendants of Esau, Genesis 36; Deuteronomy 2; 1 Chronicles 1; who lived in the Arabic countries to the east and south of Israel—the countries that were home to the *mágos*.

The content of the wise men's gifts points to Arabia (in modern-day geopolitical terms, Jordan, and the uppermost part of Saudi Arabia), cf. Isaiah 60:6. The fact they left Bethlehem without returning through Jerusalem may indicate a southern route leading to Arabia. A trip from Arabia might have been accomplished in as little as thirty days (after a suitable time to accomplish the logistics of launching a caravan). Why did Matthew say they were "from the east?" Because they came into Jerusalem on the Jericho Road, which ran east from Jerusalem. How do we know they were not Persians or Babylonians? Because those peoples are always identified in Scripture as from the north.

When gentiles living in the regions today known as Iraq and Iran—the Babylonians and Persians—when these peoples attacked Israel they followed the "Fertile Crescent" formed by the Tigris and

Euphrates Rivers, which caused them to attack from the north. They followed the Fertile Crescent north from their cities and then east into Syria, and then south into Israel and Egypt. From Israel's perspective, the Babylonians and Persians attacked from the north, so Scripture identifies them as from the north. To complete the geographical picture, a reference to countries from the south meant Egypt.

From the east means modern-day Jordan and Saudi Arabia, because the Arabic traders entered Israel by crossing the Jordan River near Jericho. The *mágos* who came looking for the "King of the Jews" were Arabians from what the Old Testament peoples named Ammon, Moab, Seir (Edom), and Midian; in modern terms, Jordan (Ammon, Moab, Seir/Edom) and Saudi Arabia (Midian). They came into Jerusalem from the east.

The caravan would have been more than three people (some assume three wise men because three types of gifts are mentioned), more likely fifty-plus. Some time for research, understanding, permission, and preparation must be granted. Assuming the "star" appeared on the day Christ was born in early September, then it could have appeared anywhere from one to six months prior to their visit to Herod in Jerusalem (see *Excursus* at Matthew 1:18.)

The wise men found the "child" Jesus in a "house." Joseph would have moved the family into a house as soon as possible after the birth. The family had not made the journey to Bethlehem just to fulfill the prophecy, Micah 5:2.

> Why did Mary go with Joseph? She didn't have to; the enrollment counted property owners. There may have been several reasons. One, Joseph and Mary were newly married, she was about to give birth, and she was alienated from her family by her supposed infidelity (getting pregnant before marrying Joseph). Under those circumstances it probably seemed best to both that Mary accompany Joseph. Two, Joseph and Mary knew Micah 5:2. Third, the enrollment gave them the opportunity to move away from Nazareth before the birth occurred. There was undoubtedly a lot of gossip about Mary's due date. As [was discussed in *Excursus* at Matthew 1:18, above] Mary went to Elizabeth's house in December when she first became pregnant, and returned to Nazareth three months later, in March. Mary was three to

four months pregnant when she married Joseph. Her clothing, a loose outer robe over an inner tunic, may have kept her pregnancy from showing when she married. But as her August-September due date approached (nine months from December), she would have been visibly more pregnant than the five to six months from their wedding would justify. By giving birth away from Nazareth, Jesus would be assumed to have been born nine months from their wedding, and the families would be spared social embarrassment. So Joseph wasn't just responding to the census, he and Mary were moving to Bethlehem to rent a house (Matthew 2:8–11), have the baby, and live in Bethlehem.[1]

The word for "child" means newborn and older. That Herod killed all infants from birth to two years old indicates his uncertainty as to the *mágos* report; he was just being ruthlessly thorough.

The "star" was not an astronomical phenomenon. It first appeared in the sky in a position relative to the location of the *mágos* that made it seem to be over the land of Jacob/Israel. Then the star disappeared. After the *mágos* visited Herod the star reappeared and led them to the house where Jesus was living—it moved, and then it stopped over the house.

Some believe the star was a comet, which appeared in the sky, then disappeared as it went behind the sun, then reappeared just in time to guide the wise men to the house. Chinese astronomers saw a supernova for 70 days in 5/4 BC, which some identify as a comet, thus accounting for it appearing, disappearing (behind the sun), and then reappearing. There was a conjunction of Saturn and Jupiter in 7 BC and in 6 BC Mars joined this conjunction. Haley's comet appeared in 12/11 BC, but this is too early.

If the phenomenon the *mágos* saw was a normal phenomenon, it would have continued to move as they moved, and stop when they stopped. But the phenomenon moved on its own, and it stopped on its own, and it distinctly located itself over the house. Might not the original sighting correspond with Luke 2:13, the multitude of the heavenly host praising God at the birth of Jesus? And the next sighting one or more of that heavenly host, an angel(s), guiding the wise men to Jesus? Regardless, "his star in

---

[1] Quiggle, *Incarnate*, 85–86.

the east" was a supernatural event, not the astronomical phenomenon the wise men thought it to be.

John 1:14 says the Word became flesh and tabernacled [dwelt] among us. If John is referring to the timing of Jesus' birth, then Jesus could have been born about the time of the Feast of Tabernacles in September. The information in Luke's Gospel supports a late August–early September birth, a few days prior to the Feast of Tabernacles.

A September birth would have given the wise men several months to prepare for and make the trip to Jerusalem before Herod died. Their visit with Herod before he died, his order to kill the children when he realized the wise men were not returning, and his death between March 29 and April 11, 4 BC., indicate the *mágos* came to Jerusalem between one to three weeks before Herod took those actions.

Translation Matthew 2:3–8

3 But having heard, Herod the king was troubled, and all Jerusalem with him. 4 And having gathered together all the chief priests and scribes of the people he asked them where the Christ was to be born. 5 And they said to him, "In Bethlehem of Judea, for thus it has been written through the prophet: 6 'And you, Bethlehem in the land of Judah, by no means are least in the rulers of Judah. For out of you will come forth a ruler who will shepherd my people Israel.' " 7 Then Herod, having secretly called the wise men, inquired exactly of them the time of the star's appearing. 8 And sending them to Bethlehem, he said, "Go. Search carefully for the child. Then, whenever you have found him, make it known to me, that I might come and so homage to him."

TRANSLATION NOTE

In v. 8, the KJV, NKJV, ASV, and BBE (Bible in Basic English) translate *paidíon* as "young child." Note that it is Herod who uses this word, not the wise men. When used literally *paidíon* means "a child recently born, a baby, infant . . . also those more advanced [in age]."[1] If, as proposed, Christ was born in September 5 BC, and the wise men are visiting prior to March 29, 4 BC, then Jesus is an infant, about seven months old. I agree with other versions that

---

[1] Zodhiates, *WSDNT*, s. v. "3813."

translate *paidíon* without the adjective. I felt "infant" would be appropriate, but to translate "young child" or "infant" would be too much interpretation of the text.

Herod calls the newly born "king of the Jews" a *paidíon*, but at 2:16 he gives instructions to kill the *país*, a child, boy or girl, from infancy to youth.[1] Herod spoke Hebrew, or more likely Aramaic, in his court, but he probably spoke Greek with the wise men. The Koine dialect of Greek was the language of trade and diplomacy between nations. As 2:16 shows, Herod was thinking of any male child from infant to two years of age, in which case *paidíon* was the appropriate word.

EXPOSITION

Herod and Jerusalem were troubled, but probably for different reasons. Herod understood the wise men's reference to "King of the Jews" to mean the Christ. But to Herod "the Christ" meant an earthly king who would usurp his throne. Others, including the religious professionals, might have wondered how the Christ could come and they not be aware of his arrival.

This is the Herod who killed his wives and several of his children; the Herod who left instructions that thousands be killed when he died so there would be mourning upon his death.

Herod does not call a meeting of the Sanhedrin, the official government council to the king, but calls the religious professionals—some of them in the Sanhedrin.

The chief priests and scribes dutifully stated the Micah 5:2 prophecy to Herod, who in turn sent the magi to Bethlehem. The words of the assembled priests and scribes do not quote the Hebrew or other known versions of Micah 5:2, and there seems to be a reference to 2 Samuel 5:2, so there is an element of interpretation in their answer.

Skeptics insist the early church created the story to fit the prophecies. The gospels were written early enough that a false testimony could have been disputed; there is no evidence for Jesus' birth anywhere but Bethlehem.

Herod's instruction to the wise men concerning doing homage to the new king was insincere, as subsequent events reveal. Herod

---

[1] Ibid., s. v. "2816."

was an Edomite. He knew he might be displaced by a king out of the Davidic dynasty.

Why didn't the chief priests and scribes go themselves to Bethlehem and search for the Christ? Herod may have forbidden them, not wanting to give an opportunity to have the religious professionals herald a new king and raise a rebellion against him. More likely, they may have arrogantly assumed gentiles could not know anything about their messiah. They were the professionals. If the messiah were to come, he would certainly come to them for their approval and assistance.

Translation Matthew 2:9–12

9 Now, having heard the heard the king, they went. And they saw the star—the one they saw in the east—going before them until it came and stood over where the child was. 10 Now when they had seen the star they earnestly rejoiced with great joy. 11 And having come into the house, they looked at the child with Mary his mother. And falling down they did homage to him. And opening their riches, they brought gifts to him: gold and frankincense and myrrh. 12 And having been warned by God in a dream not to return to Herod, they went into their country through another way.

TRANSLATION NOTE

The word I have translated "having been warned by God" is *chrēmatízō*. The word has different meanings according to context. The basic meaning is to manage a business. In relation to kings and magistrates it means to do public business, give audience, answer as to ambassadors, to warn, to advise.[1] To warn the wise men, who were in a sense ambassadors, seems appropriate to this context. In the sense of warning it can bear the meaning of an oracle, or a warning from God, cf. Hebrews 12:25. A strictly literal translation would be "having been warned." Adding "by God" seems suitable to the intended meaning of the context, because the warning came in a dream.

EXPOSITION

The supernatural phenomenon in the sky appears again to the wise men, this time to guide them to the house where Jesus was living. The star moved and then stopped: "going before them until

---

[1] Ibid., s. v. "5537."

it came and stood over where the child was."

Where was Joseph? Probably there, but Matthew focuses on Jesus: their act of homage is toward Jesus only, not Mary also. Why is Mary mentioned? The scene simply describes the facts: they came looking for Jesus and found him with Mary.

Their gifts are appropriate to an Arabian origin, and reflect the high esteem in which they held the infant Jesus, whom they believed to be a king. God warns them, via a dream (a means appropriate to their culture) not to return to Herod. The warning to the wise men need not have taken place at the house, for they probably spent the night in Bethlehem. Any good Bible atlas will show a road out of Bethlehem to the south, lending credence to the theory the wise men were from Arabia.

Some older commentators gave symbolic meanings to the gifts. For example: gold representing Christ's kingdom, frankincense his priesthood, and myrrh his burial. "I see no solid ground for such an opinion," wrote Calvin.[1] The wise men, even if one assumes they had full knowledge of all the Old Testament scriptures (if so, probably from the LXX), did not have an understanding of those scriptures greater than their Hebrew contemporaries. Only a very few persons who had been enlightened by the Holy Spirit (e.g., Luke 2:9, 11, 26, 38) understood who Jesus was (the Christ) and why he had come (salvation). The wise men were not among that number. As noted before, they were responding to Numbers 24:17.

Translation Matthew 2:13–15

13 Now after they left, behold, an angel of the Lord appears in a dream to Joseph, saying, "Get up. Take the child and his mother and escape to Egypt, and remain there until I may tell you; for Herod is about to look for the child to destroy him." 14 Now getting up he took the child and his mother by night and went into Egypt, 15 and was there until Herod's death, that might be fulfilled that spoken by the Lord through the prophet, saying, "Out of Egypt I have called my son."

EXPOSITION

God now warns Joseph to flee from Herod. Apparently this was the same day the wise men had arrived. Matthew presents this as

---

[1] Calvin, *Commentaries*, 16:137.

a recapitulation of Israel's salvation experience, beginning with the trip into Egypt, Genesis 46, the Exodus (Exodus 12), and referencing Hosea 11:1, "Out of Egypt I called my son."

Hosea 11:1 is part of a larger context that reveals God's love for his "son" Israel. There is no indication the Jews regarded this verse as messianic, but it is so used by Matthew under the influence of the Holy Spirit. Some commentators find a reference to Moses as the promised deliverer. France believes the theme is Jesus as typologically the true Israel: the childhood history of Jesus presents the dawning of the messianic age.[1] Perhaps, but Matthew's purpose is simpler: to give convincing proof Jesus of Nazareth is the Christ, the son of God.

Joseph was a carpenter, a trade requiring hard work and earning little money. How did he afford a trip to Egypt, set up his family in a strange country, and restart his business? The gifts given by the wise men funded their flight to and life in Egypt. God is always practical in his dealings with his people. Moreover, someone will a skilled trade, such as carpentry, can find work most anywhere.

If Jesus was born in September, and Herod died the following April, and the wise men visited in between those events, then why send Joseph and family to Egypt with only a few months or days remaining in Herod's life? One, God uses means to accomplish his will: the family fled to prevent Herod's soldiers from killing Jesus. Two, Matthew, guided by the Holy Spirit, believed it was to fulfill the prophecy.

Looking to the ways of the world, it took some time to work out the political ramifications of dividing Herod's kingdom to his heirs. Moreover, the time in Egypt gave time for the wise men's visit and the Bethlehem massacre to be forgotten, so Jesus could live a normal life free from pursuit and inquiry.

Looking ahead to v. 22, one of Herod's children and heirs, Archelaus, inherited the southern part of the Herod's former kingdom, and was deposed in AD 6 for misrule. Thus, we can estimate the maximum length of the Egyptian stay as beginning before Herod died in early 4 BC and ending before Archelaus was deposed in AD 6, a period of about nine years. When Jesus' parents returned to Nazareth with their child, he was old enough no one

---

[1] France, *Matthew*, TNTC, 86.

remembered, cared about, or questioned the length of Mary's pregnancy, or when Jesus had been born. They could look at the child and decide for themselves how old he was. There was no Facebook, Google, media news, smart phones, IPads, or insta-snap-gram-chat to inform the public of past events.

Translation Matthew 2:16–18

16 Then Herod, when he understood that he had been deceived by the wise men, was very angry, and he sent to put to death all the male children that were in Bethlehem and in all its region, from two years old and under, according to the time which he had inquired from the wise men. 17 Then was fulfilled that spoken by Jeremiah the prophet, saying, 18 "A voice was heard in Ramah, great wailing and mourning, Rachel wailing for her children and would not be comforted, because they are no more."

TRANSLATION NOTE

In v. 16, most versions—the KJV is an exception—translate *pais*, "a boy or girl child," as "boys," or "male children." That Herod ordered only males to be killed is reasonably assumed, because messiah was to be a male, Psalm 2:7. The noun is in the masculine gender. For the sake of clarity I have translated *pais* as "male children."

EXPOSITION

Bethlehem at the time Jesus was born is estimated to have had a population of between 300 and 1,000 people. The number of males two years of age and under would be about twenty for a population of 1,000.[1] No history other than Matthew's records this massacre, because historically it was a minor incident when compared to the number of people Herod had killed during his reign, including members of his own family.

The murder of those children from birth to two years of age does not mean Christ was two years old, or that the wise men had seen the star-like phenomenon up to two years before they met with Herod. Herod was simply being thorough by allowing a large margin for error. His margin for error also expanded the murders beyond Bethlehem to "all its region." He wanted to make sure the

---

[1] Ibid; Hagner, *Matthew 1–13*, 36.

one born king of the Jews was killed.

The weeping of Rachel in Ramah is from Jeremiah 31:15. Rachel is (figuratively) weeping for Ephraim, a tribe out of her son Joseph. She is weeping at Ramah because Jeremiah 40:1 gives Ramah as a point from which the captives of Judah and Jerusalem were carried away to Babylon. Ramah and Jerusalem were in the territory of Benjamin, Rachel's other son, and Bethlehem was on the border between Judah and Benjamin. Matthew takes a historical event and creates an analogy: the foreign king of Babylon killed many and carried away rest to Babylon; the foreign king Herod carried away the children of Bethlehem in death. Matthew has connected the Christ to two significant events in the history of Israel: the Egyptian Exodus and the Babylonian Captivity. Just as God delivered Israel from those captivities, even so Jesus of Nazareth is the Christ who will deliver Israel from captivity. The present "captivity" is sin, not Roman oppression, but Matthew builds his case slowly, saving that particular revelation for later in his Gospel.

Returning to Jeremiah's prophecy, Matthew is not saying God caused the deaths to fulfill a prophecy (Matthew does not use the "in order that" or "so that" conjunctions). Herod was solely responsible for his despicable actions. Matthew is saying Jeremiah's prophecy of the Babylonian King carrying Hebrews to Babylon is metaphorically recapitulated by Herod's despicable act. Herod is the foreign king (he was an Edomite, not a Hebrew) who has taken away Rachel's children.

The spiritual conditions—rather, the lack of genuine spirituality—in Israel when Christ was born were not unlike those in Israel thirty years later when Christ began his ministry. God allows human kind to reap the consequences of their sins. Herod was one of those consequences, God allows people to receive the leadership which their spiritual condition—their turning away from God—merits.

Evil will come, but God's providence will overrule evil for good. Messiah is saved and this incident in his history is used to demonstrate Jesus of Nazareth truly is the messiah. Once again Matthew has taken a prophecy considered non-messianic and revealed its messianic intent.

Translation Matthew 2:19–23

19 Now Herod having died, behold, an angel of the Lord appears in a dream to Joseph in Egypt, 20 saying, "Get up, take the child and his mother, and go into the land of Israel. For those seeking the life of the child have died." 21 Now Joseph got up, took the child and his mother, and came into the land of Israel. 22 But having heard that Archelaus rules Judea in place of his father Herod, he was afraid to go there. Having been warned by God in a dream, he turned into the region of Galilee. 23 And having come he lived in a city called Nazareth, so that might be fulfilled what was spoken through the prophets, that "He will be called a Nazarene."

EXPOSITION

At some point in time after Herod's death, which Joseph may have heard prior to the angel's appearance, an angel of the Lord directed him to return to Israel with his family. Interestingly, Joseph is told to go to the land of Israel, but that nation no longer existed as a political or national entity. The Romans had divided the land of Israel into several territories within the region they identified as the Syrian province. Starting at the city of Dan in the north and traveling to the city of Beersheba in the south these territories were Ituraea, Tyre, Galilee, Decapolis, Samaria, Perea, Judea, and Idumea.

However, in God's eyes, national Israel existed, waiting for its messiah. If one carefully follows Jesus' travels it can be seen that Jesus remained within the territories as parceled out to the twelve tribes by Moses and Joshua, and it can be demonstrated Jesus visited every old tribal territory except Simeon (which was embedded within the territory of Judea). Jesus ministry was to the house of Israel, regardless of the ways of the world.

Joseph was apparently returning to Bethlehem. To live with the messiah in the city of his and their ancestor David would be sensible to any who knew the scriptures. Those who sought Jesus' life were dead or no longer had any authority. But when Joseph heard Archelaus ruled in Herod's place, he was afraid. I doubt Joseph thought Archelaus would seek to kill Jesus, but he didn't want to live under his authority. Archelaus was worse than Herod in some ways; so bad that in AD 6, after about nine years of rule, the leading citizens of Judea sent a delegation to the Emperor asking to have him removed from his position.

So, God advised Joseph to go to Nazareth in Galilee. Joseph

Matthew Two

altered his course and went to Nazareth. Looking at a Bible atlas, Joseph had probably come out of Egypt into Judea along the coastal road, intending to turn toward Jerusalem and Bethlehem just north of Azotus (the Old Testament Ashdod). Knowing his fears, and looking to the future (as God does), God through a dream directed Joseph to an obscure village in Galilee: Nazareth. In response Joseph would have continued up the coastal road, probably to Ptolemais where the road named "Via Maris (the Way to the Sea) began and ran east to the Sea of Galilee. A foot path about eighteen miles west of Ptolemais ran from the Via Maris south about eleven miles to Nazareth through Sepphoris.

Nazareth was the very definition of an obscure, unimportant village. It is not mentioned in the Old Testament or in any contemporary Jewish literature. The city of Jonah, Gath-hepher (2 Kings 14:25) was two miles northeast. Sepphoris, the largest city in Galilee, was seven miles northwest.[1] Cana (John 2:1) was five miles north of Sepphoris. Nazareth wasn't the only obscure village in Galilee, but it was the one God picked for Mary and Joseph to raise Jesus to manhood. He picked it because Jesus was to grow and mature while living a completely mundane human life. The man in the God-man was a man just like us (he hungered, he thirsted, he was tired, he was angry, he wept, he peed, and he pooped just like us), so that the God-man could sympathize with our weaknesses, and be tempted in all ways, as we are (yet without sin), Hebrews 4:15. His mundane life is a testimony to his genuine humanity.

Matthew 2:23 is one of the more difficult fulfillment passages. But close attention to what Matthew does and does not say reveals his meaning. Matthew does not say "this saying made by this certain prophet was fulfilled." Rather, he made a general reference to the prophets, and an ambiguous reference to their messianic prophecies, "that it might be fulfilled which was spoken by the prophets, 'he shall be called a Nazarene.' "

There is no prophecy that specifically relates messiah to the Nazirite vow. Nor did he follow that vow, for example, he touched the unclean, ate grapes, drank grape juice, and almost certainly trimmed his hair short after the fashion of the day. One can say he followed the Nazirite ideal of complete devotion to God, but he did not take that vow nor follow its restrictions.

---

[1] Josephus, *Wars*, 3.2.4.

What may be in view here is a play on words relating to his seeming insignificance. Messiah was expected to be a warrior like his ancestor King David. But Jesus came out of obscure Nazareth, and so was called a *Nazōraios*. Matthew may have been thinking of a passage such as Isaiah 11:1, which describes a branch, *nēser* out of the root of Jesse—a shoot coming out of a cut-down stump,[1] a symbol of lowliness. Some kind of word play connecting *nēser* and *Nazōraios* may be what Matthew intended. Looking to Isaiah 53, the messiah comes as the despised Servant of the Lord. Nathaniel asked Philip, "Can anything good come out of Nazareth," John 1:46, because Nazareth was not mentioned in any prophecy—not mentioned at all in the Old Testament. Compare the chief priests and Pharisees at John 7:52.

However, Matthew is not referring to one prophet, but the general tenor of all the prophets, who describe messiah in his first advent as humble in his person and rejected by his people. France comments:

> It has been suggested that Matthew saw in the obscurity of Nazareth the fulfillment of Old Testament indications of a humble and rejected messiah; for Jesus to be known by the derogatory epithet *Nazoraios* (cf. John 1:46) was not compatible with the expected royal dignity of the messiah, and thus fulfilled such passages as Psalm 22; Isaiah 53; Zechariah 11:4–14.[2]

Matthew says, "he shall be called a *Nazoraios*" to indicate the Christ's humble origins and coming rejection by the Jewish people. First century Christians would have caught this sense, cf. Acts 24:5, because the designation "Nazarene sect," was meant to demean the Christian community. As D. A. Carson pointed out, "Matthew is not saying that a particular Old Testament prophet foretold that messiah would live in Nazareth; he is saying that the Old Testament prophets foretold that the messiah would be despised."[3]

---

[1] France, *Matthew*, TNTC, 89.
[2] Ibid.
[3] Carson, *Matthew*, 97.

Matthew Three

Translation Matthew 3:1–4

1 Now, in those days, John the Baptist comes preaching in the wilderness of Judea, 2 and saying, "Repent, for the kingdom of the heavens is near!" 3 For he is the one declared through Isaiah the prophet, saying: "The voice of one exclaiming in the wilderness: 'Make ready the way of the Lord; make his paths straight.' " 4 Now John himself, his clothing was camel's hair, and a belt of leather around his waist; and his food was locusts and wild honey.

EXPOSITION

The "wilderness of Judea" ran along the west side of the Dead Sea, up to the north end where the Jordan River emptied into the Dead Sea. The phrase "in those days," refers to the days when Jesus lived in Nazareth, 2:23. Jesus is about thirty-five years old, as is John Baptist. If, as discussed below, John began his ministry late AD 29, then Matthew passes over twenty-five to thirty years of unimportant history between 2:23 and 3:1.

The Baptist's message is simple: Messiah's kingdom is near, therefore prepare yourself by repenting of your sins. "Near" ("at hand" is another legitimate translation of *eggízō*[1]) is being used in the prophetic sense: it is the next event to occur on the prophetic calendar. The fact it is being announced means it is near in time as well. *Eggízō* is in the present tense, indicating "a state of affairs which is already beginning and which demands immediate action . . . The time for decision has already come."[2] John's exhortation to repent echoed the Old Testament message to turn away from idols and immorality and turn to YHWH (the Hebrew word used as God's personal name) in covenant obedience.

Matthew identifies John as Messiah's forerunner by reference to Isaiah 40:3. In Isaiah the "voice" preceded the coming of God. By citing the reference Matthew implies the Baptist fulfills the prophetic "voice" and Jesus of Nazareth is the fulfillment of God's coming.

John's manner of dress was apparently intended to call to mind

---

[1] Zodhiates, *WSDNT,* s. v. "1448."
[2] France, *Matthew*, TNTC, 90.

Elijah, 2 Kings 1:8, "He is a hairy man and wore a leather belt around his waist" (NKJV). For the spiritually perceptive this description and the exhortation to repent would call to mind Malachi 4:5, 6.

> See, I will send to you Elijah the prophet before the coming of the great and terrible day of YHWH. And he will turn the heart of the fathers to their children and the heart of the children to their fathers, lest I come and strike the earth with a curse.

Matthew 3:4 is the only reference in Scripture to eating locusts, although they were and are still used as food. In the wilderness locusts and wild honey would be readily available food sources. Matthew may have intended to invoke the image of Elijah who was fed by God in the wilderness. The total effect would be that John the Baptist was a prophet (per Isaiah, Malachi) who like Elijah came out of nowhere, sent by God, sustained by God, with a message from God, that God was coming to establish messiah's kingdom.

Translation Matthew 3:5–12

5 Then went out to him Jerusalem, and all Judea, and all the region around the Jordan, 6 and were baptized in the Jordan by him, confessing their sins. 7 But having seen many of the Pharisees and Sadducees coming to his baptism, he said to them, "Generation of vipers! Who instructed you to flee from the coming wrath? 8 Therefore produce fruit worthy of repentance, 9 and think not to say in yourselves, 'A father we have, Abraham.' For I say to you that God is able from these stones to raise up children unto Abraham. 10 Even now the ax is being used against the root of the trees. Therefore a tree not producing good fruit is being cut down, and into the fire is thrown. 11 I indeed baptize you in water unto repentance, but the one coming after me, he is mightier than me, whose shoes I am not worthy to carry, he will baptize you in the Holy Spirit and with fire. 12 Of whom the winnowing shovel is in his hand, and he will thoroughly clean out his threshing floor and gather his wheat into the storehouse; but the chaff he will burn with unquenchable fire."

TRANSLATION NOTE

In v. 6, and in other verses, the word *baptízō* has not been translated by every version, but transliterated: baptize. The word means "to immerse, to submerge for a religious purpose, to overwhelm, to saturate."[1] I have retained the transliterated word for the sake of familiarity, but the reader should always bear in mind the translation is "immerse," e.g., v. 6, "and were immersed by him in the Jordan."

In v. 11, last sentence, which I have translated "he will baptize you in the Holy Spirit and with fire," is in most versions (the ASV is an exception) translated "he will baptize you with the Holy Spirit." The Greek word those versions translate as "with" is *én*, which means "in, at, or by any place or thing." The idea here is means. The Holy Spirit is a person, not a thing, like water. The Holy Spirit himself is not the medium into which a person is baptized, he himself is the one who baptizes, i.e., immerses, the person into a living relationship with Christ, by his operation on and in the believer, joining the believer to Christ. Just as at Romans 6:3 the believer is baptized into Christ, even so the believer is baptized in the Holy Spirit.

EXPOSITION

John would have remained close to the roads, so he was probably baptizing near the road that goes into Perea after crossing the Jordan River near Jericho (the Jericho Crossing), just above where the Jordan empties into the Dead Sea. (See my commentary *John 1–12* for a discussion of "Bethabara across the Jordan, where John was baptizing," at John 1:28.)

John' preaching created a widespread revival movement, affecting not only the common people, but also their religious leaders. His baptism was not for the same reason as the self-baptism of proselytes or the ritual cleansings of Judaism. Those being baptized with John's baptism were not seeking ritual purification, but were making a statement about inward repentance resulting in spiritual cleansing. Their baptism symbolized the inner repentance that meant they were fleeing from the wrath to come (v. 7) when messiah would appear to judge his people.

John rejected the Pharisees and Sadducees, whom the other gospel accounts reveal as religious formalists and secularists, respectively. John's message was directed to those who would repent and confess their sins. The Pharisees believed their legalism kept them from sinning, and the Sadducees didn't believe in sin,

---

[1] Zodhiates, *WSDNT*, s. v. "907."

thus the reason for John's question, "Who instructed you to flee from the coming wrath?" There is a good bit of irony in John's question; the Pharisees would have rejected any instruction, especially from someone not trained in their schools, cf. John 7:15. So would the Sadducees.

From these professors of religion John demanded works that revealed their repentance, which in the context of their lives would have meant a denial of their beliefs. They believed they were worthy of the coming kingdom, not specifically because they were Jews, but because they were members of the Abrahamic Covenant community—gentiles also became children of Abraham when the proselytized—and the merit of Abraham guaranteed God's blessing.

They also believed their practices made them superior to other Jews. They were not coming "for" John's baptism, i.e., to receive it, but "to his baptism" to see what it was all about. John strikes to the heart of the matter, which is that they were curious, not repentant.

John may be using a devastating play on words. Isaiah states Abraham was the rock from which they were hewn, but John says any stone could be made to serve the same purpose. The Isaiah passage may have brought to mind the similarity between the Hebrew word for stone, *eben* and that for children, *ben*. No doubt John offended them by suggesting they needed to repent.

In his reference to Jesus as "coming after me" John uses *opísō*, a word meaning behind, with either reference to time, or to place. In the thirty-five New Testament uses it never has reference to time, unless the Baptist's use (here and Mark 1:7; John 1:15, 27, 30) is the exception. John is saying messiah will be recognized as a follower of John, that is, he will be baptized with John's baptism.[1] But, John ensures his hearers understand the relationship between himself and Christ. A disciple was expected to care for his master, but to carry his master's shoes was too lowly for a disciple (it was the work of a slave). The truth about the person coming after John is that he is mightier and more worthy than John.

When looking ahead to Matthew 11:2–3 (cf. Luke 7:20, "Are you the Coming One, or do we look for another?"), it seems obvious John was thinking of (what we would identify as) Second Advent

---

[1] See John 1:33.

judgments and the inauguration of the Messianic Kingdom. Jesus' messianic mission had not taken the direction John's understanding of his own mission and Old Testament messianic Scripture had led him to expect. John was expecting the Davidic/Messianic Kingdom (hence John's question in Matthew 11:3), but at this advent the kingdom would come in another form.

There are four forms of the kingdom in Scripture.

The Universal Kingdom (Kingdom of God): God's universal rule over his creation and in the kingdom of men. This kingdom is present for all time and eternity (cf. 1 Corinthians 15:24–28).

The Davidic-Messianic Kingdom, inaugurated at Christ's second advent. This kingdom fulfills the Davidic covenant (2 Samuel 7:11b–17; 1 Chronicles 17:10b–15). Christ's rule will be over all the inhabitants of the earth. The church will reign with Christ in this kingdom (2 Timothy 2:12; Revelation 5:10; 20:6).

The Mystery Kingdom: the present kingdom between the two advents of Christ. This kingdom includes true believers, people professing (not possessing) faith, rejecters of faith, and opponents of faith. The ruler is God. The church is part of this kingdom.

The Spiritual Kingdom: the present kingdom between the first advent and the rapture of the New Testament church, composed of believers only, entered only by the new birth. The Ruler is Christ, the ruled are believers. This kingdom owns no territory, claims no leader other than Christ, and has no permanent place on earth, because its members are citizens of heaven, expatriates on earth.

The forms of the kingdom that would result from Christ's first advent were the mystery kingdom and the spiritual kingdom. John Baptist was, in general, correct about the outcome of Messiah's advent: Messiah's kingdom would be established. However, he did not understand the form of the kingdom that would be established at this first advent, nor the means by which it would be established (through the crucifixion-resurrection-ascension by evangelism, discipleship and faith-in-Christ communities).

The reference to the Holy Spirit and fire are to salvation through the judgment of sins. Messiah's enemies would be conquered through his saving death on the cross. John's preparatory baptism will be superseded by the true spiritual baptism in the Holy Spirit that cleanses and saves. All that is worthless will be destroyed. Wheat and chaff are symbols for the saved and unsaved, respectively.

Translation Matthew 3:13–17

13 Then Jesus came from Galilee to the Jordan unto John to be baptized by him. 14 But John hindered him, saying, "I have need to be baptized by you, and you come to me?" 15 But Jesus said to him, "You let this pass for the present time; for thus it is proper to us to fully accomplish all righteousness." Then he allowed him. 16 Now having completed his baptism, Jesus immediately came up from the water. And behold, the heavens were opened to him, and he saw the Spirit of God as a dove descending and coming upon him. 17 And he perceived a voice out of the heavens, saying, "This is my son, the beloved, in whom I am well pleased."

TRANSLATION NOTE

In v. 17 I have translated "he perceived a voice." The Greek word translated "he perceived" is *horáō*, "to see, perceive with the eyes." The word may be used figuratively: to perceive with the mind of senses. That is the use here.[1] I translated "he" because in this use *horáō* is a second person singular verb (the singular "you.")

EXPOSITION

John began his mission in the spring of AD 29.

Excursus: When did the Baptist Begin His Ministry?

Luke 3:1 states the Baptist began his public ministry "in the fifteenth year of the reign of Tiberius Caesar." Luke could be reckoning Tiberius's regnal years from his co-regency with Augustus, beginning AD 11, making the fifteenth year AD 25–AD 26. This is the view of most modern scholars, as they try to relate Jesus' birth in 5 BC to Luke's statement at 3:23, "Jesus began his ministry at about 30 years of age." Luke 3:23 does not mean Jesus was 30 years old when he was baptized, but that he was "about 30 years of age." Luke related Jesus' age to "about 30 years of age" because culturally a male was considered to have become mature

---

[1] Zodhiates, *WSDNT*, s. v. "3708."

after 30 years of age. Jesus the Christ is King and Priest (and Prophet). King David began his reign at 30 years of age (2 Samuel 5:4). The Levites began to serve in the temple at thirty years of age (Numbers 4:3).

There is no manuscript or coin evidence the Romans ever dated regnal years from the beginning of a co-regency. Tiberius himself reckoned his first regnal year from the death of Augustus (August 19, AD 28) which was the normal Roman method. If we date his regnal years in the same manner that Tiberius dated them, the fifteenth year of his reign was August 19, AD 28 to August 18, AD 29. John began his ministry between those dates. This doesn't mean Jesus was baptized between those dates, but that the Baptist began his ministry at some point between those dates.[1]

Excursus: When Was Jesus Baptized?

To answer the question posed by the title of this excursus, the deciding issue is, in what year did Jesus celebrate the first Passover of his public ministry? If John began baptizing shortly after August 19, AD 28, when Tiberius's reign began, then an AD 29 Passover might be possible. However, we know that Jesus' public ministry encompassed four Passovers:

Passover AD 30, John 2:13

Passover AD 31: Luke 6:1 (cf. Matthew 12:1; Mark 2:23)

Passover AD 32: John 6:4 (cf. Matthew 14:13–21; Mark 6:32–34; Luke 9:10–17)

Passover AD 33, John 19:31 (cf. Matthew 27:50; Mark 16:37; Luke 23:46)

The Luke 6:1 Passover is the one some may doubt. This was the "plucking grain on the Sabbath" incident. In describing the "plucking grain" incident Luke used the term "the second Sabbath after the first." Leviticus 23:15 explains the meaning of this terminology.

> And you will count for yourselves from the day after the Sabbath [the first Sabbath after the Passover, 23:6], from the day that you brought the sheaf of the wave offering, you shall count seven complete Sabbaths (NKJV).

---

[1] Quiggle, *John 1–12*, 69.

Luke's use of this terminology is often dismissed as "a transcriptional blunder" or a dittography.[1] However, the words make perfect sense in the light of Leviticus 23:15. The number of weeks from the Passover to Pentecost was counted by the number of Sabbaths. There were fifty days, or seven Sabbaths plus one day, from the first Sabbath after Passover to the day of Pentecost, Leviticus 23:15–16. Luke's "second Sabbath after the first" agrees with the terminology the Jews used to name these weeks, and Luke's specific use means the second week after the sheaf of the firstfruits was waved before the Lord. The sheaf was waved on the day after the Sabbath after Passover (thus, during the Feast of Unleavened Bread). Luke's terminology pointed to a Passover that occurred about two weeks prior to the "plucking grain" incident. No other gospel mentions this Passover. But that is also true of the AD 30 Passover, John 2:13.

If the first public Passover was AD 29, then Jesus would have been crucified in AD 32. Astronomical data for Passover AD 32 requires a Sunday, Monday or Tuesday crucifixion,[2] but Jesus was crucified on a Friday according to John 19:31.

Therefore, Jesus' first public Passover could not have been in AD 29. John must have begun baptizing after Passover AD 29. Considering that he was baptizing in the Jordan River, the water and weather would be warmer in late spring. This would be a sufficient period of time before Jesus was baptized to allow John's followers to grow in numbers large enough to attract the attention of the Jewish leaders (John 1:19–28), and prepare the hearts of the people for the Messiah. The better date for Jesus' first Passover of his public ministry is AD 30, and his baptism between Passover AD 29 and Passover AD 30.

We can work out the latest date for Jesus' baptism (in relation to the Passover) from the events after the baptism. After he was baptized Jesus walked to the wilderness of Judea. Assuming John Baptist was baptizing at or near the Jericho Crossing, Jesus walked southwest a few miles into the desert wilderness just west of the Dead Sea, between the Sea and the mountains. We don't know where in the wilderness the temptation occurred, and I will simply use fifteen miles as the distance Jesus walked. The terrain is rough,

---

[1] Metzger, *Textual*, 116.
[2] Boyer, *Chronology*.

especially when one leaves the dirt paths, and I will estimate Jesus took five hours to walk to the site of the temptation. There he endured forty days of temptation. He then returned to where he had been baptized, another five hours. He gathered together three of his disciples, 1:38–42 (Andrew, Peter, John), and let us agree a few days passed, and then he and they walked to Bethsaida-Galilee, about three days, where he gathered two more disciples (Philip, Nathaniel). Then he went to Cana for a wedding, about three hours walking from Bethsaida-Galilee (although he could have went to Nazareth, about four hours walking, and then been invited to the wedding); the wedding could have been celebrated for as long as seven days. He then went to Capernaum, about 5.5 hours, and stayed several days. Then he returned to Jerusalem for Passover, about three to four days walking, depending on the route taken. The minimum number of days was:

Location	Time/Days	Cumulative
Wilderness	5 hours	
Temptation	40 days	40 days
Return to Baptism site	5 hours	41 days
Five disciples	2 days	43 days
To Bethsaida-Galilee	3 days	46 days
To Cana plus Wedding	7.5 days	53.5 days
To Capernaum	5 hours	54 days
Days at Capernaum?	3–14 days?	57–68 days
To Jerusalem/Passover	3–4 days	60–70 days

If all the roads we know Jesus traveled between his baptism and the Passover were laid out in a straight line the distance would be about 200 miles. Walking time at four miles per hour would be about 50 days; at three miles per hour about 67 days. Adding in the time spent at the Cana wedding and at Capernaum, I estimate about 60–70 days between the baptism and the Passover. Working 60–70 days backwards from Passover April 7, AD 30, and assuming John has included most of the details of Jesus' ministry between the temptation and the Passover, the latest date Jesus could have been baptized was in between January 22–February 1, AD 29. (Although the Jewish civil year began with the seventh month, Tishri, our September-October, God established Nisan as "the first month of the year," Exodus 12:2. Therefore I am dating AD 30 as beginning Nisan 1, i.e., March 23.)

I believe a date between the Feast of Tabernacles (late September in AD 29) and the Feast of Dedication (mid-December) is more likely. Jesus would have attended Tabernacles (a mandatory-attendance Feast), and may have attended Dedication. From one of these Feasts, knowing the time for his public ministry had come, Jesus would have left Jerusalem going east to Jericho and the Jordan River where John was baptizing. Jesus was most likely baptized between October–December (inclusive) AD 29, but not later than January 22–February 1, AD 29, and his first public Passover was Nisan 14, AD 30, which in modern terms was April 7, AD 30.[1]

Returning to the exposition. Matthew's account does not tell us whether Jesus immersed himself, or was immersed by John. His description, "having completed his baptism, Jesus immediately came up from the water" will support either view.

14 But John hindered him, saying, "I have need to be baptized by you, and you come to me?"

Matthew writes that John tried to prevent Jesus from being baptized, with the comment "I need to be baptized by you." Matthew does not explain how John recognized Jesus as different from others in the crowd. John Baptist's comments in the gospel of John (1:31–34) might seem to indicate he did not know Jesus, but the view that reconciles the Baptist's statements in Matthew and John is that John knew Jesus personally, but did not know him as the messiah.

It seems reasonable that John should know Jesus. The story of the two births (Luke 1) would have been family tradition. It also seems reasonable that John had met Jesus, because the families would have been able to meet during the pilgrim feasts (Passover, Pentecost, Tabernacles), and possibly at other times. Mary may have repeated her visit to Elizabeth many times as the cousins matured. (We don't know what the familial relationship was. We only know that Elizabeth and Mary were related, Luke 1:36, but we don't know what that relationship was. The word used in Luke, *suggenēs*, means "a relative, one of the same family" in this

---

[1] Quiggle, *John 1–12*, 69–72.

context.[1])

John Baptist's words in Matthew may have come from knowing Jesus' origin as born of the Holy Spirit, and knowing Jesus' character from contact between the two families as the boys grew to manhood, so that John may have believed Jesus had no sin of which to repent.

If family tradition and personal meetings are the background to this meeting, then John had some estimation of Jesus' character. The Baptist's clear statement in John 1:31–33 indicates, at the least, that he did not know Jesus as the one who would baptize with the Holy Spirit, until after the Holy Spirit descended on Jesus at the baptism. Therefore, John's intent in denying Jesus baptism was to say, "You don't need my water baptism because you have no need for repentance; I need you to baptize me." John knew something of Jesus the man, but did not know Jesus as the messiah.

15 But Jesus said to him, "You let this pass for the present time; for thus it is proper to us to fully accomplish all righteousness." Then he allowed him.

John came baptizing per YHWH's commandment for two purposes. The first was to prepare hearts for Messiah's coming through repentance of sin, signified by water baptism. The second was to reveal the messiah through water baptism. Jesus said, "It is proper to us to fully accomplish all righteousness." The word *dikaiosúnē*, righteousness, has the basic meaning in Matthew's gospel of the conduct God expects of his people.[2] The word *pleróō*, "fulfill, fully accomplish" is used in Matthew with the meaning "to do that which God requires." Thus, the meaning of Jesus' comment to John was, "If you and I are to fulfill all that God requires of us, then even this seemingly inappropriate act must also be included."

Why did Jesus seek out John's baptism? Jesus knew the Father's will was that he be revealed through John's baptism. It was part of the Father's redemptive plan that the Son identify himself with John's messianic proclamation. In being baptized Jesus identified himself with those people who had come to John's baptism to express the repentance that prepared them for

---

[1] Zodhiates, *WSDNT*, s. v. "4773."
[2] France, *Matthew*, NICNT, 119; Morris, *Matthew*, 64.

Messiah's judgment and kingdom.

Jesus' baptism was both the public acceptance of the messianic mantle and the public announcement his messianic mission had begun; a view agreeable to the Baptist's statement in John 1:33. John's prophetic ministry was the intended means God the Father had provided to herald the Son's messianic mission. The Father's voice of approval, Matthew 3:17, and the descent of the Holy Spirit, Matthew 3:16; John 1:32, prove the point: John's Baptism was the means through which Jesus was publicly approved as of the "Servant of God" (Isaiah 42:1 et al) and dedicated to the redemptive purposes of the messianic mission.

In saying that the messiah was revealed through water baptism, and that Jesus' baptism was his public acceptance of the messianic mantle, is not to say Jesus became the messiah through his baptism. Jesus was the messiah from the moment of his conception: Psalm 2:2, "YHWH and . . . his messiah"; Psalm 2:7 7, "YHWH said to me, you are my Son"; Isaiah 7:14, "Behold the virgin will conceive . . . call his name Immanuel"; Luke 1:31–33, "you will conceive . . . and call his name Jesus . . . YHWH will give him the throne of his father David . . . he will reign over the house of David forever"; Luke 1:11, "born to you this day . . . Christ the Lord."

There is no specific Old Testament Scripture stating messiah would be baptized, but those appointed to certain offices were anointed into that office, e.g., Exodus 29:1, 7, 20–21. Israel's kings and prophets and priests were publicly appointed to their office by the public act of anointing. Jesus' baptism was the public anointing that revealed he had been appointed to the messianic office.

John Baptist said he was sent to baptize to reveal the messiah John 1:31, "And I knew him not; but that he should be revealed to Israel, therefore I came baptizing in water." Jesus, being the God-man, knew the will of God in this matter. If John had known his cousin Jesus was the messiah, then he would not have hesitated. But he could not know until the baptism was accomplished, John 1:33.

Questions, as to when Jesus developed a consciousness of himself as messiah, and how he interpreted the Old Testament messianic-prophetic Scripture, are relevant to the baptismal event only if we intend to view the baptism as the point in time when Jesus became aware, or perhaps accepted, his messianic mission. These questions I answered above: he was born the messiah. The

God-man, whose divine nature interpenetrated, informed, and infallibly guided his human nature in every thought and action, came to be baptized because the time had become "today": that day in messiah's life when his public ministry was to begin.

Jesus came to his baptism knowing the beginning and end to which his mission would take him. Our choices concerning this matter are clear. Either Jesus stumbled through three plus years of ministry learning about his mission on-the-job; or Jesus knew every step of his mission and how it would end—had in fact, as the God-man, planned out the mission to call his disciples, train the twelve, die for the sin of his people, and see to it that his redemptive mission was continued through his followers. The conclusion, then, is inescapable: the Father required the Son to be baptized by John as a necessary next-step (the incarnation was the first-step) in fulfilling the Son's messianic and redemptive ministry.

16 Now having completed his baptism, Jesus immediately came up from the water. And behold, the heavens were opened to him, and he saw the Spirit of God as a dove descending and coming upon him.

Matthew's description will allow Jesus to self-immerse or the Baptist to have immersed Jesus. Self-immersion was the norm for proselytes or cleansing rituals, so it would not have been out-of-place here.

Jesus "immediately came up from the water," which could mean standing up in the river after being fully immersed. But since Matthew uses the preposition *apó*, "away from," it is more probable Jesus left the river and was now standing on the ground by the river.

In describing the events immediately following Jesus' coming up out of the water after his baptism, Matthew has placed his emphasis on a personal experience for Jesus alone. The pronouns are third person singular: the heavens were opened to him; he saw the Spirit of God descending and coming upon him.

This does not necessarily mean the event was seen only by Jesus. John Baptist indicates, John 1:32, he saw the Holy Spirit "descending from heaven like a dove." This does not mean the Holy Spirit manifested in the form of a dove, but that something about the appearance suggested a dove; perhaps color and gracefulness displayed in the descent and landing. The Greek word refers to a variety of pigeons and doves. The "swooping flight formed an appropriate way of visualizing the descent of the Spirit."[1]

There is little in the way of Old Testament use to connect this manifestation "like a dove" with some symbolic meaning relevant to Jesus' baptism. There is no Old Testament use of a bird directly connected in a symbolic way to the Holy Spirit. The identification of the dove as a symbol of peace (harmless as a dove) is also without clear Scripture support (see the figurative uses of "dove" at Psalm 55:6; 68:13; Isaiah 38:14; 59:11; 60:8; Jeremiah 48:28; Hosea 7:11; 11:11; Nahum 2:7.) The association of the Holy Spirit with fire (Matthew 3:11; Acts 2) is also contrary to the peace symbol.

Whether or not the assembled crowd saw something of the "heaven opened" event cannot be determined with certainty. In the moment, then, this was an experience intended for Jesus, for reasons about which we can only speculate: perhaps as an encouragement; perhaps as a token of approval; perhaps as a divine statement (to all reading Matthew's Gospel) that the Father and Spirit were one with Jesus in his messianic mission. Matthew's view is of a private experience, "the heavens were opened to him," but by incorporating the event into his gospel Matthew invites his readers to experience the moment with Jesus. Matthew intends for his readers to understand God is with Jesus in an extraordinary way, that his messianic mission has the seal of the Father's approval, and is in fact a joint-venture by the Holy Trinity.

That "the heavens were opened," does not mean the material sky, but rather the spirit domain opened (at least to John Baptist and Jesus) onto the material plane. This was not a vision, but a literal, event. The material human senses of John Baptist and Jesus were enabled to see into the spirit domain.

The descent of the Holy Spirit informs us that the Holy Spirit empowered Jesus for his messianic ministry. All of Jesus' life and every work were empowered by the Spirit. This is not to say the Spirit was not with him before his baptism, but now we are allowed to see that the Spirit empowered him for his messianic-redemptive mission. The Baptist witnesses that, "He whom God has sent speaks the words of God, for God does not give the Spirit by measure," John 3:34. Jesus received the Holy Spirit without measure, meaning he had all the spiritual power and all the spiritual gifts in abundance

---

[1] France, *Matthew*, NICNT, 122.

above what was necessary to accomplish his mission. More simply, his ability to accomplish his mission was greater than the necessity imposed on him by his mission.

The Holy Spirit empowering Jesus does not mean the deity of the God-man was inactive, or ineffective, or unable to act. The two natures of the God-man acted in perfect harmony. The deity nature acted through the human nature to accomplish the will of the God-man, without deifying the human nature. Because Christ's human nature remained human, it needed to be empowered by spiritual gifts appropriate to the messianic mission. What was true of Jesus is true of every believer: every believer is empowered by the Holy Spirit with spiritual gifts in order to perform the mission assigned by God to that believer. The messianic mission required the human nature be empowered by all the spiritual gifts in abundance.

17 And he perceived a voice out of the heavens, saying, "This is my son, the beloved, in whom I am well pleased."

Although some see this as an act of commissioning, the words do not support that interpretation. If we understand the words in the context of the event, then Jesus has correctly fulfilled the Father's will in being baptized by John. If we think of Jesus from birth to this moment, then Jesus has lived in such a way that God is "well-pleased" with him as a person, which is a significant witness to his divine and human natures and his sinless person and life.

In terms of relationship, Jesus has a unique relationship with God: "my son, the beloved." In the context of the presence of the Son and Spirit the voice must be that of the Father. Thus, the messianic-redemptive mission is in view, for the Father sent the Son as Savior of the world, 1 John 4:14. Morris writes, "the utterance reflects Isaiah 42:1 . . . modified by Psalm 2:7," and "at the very beginning of Jesus' ministry, his Father presented him, in a veiled way, as at once Davidic Messiah, very Son of God, representative of the people, and suffering Servant."[1]

Matthew tells us, later in the story of Jesus, that God repeats the same declaration (with the addition "hear him") when Jesus was transfigured on the mountain. The phrase "my son, the beloved" is used nine times in Scripture (Matthew 3:17; 17:5; Mark 1:11; 9:7; Luke 3:22; 9:35; 20:13; 2 Timothy 1:2; 2 Peter 1:17),

---

[1] Morris, *Matthew*, 68.

eight times in reference to Jesus. Three each are in Matthew, Mark, and Luke reporting the voice at the baptism; three each in the same gospels reporting the voice at the transfiguration. Luke reports Jesus' use in the parable of the vineyard, where it is meant to point to Jesus. Peter (2 Peter 1:17) uses the phrase in reference to the transfiguration, stating it is a declaration of honor and glory given to the Son from the Father. Considering these uses, the phrase may be intended as a messianic title. If so, then Matthew's readers should see in this phrase that Jesus of Nazareth was the man whom God loved, in whom he was well-pleased, the man who was God's son, whom God had anointed as the messiah of John Baptist's proclamation.

Matthew Four

Translation Matthew 4:1–2

1 Then Jesus was led up into the wilderness by the Spirit to be tempted by the devil. 2 And having fasted forty days and forty nights, afterward he was hungry.

EXPOSITION

If, as I suppose, Jesus was baptized near where the road came down from Jericho and crossed the Jordan River into Perea, then the Wilderness of Judea was a short journey to the west and south, lying in the great valley between the western shore of the Dead Sea and the eastern side of the mountain range on which Jerusalem was located.

The wilderness of Judea was and is a hot, dry, mostly unoccupied land, except where natural springs or rain runoff from the mountains make human habitation possible (e.g., Jericho, Engedi, Anathoth, Tekoa). Most of the wilderness was below sea level, descending from the 4,600 foot heights of the mountain ridges down to the Dead Sea at 1350 feet below sea level. Matthew says Jesus was led "up," but he is simply noting that he was led to a part of the wilderness that rose to an elevation above that of the Jordan River and Dead Sea; perhaps into a mountainous area, perhaps in the foothills, perhaps still below sea level. Regardless, Jesus went to an area nearly devoid of life-sustaining materials and human occupancy, so that he might be seen as depending solely on God.

Matthew and Luke state Jesus was led by the Spirit (Mark says driven) into the wilderness to be tempted by the devil (Satan), *diábolos*, a word meaning to slander or accuse. This temptation, then, was the will of God requiring obedience by the God-man.

The journey taken during the temptations, escalating in physical height from the below-sea-level wilderness, to the pinnacle of the Temple, to an exceedingly high mountain, suggests the increasing escalation or force of the temptations directed toward Jesus. The temptations began with the subtle suggestion to act independent of the Father's will by immediately satisfying his hunger, escalating to the less subtle doubt cast on God's love and faithfulness by insisting God protect him, climaxing with the blasphemously outrageous proposal to worship Satan.

First, we must note that "the temptations must be understood as the consequence of Jesus' acceptance of his divine sonship, not doubts about it"[1] Jesus did not need these temptations to overcome doubts. He was not, for example, tempted to use his divine power to prove to himself he had divine power. Because God the Spirit lead the Son to endure these temptations, one must ask, "Why was God tempting Jesus?" He wasn't. Satan tempted Jesus. Jesus was led by the Holy Spirit to endure these temptations because he is the son of God, a title that in the context of his messianic mission indicates submission to the will of God.

This testing was to demonstrate the reality of that "son of" relationship existing between God and Jesus the God-man. Would Jesus seek his own gain, or would he fulfill his mission by faithful obedience? Adam son of God (Luke 3:38) failed his test; Israel son of God (Hosea 11:1) failed their test; will Jesus son of God succeed? To show the obedience of Jesus the son through submission to God and dependence upon God is the reason God sent the Jesus to be tempted.

The word translated "tempted" is *peirázō*, which means a temptation that seeks to destroy faith by tempting to sin.[2] By enduring the temptation faith is approved. James 2:13 tells us that God himself is "untempted" and does not *peirázō* any person. Trials come in three types:

> The Cause and Effect Trial. This trial is the application of the law of sowing and reaping, Galatians 6:7, 8. In this trial you reap what you have sown. If you sow sin you reap sorrow and chastisement. If you sow obedience you reap blessing.
>
> The Spiritual Trial. This trial comes when the believer is really striving to live for the Lord Jesus. This trial has nothing to do with something you have done wrong. It is the opposition of the world and Satan to a godly lifestyle. One might also call this the spiritually maturing trial, for it is used of God to strengthen faith and mature Christian character.
>
> The Spiritually Mysterious Trial. There is no logical explanation, of any kind, for the trial being endured. This trial sometimes falls into the "life happens" category, and

---

[1] Ibid., 70.

[2] Zodhiates, *WSDNT*, s. v. "3985."

sometimes into the "spiritually maturing" category. However, no satisfactory explanation may be found this side of heaven.

The trial Jesus endured falls under the "Spiritual Trial" category. Jesus was to live his life and perform his mission according to God's rules for living, rules expressed in Scripture, as Jesus' responses to Satan clearly show. Satan's desire was to destroy the credibility and mission of the one God has proclaimed his son, and undoubtedly he never ceased trying to deflect Jesus from his mission; these three recorded temptations surely serve as an example of temptations continuing throughout Jesus' life and ministry.

God did not avoid Satan. God brought Jesus to a place and moment of intense testing by Satan to demonstrate to all the world— to those who would read these gospel accounts—that Jesus was the "son of" God, i.e., the man after God's own heart, appointed and anointed for the messianic and redemptive mission. One qualification for being the redeemer was to be the kind of "son of" God whose moral character was such that he was the perfectly sinless son of God, suitable to propitiate God for the guilt of sins. This God intended to demonstrate through the temptations.

The devil intended to destroy the faith, credibility, and qualifications of Jesus' the "son of" through his solicitations to evil, thus disqualifying him to be "God with us," disqualifying him to be the one who would "save his people from their sins," and disqualifying him to be the messiah. Satan would defile Jesus the same way he had defiled God's first "son of," Adam.

France relates Jesus' trial in the wilderness to the trial of Israel in the wilderness, which concluded with the same scriptures Jesus used to fend off Satan, citing Deuteronomy 6:13, 16; 8:3. (In context, in Deuteronomy, Moses is instructing a new generation concerning the Law before they enter the land.) Thus, in succeeding where Israel had failed, says France, the Jesus' wilderness-temptation experience is "an elaborate typological presentation of Jesus himself as the true Israel, the 'Son of God,' through whom God's redemptive purpose for his people is now at last to reach its fulfillment."[1] Perhaps this is a valid view; there are parallels in Matthew that seem intended to relate Jesus' experiences

---

[1] France, *Matthew*, NICNT, 128.

to those of ancient Israel. However, there are no scriptures that name Jesus the true Israel.

What we can say is that the trial in the wilderness was allowed and controlled by God in order to fulfill his purposes for the Christ. Satan followed his own sin nature in tempting Jesus, but as with all such actions by Satan he could go only so far as God allowed, and no further. Does this mean the temptation was not real, or that under a more severe temptation Jesus might have failed? No, it means God sovereignly kept his promises and sustained his servant in the moment of his temptations, in order to fulfill his purposes.

Whether or not "the devil's intention to 'tempt' Jesus to do wrong is subsumed under God's good purpose to 'test' his Son,"[1] is the correct view, the temptations occurred and Jesus overcame them through his faith and the power of the Holy Spirit. We should note that the source of these accounts is Jesus telling his disciples, or the Holy Spirit guiding the writers at a later date, John 16:13. The variations between the Synoptics are the result of their own personality, style, and purposes in writing, as guided by the Holy Spirit.

The trial apparently lasted 40 days, or at least Jesus fasted for forty days. His fast was partial not total. The scriptures state that after his fast he was "hungry," not thirsty. Jesus did nothing superhuman, but rather what he did fell within the capabilities of humanity's physical nature. Others, during this New Testament church age, have repeated the forty day fast in imitation of Jesus. So he certainly drank water. He may have allowed himself goat's or camel's milk; he may have eaten fruit, such as palm dates; but he did not eat meat or bread.

There were probably more temptations, and harassment, by Satan, during these forty days than the gospels record. The combination "forty days and forty nights" indicates a period of testing, and again the typological relationship between Jesus and Old Testament Israel (forty years in the wilderness) may be in view; but the forty days and nights was a real passage of time (cf., Exodus 24:18; 1 Kings 19:8), not merely symbolic.

John Baptist (and others noted in secular literature) found food in the wilderness, so it may be Jesus' fasting was by choice, not

---

[1] Ibid., 129.

necessity. Why Jesus fasted is not explained, although early readers would have assumed it was accompanied with intense prayer and serious dedication to God's will.

Translation Matthew 4:3–4

3 And having come, the tempter said to him, "If you are the son of God, speak that these stones might become loaves of bread." 4 But answering he said, "It has been written, 'Not by bread alone shall the man live, but on every word that comes from the mouth of God.' "

EXPOSITION

The "tempter" is universally recognized as a reference to Satan (cf. 1 Thessalonians 3:5), and the word is used here (versus "devil" or "Satan") to indicate his actions as well as his person. The tempter says, "If you are the son of God," clearly referring back to 3:17.

The "if" here has occasioned much confusion. Is Satan stating that Jesus is the son of God, is he questioning whether or not Jesus is the son of God, or is he asking Jesus if he questions his own deity? The question is more simple that these: Satan is saying Jesus should prove that God was right when he said, "This is my son," 3:17. Was Jesus of Nazareth really a son of God? Was God right to be well-pleased?

The term "son of" in Scripture, when not used of literal physical descent, indicates a person has the characteristics of the person or thing of which he (or she) is a "son of." A son of lawlessness is lawless, a son of the Law was obedient to the Law, the sons of Belial were idolaters. The sons of God have the moral characteristics of God. Satan was saying, "Prove God was right when he said you were a 'son of God.' " Satan wasn't asking Jesus to prove his deity—during Jesus' earthly ministry Satan did not know Jesus was God the Son incarnate in Jesus of Nazareth. Satan was demanding Jesus of Nazareth prove he truly was one of the sons of God, as God had testified.

Who did Satan believe Jesus to be? Did he believe Jesus was God the Son incarnate in a human being? Or did he believe Jesus was a human being in a faith-based relationship with God, thus a "son of" God, whom God had anointed to be the messiah? Undoubtedly the latter. Satan would not have tempted Jesus to worship him if he believed Jesus was God the Son incarnate. Satan knows "God cannot be tempted by evil" (James 1:13).

We must, therefore, wash away our presuppositions and place ourselves within Matthew's historical-cultural setting of the temptation. At this time in history Satan did not use the term "son of God" to identify Jesus as the God-man but as a human being in a faith-based relationship with God possessing the moral characteristics of God. To Satan, Jesus of Nazareth was yet another in a long-line of "sons of God" that he would defile, as he had defiled the first son of God, Adam.

The "if" ("if you are the son of God") performs a certain grammatical function known as a condition of the first class. This is a "simple conditional assumption with emphasis on the reality of the assumption (not of what is being assumed); the condition is considered a real case."[1] The tempter is stating a condition that was presented as reality, but he is questioning whether the condition is factual by demanding Jesus furnish proof. Satan could be viewed as saying, "I assume as true that you are the son of God, so prove it by commanding these stones to become bread." Or, he could be viewed as saying, "In view of the fact that you are the son of God, command these stones to become bread," this last being slightly a more subtle way of demanding proof.

Regardless of how one might understand the statement, Satan is providing Jesus the opportunity to act independent of God's will. Adam self-originated sin when he decided to choose his way in life in disobedience to God's will (Genesis 2:17; 3:6). Will Jesus seek his own way or will he honor God?

Although there is no divine revelation we know of that required Jesus to fast, there is a divine intent that Jesus' faith and obedience be tested. God agreed with and cooperated with this test of Jesus' faith. Here we do not see manna falling from heaven for Jesus, as God made it appear for Israel. Jesus determined a time of fasting was an appropriate response to this period of testing, and the obvious response of the divine will reveals that the decision to fast was approved. What was required, then, was that Jesus endure the consequences of his choice to worship through fasting.

Put another way, the claim Jesus was a "son of" God was to be tested (4:1; Mark 1:12; Luke 4:1). Because "son of" defines the

---

[1] Morris, *Matthew*, 73, n. 11.

character of one's humanity, Jesus chose to endure the trial through the natural limitations of his humanity: he fasted. To endure through the trial and overcome the temptations that were part of the trial he depended on the resources available to every "son of" God. By this means he revealed the claim was true.

The consequences of the fasting are used by Satan to tempt Jesus. The first temptation was an appeal to the lust of the flesh as well as to the pride of life: to satisfy hunger as well as to self-determine in defiance of God. The point is not that God specifically forbade Jesus to provide for himself during his fast in the desert; he did not. The point is that the way of the messiah in his first advent was lowliness, complete dependence on God, and to make his way in the world as a spirit-filled man, not as the omnipotent God. He was the omnipotent God, but he chose to be dependent on the Father and Spirit to provide his needs.

Jesus' use of his omnipotence was always for the good of others, not specifically for himself. There would come times when a display of his omnipotence was appropriate, e.g., commanding wind and wave to be still, knowing the thoughts of others; commanding demons to depart; healing diseases. But these works were not performed apart from his humanity. His deity nature worked through his Spirit-filled and spiritually gifted human nature.

Though Jesus the God-man had two natures, he was one person and acted as one person, because a nature is not a person, it is part of a person. The two natures of Christ concurred and cooperated so that the omnipotent power of the deity nature acted through the human nature. In the incarnation the substance and properties of each nature remained unchanged and unimpaired. His deity remained deity and his human nature remained human. Acts proper to deity are often spoken of as performed by the man Christ Jesus. This is the Scripture's way of telling us that his human nature was so interpenetrated by his deity nature that attributes properly belonging to deity acted through his human nature. Jesus the Christ stilled the storm, healed the blind, raised the dead, created bread and fish in his hands, and did other acts proper to deity.

For example, at the feeding of the 5,000, we see the Spirit-led man doing the will of God: Jesus looked up to heaven and gave thanks before he broke the bread, divided the fish, and multiplied both through an act of creation by his own omnipotence.

Such displays of his omnipotence during his public ministry

were for the benefit of others, not for himself. Compare Luke 24:30; after the resurrection Jesus personally blessed the bread, an act of God.

The book of Hebrews 2:7, 9–10, 14 makes it clear that God the Son joined humanity to his deity so that he would be the same flesh and blood and mortality as those whom he came to save, and experience death on their behalf. Therefore his way in the world was not to exercise the prerogatives of deity, but to depend on the providence of God through humble obedience to God's will; to be made a little lower than the angels, i.e., to be human. Human beings cannot command stones to become bread.

The temptation was genuine. Jesus was both hungry and, from Satan's point of view, could call upon God for the power to turn stones into bread. Let us remember, though, that temptation is a solicitation to do wrong, not the wrong itself.

Jesus' way in the world was to live according the Word of God, which required him to live according to the limitations of his humanity. "To use his powers to satisfy personal needs would be to deny all this."[1] Deuteronomy 8:3 provided an appropriate expression of the Word relevant to this temptation. The will of God, not the necessities of living, is the rule of life. Jesus references "every word." The word of God is profitable in its entirety: we neglect the parts at our peril; we obey the whole to our profit. In that light notice Jesus does not use a Scripture applicable to the messiah alone, but one that is valid for all persons. "Jesus overcame temptation with resources open to each of his followers. Obedience was important for him, and it is important for us."[2]

Translation Matthew 4:5–7

5 Then the devil takes him to the holy city and sets him upon the highest point of the temple, 6 and says to him, "If son of God you are, throw yourself down. For it has been written: 'To his angels he will give command concerning you,' and 'In their hands they will bear you so at no time may you strike your foot against a stone.' " 7 Jesus said to him, "Again it has been written, 'You will not put to the test the Lord your God.' "

---

[1] Ibid., 73–74.
[2] Ibid., 74.

EXPOSITION

Because Jesus responded with God's word to the first temptation, the tempter, who Matthew now calls the devil, adapts and uses God's word as the basis for his next temptation. The temptation in the garden began with the serpent using some of God's Word, but not all of it. Luke makes a closer parallel to Adam's temptation experience by placing the genealogy, 3:23–38, between the baptism and the temptation—Jesus is a son of God as was Adam. God had said,

> Genesis 2:16–17, You are may eat from any tree in the garden; but you must not eat from the tree of the knowledge good and evil, for when you eat of it you will surely die.

But the serpent said,

> Genesis 3:1, Did God really say, "You will not eat of every tree of the garden."

God had stated the positive, then the negative. Satan stated only the negative. Satan misquoted and misused Scripture.

Here in Matthew Satan misquotes and misuses Psalm 91:11, 12 in a very subtle way. The Psalm explains that God's providence will protect the believer. Satan makes an application to Jesus-son-of-God. The Psalm reads:

> For he will give his angels command to guard you in all your ways. In their hands they will carry you, so you do not strike your foot against a stone.

But Satan said:

> For it has been written: "To his angels he will give command concerning you," and "In their hands they will bear you so at no time may you strike your foot against a stone."

We see that Satan left out the important words, "To guard you in all your ways." The Psalm was written for all who trust in the Lord. The omitted words are important not only to Jesus but to every believer. In the case of Jesus his "way," as I explained above, was to live according to the will of God in submission to and dependence upon God. Satan is suggesting Jesus prove God will protect him, but the promise is applicable only to those persons who live according to the way of faith in, dependence upon, and submission to God. To put God to the test is not part of the way of

God.

The way of every believer is to have faith in God's promises of protection, not to demand God prove his promises. When a believer has genuine God-given faith in the promises, that faith is itself the reality and demonstration of the promises. The reality of those promises is really present with the believer: not wished for, not wondered about, not an anxious "I hope so," but the steadfast assurance that the promises are real, genuine, imminent.

By faith I am absolutely and completely assured of the reality of the things God has promised, and I do in fact by faith hold those promises in the hand of my soul as a present reality and possession. "Now faith is the title deed[1] of things hoped for, the objective demonstration[2] of the spiritual reality of things not seen," Hebrews 11:1. (See my commentary on Hebrews.) Jesus' way was not to doubt God could and would protect him; to not require a demonstration to support his faith; his way was to have confident trust in God's promise of protection; His way was to let faith itself be the sufficient demonstration of the promise.

There is some question as to whether or not Satan physically transported Jesus to the Temple, or if he was there in a vision (cf. Daniel 8:2, physically in Shushan but in a vision 350 miles east of Babylon in Elam). The reason for this question is the seeming impossibility found in the next verse, v. 8, a mountain high enough to show Jesus "all" the kingdoms of the world. Whether Jesus was taken to the pinnacle of the temple (and later the high mountain) in a vision or in physically reality, the temptation was real.

One might argue that for the temptation to be real the threat of destruction by jumping off the highest point of the temple had to be real. This view misses the point of the temptation, which was to choose between having faith in the promises, or make God prove his love, providence, and promises. In other words, doubt is internal. Therefore, a vision would be sufficient for the purpose of the temptation.

Some commentators believe the omission of "in all your ways" is of no significance. Hagner, France, Morris, and Hendrickson, admit these words have some force in the Psalm, but that their

---

[1] Moulton, *Vocabulary*, 659–660.
[2] Zodhiates, *WSDNT*, s. v. "1650."

omission by Satan "is probably of minor importance.[1] In the view of Hagner et al, Satan is suggesting Jesus create a circumstance wherein God will be obligated to act to save his Son's life, or require the angels to act on God's command to protect the Son.

However, when these words are omitted, the Psalm passage reads as though God promises to protect the righteous person no matter what he or she does. This is the way Satan would have us interpret God's will. Didn't Jesus just tell us, v. 4, that "every word that proceeds from the mouth of God" is important? Satan changes and omits words so he might twist the meaning to his own purposes and advantage.

Jesus rejects Satan's deliberate misuse of the Psalm. In response to this temptation Jesus quotes Deuteronomy 6:16. The preface to this verse in Deuteronomy is v. 13, "You shall reverence YHWH your God and serve him," and the epilogue is v. 17, "You shall diligently keep the commands of YHWH your God." These were, significantly, things Satan did not do, the point where Adam failed, and in which Israel had only limited success. Faith does not need to see proof of God's promises, faith itself (as being given by God) is proof of the reality of the promises; obedience is the proof of faith. To borrow from the theme of Hebrews 11, by faith the Son of God worked out the will of God through his life and throughout his life.

Translation Matthew 4:8–11

8 Again, the devil takes him to a very high mountain, and shows to him all the kingdoms of the world and their glory, 9 and he says to him, "These things, to you I will give all, if falling down you will worship me." 10 Then Jesus says to him, "Go away, Satan! For it has been written, 'The Lord your God you will worship, and him alone you will serve.' " 11 Then the devil leaves him, and look, angels came and ministered to him.

EXPOSITION

The devil could have physically taken Jesus to the top of an exceedingly high mountain and physically showed him all the relevant kingdoms of the then-biblical world; or at least the territory

---

[1] Hagner, *Matthew 1–13*, 67; France, *Matthew*, NICNT, 133; Morris, *Matthew*, 75; Hendrickson, *Matthew*, 229.

encompassed by these kingdoms. Or he could have, on the top of a high mountain, made all the kingdoms of the world pass before Jesus' eyes as in a vision. If we allow this last as possible, then it is a short step to admitting a vision in the wilderness, versus physical transportation.

The most likely sense is that Satan caused it to appear to Jesus' senses as though he was on a high mountain, and created a vision that displayed all the kingdoms Satan claimed as his own. It is significant Jesus was shown the "glory" of "all the kingdoms of the world." The glory of man's kingdoms is both tangible and intangible. From the great distance of "a very high mountain" the only visible tangible asset would be the lands so ruled, and the intangible would not be visible at all under an interpretation requiring the physical transport of Jesus to a high mountain. Satan caused Jesus to see a vision of some sort, though not necessarily a trance-like state, and we might imagine this as a visual display, like a movie projection in our day.

Satan says, "All these things I will give you," as though they were his to give. In Luke's account Satan claims the authority and splendor of these kingdoms have been given to him, and he can "give it to anyone I want to." Some little truth and much error are evident in these statements. Satan has the power and authority to influence men to sin, and to create the means for men to act on the temptation of sin, and to guide men into positions of power and authority within the political, economic, military, and religious systems he has created to further man's sinful rebellion against God. His authority, however, is exercised by permission, and his power is limited in its exercise according to God's will. Satan creates circumstances and influences man, but it is God who has determined the appointed times and boundaries of man's habitation" (Acts 17:26, cf. Daniel 7:2; Revelation 7:1). Moreover, the price of worshiping Satan is to suffer Satan's fate. What Satan can give has no eternal value.

The tempting offer is to worship Satan for personal gain. This seems to be an offer of the messianic kingdom without the required suffering of the king. However, it is simply an offer of worldly gain in exchange for wrong worship. In every temptation Satan appeals to Jesus' human nature, because he believed Jesus was fully human, not deity-in-humanity. In the first temptation Jesus' humanity suffered hunger, which power given by God could relieve.

Satan believed the messiah had been given power for his mission and could choose to exercise that power. Compare Revelation 13 where Satan's beast and false prophet have supernatural powers (actually performed by fallen angels, cf. Revelation 16:13).

In the second temptation Jesus the Christ could have acted in a way that might cause his physical death, which the angels had been commanded to prevent (until the crucifixion). This is an appeal to pride. "Even the angels," the Christ might be expected to say, "are subject to me." The angels were not subject to the Christ during his earthly ministry, compare Matthew 26:53, they are subject, as is the Christ, to the Father.

In the third temptation Satan appealed to the innate necessity of human nature to worship. God designed within human nature an awareness of himself resulting in an instinctive need to worship God. This is seen in that when human kind rejects God, they develop objects to satisfy their need to worship. Satan understands this. As a created being he also feels this instinct and rejects it by worshiping himself. In the future his man of sin, his beast, will worship himself, his ambition, and what he believes to be his own power, cf. Daniel 11:38.

But worship belongs to God alone, and Satan knows this also. Satan has always desired to be worshiped by God's creatures, human and angel. When Satan sinned, his sin was not only pride in himself, Ezekiel 28:17, but the desire for worship, Isaiah 14:13–14. God allows him to create an appearance of worship through idols and other indirect means, but never to receive direct worship. Even during the Tribulation Satan receives worship through the beast and false prophet, Revelation 13:4.

Here, in this third temptation, Satan appeals to Jesus to worship him in exchange for worldly gain and the rule of the world. Underneath this offer is the old desire for God to acknowledge that Satan is (in his not so humble opinion) as worthy of worship as is God. Jesus' response, from Deuteronomy 6:13, clearly addresses both appeals: only God is worthy of man's worship. Jesus-son-of-God will worship God alone. Note that at the end of his earthly mission Jesus declares he has been given "all authority in heaven and on earth," that is, authority over the spirit and material domains, Matthew 28:19. Jesus achieved through obedience that which Satan offered through disobedience.

We should not think it strange that Jesus proclaims God as his

God, and that Jesus worships God. Jesus the Christ is God-man, that is, he possesses the natures of deity and humanity. The human nature of the God-man must worship, because humanity was designed by God to worship God. Because the human nature in the God-man is genuine humanity, he must worship. He chose to give his worship to the only appropriate proper object for worship: God.

In responding to the tempter and devil, Jesus calls him "Satan" (the first of four uses in Matthew), a word meaning "slanderer," which seems appropriate to the circumstances. Satan has committed blasphemy by asserting that he has a right to receive worship, which rightly is directed to God only. He has asserted that he is equal with God. Jesus commands Satan to "Go away." Satan must feel the power of the command, but it is the power of God exercised on behalf of his servant who has proven that he is truly a "son of" God.

Jesus decisively rejects the temptation and the tempter. It is important we see that Jesus rejected these things and this evil person using means available to any believer: obedience to God's Scripture, faith toward God alone, faith in God's faithfulness. The extant of the obedience and faith required is available to every believer: one is to serve only God. God alone and only God is the proper object of worship, obedience, and service.

After these things angels came in response to God's promise, Psalm 91:11–12, and served Jesus. No doubt they gave him food, drink, and strengthened him spiritually (cf. Luke 22:43).

Translation Matthew 4:12–17

12 Now having heard that John had been arrested, he withdrew into Galilee. 13 And having left Nazareth, he came and dwelt in Capernaum, which is by the seaside, in the regions of Zebulun and Naphtali, 14 that might be fulfilled that spoken by Isaiah the prophet, saying, 15 "Land of Zebulun and land of Naphtali, way of the sea, beyond the Jordan, Galilee of the gentiles, 16 the people sitting in darkness have seen a great light and those sitting in the country and shadow of death a light has dawned on them." 17 From that time Jesus began to preach and to say, "Repent, for the kingdom of the heavens has drawn near."

TRANSLATION NOTE

The word translated "arrested" in v. 12, or "put in prison" in

Matthew Four

other versions, means "to deliver over or up to the power of someone . . . as to magistrates for trial or condemnation."[1] The subsequent history of the Baptist justifies the translation "arrested," or "put into prison."

EXPOSITION

Matthew passes over the six months of Jesus ministry after the temptation, which is covered in John 1:19–4:4 and Luke 3:19–20. In those six months Jesus went to Galilee, where he performed the miracle at Cana and visited Capernaum (John 2:12). Then he returned to Jerusalem, where he cleansed the Temple, experienced the first Passover of his ministry (AD 30), met with Nicodemus, and returned to Galilee through Samaria (John 4).

When he went to Jerusalem for his first ministry Passover, the disciples he had chosen in John 1:35–51 (Peter, John, Andrew, Philip, and Nathaniel) were with him, but when he returned to Galilee, John 4, Andrew, Peter, and John returned to their fishing, Matthew 4:16–22, because they had a business to run and families to feed.

While these are fishing, Jesus takes a preaching tour of Galilee, (Matthew 4:17; Mark 1:14–15; Luke 4:14–15), heals an official's son (John 4:46–54), was rejected at Nazareth (Luke 4:16–30), left Nazareth, and made his home at Capernaum (Matthew 4:13; Luke 4:31). Now it is time to call Peter, Andrew, James, and John to full time discipleship (Luke 51–11).

John says, 4:1–4, Jesus went to Galilee when he knew "that the Pharisees heard he was making and baptizing more disciples than John." Mark says Jesus went to Galilee "after John was arrested." Luke records the arrest out of chronological order, then reports the baptism, the genealogy, and the temptation, and then states, "Jesus returned in the power of the Spirit to Galilee." Matthew says that when Jesus "heard that John had been arrested, he withdrew into Galilee." These are simply different perspectives of the same event.

How Jesus heard the Baptist was arrested is not stated in the gospels. Nor is the length of John's ministry after Jesus was baptized, although according to John's gospel John Baptist's ministry lasted until sometime after the first Passover. The

---

[1] Zodhiates, *WSDNT*, s. v. "3860."

Synoptics take up the story after John was imprisoned.

What seems the most likely order is that after the Passover and Nicodemus events (John 2:13–3:21), Jesus continued to minister in Judea (John 4:1–2). He heard the Pharisees were comparing John's ministry to his, and then he heard John was arrested, and upon hearing of John's arrest he left Judea, passed through Samaria to meet the woman at the well, and thus returned to Galilee. There he conducted an extensive ministry lasting about two and one-half years, with trips to Jerusalem for two Passovers, Luke 6:1, John 6:4, and at least one other feast: Woodgathering in August or Tabernacles in late September, John 5. While in Galilee he made short trips into Tyre and Sidon, the Decapolis, and to Caesarea Phillipi.

Matthew's gospel gives the impression John Baptist was imprisoned shortly after the baptismal event and then Jesus went to Galilee. The Synoptic Gospels tend to focus on the Galilean ministry but John's Gospel focuses on the Judean ministry. That is why the Synoptic Gospels ignore events of the first six months, and John doesn't.

Matthew is concerned with the fulfillment of messianic prophecy. The prophecy in vv. 14–16, Isaiah 9:1–2, required an extensive ministry in Galilee. Thus, from Matthew's point of view, Jesus went to Galilee to fulfill the prophecy of Isaiah. The notation, "Galilee of the gentiles" (gentiles is literally "nations") indicates Jesus' mission includes the Abrahamic prophecy of "blessing to all nations" (Genesis 12:3; 18:18; 22:18; 26:4; 28:14.) Assuming Matthew's gospel was written ca. AD 58–60, the point was important to the Hebrew-gentile churches. However, although there were several gentile cities in Galilee (e.g., Tiberius just south of Capernaum, Sepphoris a few miles northwest of Nazareth), Jesus is not said to have visited any of them.

Matthew tells us Jesus left Nazareth to live in Capernaum. Luke tells us it was because the people at Nazareth had rejected him, 4:16–31. As the eldest son he may have moved his mother and other members of his family to Capernaum (this was after the wedding at Cana); or, more likely, Mary was living in Nazareth with James, the next oldest.

Jesus came to Galilee to minister in the former tribal territories of Naphtali and Zebulon. Nazareth was located in what had been Zebulon, and Capernaum was in the former Naphtali. A comparison between the tribal allotments stated in Joshua and the Galilean territory in the time of Christ reveals the region of Galilee incorporated most of the territory assigned to Naphtali (to the city of Kadesh), all of Zebulon, part of Issachar (excluding the most southern part), part of Asher (incorporating the east side of Asher's territory), and a small part of the most northern region of West Manasseh. In Jesus' time these tribal areas (Naphtali, Zebulon, Asher, Issachar, Manasseh) were broken up into Galilee, Tyre, Iturea, Samaria, and the Decapolis.

Some commentators state Jesus left Israel's territory when he went to Tyre and Sidon, to Caesarea Philippi, and to the Decapolis; some include Perea in this list. However, Jesus never left the original boundaries of the land as given to the twelve tribes by Moses and Joshua. Caesarea Philippi was located in the old territory of Naphtali. If Mount Hermon (northeast of Caesarea Philippi) was the site of the Transfiguration, then Jesus was in the territory of East Manasseh. When he went to Tyre and Sidon he was in Asher. The Decapolis was located in East Manasseh, Issachar, and Gad. Samaria was within West Manasseh. Perea was located within the territories of Gad and Reuben. To complete this list: Judea was within the territories of Ephraim, Benjamin, Dan, and Judah. Idumea was within Judah and Simeon.

Jesus never left the original boundaries of the land of Israel. He ministered directly to some gentiles, and many more gentiles saw him and heard him speak. But, he was sent to the lost sheep of the house of Israel, and he shepherded the sheep of that pasture, Psalm 95:7; Jeremiah 3:15; 23:4–6; see also Psalm 74:1; 79:13; 100:3; Ezekiel 34:12, 31; John 10:9.

Matthew reports Jesus moved to Capernaum. This may have been because Nazareth had rejected him, Luke 4:16–31, but Jesus had already visited there with his mother and brothers (John 2:12), so it seems likely he had already made plans to move to Capernaum. Capernaum's population (estimated at 1,000 to 15,000) was larger than Nazareth, and it was a busier city, very involved in the fishing industry supported by the Sea (Lake) of Galilee. Thus it had people coming in and out of the city to ply their trade and purchase goods and services. Its importance is seen in the presence of a Roman outpost (the Centurion, Matthew 8:5), government administrative officials (John 4:46) and a customs (tax) post (Matthew 9:9); together these indicate a city of local administrative and economic importance. Capernaum conducted an Empire-wide trade in the small fish taken out of the Sea of Galilee, which were dried and salted for sale and consumption through the Roman Empire.

Matthew has abbreviated and interpreted the Hebrew version of Isaiah 9:1–2 to communicate the sense of the prophetic fulfillment. The original passage begins with the gloom of judgment, gives the prophecy substantially as Matthew has given it, concludes with joy, and leads into the "Unto us a child is born" prophecy. Matthew's use highlights the geographic features and emphasizes a link between Galilee and the dawning of the light, so that in both Isaiah and Matthew the dawning of the light is the messianic prophecy of the child who brings salvation and the kingdom.

Matthew incorporates Isaiah's (9:7) kingdom reference in 4:17. gentiles would be living in territories originally given to the tribes of Naphtali and Zebulon, in Isaiah's time, ca. 742–680 BC, depending on when the prophecy was given, for the Assyrian conquest was 722 BC. At the least the prophecy foresees the Assyrians.

By the time of Christ these northern territories had been overrun by many gentiles: Assyria forcibly immigrated their own people into Israel to populate the land (creating the Samaritans). The empires of Babylonia, Persia, Greece, and Rome (which set up military, political and administrative offices) also sent their people into the region. There was a substantial gentile population in Galilee.

Isaiah notes the people "walked" in darkness, but in Matthew they "sit" in darkness. The movement from walking to sitting is a metaphor indicating spiritual darkness has become a spiritual state: the activities of life are being conducted in the sphere of spiritual darkness.

To sit in the "shadow of death," indicates a grievous lack of spiritual life; the prospect for a person sitting in spiritual darkness is spiritual death. The movement from darkness to light—from hopelessness to hope in Isaiah's prophecy, from sin to salvation in Matthew—indicates the anticipated result of messiah's ministry, as a result of the new kingdom of the heavens, which was at hand in the person of the messiah.

Finally, Matthew incorporates Isaiah's "by way of the sea,

beyond the Jordan." In Isaiah the phrase, "by way of the sea," probably meant a beaten path running west from the Lake to the Mediterranean. The Romans paved the path and named it the *Via Maris*, which translates to "The Way of the Sea," meaning the way to the Mediterranean. Galilee of the gentiles was by the way of the sea.

The phrase "beyond the Jordan" normally refers to the east side of the Jordan River, which would be gentile territories in Isaiah's time, but the territories of East Manasseh and Gad in an earlier time. However, if Isaiah is viewing Naphtali and Zebulon from the perspective of the conquering Assyrians, then this makes sense. As viewed from the east side looking west, Galilee would be beyond the Jordan.

In reference to the nations Matthew could be using "beyond the Jordan" in a metaphorical sense to mean non-Jews physically or religiously outside of Israel. Or, he could mean Jesus' ministry extended from Galilee eastward beyond the Jordan, which it did. We know Jesus made a few trips into the Decapolis and Perea (East Manasseh and Gad). However, as it seems Matthew is using Isaiah to describe the area in which Jesus would minister, which was Naphtali and Zebulon, he probably adopted Isaiah's point of view to describe, in general terms, the nominal boundaries of Jesus' ministry.

17 From that time Jesus began to preach and to say, "Repent, for the kingdom of the heavens has drawn near."

John Baptist proclaimed this same message of repentance in view of the coming kingdom. Now Jesus has taken up the proclamation of the kingdom in a land that has been neglected by its spiritual leaders, to the point that the people have settled into the state of spiritual darkness in the country and shadow of spiritual death.

There is doubt as to why Jesus repeats the Baptist's message. France believed Matthew "has taken the traditional account of Jesus' preaching and extended it back to John; that he [Matthew] began with John and then chose to introduce Jesus in the same terms."[1] This is a disappointing view in a generally useful commentary. Matthew did not create the story—none of the Four

---

[1] France, *Matthew*, NICNT, 144.

Gospels include fictional elements; Matthew tells us the story of John Baptist and Jesus.

Jesus began with the message of the kingdom because the kingdom was not present, yet, but it was, as Old Testament prophecy was currently understood, the next event on the prophetic calendar (the New Testament church era was still a mystery yet to be revealed). Even though the king was present, he had not assumed his throne, but continued to prepare the people for his messianic mission, which was one of judgment, salvation, and then the kingdom.

Second, John, and then Jesus, had proclaimed this message outside of Galilee. John Baptist apparently never went into Galilee. According to the Gospel accounts, the closest John Baptist came to Galilee was when he was baptizing at Aenon near Salim, John 3:23. These two towns were located a little south of Scythopolis, near the Jordan River, just north of Samaria in that part of the region of the Decapolis that extended west of the Jordan to the border of Galilee. Jesus had been preaching in Judea before he left for Galilee, John 4:1–4. The proclamation of the kingdom was therefore appropriate in this new unevangelized territory of Galilee.

The phrase "from that time Jesus began" *apó tóte árchomai ho Iēsoús* (vocabulary forms), is one of Matthew's structural markers dividing his gospel story. The phrase signals a new phase of Jesus' ministry has begun. From this point forward, to 16:21 (where the phrase is repeated to signal a new phase of Jesus' ministry) Jesus will actively promote the messianic kingdom.

Translation Matthew 4:18–22

18 Now walking by the Sea of Galilee he saw two brothers, Simon called Peter and Andrew his brother, casting a large net into the sea, for they were fishermen. 19 And he says to them, "Follow me and I will make you fishers of men." 20 Now immediately leaving the nets, they followed him. 21 And having gone on from there he saw others, two brothers, James the son of Zebedee and John his brother, in the boat with Zebedee their father, mending their nets, and he called them. 22 Now having immediately left the boat and their father, they followed him.

EXPOSITION

The simplicity of Jesus walking by the Sea of Galilee in v. 18 is in contrast to the great multitudes following him a few days later, v. 25.

Matthew makes it seem these men did not know Jesus until they were formally called as his disciples—the intent of "follow me." It is possible that this is all he knew, e.g., he asked Peter (or Andrew or John) "When did you become disciples," and this was the answer.

We know from John's Gospel that Peter, Andrew, and John had already met Jesus and accompanied him to many places; I have briefly discussed the events following the AD 30 Passover (see also my commentary *John 1–12*). To expand the previous discussion: after the AD 30 Passover, Peter, Andrew, John, Philip, Nathaniel, probably James and possibly others went with Jesus on a preaching tour of Judea, which lasted until Pentecost, fifty days after Passover. Then, Jesus hearing about John Baptist's imprisonment, returned to Galilee through Samaria, John 4. Upon reaching Galilee these men returned to their fishing business while Jesus conducted a preaching tour of Galilee. The preaching tour of Galilee was completed while the men worked at their business. So the question is, "Why does Jesus call these four men to full time ministry now?"

These men had already committed to being followers. But later they would be called to be apostles, and then after the resurrection/ascension they would continue Jesus' ministry. As a prerequisite to their future they needed to commit to being full-time disciples. A full-time disciples lived with, cared for, and learned from their Master. They needed to be called to that commitment.

Unlike the habits of Judaism, in which the disciple chose his master, Jesus chose those disciples whom he would train to take up his evangelistic and ecclesiastical mission. That is the way of the Holy Spirit with men: he calls them well before they are needed, so he may forge and temper the blade before the battle. Jesus calls them to himself before the storm of popularity breaks upon him.

We might think of this scene as representative, i.e., Jesus choosing others in a similar manner. We hear nothing of when or how others might have been called; undoubtedly some joined themselves to Jesus and some Jesus personally called. The risen and ascended Jesus calls men and women to himself through the act of salvation, using the evangelistic and discipleship mission conducted by his followers. Matthew shows the personal call of these four men to discipleship, perhaps because he was chosen in a similar manner (9:9), but without the prior relationship those men

Matthew Four

had enjoyed.

The point of view Matthew presents to his readers is that the newly-called disciples immediately left their employment and followed, without a prior meeting with Jesus (just as Matthew had been called). From that particular point of view we may say in explanation they had probably heard his preaching in Capernaum, and their immediate response points to the charisma of Jesus' personality, the motivation felt in his preaching, and the compelling pull of the Holy Spirit upon their souls (we should never forget the super-natural aspects of Christianity).

Matthew explains none of this, just as he does not explain why Simon was called Peter (John 1:42). Jesus calls them saying, "Follow me," *dúete opísō mou* (vocabulary forms). The key word is *opísō*, which when used with *dúete*, "come," has the meaning of "follow me as a disciple." They understood they were being called to another vocation, to follow as a disciple the person they believed might be, probably was, the messiah, the one John Baptist had proclaimed to be the lamb of God who takes away the sin of the world.

James and John did not leave their fishing business but stopped working at it. According to 8:14, they were not required to sell and leave all. Their father had employees (Mark 1:20) to help him in the business he ran with his sons James and John, and their partners Peter and Andrew (Luke 5:10). Their families had continuing income while these four followed Jesus, and it may be sons of the four men worked in their place (we know Peter was married, and see 1 Corinthians 9:2). In these times disciples literally followed their mentor as he walked around, so they knew they would be away from home, family, and business. What they knew of Jesus was apparently very compelling.

(They saw their families each time Jesus returned to Capernaum, and they may have worked their fishing business from time to time during their time with Jesus. They are not mentioned in John 11, and Jesus returned to Galilee after raising Lazarus for one final tour, and possibly to gather all his disciples before the last Passover. No gospel specifically records his return to Galilee, but after John 11:54, when he is in Ephraim, the Synoptics locate him traveling through Samaria, Galilee, Perea, Jericho, Bethany, and finally arriving at Jerusalem for the AD 33 Passover, Matthew 19:1—26:13; Mark 10:1—14:9; Luke 17:11—19:28; John 11:45—12:11.)

The notice that they were fishermen explains why Jesus found them at the lake, and leads to the analogy "fishers of men," which may be from Jeremiah 16:16, "Behold, I will send for many fishermen," says the Lord, "and they shall fish them," a verse with connection to the messianic kingdom. The term "men" is of course to be understood as meaning human kind, i.e., men and women.

Translation Matthew 4:23–25

23 And he went in all Galilee, teaching in their synagogues, and preaching the gospel of the kingdom, and healing all disease and all sickness among the people. 24 And the news of him went out into all Syria. And they brought to him all the sick having varied diseases and pains, oppressed and being inhabited by demons, and being epileptics and paralytics; and he healed them. 25 And great crowds followed him from Galilee and the Decapolis and Jerusalem and Judea and beyond the Jordan.

TRANSLATION NOTE

In v. 24 the word translated "epileptics" is *seleniázomai*, "to be moonstruck, to be a lunatic."[1] The word describes what we now know to be epilepsy. The ancient peoples observed the disease and thought it was more pronounced during certain lunar phases. Epilepsy was first proposed as an organic disease in 1873, and studies from 1859–1906 defined it as a neurological disorder.

In v. 24 the words "being inhabited by demons" translate *daimonízomai*, "to be in the power of a demon."[2] Most name this "demon possession," but spirit beings can merely inhabit a soul, they cannot own it; every human soul belongs to God the Creator.

EXPOSITION

In vv. 23–25 Matthew gives his readers a summary of what is to follow in chapters five through nine, and we find 4:23 substantially repeated at 9:35 (perhaps forming an inclusio?).

We should see in this description of events a picture of Jesus as the itinerant preacher and teacher, and the effect of his ministry on Galilee. "In all Galilee" does not of course mean every inch of the region, or even every city, town, village, road, bypath, field,

---

[1] Zodhiates, *WSDNT*, s. v. "4583."

[2] Ibid., s. v. "1139."

valley, hill, or mountain. The phrase has the sense of "throughout." As an itinerant teacher/preacher Jesus would have "necessarily repeated approximately the same material again and again and faced the same problems, illnesses, and needs again and again."[1]

Matthew's material is a representative sampling of Jesus' teaching, preaching, and healing activities. This becomes more evident when we evaluate the testimony of Josephus, writing one generation later. Josephus said Galilee had 240 cities and villages and each had a population of no fewer than 15,000 persons.[2] Although this estimate, especially of the population (a total of 3,600,000) was probably exaggerated, it still indicates the enormous physical activity required of Jesus. At the rate of two villages or towns per day, with no time off for Sabbath (impossible), it would have taken four months to visit them all. Yet, Matthew seldom places Jesus in a village, unless he is at a synagogue. Jesus preferred the open fields and meadows where great numbers could congregate, leading one to believe the crowds came to him as he approached a city or village.

Jesus' teaching may have focused on the Torah, of which the sermons on the mountain (Matthew 5 ff.) and the plain (Luke 6 ff.) provide samples (These may have been the same sermon, as Luke's "on a level place" may simply indicate a meadow or other flat expanse on the side of a mountain.[3]) France says the "mention of 'synagogues' . . . in first century Galilee may denote village assemblies rather than buildings erected for worship as such"[4] and he references two archaeological studies disputing the idea of a synagogue building in every Galilean town. Matthew does not record a discourse in a synagogue, or even a house, so perhaps Jesus' teaching (versus preaching) was limited to those cities (e.g., Capernaum) that had a synagogue. This seems doubtful, and it is more realistic to assume each village had some structure or area set aside for worship and religious instruction, not matter how simple it may have been. But for Matthew, the thought is the message, not the venue.

Jesus' preaching was about the gospel of the kingdom. The

---

[1] Carson, *Matthew*, 121.
[2] Josephus, *Life*, 45; *Wars*, 3.3.2.
[3] Hagner, *Matthew 1–13*, 80.
[4] France, *Matthew*, NICNT, 149, n. 6.

gospel ("good news," *euaggélion*) of the kingdom is in context the rule of God on the earth, specifically in the person of messiah. Matthew's use of the term, "the kingdom," may be an abbreviation of the longer "Kingdom of God," or "kingdom of the heavens," but, regardless, the message in context is that the good news being preached is concerned with God's sovereign rule.[1] Since Matthew chooses to distinguish between Jesus' teaching and his preaching, it is likely the preaching took place in the more informal outdoor setting where the crowds gathered to hear him, versus teaching in a synagogue or some other suitable structure.

Matthew tells us that Jesus healed "all disease and all sickness among the people." No single case of illness brought to Jesus was left unhealed. "All disease and all sickness" must be limited to the kinds of illnesses occurring in the places where Jesus was ministering.

The term Syria admits of two descriptions. Syria may be strictly defined as the region north of Galilee (the predominantly Jewish perspective),[2] but probably means the Roman province that incorporated Syria proper and Syria-Palestine (Iturea, Tyre, Galilee, Samaria, Judea, Idumea, Perea, Decapolis).[3] We see in v. 25 that this is Matthew's perspective.

The "great crowds" that followed Jesus should be understood as occupying a middling position: not opposed to Jesus, but not disciples.[4] The crowd included the curious, those in need (v. 24), and out of the crowd came a few true disciples. Interestingly, reference to Samaria or Samaritans does not occur in Matthew (or Mark), and the list in v. 25 goes around Samaria. "Beyond the Jordan" refers to Perea. The word "Decapolis" literally means the "ten city area."

As his fame spread, so did the burdens of ministry. "All the sick" doesn't mean every sick person without exception throughout all Syria, but that many coming to Jesus were sick, and those who were not sick brought their sick relatives or friends with them. Matthew distinguishes organic disease and demon-caused

---

[1] France, *Matthew*, NICNT, 151; Morris, *Matthew*, 88.
[2] Hagner, *Matthew 1–13*, 80.
[3] France, *Matthew*, NICNT, 151.
[4] Morris, *Matthew*, 90.

maladies. When Jesus healed the demonized he did so by casting out the demon. Scripture always distinguishes between organic and demon-caused. The healing of various diseases were kingdom blessings indicating the kingdom was at hand.[1]

---

[1] Carson, *Matthew*, 121.

Matthew Five

Translation Matthew 5:1–9

1 Now seeing the crowds, he went up on the mountain. And when he had sat down his disciples came to him, 2 and opening his mouth, he taught them, saying, 3 "Blessed the poor in the spirit, because theirs is the kingdom of the heavens. 4 Blessed those mourning, because they will be comforted. 5 Blessed the meek, because they will inherit the earth. 6 Blessed those hungering and thirsting for righteousness, because they shall be filled. 7 Blessed the merciful, because they will receive mercy. 8 Blessed the pure in heart, because they will see God. 9 Blessed the peacemakers, because they will be called sons of God."

EXPOSITION

The function of the principles and precepts Jesus taught on the mountain was threefold. First, the messianic king publishes the laws of his kingdom. Second, the king declares the rule for entry into the kingdom, which is not works, but righteousness of a different quality than that the scribes and Pharisees professed to possess (Matthew 5:20). Third, the king proclaims the moral and ethical rules members of the kingdom must practice as the normal and habitual course of their life.

When we consider these three reasons as a whole, it is apparent that only by the grace of the king can any person enter the kingdom, and only by his grace can a member of the kingdom live according to his rules for kingdom citizens.

The scribes and Pharisees believed that they were righteous because they practiced strict adherence to the letter of the law. The facts, however, were different. The law demanded more than outward conformance in one's words and actions, and this is what Jesus explains in his sermon. Righteousness is the result of inward spirituality, obtained only by grace through faith in the Savior King, and expresses itself in righteous thoughts, attitudes, words, and deeds.

The level of righteousness required for entry into the kingdom was impossible to attain by mere adherence to the letter of the law, still less by tradition or inheritance. In other words, neither descent from Abraham nor strict adherence to the details of the law could be sufficient to merit heaven. If a matter of descent, then everyone could enter. If a matter legal obedience, then only the scribes and Pharisees would have merited heaven. If one would attain the righteousness required to merit the kingdom, then it must be by a means that exceeded the righteousness of the scribes and Pharisees. This was patently impossible under the explanation Jesus gave of the spiritual demands of the law.

Looking to other scriptures in the Four Gospels and the epistles, righteousness is obtained only through personal faith in Jesus as Savior. Jesus came to seek and save the lost, Luke 19:10. Through faith in him the sinner is changed: born-again to spiritual life, the righteousness of Christ imputed to him/her. The believer is given new life, new wants, new desires, godly values, new goals for life, and the assurance of eternal life. He/she is able to live righteously because Christ has made him/her righteous. Only through saving faith in Christ can one's righteousness exceed that of the scribes and Pharisees.

Turning back to the sermon, Matthew says Jesus was on the mountain. Luke (6:17–49) says Jesus was on a level place. Luke could mean a separate time of teaching, for as noted above Jesus probably repeated his message as he went from place to place. Luke probably meant this event took place in a broad meadow on a mountain. Jesus was seated on a place higher than the crowd, and the crowd gathered in the meadow near to where Jesus sat.

Luke says people came from Judea, and Jerusalem, and from the seacoast of Tyre and Sidon, possibly suggesting some high place near the seacoast, but in fact the entire region of Tyre and Sidon, as lying between Galilee and the Mediterranean Sea, was considered as near the seacoast.

Matthew does say "the" mountain, but the definite article has no precedent, suggesting it was well-known to Matthew's original readers. The words can be used to mean a mountainous area or perhaps high hills, as in the hill country to the west and north of the Sea of Galilee. In common speech any hill significantly higher than the surrounding land was a called a mountain. For example, Mount Carmel near the Mediterranean Sea coast is 800 above mean sea level (MSL). The Mount of Olives (2732 feet MSL) is 400 feet higher than the Kidron Valley (2320 feet MSL), and 300 feet higher than the temple mount in Jerusalem (2440 feet MSL). Most mountains in the Bible are less than 3,000 feet above MSL. Regardless, the sermon was delivered on a level place at a location high enough to qualify as a mountain to Matthew. Luke notes a crowd of his disciples and many people were present, while Matthew focuses on the disciples. The appeal is evangelistic, 5:20, but the content is for disciples.

The sermon begins with a series of sayings known as "beatitudes," a declaration of blessedness, identified by the formula introduction, "blessed." The Greek word for "blessed" is *makarios*, which is not a verb (as often mistranslated) but a plural adjective. The adjective describes a person "in a 'happy' situation, one which others ought to share . . . Beatitudes are descriptions, and commendations, of the good life"[1] the believer has in Christ.

These several beatitudes should be taken together as expressing the general character of a member of the kingdom. In other words, there are not some who are poor in spirit, others who mourn, and still others who are respectively meek, merciful, pure, etc. These ethical characteristics define the character of the blessed/happy person living in the kingdom (much as 2 Peter 1:5–7 describe the characteristics of the spiritually mature believer).

The poor in spirit are those who are humble toward God, Isaiah 66:2. The Greek language had two words for the poor. The *pénēs* poor, not the word used here, earned his bread by daily labor, but must labor daily for his bread.[2] He/she had the necessities, but nothing extra. The *ptōchós* poor, the word used here, had nothing. The *ptōchós* poor were helpless, in abject poverty, possessing nothing, in complete destitution, and must beg for his or her daily living.[3]

In the context of the kingdom, the *ptōchós* poor are the ones who gladly submit to God's rule because they have no spirit of rebellion; they have no desire to make their way in life apart from God's guidance. All their righteousness comes from God not from themselves. Their humility consists of knowing they must depend on God for every need. Because they are spiritually destitute of their own righteousness, they are prepared to be filled by the grace and righteousness of Christ.

The consequence (*not* reward; *not* merit) of depending on God

---

[1] France, *Matthew*, NICNT, 161.
[2] Zodhiates, *WSDNT*, s. v. "3993."
[3] Ibid., s. v. "4434."

for righteousness (being *ptōchós* in spirit) is membership in the kingdom. Membership in the kingdom is obtained only through Christ's righteousness imputed to the believer who has been saved by grace through faith, not by his or her own works or merit.

Those who mourn may be described as happy/blessed because they shall be comforted. This is grief because of what is wrong in the world. They mourn over the way God's cause is rejected and his people despised. Compare Isaiah 61:2–3; Psalm 119:136. Believers will be comforted when they see Christ triumph over sinners who oppose Christ and persecute them.

Those who are meek shall inherit the earth. The meek are those who patiently endure wrong while waiting for God to judge their cause. They do not assert their right to justice and equity, but endure with humility through dependence on God. "It is," said Morris, "Christian to be busy in lowly service and to refuse to engage in the conduct that merely advances one's personal aims."[1] The humility that denies self-assertion and does not aggressively insist on his or her rights takes great strength of character, for it abstains from creating personal advancement or taking personal vengeance. When the unrighteous are removed from the land, those who suffered and endured injustice and inequity from the wicked will inherit the earth, Psalm 37:9–11. "Others claim their rights, but the meek are concerned about their duties."[2]

"Blessed the meek" sounds as though God disapproves of ambition, of bettering one's position in the world. God has nothing against ambition, except when it is pursued for its own sake, or when it injures others, or when ambition replaces God as the focus of one's life. Christ and his kingdom must always be the focus of life. A believer is not to spend his/her love on things of the world, 1 John 2:15–17, but on Christ.

According to the next beatitude, those who hunger and thirst for righteousness shall be filled. The physical sensations are used metaphorically to express deep and intense longing, the must-be-satisfied necessity, required to be a vital participant in God's rule. It is more than desire to see the world ruled by God's righteous standards. The focus is inward, it is moral character: to intensely desire to be possessed and ruled by that righteousness which

---

[1] Morris, *Matthew*, 98.

[2] Ibid., n. 21.

comes only from a relationship with Christ. It is to want to live as God requires; compare John 4:34. As noted before, one can only be happy/blessed by grace alone. So too here, this is not righteousness self-achieved but the righteousness of God filling the soul to empower living as God requires. God fulfills the longing for righteousness. The word "filled," means fully satisfied, well filled, stuffed.

Those who are merciful will obtain mercy. Mercy delays judgment or relieves suffering. Here is one's relationship with God working itself out in daily life. There is an equity or balance in God's justice that gives against that which has been given, for true justice is giving what is due, positive or negative, neither less nor more. The moral expression of sowing and reaping is in view. As a general rule of God's justice, those who are themselves merciful toward others will receive mercy. God blesses those who live according to God's rules for living. "There are people who show by their habitual merciful deeds that they have responded to God's love and are living by his grace."[1]

The pure in heart will see God.

> The heart refers to the personality: the seat of moral reflection, choice of the will, and pattern of behavior. The term includes all the mental processes, feelings, affections, and emotions, along with the internal motivations, leading to one's decisions and responses to life situations.

In the biblical view of man, his moral and religious condition lies in his heart. In the context of this view the term "pure" indicates the moral and religious condition of the soul that brings one into a spiritual condition suitable to see God. To see God in the context of a pure heart is not physical sight in the here and now, nor a vision, nor a dream. God is Spirit (John 4:24), no one has seen God at any time (John 1:18; 1 John 4:2), but the Son declares God to whom he will (John 14:6). Those who are pure in heart—believers in Christ as Savior—will see Christ because they have been spiritually transformed to be like him, 1 John 3:2. Everyone who has this confidence, that he will see God in the person of Jesus Christ, keeps him/herself pure even as God is pure, 1 John 3:3. Purity in heart is the spiritual transformation that occurs at salvation, and the

---

[1] Morris, *Matthew*, 100.

righteous life lived as a consequence of salvation.

The peacemakers shall be called sons of God. Most commentators discuss this verse in terms of the word peacemakers. But understanding begins with the consequence: they shall be called sons of God. The term "son(s) of God" always indicates a faith-based relationship with God. The unfallen angels are sons of God because they had faith and did not follow Satan. Saved persons are sons of God because they have a saving relationship with God through faith in Christ as Savior.

Peacemakers are sons of God because like God they seek the lost with God's message of salvation in Christ. The message of salvation is their work as peacemakers. Salvation reconciles the sinner to God, which makes the saved person to be at peace with God, thus those who give the message of salvation through Christ are peacemakers.

When one is in a state of peace with God, then one can live out the consequences of that peace by being at peace with others, Romans 12:18, and bringing peace to others. A peacemaker shares the story of his/her peace with God through the gospel of salvation in Christ, so others can experience peace and in turn become peacemakers. Making-peace between God and sinners through proclamation of the gospel of salvation is the first function of a peacemaker.

The call to the believer concerning peace is always personal, e.g., Psalm 34:15, "Depart from evil and do good; seek peace and pursue it." In the almost 400 uses of the term "peace" in Scripture, the believer is never called to make peace between warring sinners. Scripture states, in many places and many ways, that there is no peace for the wicked—the unsaved person—apart from salvation.

This is not to say believers should not be agents of peace wherever they go, because wherever a believer goes he should bring with him that quality of peaceableness and disinclination to conflict that characterize those who are at peace with God. The believer should actively overcome evil with good, Romans 12:21. But the primary function of a peace-maker is to practice the ministry of reconciling sinners to God through the Gospel of Salvation, 2 Corinthians 5:18–19.

Translation Matthew 5:10–12

10 "Blessed those having been persecuted because of

righteousness, because theirs is the kingdom of the heavens. 11 Blessed are you when they may revile you and may persecute you, and may say all kinds of evil against you, lying on account of me. 12 Rejoice and leap for joy, for great is your reward in the heavens, for so they persecuted the prophets before you.

EXPOSITION

If we keep in mind that Jesus is speaking about membership in a kingdom that does not yet rule over the earth, then the blessedness of the persecuted will be more understandable. Remember that at the beginning of this chapter I said the beatitudes are the king announcing the qualification for membership in his kingdom, that the qualification for membership is righteousness by grace, and that the beatitudes are the ethical standards of behavior for the members of the kingdom. To these three we must add a fourth, that the rule of the king was not intended for his first advent, but his second. Today Christ rules in the hearts of his saved people. He was born to rule all nations with a "rod of iron," Psalm 2:9; Revelation 2:27; 12:5; 19:15 (all uses). But that aspect of kingdom rule, as is evident from the Scripture cited, takes place at the second advent.

The kingdom in the first advent period, which is from the ascension to the second advent, is in the souls of men as the king rescues them from sin and empowers them to live according to the ethical standards of the kingdom—the standards we find in this sermon. This phase of the kingdom is the spiritual rule of God in the hearts of those who believe on Christ as Savior. The day when the king will rules with a rod of iron is coming, but until that day his followers will be persecuted by those who deny him his right to rule in their life.

Therefore, those who are righteous (their salvific state makes them so) and practice righteousness (empowered by the Holy Spirit to so live) will be persecuted by those who are unrighteous, as their sins are exposed by the righteousness of the saved. The born-again are members of the kingdom of the heavens, which is the kingdom of God's rule over all creation. Therefore, whatever unrighteous men do to a righteous person is of no eternal consequence, because the king overrules all tribulations for good.

When persecution, insult, and evil come upon the believer, he/she is to be comforted by two thoughts. One, his/her reward in heaven is great. Not the reward of membership in the kingdom (salvation by grace through faith is the only means of entry into the kingdom), but the reward due a member of the kingdom who has suffered for righteousness sake. The reward is given for patient and continuing endurance of persecution.

Second, the persecuted believer stands with others, the small and great of the kingdom, who also suffer. He stands among that great cloud of witnesses to God's faithfulness (e.g., Hebrews 11:1–12:2). Therefore a believer should not become discouraged when the world actively stands in opposition to his or her faith. The believer is actively engaged with the world as an ambassador of Christ, bringing the message of reconciliation with the king to those who are in rebellion against him. The believer is actively living out the principles of the kingdom, outing him/her to the world as a stranger and foreigner, making them a target for persecution because of their spiritual incompatibility with the world and its members. Those who are members of the kingdom will be persecuted until the king returns to rule with his rod of iron.

Translation Matthew 5:13–16

13 "You are the salt of the earth; but if the salt is no longer salty, with what shall it be salted? It can be used for nothing any longer, except to be thrown out to be trampled by men. 14 You are the light of the world. A city is not able to be hidden setting upon a hill. 15 Nor do they light a lamp and put it under a basket, but upon the lampstand, and it shines for all those in the house. 16 Thus, let shine your light before men, so that they might see your good works and they should glorify your Father in the heavens."

EXPOSITION

These verses are the contextual connection between vv. 1–12 and v. 17ff. The members of the kingdom have an obligation to live according to the rules of the kingdom. By so living they extend the reach of the kingdom to others.

That they can so live is a result of their salvation. That they must diligently practice the Christian life is the reality of having sin—the principle of evil—resident in human nature, even saved, born-again human nature. Scripture tells the believer that they are new creatures in Christ who can live by God's rules for living, and at the same time exhorts them to actively practice and live by those rules, because indwelling sin always tempts believers to not live by God's rules (James 1:14). The Christian life—the kind of life one is to live after salvation—is the product of grace, but personal effort is the means by which the ends of that grace—a righteous life—are achieved. That God provides the power, understanding, and guidance to live by grace requires the believer to use these God-provided means to so live.

Three analogies are used to make this point. The first is salt. Salt is a flavoring. Salt is also a preservative because bacteria will not grow in salt. The "earth" in this saying, as well as the salt, is to be understood metaphorically. The earth probably indicates humanity, and the salt serves to flavor and preserve all that is good and useful in humanity. The members of the kingdom preserve righteousness on the earth by their testimony in gospel proclamation and the manner in which they live their life. By being salt they hinder the corruption of sin and promote righteousness in sinners; if not by their testimony of salvation then by their righteous example and warning.

If salt loses its saltiness, then it has lost its function. Literal salt is pure sodium chloride and naturally has the quality we define as saltiness. However, salt in the ancient world was not always pure, because it was mainly harvested from salt water evaporation, thus the sodium chloride was mixed with other minerals. It was possible for the sodium chloride to leach out. The minerals left behind were good for nothing. Christians must not respond to persecution by abandoning their mission to live righteously and preach the gospel of peace with God in Christ. Christians must respond to God's commandments by practicing the intent of the King's kingdom laws.

The second and third illustrations reflect Christians as the light of the world. In Scripture light is a symbol of knowledge, wisdom (knowledge used in morally right ways for morally right ends), moral purity, holiness, righteousness, etc. As the light of the world believers possess and exhibit the light of God in their righteous behavior and gospel testimony. Their shining example is first likened to a city set atop a hill, thus always visible and visible from afar. The second example is a lamp in a house. The lamp the Bible speaks of was a shallow bowl (sometimes the bowl had a hard covering) filled with oil in which a wick was floated. The oil-filled dish with burning wick was the lamp, and it was set on a lampstand to give light throughout the house. When light is wanted the lamp is not put under a basket.

Christians are not to hide their status as members of the spiritual kingdom; being a disciple, practicing discipleship, and making disciples is not an option; it is the nature of a lamp to shine. To not shine is the same as losing one's saltiness. The lamp of faith is to shine before men in such a way that men can see God in the good works of the members of the kingdom, and hear their testimony of saving faith in Christ. Whether sinners reject or applaud godly works and testimony, God is glorified.

There is, in some minds, a question as to the source of the Christian's light. The light of the Christian is Christ, but it is not a reflected light. Christ says an emphatic "you" are the light," and an emphatic "your" light. Christ dwells within the saved soul. The light is Christ shining out through the believer in righteous thoughts, attitudes, words, and deeds. This light can be dimmed if the believer engages in acts of sin, or hides away his relationship with Christ by being silent or withdrawing from the world. Letting out the light within is a shared activity: Christ supplies the light, and the believer lets it shine by not putting it under the basket of sin, by not retreating from the top of the hill of testimony.

Finally, this is Matthew's first use of the term "Father" to refer to God. Although this designation of God was not unfamiliar to the Jews, it was not in common use. Jesus brought out this truth, altering forever the way the righteous think of their relationship with God.

Translation Matthew 5:17–20

17 "Think not that I came to destroy the law or the prophets. I have not come to destroy but to fulfill. 18 For truly I say to you, until the heaven and the earth may pass away, never no never will one iota or one point from the law pass away until all may be accomplished. 19 Whoever then may break one of these commandments, even the least, and may teach so to others, he will be called least in the kingdom of the heavens; but whoever may practice and may teach them, he shall be called great in the kingdom of the heavens. 20 For I say to you, that unless your righteousness may abound above the scribes and Pharisees, never no never might you enter into the kingdom of the heavens."

EXPOSITION

These verses serve as an introduction to the verses that follow. The conflict is between the true meaning of the law and those who outwardly appear to have followed the law, but inwardly have broken the law and teach others to do the same.

Specifics in this conflict will be introduced by the phrase, "you have heard." Jesus will teach the true meaning of God's commandments. What is in view is the whole of Scripture, encompassed in the phrase, "the law and the prophets." Scripture is a simple unity of many parts. Christ came to fulfill all those several parts of the law relevant to himself as Messiah and Savior. The unity of Scripture will remain whole and unbroken as every part is fulfilled.

The *iota* was the smallest Greek letter, but here probably refers to *yodh*, which was the smallest letter in the Hebrew alphabet. The "point" was a tiny projection on some Hebrew alphabet characters to distinguish them from other characters whose appearance was the same except for the point. Even the smallest parts of the Scripture are important and will be fulfilled. To break the least of the commandments is to break the unity of Scripture, thus to break all.

The phrase "least in the kingdom of the heavens," in the overall kingdom concept underlying this sermon, means the person who is least is not a member of the kingdom. The kingdom is the rule of God. To be a member is to be submissive to God's rule; to be disobedient characterizes those who are unsaved. The saved propagate the kingdom as salt and light; the unsaved teach others to break the commandments.

There is undoubtedly a warning to the scribes and Pharisees in v. 19. Those who personally obey the Scripture and teach others to do the same—through the message of salvation, personal manner of living, and instruction in righteousness—are greatest in the kingdom, fulfilling the goals of the kingdom. We have previously discussed v. 20 as the key verse in the sermon. Here it introduces the contrast between the King and kingdom members who teach others to obey Scripture, and the Jewish leaders who taught others to obey their traditional interpretations.

An interesting aspect of Jesus' teaching is first seen in v. 18 and repeated in Matthew thirty-one times (and seen in the other gospels). The word translated "truly" is the word we transliterate "amen." This word was used among the Hebrews and Christians to show an approval of the words of others. Jesus himself is the truth; he himself is the confirmation of every word spoken by God. Jesus is affirming that what he says is truth, and may be using *amen* as an invitation to the reader to assent to the truthfulness of these affirmations.

Translation Matthew 5:21–26

21 "You have heard that it was said at the beginning, 'You shall not murder,' and 'whoever shall murder will be liable to the judgment.' 22 But I say to you, that any person becoming angry with his brother without cause will be liable to the judgment. Moreover, any person who may say to his brother, 'Raca' will be liable to the Sanhedrin. Moreover, any person who may say 'Moros' will be liable to the fire of Gehenna. 23 Therefore if you should offer your gift at the altar, and there you should remember that your brother has something against you, 24 leave your gift there before the altar, and go away. First be reconciled to your brother, and having returned offer your gift. 25 Become friends with your accuser quickly, while you are on the way with him, that the accuser never deliver you to the judge, and the judge to the officer, and into prison you will be cast. 26 Truly I say to you, you will never no never come out from there until you should pay the last coin."

TRANSLATION NOTES

In v. 21 the word translated "at the beginning" is *archaíos*, "old, expressing that which was from the beginning . . . whatever that beginning may have been."[1] The example given by Zodhiates is Acts 21:16, "Mnason of Cyprus, an *archaíos*," variously translated as an early/old/aged disciple. Mnason was "not necessarily an elderly disciple, but one who had been a disciple from the beginning of the faith, from the day of Pentecost."[2]

The modern translations of *archaíos* at Matthew 5:21 are: NKJV, ESV, those of old; NIV, the people long ago; HCSB, NLT, our ancestors. These translations look back to the original word given at Mount Sinai, circa 1445 BC. However, that is not what Christ is referring to.

Christ is referring to the traditional interpretations of the Law—interpretations that were repeated by the current generation of professional theologians, i.e., the scribes, Pharisees, and

---

[1] Zodhiates, *WSDNT*, s. v. "744."
[2] Ibid.

Sadducees. The key factor I used in translating *archaíos* "at the beginning" was Jesus' word, "You have heard that it was said." To paraphrase Jesus, he said the crowd, "You have been told, 'This is what God's Word given in the Law means,' but those interpretations are wrong. I am going to tell you what God meant when he gave the Law."

Therefore *archaíos* does not refer to the Law, but to the traditional interpretations and interpreters of the Law that dated to the beginnings of the professional religious classes of first century AD Jewish society: the scribes, Pharisees, and Sadducees. Of first importance were the scribes, post-Ezra, (circa 445 BC) who developed into the professional theologians, followed by the Pharisees and Sadducees, which parties developed in the post-Maccabean age (circa 165 BC). Each party quoted or cited the traditional interpretations from their ancestors, and it is that interpretation to which Jesus referred when he told his listeners, "You have heard that it was said."

In v. 22 there is a manuscript variation. Some manuscripts read, "angry with his brother will be subject to the judgment." Other manuscripts read, "angry with his brother without cause will be subject to the judgment." Each reading is found in manuscripts of Western, and Byzantine origin. Jesus says there are times when anger is appropriate, e.g., his anger at Mark 3:5. Therefore I have included the phrase "without cause" as the genuine reading of the text.

EXPOSITION

Here is the first of the contrasts between the Jewish teachers of the law and Jesus the living truth and interpreter of God's commandments. The opening "you have heard" reflects both the oral manner in which the law was learned and the traditional interpretations given to the law by its teachers. The population was not generally illiterate, but writing materials were expensive, and books were scarce because hand-copied.

Long works of literature, like the Old Testament, or even the Torah (Pentateuch), were generally unavailable to the public. There might be a copy of the Torah and those parts of the Scripture read during the feasts in the local synagogue, but these would be great rolls of papyrus on scrolls. Therefore, disciples learned the Scripture and the traditional interpretations of the great Rabbis by rote memory. The common people learned through the reading and teaching of the local synagogues. They had heard the Scripture with rabbinical commentary, and what they had been taught was what they knew. Now we see the gravity of the preceding warning, v. 19, concerning breaking the Scripture and teaching others to break it in the same manner.

Jesus set Scripture free from these traditional interpretations. Many were not wrong, but the emphasis was on keeping the letter of the law, versus its intent. A philosophy had developed, after the Babylonian captivity, that if one kept rules more stringent than the Scripture commandments, then one could never disobey the Scripture. In practice the traditional interpretations grew in number greater than God's commandments, and grew in form and intent separate from the commandments. The result was a complex body of rules that often contradicted God's commandments, or through obedience to the traditional rules forced disobedience to God's commandments.

21 *"You have heard that it was said at the beginning, 'You shall not murder,' and 'whoever shall murder will be liable to the judgment.'*

In relation to this first conflict between what God said and what the Rabbis taught, it must be admitted that the Scripture said, You shall not murder, Exodus 20:13. Jesus is not disputing this commandment. That specific passage does not speak of judgment, but others do, e.g., Exodus 21:12, and the interpreters of Moses concluded that murder would result in judgment. Jesus did not dispute any of this.

What Jesus did teach is that the law is also spiritual in nature. The Law looks to internal motivations as well as outward actions, condemning the intent as well as the deed. The Ten Commandments are not the whole law. The Ten are explained in the other parts of the law. For example, "You shall not murder" is explained by Leviticus 19:17 to include "you shall not hate your brother in your heart."

In a series of three comments Jesus explains how inward motivations are equivalent to outward actions (anticipating v. 28). The first is anger without cause. There are times anger is appropriate. Anger toward the effects sin has against others is appropriate, Mark 3:5. Anger without cause is malice: the desire to inflict injury, harm, or suffering, an evil intent toward another.

The second inward motivation equivalent to murder is summed in the word "raca," a transliteration of the Greek *rhaká*, which is "a word of contempt meaning empty, worthless, foolish."[1] Jesus says that when you judge a person as worthless, you are saying that person is not fit to live. Two modern examples: 1) unborn children, says the abortionist, have no immediate value, so abortion is not murder but the destruction of something unwanted; 2) those who cannot believe in our religion, says the fanatic, are worthless, their lives are empty, so it is right to execute them. One more: the elderly, the sick, the diseased, the paralyzed, the mentally challenged (the homeless, the drunk, the addict: pick a category) cannot contribute to society, says the secularist, instead they burden society, so euthanasia is appropriate for the worthless of society. Judging someone to be of worthless character or contribution in relation to society, others, or one's self is saying they are disposable people who should be disposed of. Jesus calls that attitude murder.

The third inward motivation equivalent to murder is summed in the word *mōrós*, which I have transliterated rather than translate. *Mōrós* means "silly, stupid foolish." The English word "moron" is derived from *mōrós*. It is a more serious reproach than *rhaká*, which scorns a man by calling him stupid, whereas *mōrós* scorns him concerning his heart and character."[2] Jesus calls the attitude expressed by this word, murder.

The three conditions, and the escalating liability to judgment, the Sanhedrin, and the fire of Gehenna, show an increasingly condemning attitude toward others. All who judge others as "not fit to live" are liable to judgment, up to and including eternal punishment—which is what the reference to Gehenna indicates.

Verses 23–24 make the point in a different way. One cannot properly worship God Creator and Savior if he/she is in conflict with a fellow believer. I say, "fellow believer," because Jesus names the offended person "brother." To the Jew every other Jew was a brother (or sister) in the Lord. The Hebrew people were literally descendants of one man, Jacob, who was himself the child of Isaac, the child of Abraham. Moreover, they were joined together by one

---

[1] Zodhiates, *WSDNT*, s. v. "4469."

[2] Ibid., s. v. "3474."

religion, YHWH worship, which caused every proselyte to also be a brother or sister.

Applying that truth to Christianity, believers are related to one another by faith in Christ. Therefore, if a believer is at worship or prayer or Christian service, whether public or private, and remembers his brother or sister in Christ has "something against you," the matter should be resolved before continuing. The apostle John learned this lesson from this teaching, 1 John 3:14–15, "He who does not love his brother abides in death. Whoever hates his brother is a murderer"; 1 John 4:20, "If someone says, 'I love God,' and hates his brother, he is a liar; for he who does not love his brother whom he has seen, how can he love God whom he has not seen?" One cannot offer himself to God if he does not love his brother. Jesus is making the point that God sees to the heart of the matter—your heart. The worshiper should take the initiative to make reconciliation.

Verses 25–26 make the same point in different way. The "accuser" means an adversary in a lawsuit. In the example the two of you are on your way to the judge, because you cannot work out the problem between yourselves. To reconcile "now" is the need of the hour, because when you face the judge the time for reconciliation is past. The case Jesus sets up assumes you are (or at least may be) the one in the wrong. However, whether you are the offended party or the offending party, you, as the believer and member of the kingdom, should be the one to take the initiative to reconcile. In each of these examples (vv. 22–25), the responsibility for peace, reconciliation, right attitudes, and right behavior is on the part of the member of the kingdom.

The concluding verse (v. 26) views an eschatological eternal judgment for those who continue in such behavior (i.e., physically die without repentance from sin and faith on the Savior). Eternal judgment is the end of those who are not kingdom members. Jesus used the fires continually burning in the city trash dump, the Valley of Hinnom, as an example of eternal punishment. The "fire of Gehenna," v. 22, is a symbol of that eternal judgment whose place is the lake of fire, Revelation 20:11–15, as is the prison, v. 25. (The word *hádēs* is often mistranslated as "hell" but Gehenna/lake of fire is the true hell.) The eternity of that judgment is expressed in v. 26, in the phrase, the last coin—a reference to the smallest Roman coin. Those imprisoned in the lake of fire are sinners; they had no merit nor can they earn any merit, because they rejected the only person, Jesus the Christ, who has the merit needed to save their souls from an eternity of punishment.

Translation Matthew 5:27–30

27 "You have heard that it was said at the beginning, 'You shall not commit adultery.' 28 But I say to you that anyone looking upon a woman to lust for her has already committed adultery with her in his heart. 29 But if your right eye leads you into sin, take it out and cast it from you; it is advantageous for you that one of your members should perish, and not all your body be cast into Gehenna. 30 And if your right hand leads you to sin, cut it off and cast it from you; it is advantageous for you that one of your members should perish, and not all your body be cast into Gehenna."

EXPOSITION

Jesus repeats the prohibition against adultery exactly as it appears in Exodus 20. The ancient world viewed sexual intercourse with a married woman as a violation of the husband's property rights, but viewed it as allowable when a married man had sex with an unmarried woman. In no case was sexual activity outside of marriage viewed as appropriate for a married woman. God does not make or support these distinctions in his Word. Throughout the Bible, adultery is forbidden to any married person.

Jesus' concern is for the inner thoughts and disposition that can lead to lust and may lead to immoral action. One would be wrong to think the Old Testament did not address the inward motivation of sexual lust: Exodus 20:17; Deuteronomy 5:18, "You shall not covet your neighbor's wife." Proverbs 6:25, "Do not lust after her [the seductress] beauty in your heart." Proverbs 11:6, "The unfaithful will be caught by their lust." In v. 28 Jesus is not expanding the commandment, he is clarifying that moral corruption begins in the soul.

In vv. 29–30, Jesus cautions against allowing those thought processes, attitudes, and actions concerning sexual lust to take hold. Just as Joseph fled from Potiphar's wife and Paul tells the Thessalonians to "flee fornication," even so the believer should cut himself off from those avenues by which improper sexual thoughts enter into the soul and grow into immoral lust.

Jesus is not telling us to literally pluck out an eye or cut off a hand; he is using a hyperbole for effect. This may be seen in the use of "right eye" and "right hand." In the ancient world the right hand was symbolic of the action of one's will, because the right hand was the dominant hand (for the majority). The right hand symbolized power and authority, and by metonymy symbolized thought, impulse, effort, commitment, loyalty, honesty, inheritance, and blessing. The same ideas apply to the eye, because sight leads to decision. The idea of the right hand and right eye is thought or impulse leading to sin. What is at fault is not the physical part of the body, but the inner motivation, just as in the previous section concerning murder.

Whatever may lead a person to wrongful desires should be avoided, removed, and otherwise removed from one's life. If, for example, the believer who has a problem with alcohol keeps going into a bar, or worse, continues to work in a bar, he has let his eye and his hand lead him into sin. Even so, the believer should cut out of his life those activities that can lead him/her into temptation and sin.

The hyperbole extends to judgment; illicit sex won't cast you into Gehenna/hell, but it is a symptom that you may not be saved and are on your way to hell: people freely make the choices that lead to lust and sin, or to faith and righteousness.

Translation Matthew 5:31–32

31 "Now it was said, 'Anyone who should divorce his wife, let him give her a written notice of divorce.' 32 But I say to you, that any man divorcing his wife except on account of sexual immorality causes her to commit adultery; and whoever it may be should marry a woman having been divorced commits adultery."

EXPOSITION

> Jesus is referencing Deuteronomy 24:1–4.
>> When a man takes a wife and marries her, and it happens that she finds no favor in his eyes because he has found some uncleanness in her, and he writes her a certificate of divorce, puts it in her hand, and sends her out of his house, when she has departed from his house, and goes and becomes another man's wife, if the latter husband detests her and writes her a certificate of divorce, puts it in her hand, and sends her out of his house, or if the latter

husband dies who took her as his wife, then her former husband who divorced her must not take her back to be his wife after she has been defiled; for that is an abomination before the Lord, and you shall not bring sin on the land which the Lord your God is giving you as an inheritance. (NKJV)

This law is among a series of miscellaneous laws that Moses gave Israel just prior to their entry into the land under Joshua's leadership. The law does not command or encourage divorce but recognizes that divorce will happen—was happening—among the people.

In the case cited by Moses the man no longer desired to be married to his wife because of "some indecency," an undefined term, though not adultery, which was punishable by death. The cultures of ancient days considered women property of their husband. If she was sent away without a certificate of divorce she remained legally attached to him. The divorce certificate was for her protection, because it legally dissolved the marriage, thus leaving her free to remarry.

A single woman had no means of support in the ancient world except for husband or family. To simply kick her out of the house was to leave her destitute. Thus, Moses provided a remedy for an existing circumstance, a remedy that severed her legal "property" relationship with her husband and allowed her to remarry.

The case example goes on to suppose a second divorce, or the death of the second husband. In those circumstances the first husband could not remarry the wife he had earlier divorced. This may have been intended to prevent a cycle of marriage-divorce-remarriage for some type of gain (e.g., 24:5, to gain further deferment from military service), or prevention of frivolous divorces, or to keep a woman from being treated like property that could be disposed of and then obtained again. However, the more likely reason she could not return to her first husband, is that by marrying a second time the woman had established a "one-flesh" relationship with the second husband, which permanently ended the one-flesh relationship she previously had with the first husband. For the first husband to take her back would in essence be adultery with the wife of another man.

In relation to v. 32, it is this last that Jesus (probably) had in mind. The one-flesh relationship that is the bond of marriage, Jesus says, can only be broken when a spouse commits sexual activity with a person not his or her spouse. Thus, to marry a woman having been divorced (sexual consummation is assumed) is to break the bond of her former relationship.

This breaking of that bond technically constitutes adultery. The certificate of divorce dissolved the property relationship, but could not break the one-flesh bond. Only sexual activity apart from marriage can break it. Thus, when Jesus states that he who divorces his wife for a cause other than her adultery is causing her to commit adultery when she remarries, he is not assigning blame to the woman who was divorced, but to the man who divorced her.

The spouse who commits the act of divorce against his or her spouse is causing the former spouse to commit adultery when he/she marries another. The sexual activity of the second marriage breaks the bond of the first, and that sexual activity is technically adultery. We should keep in mind that this is not Jesus' only word on the subject of divorce (cf. 19:3–121), and the whole should be considered, not merely the parts. At Mark 10:11–12 Jesus said,

> And he said to them, "Whoever may divorce his wife and should marry another commits adultery against her. 12 And if the woman has herself divorced the husband and should marry to another, she commits adultery."

In the Mark passage Jesus makes it clear that the person committing the act of divorce, whether the husband or the wife, is the one who has sinned. (A woman could divorce her husband in first century Judaism, although she had to petition the court to do so, whereas he could simply write out a notice of divorce). The innocent party—the one against whom the act of divorce had been committed, was free to remarry. Compare 1 Corinthians 7:10–11 where Paul states the same as Jesus at Mark 10:11–12. Compare also 1 Corinthians 7:15, abandonment by an unbeliever. In either case—abandonment or the victim of divorce—the person divorced or abandoned was not the sinner, and sexual consummation of a second marriage was not a sin.

The King's rule for members of his kingdom was to work out their problems and remain married. Sometimes, however, one or both spouses give up and divorce occurs.

Translation Matthew 5:31–32

33 "Again, you have heard that it was said at the beginning,

'You shall not swear falsely, but you shall keep your oaths to the Lord.' 34 But I say to you not to swear at all: not by heaven, because it is God's throne; 35 not by the earth, because it is the footstool for his feet; not by Jerusalem, it is the city of the great King; 36 not by your head will you swear, because you are not able to make one hair white or black. 37 But let your word be 'Yes,' 'Yes'; 'No,' 'No'; now more than these comes from evil."

EXPOSITION

The scriptures connected in this statement (Jesus does not quote, he combines) are Leviticus 19:12; Numbers 30:2; Deuteronomy 23:21; Psalm 50:14; Zechariah 8:17. Jesus is not declaring a strict prohibition against oaths, because Jesus himself took an oath, Matthew 26:63–64. The point being made is found in v. 37. The integrity, honesty, and reputation of the believer should be such that his word is not open to more than one interpretation; that he does not have to guarantee the truthfulness of his word by an oath.

(In some circumstances, such as testimony given in a court of law, unbelievers demand an oath as a guarantee against lying. The believer must live in the world and therefore must conform to the world in harmless matters, such as promising to do what his born-again nature would naturally lead him or her to do: tell the truth.)

Those who follow Jesus must speak the truth; it should never be necessary for a believer to confirm his/her word by appeal to God, to some religious icon or location, nor by one's self. To have to confirm the truth by an oath comes from evil (some versions translate "the evil one."). This word from Jesus reflects his historical circumstances where oaths, such as he examples, were common and expected. In our vastly more secular world oath-taking is not so common, or has been reduced to "I swear," a meaningless oath whose guarantor is the oath-taker.

Translation Matthew 5:38–42

38 "You have heard that it was said, 'Eye for eye and tooth for tooth.' 39 But I say to you, resist not the evil; but whoever might strike you on your right cheek, turn to him also the other; 40 and to the one willing to sue you and take your shirt, let him have your coat also; 41 and whoever may compel you to go one mile, go with him two. 42 To the one asking, give; and you should not turn away from the one desiring to borrow from you."

TRANSLATION NOTE

In v. 39 the word *rhapízō*, strike, originally meant to beat with rods, but in the New Testament is used in the sense of "to hit with the open hand, to cuff, slap, especially the cheeks or ears, with the accusative (Matt. 5:39 where it means to strike)."[1]

In v. 40 where I have translated "shirt" and "coat" (following the HCSB); the original is "tunic" and "cloak."

EXPOSITION

Jesus is speaking against personal retribution in civil matters. The civil portion of the Old Testament Law was for government to enforce by appropriate legal means. The words in v. 38 come from Exodus 21:24; Leviticus 24:20; Deuteronomy 19:21. The Exodus passage, 21:12–27 refers to legal remedy for injury caused by violence. The Leviticus passage, 24:17–22, also refers to legal remedy for injury caused by violence. The Deuteronomy passage, 19:15–21, refers to legal remedy to be applied to a false witness.

What is evident in these passages is that the law refers to legal retribution, not personal retribution. Yet, personal retribution was how these verses had been interpreted. In the correct view as applied to v. 39, those offended were not to seek personal redress; suitable legal remedies should be sought to maintain public order.

The Christian should avoid escalating personal conflict. In countries where Christianity is the underdog this could lead to harassment and persecution; a non-confrontational attitude could lessen the anger of the enemy. One should note that for a right handed person to slap another on the right cheek would require a back-handed slap. This was not only physical injurious but was considered a humiliating insult (cf. Isaiah 50:6).

The thought in v. 40 is *not* to give away your possessions to every person who asks or begs, but is a response to legal action. People's dress in these times consisted (from skin out) of a loin cloth, a tunic from shoulders to knees (to ankles for women), a cloak (the outer garment), a belt (or sash) around the waist, a head covering, and sandals or shoes. A tunic functioned in some ways like a shirt. The Old Testament forbade taking a person's cloak (Exodus 22:25–27; Deuteronomy 24:12–13), so the action

---

[1] Zodhiates, *WSDNT*, s. v. "4474."

envisioned may be taking the tunic/shirt as a pledge for a debt. Jesus says the proper response when being sued for your shirt is to also give the person your more valuable outer garment. (cf. 1 Corinthians 6:7; perhaps also Romans 13:8).

The circumstance in v. 41 was a condition of Roman occupation. Under Roman law a soldier could compel the citizen of an occupied country to carry the soldier's military gear for a Roman mile (4,854 feet). This imposition was deeply resented by the people of Palestine. Jesus says the believer is to go well beyond the demanded service; in a larger sense the believer is to put up with unreasonable and disliked demands. What is in view is attitude, not necessarily the action.

Verse 42 expresses the point at issue in vv. 38–41. The believer need not be insistent as to what he or others may consider his natural or legal rights, but is to understand "right" as those rules of living that regulate his attitudes and behavior as a member of the kingdom, even if this results in a loss (temporary or otherwise) of those natural and legal rights. Verse 42 insists the believer make generosity a characteristic of his/her behavior, without judging if the person asking is deserving or undeserving. This is not limited to material goods, which the believer may not have (or may not have what is being asked), it includes kind words and good counsel. One should be willing to give what one has to meet the circumstances.

Let us also understand that these verses do not contradict other scriptures requiring the believer to meet the various needs in his life, such as caring for self and family, providing food and home, meeting financial obligations, and yes, even satisfying reasonable desires. The believer whose life is regulated by Scripture has his priorities in the proper order: God, family, others, self. The believer must take care of his (or her) own spiritual and material needs, otherwise he/she has nothing with which to minister to others. Family begins with one's immediate family, and in some circumstances extended family may be classed with "others." As we have been given, so let us give.

Translation Matthew 5:43–48

43 "You have heard that it was said, 'You will love your neighbor and you will hate your enemy.' 44 But I say to you, love your enemies, and pray for those persecuting you; bless those cursing

you, do good to those misusing you and hating you, 45 so that you may be sons of your Father in the heavens. Because he makes his sun rise on evil and good, and sends rain on righteous and unrighteous. 46 For if you love those loving you, what reward have you? Do not also the tax-collectors do the same? 47 And if you greet your brothers only, what more do you? Do not also the gentiles do the same? 48 Therefore you will be perfect, just as your heavenly Father is perfect."

TRANSLATION NOTE

In v. 44 the clause "bless those cursing you, do good to those misusing you and hating you" is considered by the moderns as "not originally present in Matthew's account of the Sermon on the Mount, their omission in early representatives of the witnesses [various manuscripts] would be entirely unaccountable. The divergence of readings among the added clauses likewise speaks against their originality."[1] The clause is considered to have been imported from Luke 6:27–28 by later scribes.

The manuscripts Metzger lists are from the Western, Alexandrian, Eastern (Syrian), and Egyptian groups. There are four Egyptian manuscripts, dated between AD 200 and 400. If an assumed common ancestor was missing the clause, then it is understandable why the clause is missing in the four extant Egyptian manuscripts. Manuscripts Aleph and B of the Alexandrian group, also cited, are the only manuscripts from the fourth century; a likely common ancestor would affect Aleph and B. The same might be said for the others. Metzger doesn't mention the Byzantine group.

Irenaeus (AD 130–202) is often cited as not using the clause, writing, "Love your enemies and pray for those that hate you."[2] However, it will be noted he joins the first and last parts, omitting the middle. I have placed in brackets the part Irenaeus omits: "[But I say to you,] love your enemies, and pray for those [persecuting you; bless those cursing you, do good to those misusing you and] hating you." It would seem Irenaeus knew the entire verse and used what suited his purpose. Irenaeus was born in Turkey and knew Polycarp of Smyrna. He would have known the Eastern

---

[1] Metzger, *Textual*, 12.
[2] Roberts, *ANF*, 1:447.

(Syrian) group missing the clause and Byzantine group of manuscripts containing the clause.

Cyprian (AD ca. 200–258) is also cited as not knowing the disputed clause. He quotes from Matthew 5:44 three times, each time leaving out "bless those cursing you, do good to those misusing you and hating you."[1] Cyprian was born in Carthage, North Africa, and would have known the Alexandrian, Western, and Egyptian manuscripts which do not have the clause.

If one depends solely on the manuscripts out of North Africa (Alexandrian, Western, Egyptian) then the clause is not original. When one adds in the Byzantine group, then its originality is less in doubt.

The fact is modern Language Authorities universally dismiss the Byzantine group of manuscripts, from which the KJV has its text. They are not the oldest, but they are the most numerous, providing a large base from which to judge scribal errors and additions. It is possible the clause was not original to Matthew and later imported into Matthew from Luke. Nevertheless, looking at Irenaeus and the Byzantine group of manuscripts, I have decided to retain the clause in the verse.

In v. 47 some manuscripts read *telōnēs*, tax-collector, versus *ethnikós*, nations, i.e., gentiles. I decided to use *ethnikós* to maintain the progression: v. 45, unrighteous, v. 46, tax-collectors, v. 47, gentiles.

EXPOSITION

Jesus is stating (or summarizing) the popular teaching of the day. The commandment to love one's neighbor is stated in the law at Leviticus 19:18. However, the Old Testament nowhere teaches that one's enemy is to be hated. There are times when a negative or opposite statement is reasonably implied from a positive statement; it is a principle of logic that a positive statement of truth implies that the opposite is also true. This was what the people had been taught. However, this teaching ignored other positive commands throughout the Old Testament, such as, Proverbs 25:21, "If your enemy is hungry, give him bread to eat; and if he is thirsty, give him water to drink" (NKJV) The teachers were setting a lower standard, just as they did with Leviticus 19:18, which commands

---

[1] Ibid., 5:485, 495, 546.

the believer not just to love his neighbor, but to love his neighbor just as he would love himself.

Skeptics and Christians alike have problems with vv. 43, 44. These problems center in three concepts: who is my neighbor, what is an enemy, and what is love? In the Leviticus passage there is little doubt the neighbor was a fellow Israelite. Leviticus 19:17 speaks of one's brother and neighbor; v. 18 speaks of the "children of your people" and a neighbor. In 1 Samuel 14:20 the term is used of another nation, the Philistines, who were fighting one another, "every man's sword was against his neighbor."

In the Old Testament view the term neighbor implies an innate relationship, whether by birth, race, national origin, etc. For example, 1 Samuel 15:28, "So Samuel said to Saul, 'YHWH has taken the kingdom of Israel from you this day and given it to your neighbor, who is better than you,' " That "neighbor" was David, who had nothing in common with Saul except they were both Israelites. Proverbs 27:10 says, "Do not forsake your own friend or your father's friend, nor go to your brother's house in the day of your calamity; better is a neighbor nearby than a brother far away." In this instance, to the Israelite reading Proverbs, the neighbor was a man of his own race.

Jesus broadens the concept of neighbor in the parable known as the Good Samaritan. A neighbor is the one who is present to help in a time of need, and a neighbor is one who needs help. It is this reciprocal relationship that redefines neighbor to include others besides those with whom we have an innate relationship. A neighbor can be someone you don't know who needs help, and you become his neighbor when you provide the help. The Proverbs 27:10 citation indicates this point of view, even in Old Testament Israel, where the person living next door may not have been a fellow Israelite.

Nor was this a new thought. The concept of who is my neighbor is extended in Leviticus 19:34 to "the stranger [foreigner/non-Israelite] who dwells among you," saying that you shall love him as you love yourself. In Christianity the innate "neighbor" relationship is common salvation in Christ, but this does not prevent the believer from acting the part of a neighbor to any who are in need.

This, then, is the point. In both Old and New Testament a neighbor is someone with whom you have an innate relationship, and a neighbor is someone who needs the help you are able to provide. The Christian is to be a neighbor to all by showing mercy and giving help (in mundane or significant ways) to meet the need of the moment. In the Good Samaritan parable the man needing help was not the Samaritan's innate neighbor, but the Samaritan made him his neighbor and became his neighbor when he met his need.

Who is an enemy? An enemy is someone who is actively opposed to you. However, you are not actively opposed to him, unless forced to defend yourself, defend another to whom you are a neighbor, or are defending righteousness against unrighteousness for the sake of right and the glory of Christ (defense is not always physical violence).

An enemy is not merely one who disagrees with you. A person must actively engage in hostility (not necessarily physical hostility) toward you to be an enemy. Saul became David's enemy, 1 Samuel 18:29. The pagans in the land were the enemy of Israel because they actively opposed God. Elijah was Ahab's enemy (1 Kings 21:20), because Ahab opposed God and Elijah was God's sword to execute justice upon Ahab and idolatrous Israel. An enemy is the one who hates the righteous, Psalm 106:10, pursuing the righteous person in order to do harm.

The believer is not to reciprocate with the same hatred. Proverbs 24:17, "Do not rejoice when your enemy falls, and do not let your heart be glad when he stumbles" (NKJV). Why? Verse 18, "Lest the Lord see it, and it displease Him, and He turn away His wrath from him" (NKJV). Why would God turn away his wrath from your enemy? Because hatred is not righteous. The way of the righteous is not to act like the unrighteous. The enemy hates, a citizen of the kingdom acts in the best good of others (he/she loves).

In Psalm 139:21–22 David says he hates those who hate God, he hates them with a perfect hatred and counts them as enemies. A "perfect hatred" is without malice. It is a righteous indignation that recognizes the unrighteous actively oppose God; but the righteous actively oppose sin. A "perfect hatred" is the hatred of wickedness as wickedness, the righteous soul joining with God in his (God's) opposition to evil. Note how David ends this Psalm, vv. 23–24, with an appeal to God to search out any wicked way in David's own soul. David would count himself as God's enemy—as his own enemy—until any wicked way within him was purged.

Love is misunderstood when separated from the meaning established by biblical use. Love may express itself in affection and sentiment, but emotions are not love, they are the result of love.

> Love is a decision of the will to actively seek the best good for another person, without expectation of recompense, reciprocity, or recognition for one's self, and without consideration of merit or demerit in the one so loved.

Seeking the best good can be expressed in many ways. One can meet material, emotional, mental, or spiritual needs. Leviticus 19:17 is very clear that rebuking sin in your neighbor is love and abetting his sin by saying nothing is hatred. Sin separates a person from God; a rebuke may lead to repentance and salvation; saying nothing, doing nothing, is a statement that you are willing to allow your neighbor to be lost from God. What greater expression of hatred can there be?

God, says Jesus, acts in a loving way toward those who actively oppose him in their sinful state. God is kind and merciful to his enemies. He makes the sun to rise and the rain to fall on those who are evil as well as those who are good—God gives the wicked the ability to live and prosper in the world.

We know God sends his people with the salvation message to rebuke sinners of their sins. The believer is to be like God: he is to seek the good of others; salvation is the best good. Verse 44 is simply a way of saying do not act like the unrighteous when they act like sinners toward you. Rather, act like a righteous person toward them: do good not evil; pray for their needs.

Jesus gives examples of the behavior he promotes as godly. Do not act in retribution but pray and bless. God acts in retribution only after suffering long with the sinner. Retribution belongs to the Lord only—for he is the one whom sinners are opposing; believers are objects belonging to God who receive the sinner's opposition.

The second example is in v. 46. In the Jewish view, few were considered more wicked than tax-collectors. Tax collection was a franchise business the Roman government sold to individuals and corporations. To win the franchise the prospective franchisee competitively bid a certain amount of money to collect in taxes to be paid to Rome. Then, like any business, they collected more money than needed to satisfy Roman taxation in order to make a profit for themselves. Many collected a very large profit, using their position as *de facto* members of the Roman government to extort more money than was needed. They were hated for forcing Israel to support the Roman oppressors, for making a profit out of the misery of Israel, and for the dishonest practices by which they enriched themselves at the expense of their own people.

Therefore this example is very soul-searching. Even tax-collectors love those who love them. What are you doing that makes you different than them? Verse 47 is much the same, but the progression—the unrighteous, the tax-collectors—culminates with the most hated group, the gentiles: all who were not Jews. The gentiles were the highest example of unrighteousness, universally considered unclean, idolaters, thieves, and murderers. (Jesus is using the views of others to make his point.)

The unrighteous, the tax-collectors, and the gentiles are kind and friendly to one another but opposed to the righteous. They have two standards of behavior. The believer must have one standard of behavior: to be kind, as God is kind, to all. Jesus is not saying believers must trust the wicked, or must seek out their companionship, or actively engage in conflict with the wicked. Jesus opposed the unrighteous scribes and Pharisees with strong words. Love does not flee from controversy and is not afraid to rebuke. The believer is a tiny island in a sea of worldly wickedness. The unrighteous will seek out the believer: either to persecute them or to seek an answer for the hope believers have in Christ. When that happens, the believer's behavior is to be like God's and unlike theirs.

The concluding v. 48 says that by practicing God's standards of behavior the kingdom member becomes "perfect," *téleios*, as "your Father in heaven" is perfect, *téleios*. The word *téleios* has the idea of reaching the goal, thus to achieve a state of being full, or complete.[1] *Teleiōs* means perfect when applied to God but not when applied to human beings. When applied to believers *téleios* has the idea of spiritual maturity. The maturing believer thinks and acts more and more according to God's rules for living—the same rules God applies to his own behavior, the same rules Jesus followed—and in this he becomes, in later New Testament terms, Christ-like in his attitudes and behavior. He acts like the son of God his salvation has made him to be.

---

[1] Zodhiates, *WSDNT*, s. v. "5046."

Matthew Six

Translation Matthew 6:1-4

1 "But beware your righteousness is not practiced before men in order to be seen by them; otherwise you will have no reward from your Father in the heavens. 2 Therefore when you practice compassion toward the poor, do not sound a trumpet before you, as the hypocrites do in the synagogues and in the streets, that they might have glory from men. Truly, I say to you, they have their reward. 3 But when you practice compassion toward the poor, do not let your left hand know what your right hand is doing, 4 so that your compassion toward the poor may be in secret; and your Father, the one seeing in secret, will reward you."

TRANSLATION NOTE

In vv. 2–4 the word translated "compassion toward the poor" is *eleēmosúnē*, "mercifulness, compassion."[1] In the New Testament, through a figure of speech known as the metonymy of effect for cause, it is translated alms, charity, money given to the poor, giving, giving to the needy, give to the poor. When this word is used it indicates active compassion or mercy, hence my translation, "compassion toward the poor."

In vv. 4, 6, and 18 the earliest Western manuscripts end with "will reward you," but other manuscripts end with "will reward you in the open." If this condition was in one verse only, then it would be more likely a scribe accidentally failed to copy "in the open" than having added those three words. In that case, "in the open" would be considered part of the original text. However, when the same condition occurs in three different verses, it is likely a scribe deliberately added words in a well-intentioned effort to make the text better in a way that seemed good to the scribe (something New Testament scribes were known to do). The addition of "in the open" seems designed to provide an explicit antithesis to the preceding "in secret."

I also considered the theology created by adding "in the open." God does see all, so he does see "in secret." When compassionate giving is done without public acknowledgement (privately,

---

[1] Ibid., s. v. "1654."

secretly), God who knows all things knows what was done. However, it is not always true that God rewards openly those things done privately. Sometimes God's rewards are done in secret, because they are the intangible things of increased faith, or the satisfaction of knowing one has pleased God, or increased understanding, or more intimate fellowship.

I also noticed that adding the words "in the open" creates the very condition Christ is speaking against. If the Father rewards compassionate giving in the open then the act of giving may become known by others, and thus one will be rewarded with the approval of others.

Based on these textual, doctrinal, and contextual reasons I decided not to include "in the open" in my translation.

EXPOSITION

The kingdom rules in this chapter might be titled, "How to practice your faith." Three activities are used as examples: compassionate giving, prayer, and fasting. In each the focus of the practice is God not man. At issue is the attitude—the intent of the heart—underlying the practice of one's faith: is God the intended focus and ultimate recipient of our faith? Or are we practicing the mechanics of faith so as to be recognized by fellow believers as a faithful man or woman? Compassionate giving should be private, the meaning of "do not let your left hand know what your right hand is doing."

The word "reward" in v. 2 is the ordinary word for a commercial receipt—a cash register receipt for something purchased.[1] The vocal and very public giver has purchased a reputation. Today there is a business of keeping and publishing lists of charitable institutions (both those who give and those who receive), charitable contributions, and those who make such contributions. Many governments (USA comes to mind) give tax relief for charitable giving.

To all this Jesus replies that it is not Christian giving if the intent in giving is to make the giving widely known. In Jesus' day there were no charitable institutions, but there was widespread poverty, thus a broad opportunity for individual compassionate giving. Many took advantage of this opportunity to show by their giving just how

---

[1] Morris, *Matthew*, 137.

religious they were. Their intent was to gain a reputation.

Public giving at the Jerusalem temple provides an example. On the outer wall of the court of the women there were thirteen funnels set into the wall that led to thirteen chests inside the wall to receive money dropped into the funnels. The funnels were called "trumpets" because they were narrow at the opening and wide at the end that dumped into the chests.[1] Each trumpet was marked with the object the contribution would benefit, such as purchasing wood for the altar, supporting orphaned children and widows, buying animals for the daily sacrifices. Luke 21:1 (Mark 14:41) shows how the wealthy could use these trumpets to "trumpet" their giving.

Jesus says the intent of compassionate giving should be to help others and then to trust in God to provide the appropriate reward for faithful practice. The focus is not on being rewarded, but that God's approval—however that approval is manifested—is superior to men's reward. Compassionate giving should be considered a service to God, by which, in acting like God by being kind to others, and by being a neighbor to those who need a neighbor, the believer is doing the works of God.

A word about the USA practice of not taxing compassionate giving. I have noticed that when this practice is in some way threatened, Christians seem to rise up as one man against this "threat." What does it matter if giving is tax free? Our heavenly Father sees and knows and rewards accordingly. This rule of taxation is actually a piece of social engineering, a governmental leash to restrict the historical activity of the church to address and seek redress of social injustice and cultural wrongs. The tax-break is threatened if a church discusses so-called "political" issues. Why is the USA Christian community allowing itself to be threatened by the world in this manner? Is a tax break for compassionate giving the kind of open reward Christ speaks against? Let Christians be content that their Father, the one seeing in secret, rewards them as he sees fit.

Translation Matthew 6:5–8

5 "And when you pray, do not be like the hypocrites, because they love to pray in the synagogues and in the corners of the

---

[1] Edersheim, *The Temple*, 25.

streets, standing to pray, so that they may be seen by men. Truly, I say to you, they have their reward. 6 But you, when you pray, go into your room, and having shut your door, pray to your Father who is in secret; and your Father seeing in secret will reward you. 7 Now when praying, do not repeat the same thing over and over again like the pagans; for they think that in their many words they will be heard. 8 Therefore do not be like them. For the Father knows of what things you have need before you ask him."

TRANSLATION NOTE

In v. 7 the word *battologéō*, usually translated "vain repetitions," "babble," or "empty phrases" I have translated, "repeat the same thing over and over again." The word means "to speak foolishly, babble, chatter . . . much talk without content, repeating the same thing over and over again, useless speech without distinct expression of purpose."[1]

EXPOSITION

Prayer is a communication between a son of God and his/her heavenly Father. There are times when public prayer is appropriate, because it is intended to be an expression of prayer for all those gathered within hearing. That is not the practice Jesus is addressing. The "religious" among the populace would pray in public without an intent or purpose other than to show that they were a devout and religious person. This is a sort of "charitable giving" to God, i.e., giving God the gift of your time so others can see how gracious and devout you are.

In addition, the then-current practice (still in use today) was to repeatedly say the same prayer in an effort to force God to pay attention. This is what the pagans did, because they had no assurance their gods would pay attention, unless annoyed, or excessively flattered, by the incessant repetition.

On the other hand, the believer has faith in an omniscient God who knows the need before asked. Why pray if God knows? Prayer is not to inform God of the need or desire, but is an act of worship toward the loving God who meets needs and answers appropriate desires. Prayer declares the sufficiency of God and the dependence of the believer. God has decreed prayer as a means by which he

---

[1] Zodhiates, *WSDNT*, s. v. "945."

will accomplish his purpose, plans, and processes. Prayer is a means by which the believer worships God by declaring God's majesty and the believer's dependence on God. The reward is not an open show, like the hypocrites whose praying in the open is their reward, but the believer's reward is God's approval.

Translation Matthew 6:9–15

9 "You, therefore, pray in this manner: 'Our Father, who is in the heavens, your name be sanctified, 10 your kingdom come, your will be done, as in heaven also upon earth. 11 Our daily bread give us today, 12 and forgive us our offenses, even as we have forgiven those who offend us. 13 And bring us not into a state of trial, but deliver us from the evildoers.' 14 For if you forgive men their wrongdoing, your heavenly Father will also forgive you. 15 But if you do not forgive men their wrongdoing, neither will your Father forgive your wrongdoing."

TRANSLATION NOTES

In v. 13 I have translated the familiar "lead us not into temptation," as "bring us not into a state of trial." That is the translation suggested by Zodhiates.[1] The word is *peirasmós*.

> Satan tempts, *peirázō* (James 1:13, 14) in a malicious effort to destroy faith. God tests or tries, *peirasmós*, to assess, improve, and approve faith.[2]

> A *peirasmós* could be a "life happens" difficulty brought about by the circumstances, or adversity, affliction, or sorrow from God for the purpose of proving faith. Thus, in James 1:12, "blessed is the person who endures a *peirasmós*," a trial. God may send a trial, *peirasmós*, but he does not send temptation, *peirázō*.[3]

> What James is teaching would be plainer if all Bible versions had translated *peirasmós* as "trial" and *peirázō* as "temptation" or "solicitation." Count it all joy when you fall into trials. . . . Blessed is the person who endures a trial. . . . Let no person say when he is tempted, 'I am solicited to sin [*peirázō*, tempted] by God'; for God is untemptable by

---

[1] Ibid., s. v. "3986."

[2] Quiggle, *James*, 9.

[3] Ibid., 66.

Matthew Six

evil, nor does he himself solicit [*peirázō*] anyone to evil.[1]

In v. 13 I have translated the phrase *ton ponērós* as "the evildoers." Literally the words are "the evil" with *ponērós*, evil, in the neuter gender. In his/her daily life a believer struggles against internal and external influences that seek to change their thoughts and actions. Temptation from within and without seeks to lead the believer to commit an act of sin. The believer also struggles against the unsaved; evildoers are the unsaved who oppose Christ and his saved people. These seek to prevent believers from living like Christ.

Satan, the primary *ton ponērós*, is overcome representatively, not directly. Literally it is sinful persons that are overcome—persons who serve Satan's purposes by serving sin. By overcoming evildoers one has overcome Satan. The saved fight spiritual battles, but they do not fight in the spirit domain. The believer's fight is in the material domain against *ton ponērós* opposing Christ and his saved people.

In v. 13, the familiar doxology, "Because yours is the kingdom and the power and the glory forever. Amen," is not present in the oldest manuscripts. It appears, along with variations in the wording, in later manuscripts. "The use of this doxology arose when this prayer began to be used as a liturgy to be recited or to be chanted in public worship."[2] The words are not present in Luke's version, 11:2–4, either. Additionally, although Jesus used "amen" to begin a sentence ("'Truly' I say to you") he never used "amen" at the end of a sentence, unless this is the only instance (for 28:20 see comments there). For these reasons I have not included it as part of the translation.

In v. 14 the word I translated "wrongdoing" is usually translated "trespasses." The word is *paráptōma*, fault, error, lapse, mistake, wrongdoing."[3]

EXPOSITION

The prayer in vv. 9–13, is not to be woodenly repeated as a one-size-fits for all occasions. This is a model of the elements of prayer. These elements are succinctly stated by Paul in Philippians

---

[1] Ibid., 67.
[2] Robertson, *Word Pictures*, 1:55; cf. Metzger, *Textual*, 13–14.
[3] Zodhiates, *WSDNT*, s. v. "3900."

Matthew Six

4:6. Prayer is worship, prayer asking for oneself (supplication), prayer is asking for others (intercession), and prayer is thanksgiving. All these elements of prayer are to be presented to God in an attitude of the assurance of faith, not the anxiety of unbelief.

"Our Father" recognizes the relationship the believer has with God in Christ. In this prayer in Matthew (and Luke), Christ anticipates later New Testament doctrine to be taught by the Holy Spirit (John 16:13). Because God is "the God and Father of our Lord Jesus Christ," e.g., Ephesians 1:3; 1 Peter 1:3, and the believer is "in Christ," e.g., 1 Peter 5:14, then God is also the God and Father of the believer.

Sanctification means to be set aside for one specific purpose and no other purpose. The censors in the tabernacle/temple were used there, and nowhere else. My toothbrush has been sanctified to one use and nothing else. Thus sanctification is both dedication and separation. Salvation sets a believer apart from sin and dedicates him/her to God, thus he/she is sanctified—and is to practice that sanctification by a morally pure and righteous manner of life.

The petition "your name be sanctified" is recognition that God—the name represents the person—is above all else and separated from all that does not bring glory to him. "Your name be sanctified" understands God is morally pure (holy), and is a promise from the believer to worship God in a manner that respects his moral purity. "Your name be sanctified" is a promise to invoke God in a manner that respects who he is as God, and not use his name vainly.

Three petitions follow in quick succession. "Your kingdom come" looks toward Christ's kingdom on earth. Jesus the Jew and messiah is addressing fellow Jews expecting the messiah and (even at this early date in their relationship with Jesus) hoping Jesus is the messiah. The subject most associated with the messiah was renewal of the Davidic Kingdom. New Testament Christians also anticipate the coming Davidic kingdom when they (with national ethnic Israel) will rule with Christ, Hebrews 12:28; Revelation 5:10.

"Your will be done" also anticipates the messianic kingdom when the messiah "will rule them with a rod of iron" (Psalm 2:9; Revelation 19:15) enforcing his standards of righteousness in his kingdom. The petition also looks toward the Kingdom of God (God's universal rule over his creation for all time and eternity) when Christ will "deliver the kingdom to God the Father," 1 Corinthians 15:24.

The petition "as in heaven also upon earth" recognizes God's will is always accomplished in heaven. There are three heavens in Scripture. The earth's atmosphere; the second heaven which is the domain of spirit beings; the third heaven—a specific location in the second heaven—where only holy angels and redeemed men dwell. God has given human kind a brief glimpse of the third heaven in Revelation 4, 5. Right now God allows fallen angels and human beings to act contrary to his will—but he makes the wrath of man to praise him (Psalm 76:10) and makes all things work together for the good of his saved people (Romans 8:28). There will be a time when all things on the earth are done according to God's will in messiah's kingdom, just as in the heavens.

The petition for daily bread is for all the necessities of life. In the ancient world bread was the daily food for all peoples, sometimes the only food. In the thinking of the ancient world, bread was the staff and stuff of life. Thus the petition for daily bread would have been understood as responding to physical and spiritual needs.

Verse 12, with vv. 14–15, states an important biblical principle: believers are to act like the sons of God they are. Since God forgives, believers are to forgive. What is *not* in view is salvation: this is prayer by a believer, not a prayer to become a believer.

How, then, might a believer expect God to forgive his or her wrongdoing against God, if that believer is not willing to forgive the wrongdoing others commit against him/her? Forgiveness is showing mercy, being kind and compassionate, and demonstrating Christ in us to those in desperate need of Christ. Morris, puts it this way.

> It is not that the act of forgiving merits an eternal reward, but rather it is evidence that the grace of God is at work in the forgiving person and that the same grace will bring him forgiveness in due course . . . Jesus is saying that to fail to forgive others is to demonstrate that one has not felt the saving touch of God.[1]

There are two petitions in v. 13, the first related to the second. The petition "bring us not into a state of trial" is further explained

---

[1] Morris, *Matthew*, 149.

by "deliver us from the evildoers." God uses a trial to assess, improve, and approve faith. Some trials are brought about by life's circumstances. Other trials are the result of dealing with "evildoers," i.e., the unsaved opposing Christ and his saved people. The word "evildoers" is a translation of the phrase *ton ponērós*, "the evil."

> I understand *ton ponērós* in the wider sense of persons doing evil, versus the narrower sense of Satan (most commentators). In other words, I take a more practical, earth-bound view of the struggle against evil. While it is true a victory over evil deeds and evil persons—whether through a righteous life or a righteous death—can be named a victory over Satan and his evil angels, because he/they are the source of much evil in the world, it is not Satan and his fallen angels the believer fights.[1]

All trials are to be endured through submission to and dependence upon Christ. The Bible promises to make a way to endure through trials, 1 Corinthians 10:13. Here, Christ states it is proper to ask God to prevent trials from evil doers.

Translation Matthew 6:16–18

16 "Now, whenever you fast, do not be like the hypocrites with sad faces. For they disfigure their faces, so that they may appear to men to be fasting. Truly I say to you, they have their reward. 17 But you fasting anoint your head and wash your face, 18 so that you may not appear to men to be fasting, but to your Father who is in secret; and your Father seeing in secret will reward you.

EXPOSITION

Fasting, which is voluntary in Scripture, was mandatory under rabbinical interpretations policies regulating religious actions. For the religious, public fasting was a way of demonstrating their piety.

Biblical fasting is a private means of expressing mourning, repentance, devotion to God, or focus on God's will. Most fasting in the Bible is for mourning or repentance. Fasting is usually accompanied by prayer as the means to express devotion and focus. The religious castes among the Jews had turned it into mere religious formality and duty.

Jesus' complaint is the same as previous: some were doing a

---

[1] Quiggle, *John's Epistles*, 96–97.

religiously-oriented work for publicity and reputation. If the fasting person looks like he/she is suffering, then they must be suffering for their faith, and therefore have gained the praise of men for their religious devotion. Jesus puts the focus back on God.

Translation Matthew 6:19–23

19 "Do not store up for yourselves treasures upon earth where moth and rust destroy, and where thieves break in and steal, 20 but store up for yourselves treasures in heaven, where neither moth nor rust destroy and where thieves do not break in nor steal. 21 For where your treasure is, there will be your heart also. 22 The lamp of the body is the eye. Therefore if therefore your eye is healthy, your whole body will be full of light. 23 But if your eye is evil, all your body will be full of darkness. If therefore the light that is within you is darkness, how great that darkness!"

EXPOSITION

What is the believer's reward when piety is practiced according to biblical standards? The reward is a secured treasure in heaven. The treasure in heaven is not in material things, but in a relationship with God in Christ. This treasure is experienced in part in the here and now and in full in heaven. Christ has purchased blessings and an inheritance for the believer, Ephesians 1:3ff.[1]

> Eternal life as that quality of life which is vitally communicated from God to the believer.
>
> Spiritual understanding leading to the knowledge and practical application of the Scripture.
>
> Spiritual perception that gives a sense of the immediate presence of God and a sense of prayer heard and answered.
>
> Spiritual victory to limit the power of sin's temptation and pleasure.
>
> Godly love to pay attention to and care for the spiritual and physical well-being of others through selfless acts of love and good works.
>
> Persevering faith that enables continuing belief and practice of the truth throughout life.
>
> Godliness, which is God manifested in the believer when

---

[1] Quiggle, *Ephesians*, 11.

Matthew Six

he/she lives a righteous life.

Christ-like dependence upon God and complete trust in his providence and power.

Christ-likeness, which is having and practicing the moral values, holiness of life, and certainty of purpose that characterized Christ, in order to actively pursue fellowship, obedience, and service to God to fulfill his purposes and plans for my life.

There is also "an inheritance not-corruptible and not-defiled and not-fading, reserved in heaven for you," 1 Peter 1:4.[1] Paul prays at Ephesians 3:14–21 for God to give the believer the fullest understanding possible of all the unfathomable blessings they have in Christ, which includes those received now, and those yet to be received in the yet-future of heaven. The believer's treasure in heaven truly exceeds all possible earthly, material treasures. The believer adds to his/her treasure by living a Christ-like life, re: the rewards to be received after this mortal life has ended, 1 Corinthians 3:14.

Verse 21 makes the point that people put time and effort into the things they value. In v. 22 the key word is *haplóos*. "When the eye accomplishes its purpose of seeing things as they are, then it is *haplóos:* single, healthy, perfect."[2] Metaphorically it means without duplicity (deceitful in speech or actions), hence it is sometimes translated "single."

As the "lamp" of the body," the eye shines light into the mind/soul. The point is not physical sight as much as mental perception, knowledge, understanding; from there it becomes a figure of morality versus immorality, for to understand truth is to live morally. If the "eye," which is to say one's character, is spiritually healthy, then the person sees things as they really are.

Thus, a healthy eye sees the truth, and the truth creates a moral person. The phrase "if your eye is evil" moves from the physical illustration to the heart of the matter, substituting eye-as-lamp for immoral things a person might see and think upon and wrongfully desire. Here Paul's admonition sheds "light," on the subject, Philippians 4:8, "As to the rest, brethren, whatever is

---

[1] Quiggle, *1 Peter*, 23 (Translation).
[2] Zodhiates, *WSDNT*, s. v. "573."

truthful, whatever reputable, whatever just, whatever pure, whatever acceptable, whatever of good report—if any virtue and if any praiseworthy—think on these things."

Translation Matthew 6:24–30

24 "No one is able to serve two masters; for either he will hate the one and the other he will love, or he will be devoted to the one and the other he will hold in contempt. You are not able to serve God and the god of materialism. 25 Therefore I say to you, do not be anxious about your life, what you should eat or what you should drink; nor your body, what you should put on. Is not one's life more than food and the body more than clothing? 26 Consider the birds of the air, that they sow not, nor do they reap, nor do they gather into barns; and your heavenly Father feeds them. Are you not much more valuable than they? 27 Can any of you by being anxious add to his lifespan one hour? 28 And why are you anxious about clothing? Consider the lilies of the field, how they grow: they neither toil nor spin; 29 But I say to you that not even Solomon in all his glory was clothed like one of these. 30 Now if God thus clothes the grass of the field, being here today and tomorrow thrown into the furnace, will he not you much more, you of little faith?"

TRANSLATION NOTES

In v. 19 the word *mamōnás* is usually transliterated "mammon." Some translations capitalize the word to indicate Jesus uses it as a personification of materialism. Some versions translate *mamōnás* as "money" which misses the point Jesus is making. The word is "a comprehensive word for all kinds of possessions, earnings, and gains, a designation of material value, the god of materialism."[1] Because the contrast is between a personal God and *mamōnás*, it seems likely Jesus is personifying *mamōnás* as an idol opposing God. Therefore I have translated the word as "god of materialism," i.e., the false deity people create when covetousness becomes idolatry.

In v. 27 the word *hēlikía*, translated here as "lifespan" and in other versions "stature," means age in the sense of physical maturity or lifespan, or physical size in the sense of height.[2] In

---

[1] Ibid., s. v. "3126."

[2] Bromiley, *TDNT*, 2:941–943.

classical Greek and the Egyptian papyri it is overwhelmingly used in the sense of age.¹ At Luke 19:3 the word undoubtedly means stature, but elsewhere the meaning is physical age/maturity. For example: Ephesians 4:13; Hebrews 11:11; John 9:21.

At Luke 2:52 the choices are "Jesus increased in wisdom and maturity" or "Jesus increased in wisdom and grew taller." Luke's meaning is the maturity that comes with age, not physical height.

Here in Matthew 6:27, the context "life" in v. 25 favors a translation indicating age, i.e., "lifespan." The associated *pēchus*, "cubit" must here mean a measure of time, not physical height. The cubit was a measure of eighteen inches, which puts Jesus in the awkward position of asking which of you can add one and one-half feet (half a yard) to his height? Or, in the historical context, "which of you can change his height from five foot six to seven feet?" The better translation of cubit in this context is an unspecified measure of time. "That worry shortens life is the fact that adds point to the irony. The desire to turn a six-footer into a Goliath is rather a bizarre ambition."²

EXPOSITION

Verse 24 is a simple principle used to express a spirituality reality. Either the believer seeks God's approval and God's reward, or he is serving himself for worldly gain. Service for God must be wholehearted, because you cannot properly divide your loyalty between the things of the world and God.

In v. 25 Jesus is not condemning a proper worry that plans for the future. He is speaking of anxiety that cannot affect the outcome of events. If one serves God, which implies trust in and obedience toward him, then there is no need to have anxiety about the normal and necessary things of life. No amount of anxiety about the future will serve to improve the future. Again, Jesus is not saying do not plan for the future, he is saying do not excessively worry about the future.

There are principles to follow when faced with difficult circumstances.

Don't role-play the solution. God doesn't need your help. He

---

[1] Ibid.; Moulton, *Vocabulary*, s. v. "2244."
[2] Moulton, *Vocabulary*, s. v. "2244."

waits for your cooperation.

Don't DIY and afterward ask God to bless your solution. He probably won't. God blesses works that conform to his Word.

Don't go around an immovable obstacle. It is there for a reason. If God wants it removed only prayer will remove it.

Don't try to resolve a problem by yourself. Believers are a community. Every believer needs a counselor. Every counselor needs counselors.

When a door is closed, don't force it open. The right doors open with reasonable effort. The wrong doors open just enough to tempt you to sin.

Do what the Word says. God's will is found on the path. Problems tend to fix themselves when one is on the path.

Ask in faith for the things God has promised. Receive by faith whatever God gives. A "Yes" or a "No" from God should be received with identical thankfulness, trust, and praise.

The Christian life is one of dependence upon God. This includes properly using the resources God brings into your life, as well as waiting to see what resources God will provide. It includes planning for the future according to your resources, as well as waiting to see what the future will bring into your life. Sometimes the best thing a believer can do is "Be still, and let God be God."

Jesus examples this attitude in vv. 25, 26. Food and clothing represent the necessities of life. Although sometimes it seems the necessities are the whole of life, Jesus assures us that our value as persons far outweighs the things required for living. He also assures the believer that God will provide the necessities. The birds and the flowers in the field are examples of how God abundantly supplies the needs of his people. His saved people are worth much more than birds and flowers. Of course, God's idea of necessities may not be as extravagant as ours, and one must adjust to God's view of what we need. Anxiety about the necessities of life—anxiety about any of life's circumstances—won't change anything, except to decrease your lifespan.

Will God care for and provide for his people. Jesus answers, "Yes," an answer backed up by the man who during three years of ministry traveled across the width and length of Israel with nothing to call his own. He depended on God to provide food and clothing and shelter and protection. That God provided through others does not diminish the fact that it was God providing. Was Jesus from time to time cold, and wet, and tired, and hungry? Yes, but he was never anxious.

It is necessary to add that Jesus' mission—the one he was given by God, to be messiah and Savior—necessitated his manner of life during those three years of public ministry. Before that Jesus earned money to buy necessities through the hard manual labor of carpentry.

Translation Matthew 6:31-34

31 "Therefore do not be anxious, saying, 'What shall we eat?' or 'What shall we drink?' or 'What shall we wear?' 32 For all these things the gentiles seek to acquire. For your heavenly Father knows that you need them all. 33 But seek first the kingdom of God and his righteousness; and all these things will be added to you. 34 Therefore do not be anxious about tomorrow, for tomorrow will be anxious about itself. Sufficient to the day is its trouble."

EXPOSITION

The "therefore" is based on the preceding, expanding the thought of God's deliberate care for his people. God knows what each believer needs. A member of the kingdom needs to focus on two things: their part in the kingdom; the concerns of today. "Today" is an important term in Scripture, indicating the need for an immediate response to God. In an important and real sense God lives in the present of today, because every moment of time is a present "now" to God. The believer must respond to God in his or her present today. This does not mean one cannot make plans for tomorrow. It means trust in God to meet the needs of today and tomorrow

Matthew Seven

This chapter appears to be a series of independent sayings without a unifying theme. This is not unusual in wisdom literature. For example, see Proverbs 17, where each sentence is an independent proverb.

Translation Matthew 7:1–5

1 "Do not judge, that you should not be judged. 2 For with whatever judgment you judge, you will be judged; and with whatever measure you measure, it will be measured to you. 3 But why do you look at the splinter that is in your brother's eye, but in your eye not notice the beam? 4 Or how will you say to your brother, 'Permit that I might take out the splinter from your eye,' and look, the beam is in your eye? 5 Hypocrite, first take out the beam from your eye, and then you will see clearly to take out the splinter from your brother's eye."

TRANSLATION NOTE

In vv. 3–5, the word I have translated splinter is *kàrphos*, "anything that is dry and light, such as straw, stubble, chaff, a little splinter of wood, a mote."[1] I chose to translate "splinter" as agreeable to the word it opposes, *dokós*, which means "a beam or rafter used in building, a joist."[2] A freer translation: "Remove the giant piece of wood in your eye before trying to remove the tiny piece of wood in your brother's eye." Both splinter and beam are used as metaphors for a character flaw.

EXPOSITION

The kind of judging Christ speaks against is condemnation. Judging in the sense of discernment is recommended in Scripture, e.g., Proverbs 15:21; Philippians 1:9. Nor is Christ speaking against critical thinking that discerns truth from error.

The kind of judging Christ speaks against is negative criticism that reaches a conclusion the other person should be condemned for his/her character flaws. This is also the kind of negative judgment that concludes a person has no value (compare

---

[1] Zodhiates, *WSDNT*, s. v. "2595."

[2] Ibid., s. v. "1385."

comments at 5:22). Only God is allowed to judge in the sense of condemnation, because there are no flaws in his character: he sees all things rightly.

The verb in v. 1 is in the present tense: "Do not make judging others a practice or habit"; "do not let judging others become habitual." The condemnation kind of judging is intolerant; it sees the faults in others without intent to help or empathize. This kind of judging is when one maintains the habit of criticism for its own sake, giving in to the desire to expose the faults of others while intending to ignore faults in one's self.

The "speck" and "plank" analogy probably indicates focusing on something insignificant in others while at the same time ignoring something significant in one's self. The example, vv. 3–5, supports either of two views. A general view would be the hypocrisy that criticizes others while failing to exercise an appropriate self-criticism. A more specific view would be the hypocrisy that condemns in another the same or similar problem existing in the one judging. This sort of criticism of other people's failings is not acceptable.

The believer should apply the standards of righteousness to him or herself first, recognizing their failings. To self-criticize is to develop discernment and humility; it is to remove the beam in one's own eye to be able to see clearly enough to help a brother or sister in Christ with the splinter in their eye. Self-criticism is necessary so that when the believer does evaluate another's actions, he/she may do so without hypocrisy and with understanding, and perhaps with empathy.

Why is evaluation of others necessary? To know how to interact with those who claim Christ as Savior, but are lost. To know how to interact with a brother/sister who is habitually committing acts of sinning without the necessary repentance and confession to God for forgiveness and cleansing (1 John 1:9). In other words, to help others.

One should not conclude Jesus is commanding sinless perfection before a discernment may be made. But the believer discerning the character or actions of others should be living a habitually righteous life by having their own sins confessed, repented, and forsaken. Then he or she is morally prepared to offer sympathy, prayer, assistance, or even an appropriate rebuke. Jesus' warning is against hypocritical criticism.

The reciprocal statements in vv. 1 and 2 indicate hypocritical criticism rebounds against the hypocrite: 1) in this life as others discern and form an opinion about the critic's own behavior, and 2) at the final judgment conducted by God that all must face (believers, 2 Corinthians 5:10; unbelievers, Revelation 20:11–15). This is not 'karma" but justice. The concept of karma means a reward, good or bad, through reincarnation. Justice means a person receives that which is exactly due their works, whether a reward or punishment, both in this life and in the eternal life to come.

Translation Matthew 7:6–11

6 "Do not give what is holy to the dogs; nor cast your pearls before the pigs, so they may not treat them with contempt, and then turn and tear you to pieces.

7 Ask and it will be given to you; seek and you will find; knock and it will be opened to you. 8 Because everyone asking receives; and the one seeking finds; and to the one knocking it will be opened. 9 Or which man of you, whom his son will ask for bread, he will not give him a stone, will he? 10 Or also he will ask for a fish, he will not give him a serpent, will he? 11 If therefore you, being evil, know to give good gifts to your children, how much more your Father who is in the heavens will give good things to those asking him"

TRANSLATION NOTES

In v. 6, contrary to my usual practice, I have given the figurative sense rather than translate each word. The word *katapateō*, "to trample upon" has the figurative meaning, "to treat with the utmost contempt and indignity."[1]

In vv. 8 and 9, the use of the negative *mḗ* casts the turn of phrase in a manner unusual for English speakers. In English one would say (as in the HCSB), "What man among you, if his son asks him for bread, will give him a stone?" or "will give him a serpent?" But the text reads (in word order), v. 8, "not a stone will he give him?" and in v. 9, "not a serpent will he give him?" The negative *mḗ* is an adverb modifying the verb "will he give." *Mḗ* expresses the negative sense of "will, wish, or doubt [that] implies one conceives

---

[1] Zodhiates, *WSDNT*, s. v. "2662."

or supposes a thing not to exist."¹ A more accurate translation incorporating the negative *mḗ* is, "he will not give him a stone, will he?" and "he will not give him a serpent, will he?"

EXPOSITION

It is difficult to see how v. 6 fits into either the preceding or succeeding instructions. Carson suggests a possible connection with the preceding verses. "Disciples exhorted to love their enemies (5:43-47) and not to judge (7:1) might fail to consider the subtleties of the argument and become undiscerning simpletons. This verse guards against such a possibility."² I will consider v. 6 as an independent instruction.

In the ancient world of the Middle East dogs were not pets, they were scavengers, and therefore unclean. Pigs had been declared unclean by the Mosaic Law. Dogs and pigs can become violent and attack.

There is no specific content described for "holy" or "pearls," indicating these are being used as general terms for things sacred and righteous, i.e., intangible things that are morally good. One must be careful not to understand v. 6 in an anti-evangelistic way. The good news of salvation in Christ can turn dogs and pigs into holy and righteous believers.

An unbeliever does not comprehend sacred and righteous things, Romans 8:8; 1 Corinthians 2:14. The Scripture, Christ, Christians, worship, fellowship with God and fellow believers, obedience to authority, service to God and toward others, and all those other sacred and righteous things that comprise faith in Christ and the practices of Christianity are foreign and incomprehensible to the unbelievers. As an historical example, the ancient Greeks and Romans, in the second through third centuries, believed Christians sacrificed babies, ate human flesh, drank blood, and engaged in sexually immoral practices based on a corrupted view of basic Christian practices, such as Communion (Lord's Supper). The general rule of this instruction is that what is sacred or precious in the kingdom should not be indiscriminately shared with people who are unable to appreciate its sacred and precious quality. An unbeliever is ready to listen when the Holy Spirit has made them

---

[1] Ibid., s. v. "3361."
[2] Carson, *Matthew*, 185.

ready.

In vv. 7–11 the point is that prayer is effective because answered by the believer's wise and loving heavenly Father. This basic understanding of prayer is important in view of the escalating intensity of ask, seek, and knock. These verbs are present tense participles indicating habitual action: asking, seeking, knocking.

Prayer is not answered because of persistence, but because God loves his people. The persistence required reflects our needs, not God's. People are inclined to give up when there is not an immediate response to their prayer. Prayer does not force or persuade God to act. God is sovereign, his timing is not ours, and the believer is to realize prayer is a God-ordained means to accomplish God's will, not a lever to move God to act according to our will. Why some prayers are immediately answered and others not answered until much prayer over much time has passed between the believer and God is a question that cannot be answered, except by knowing the sovereignty of God works through man's responsibility to infallibly accomplish God's will.

The believer's responsibility is to pray; God has made himself responsible to respond. Someone has noted God answers prayer in four ways.

"No, I love you too much," meaning we have asked for something that is inappropriate or harmful to our welfare. In this instance one should cease to pray that prayer.

"No, not yet," because the request is good, but the timing is "not yet." In this instance prayer should continue.

"Yes, but what took you so long to ask," meaning God's timing in giving was waiting for the means by which it was to be given: our prayer.

"Yes, and here is more," as God not only grants the request but adds to it as he knows is needful for our welfare, or for the person for whom we are interceding.

In one view of the passage, "Asking" may indicate one knows what to ask for, "Seeking" may indicate uncertainty, and "Knocking" may imply a closed door. However, the progression indicates the one praying knows what he/she is asking for, knows that as he seeks it he will find it, and that when he knocks the door will be opened. The one praying knows God answers prayer, and therefore is persistent in praying.

The three actions indicate the effectiveness of prayer. The verbs are in the present tense, indicating the importance of continuing action; in a word, persistence. Doors may be closed, but prayer opens them. The two examples of vv. 9–10, and the conclusion of v. 11, reinforce the point: God answers prayer because he is a wise and loving heavenly Father. Therefore pray and get answers.

Translation Matthew 7:12–14

12 "All things therefore, all that you might desire that men should do to you, so also you do to them, for this is the law and the prophets.

13 Enter through the narrow gate; because wide the gate and broad the way leading to destruction, and many are those entering through it; 14 because narrow the gate and difficult the way leading to life, and few are those finding it."

EXPOSITION

In relation to the immediately preceding verses, the incentive for doing good to others is the example of the Father's goodness.[1] However, there is a larger view to be considered. The "therefore" incorporates the ethics of kingdom conduct from 5:17–7:11. Members of the kingdom not only act different from the world, they interact with the world according to a righteous standard. The beatitudes (incorporated into the "therefore" by 5:17–20) describe not only the character of the kingdom member, but indicate how that character should work out in practice. Christ is come to fulfill the law, and the sections on murder, adultery, marriage, going the second mile, loving your enemies, etc., are ethical rules for kingdom conduct.

In 7:12 Jesus sums up his kingdom ethics by succinctly stating the spiritual intent of the law that will be fulfilled through him and by his followers. This, then, "is of the spirit rather than the actual words of the law. It is a principle so all-embracing that . . . it actually 'is' the law and the prophets [a principle] which underlies the ethical demands both of the law and of the prophets."[2] To love your neighbor as yourself (the subtext) was to treat him in the same

---

[1] Morris, *Matthew*, 172.
[2] France, *Matthew*, NICNT, 282, 283.

manner as you want to be treated by him. One should know all the rules, but by fulfilling this one rule he will fulfill all the others.

The concluding sections, vv. 13–14, 15–20, 21–23, 24–27, are not more discipleship instructions, but state the necessity for a positive response to the preceding instructions. The positive response required is a wholehearted commitment to Jesus. Anything less than complete commitment disqualifies a person from kingdom membership, because saving faith *is* a complete commitment to Jesus as one's Savior.

The first required response to the kingdom is presented in parallel antithetical statements:

Enter through the narrow gate:
because wide the gate and broad the way leading to destruction;
because narrow the gate and difficult the way leading to life.

Many will enter through the broad gate;
Few will find the narrow gate.

Morris, see the two paths as leading to their respective gates.[1] According to France, the majority reading of the manuscripts is that one enters the gate, wide or narrow, and continues on the respective path, wide or narrow, to destruction or to life.[2]

The narrow path may be viewed as leading to the gate of salvation, thus becoming saved is in view; or as leading from the gate of salvation, thus the Christian life post-salvation is in view. Both views have merit, as long as a biblical perspective is maintained. If the narrow path leads to the gate of salvation, we must not view the narrow path as obtaining salvation through the merit of struggling along the narrow path. No virtuous struggle, no matter how long endured, and no number of good works, not matter how much good may be done, will merit salvation.

If the narrow path leads to salvation, then it is narrow because there are many false ways branching off the path to deceive the sinner into believing he or she is saved. Or the sinner will fight against the truth of his/her native spiritual state, reluctantly taking

---

[1] Morris, *Matthew*, 174.
[2] France, *Matthew*, NICNT, 287, n. 15

one step after another to the gate, struggling to accept him or herself as a sinner needing Jesus Christ the only Savior. The sinner will struggle against the truth until convicted the narrow path is the only path.

If the narrow path leads away from the gate of salvation, then the path illustrates the believer's way in the world post-salvation. The world never stops trying to seduce the believer off the path. Temptation and false doctrines and apostates and heretics branch off the path at almost every step. The believer's way in the world is hard and narrow, but the path leads to a happy and productive eternity with Jesus. The Father, and the Son, and the Holy Spirit work with the believer while he/she is on the path in order to ensure his or her perseverance through life and death into the eternity secured by Christ's propitiation for sins.

Therefore, whether we view the narrow path as leading the sinner to salvation, or as taking the believer into eternity after salvation—I believe both views are true to experience— there is one path and one way and one gate and one Savior.

Those on the narrow path are going in the opposite direction to those on the broad way. That is to say, the narrow path runs down the middle of the broad way to destruction. The narrow path runs north, the broad path south; the narrow path always climbs upward, the broad path runs down, down, down to destruction So those on the narrow path are going against the flow of those on the broad path. The people on the narrow way are being constantly shoved, jostled, pushed, punched, elbowed, and otherwise opposed by the mass of others going the wrong way, because those going the wrong way believe with all their heart their broad way is the right way. This is a good illustration as to why the narrow way is a difficult way, and why so few are willing to find and walk the narrow path.

I tend to view the wide gate at the head of the broad path. All human beings are born sinners. They are from conception on the broad way leading to destruction. They continue on the broad way all their life, until someone points out the difficult narrow path and the equally narrow gate. Sinners make a choice against Christ (the wide gate) or for Christ (the narrow gate) and either continue on the path to destruction, or take the path to eternal life.

Can the choice to reject the narrow way be changed? Of course, these verses are a metaphor for choices. During this mortal life a sinner can at any time repent and believe and enter the narrow gate to the narrow way leading to life: whosoever will may come. Only physical death prevents the choice to believe and be saved, because the power of death is to confirm the sinner's choice to reject Christ, and seal his/her eternal destiny in the lake of fire.

Some manuscripts eliminate the words "the gate" in v. 13, in the phrase the wide gate to the broad way. Metzger wrote, "on the whole it seemed best [to the United Bible Societies Editorial Committee] to follow the reading of the overwhelming weight of the external evidence, and to account for the absence of the word in one or both verses as a deliberate excision made by copyists who failed to understand that the intended picture is that of a roadway leading to a gate."[1] (Metzger's choice is to see a path leading to the gate, not away from it.)

The choice between eternal life and eternal separation from God is not new: compare Deuteronomy 30:19; Psalm 1:6; Jeremiah 21:8. The narrowness of the gate—it is the gate to eternal life—indicates it must be diligently sought, and an effort made to enter in. This is not salvation by works: one enters through the narrow gate by grace through faith and then continues his or her life of faith by grace on the narrow and more difficult way. To seek the gate and enter the way is to realize one is going the wrong way in life (conviction), turn away from what one has previously believed (repentance), and accept a new way (saving faith/born-again), with new rules for living (becoming Christ-like).

Salvation gives one a new life with new needs, new desires, new goals, and eternal life with God in Christ. The life of discipleship is the living out that new life. The new life is difficult just because it is not the way of the world. Because it is not the way of the world, few seek out and find the narrow gate and way to new life; the broad path is easier. The narrow gate and way lead to eternal life and heaven; the wide gate and broad way lead to eternal separation from God and eternal punishment.

Translation Matthew 7:15–20

15 "Beware of false prophets, who come to you in sheep's clothing, but inwardly they are ravenous wolves. 16 By their fruits you will know them. They don't gather grapes from thornbushes,

---

[1] Metzger, *Textual*, 16.

or figs from thistles, do they? 17 So every good tree produces good fruits; but a bad tree produces bad fruits. 18 A good tree is not able to produce bad fruits, nor can a bad tree produce good fruits. 19 Every tree not producing good fruit is cut down and into the fire is thrown. 20 Therefore then, by their fruits you will know them."

EXPOSITION

Don't follow after false prophets. Recognize them as false by the results (fruit) of their doctrine and life. False doctrines are a fruit of unbelief; an unrighteous life is a fruit of false doctrines. True doctrine produces a righteous life in accordance with the details of the kingdom sermon.

The requirement to "beware of false prophets" was familiar to Israel. Throughout much of their history the people had followed prophets that contradicted God's word and denied the genuine prophets God continued to send to recover them from idolatry and immorality.

The New Testament also warns against false prophets. The job of the New Testament believer to beware false prophets is a little easier than that of the Hebrews. For example, in 1 Kings 22 Jehoshaphat had to decide between two prophets, both of whom claimed, "thus says the Lord." The "word of the Lord" was not complete as it is today. Today any person with a "thus says the Lord" kind of statement that contradicts the completed written word—adding to it, taking away from it, contradicting it—is a false prophet.

The term "prophets" need not mean those who make predictions of future events; a false prophet is anyone one who falsely claims to speak in the name of God. The term "false prophet" refers to any person who makes an interpretation (preach, teach, evangelize) that is opposed to the plain and normal sense of the words of Scripture. These false prophets put on a harmless front, but their purpose is to take all they can from others for personal gain. The fate, v. 19, of false prophets, and presumably of those who wholeheartedly and blindly follow them, is to be cut down (death) and thrown into the fire, a metaphor for eternal punishment. The "therefore" in v. 20 brings this section to its conclusion.

Translation Matthew 7:21–23

21 "Not everyone saying to me, 'Lord, Lord,' will enter into the kingdom of the heavens, but the one doing the will of my Father who is in the heavens. 22 Many will say to me in that day, 'Lord, Lord, did we not in your name prophesy, and in your name cast out demons, and in your name perform many miracles?' 23 And then I will declare to them, those working lawlessness, 'Because I never knew you, you depart from me.' "

EXPOSITION

The first word in v. 21 is *ou*, the unconditional, objective negative that means absolutely not. The only persons entering into the kingdom of the heavens will be those persons who are doing the will of the Father in the heavens, no exceptions. Jesus unequivocally stated the Father's will at John 6:29, "believe in him [Jesus the Christ] whom he [God] has sent." No amount of sincere verbal profession by those who don't believe, no amount of good works by those who don't believe, no amount of religious duties by those who don't believe will save their souls from the penalty due the unsaved.

The declaration, v. 21, is followed by an example, vv. 22–23. Profession is not salvation. Preaching and prophesying are not salvation. Good works are not salvation. Following closely on the admonition to recognize false professors by the fruit of the lives (doctrines and practices) Jesus declares that it will not be mere professors of religion who are saved, but only those who are true members of the kingdom.

Genuine members are known by their response to the call to kingdom membership, which is saved through grace alone, by faith alone, in Jesus the only savior. Genuine membership in the kingdom is demonstrated by living a life of faith by grace after salvation. To profess faith is easy; to live by faith requires genuine salvation.

Note that genuine salvation is indicated by Jesus' use of the term "my Father." This relationship, "father," is produced in genuine believers as they are adopted by the Father as sons of God. Genuine kingdom members are not saved by works but by a relationship with God through saving faith in Christ. The false professors use the Name, but never call on the Lord in order to be saved. They will protest to Jesus "in that day," the day of their judgment, that they are genuine believers because they have performed many works in his name.

The term "that day" refers to their day of judgment, and eschatologically to the final judgment of unsaved sinners. Jesus is speaking to national ethnic Israel. When Christ returns and inaugurates the Davidic Kingdom, he will judge who of national ethnic Israel will be permitted to enter the kingdom, Matthew 24:31; Ezekiel 20:33–38. Christ will also judge who of the gentiles will be permitted to enter the kingdom, Matthew 25:31–46.

Jesus could not say more clearly that works do not save. These religionists will protest, "We spoke in your name and therefore on your behalf; we cast out demons in your name and therefore on your behalf; we did many wonders in your name, and therefore on your behalf." Jesus will say to them, "I never knew you," because they never knew him as personal Savior. When he commands they depart, it is to physical death, and their souls into hades to await the Great White Throne judgment, followed by eternal imprisonment in the lake of fire (Revelation 20:11–5). Their works, although they may have been good in and of themselves, or in what they accomplished, were nevertheless unlawful because not done by Jesus' authority and by his power.

Translation Matthew 7:24–27

24 "Everyone therefore, whoever hears these my words and does them, will be like a wise man who built his house upon the rock, 25 and the rain came down and the floods came and the winds blew, and fell against the house, and the house did not fall, for its foundation was upon the rock. 26 And everyone hearing my words and not doing them, he will be like a foolish man who built his house on the sand, 27 and the rain came down and the floods came and the winds blew, and fell against the house, and it fell, and its fall was great."

EXPOSITION

The house and the rock are used as metaphors. The house represents a person's manner of life. The rock is the solid foundation of saving faith in Jesus and a manner of habitual righteousness lived by God's grace in the believer's life. The rain and floods and winds are the varied trials of mortal life, including the final trial, physical death.

The person who has saving faith in Jesus, and whose life is Christ-like, has built upon the rock of salvation, the Scriptures, and faith in God in Christ. When life's trials come, the response will be according to Scripture and faith. When the final trial comes, physical death, the house will remain standing, because that person has eternal life in Christ.

The sand represents a life built on the principles and values of the world. This is the unsaved person who rejects Christ as Savior. Their life ebbs and flows, waxes and wanes according to their worldly circumstances. They cannot stand during life's trials. When the final trial of physical death comes, their house will fall eternally.

The person who is saved is the person who has faith in Jesus and lives out his faith according to these righteous "rules" of the kingdom. There are no exceptions. Anyone who would be saved must believe in and follow after Jesus. The parable is so clear no further explanation is needed.

Translation Matthew 7:28–29

28 And so it was when Jesus had finished these words, the crowds were astonished at his teaching, 29 because he was teaching them as having authority, and not as their scribes.

EXPOSITION

The scribes and other teachers of the law taught by citing the (sometimes conflicting) opinions and interpretations of the great Rabbis of the past. If they gave their opinion it was confirmed by an appeal to the Rabbis. Jesus declared the truth on his own authority. He expected them to believe him and adjust their lives accordingly.

Their astonishment also reflects the content of his teaching. He had declared the common interpretations of the day false, replacing them with his interpretation. More than that, Jesus' teaching assumes himself as "the proper object of people's allegiance and the arbiter of their destiny (5:11–12; 7:21–24, 26)."[1]

---

[1] France, *Matthew*, NICNT, 299.

Matthew Eight

Translation Matthew 8:1–4

1 Now he having come down from the mountain, great crowds followed him. 2 And look, a leper having come knelt before him, saying, "Sir, if you are willing, you are able to cleanse me." 3 And having stretched out the hand, he touched him, saying, "I am willing, be cleansed." And immediately his leprosy was cleansed. 4 And Jesus says to him, "See that you tell no one, but go, show yourself to the priest, and offer the gift that Moses commanded, for a testimony to them."

TRANSLATION NOTE

In v. 2 two words are used which most versions translate "worship" and "Lord," following the convention established by the KJV and earlier versions. The word usually translated "worship," which I have translated "knelt before" (cf. HCSB) is *proskunéō*.[1] This word can mean to show respect to a person or it can mean to worship deity. The other word is *kúrios*, which may mean "sir," "master" (a disciple to his teacher or a slave to his/her owner), or "Lord," either meaning the person a servant works for, a king, or God.[2] I have translated *kúrios* here with "sir."

There was no prior relationship between Jesus and the leper, so "master" is not proper, nor "Lord" as a servant to his master, or a subject to his king. I think it unlikely the leper believed Jesus was incarnate deity. The leper may have believed Jesus was a prophet; he may have believed Jesus was the messiah; but he did not believe Jesus was God incarnate. No one in Israel did, including the apostles, during the time of Jesus' earthly ministry. Therefore "Lord" is inappropriate for *kúrios* and "worship" is inappropriate for *proskunéō*.

Elisha the prophet healed the Syrian Naaman of his leprosy (2 Kings 5), though not in the same manner, but it was an example of God working through a man which he (God) had anointed (as a prophet); the leper may have been expecting something similar. The leper was being polite and respectful. The leper thought Jesus

---

[1] Zodhiates, *WSDNT*, s. v. "4352."
[2] Ibid., s. v. "2962."

could heal his leprosy. Thus, the man knelt as a sign of respect and said "Sir."

The messiah was God's anointed to deliver Israel, just as God has previously anointed men to be priests and prophets and kings. Jesus listed healing leprosy as a sign that identified him as the messiah, Matthew 11:5. There is no Old Testament Scripture that says the messiah will heal leprosy, but Jesus may have been thinking of the general blessings of messiah listed in Isaiah 61:1 (cf. Isaiah 29:18; 35:4–6).

Throughout this commentary, I have translated *proskunéō* as knelt "or bowed" and *kúrios* as "sir" or "master," unless the context clearly indicates an acknowledgment of Christ's deity with corresponding worship, or if *kúrios* is being used with respect to royalty.

EXPOSITION

Matthew has shown us Jesus teaching and preaching, 5:2–7:29. Now he shows us Jesus healing. Just as Matthew selected certain teaching/preaching events out of the larger number of occurring as Jesus traveled about Galilee, so too Matthew has selected certain healing events out of the many that occurred.

Matthew's first selection is Jesus healing leprosy. In the ancient world leprosy was the common name for several skin diseases, including the disease we know today as leprosy. Biblical leprosy probably included psoriasis, eczema, certain persistent fungal infestations (because a house and clothes could have leprosy), and true leprosy (Leviticus 13, 14), known now as Hansen's disease.

Today, diseases such as eczema and psoriasis can be treated, but not cured. Fungi can be cured. In 1873 Hansen's disease was identified as a bacterial infection and a cure soon followed.

In the ancient world there was no cure for any of the diseases identified as leprosy. People with these diseases were shunned for fear of infection. In reality, neither psoriasis nor eczema are contagious, although psoriasis can be inherited. Hansen's disease is contagious, but not very contagious, because 95% of human beings have a natural immunity.

In the ancient world biblical leprosy was feared and those having leprosy were "unclean" and therefore shunned by society. They were required to live apart from their fellow men. A person with leprosy was not allowed to come near individuals or the places where they lived, so this leper's faith in approaching Jesus is remarkable. The small detail of Jesus meeting the leper as he came down from the mountain is in accordance with this policy of complete isolation from human society, as it would have been well outside any village, town, etc. Jesus may have been alone, or surrounded by only a few people, but more likely the crowd parted as the leper came through the crowd shouting out his warning, "Unclean!"

This leprous man showed respect for Jesus by kneeling before him. Whether he thought Jesus a prophet or the messiah, respect was required. Respect for Jesus and for God was also given by the man in his request: "If you are willing." He knew the works of the prophets were at the discretion of the prophets, but that the power to heal came from God alone, working through the prophet. A prophet had direct communication from God, so a prophet would know if healing was allowed for this particular man—would know if it was God's will. The assembled crowd knew this also. What they saw and understood was that Jesus was willing, and therefore it was apparent God was willing, so in their view the man was healed by the power of God working through Jesus.

One of Jesus' frequent actions was to touch the unclean and diseased as he healed them. In the case of this leprous man the crowd, and the man, would have been astounded that Jesus touched him. Leviticus 7:20 clearly stated, in unambiguous terms, the person who touched any unclean thing shall himself become unclean (the meaning in context of "cut off from his people.") They must have asked themselves, as they saw Jesus stretching out his hand, v. 3, "How can a holy man, a prophet of God, touch the unclean? Will he not become unclean himself?" They did not know, until the work was done, that Jesus' touch was healing, preventing Jesus from becoming unclean. It is worth noting that Jesus did not have to touch the man to cleanse him; it was a touch of compassion. When Jesus touched the man it was the first time the man had been touched by a clean person since contracting leprosy; perhaps by any person.

The command to tell the priest may have served several purposes. One, Jesus did not need the immediate "advertisement effect" to increase his popularity and cause the crowds to become larger (cf. Mark 1:40-45). The ritual with the priests took eight days, after which the man could be expected to tell family and friends how he had been cured. The three to four days for a trip from Galilee to Jerusalem, plus eight days for the ritual and offerings, then the return trip to Galilee— about two weeks total—would have lessened the "advertisement" effect of the man's testimony.

Two, Jesus' instructions to the healed man were in accordance with the Law of Moses, Leviticus 13—14, which stated what was required to restore the cured leper to society. Three, the priests could validate a healing as genuine, but could not themselves heal, so by showing himself to the priest the man would be giving an irrefutable witness of Jesus' authority as the messianic king.

The testimony to "them" could refer to the examination by a priest, and through him to all the professionally "religious," i.e., the priests, Levites, scribes, Pharisees, and Sadducees. The "them" might possibly refer to society in general, or the man's family and friends, as teaching them that what was unclean was made clean. Regardless, if the man did as he was instructed, it would be a powerful testimony confirming Jesus as God's anointed. The Old Testament mentions only a two instances of cleansing from leprosy, Numbers 12:10–15; 2 Kings 5:14. In the New Testament two such healings are recorded: Matthew 8:3 (parallel passages Mark 1:42; Luke 5:13) and Luke 7:12.

Translation Matthew 8:5–13

5 Now having entered into Capernaum, a centurion came to him, pleading with him, 6 and saying, "Sir, my servant is lying in the house, paralyzed, in terrible pain."

7 And he says to him, "I will come and heal him."

8 But the centurion answering said, "Sir, I am not worthy that you should come under my roof. But only speak the word, and my servant will be healed. 9 For I also am a man under authority, having under me soldiers I set in order; and I say to this one, 'Go,' and he goes; and to another, 'Come,' and he comes; and to my servant, 'Do this,' and he does it."

10 Now having heard, Jesus marveled, and said to those following, "Truly I say to you, among Israel I have found no one with so great faith. 11 Now I say to you, that many from east and west will come and will recline at the table with Abraham, Isaac, and Jacob in the kingdom of the heavens. 12 But the sons of the kingdom will be cast out into the outer darkness; there will be weeping and gnashing of teeth."

13 And Jesus said to the centurion, 'Go. As you have believed, be it to you.' " And his servant was healed in that hour.

TRANSLATION NOTES

I have, for this one instance, arranged the narrative in the form of dialogue. Too often we read the Scriptures with a little pause at the end of each verse, as though each verse was a complete sentence; but the conversation between Jesus and the centurion extends across verses. Conversation has a dynamic that should not be missed. I have presented that dynamic here.

In v. 6 the word translated "paralyzed" is *paralutikós*, "paralyzed, palsied . . . loss of motor power in a muscle or set of muscles."[1] It is doubtful palsy is intended, as true palsy is temporary facial paralysis. While pain may be experienced with palsy, a person truly paralyzed in his or her extremities does not experience pain. Because the man is in terrible pain, I believe he was experiencing a herniated vertebrae disc, probably affecting the lower extremities, a condition more commonly known as sciatica, a compression of the spinal nerves in the lumbar region. The centurion used *paralutikós* to describe the observed phenomena, not the medical condition. In cases of severe disc herniation, any movement causes terrible pain, resulting in the person lying down and making every effort not to move, effectively "paralyzing" the person.

In v. 11, some versions translate *anaklínō*, "to lay down, to recline," with the word "sit." The HCSB translates recline and adds an explanatory "at the table." Those words are not in the text, but in Jesus' time *anaklínō* was used of reclining in order to eat. Instead of chairs, the ancients used a low couch set perpendicular to a low table. They leaned on their left elbow and took food from the dishes with their right hand. In this posture a person could lean back and speak privately to the person reclining to his left. This explains John 13:23, 25, explains Matthew 26:23, and explains what Jesus was doing at John 13:26.

EXPOSITION

The focal point of this story is not Jesus' authority to heal, whether in person or from afar, but his interaction with a gentile, showing that messiah's work was intended to affect all the world,

---

[1] Zodhiates, *WSDNT*, s. v. "3885."

Matthew Eight

not just Israel.

Luke 7:1–10 tells us the centurion "sent some elders of the Jews" to represent him and his request to Jesus. It is difficult to imagine a Roman centurion as a proselyte to Judaism—a gentile convert to Judaism circumcised and baptized. There are two possibilities. One, as part of the Roman government, the elders may have had necessary contact with the centurion in the course of conducting government business. Two, the centurion may have been a "God-fearer." That was what Jews called gentiles who associated themselves, to some degree, with Jewish worship, were interested in Jewish morality and monotheism, but were not obedient to some aspects of the Jewish Law, such as circumcision. Either choice is as likely as the other.

Matthew cuts out the part about the elders representing the centurion because he does not want to distract from the interaction between Jesus and a gentile. Matthew says the centurion came to Jesus, but Luke says after the elders made their plea, Jesus said, "I will come and heal him," and went with the elders to the centurion's house. Then, Luke tells us that before Jesus reached the house the centurion "sent friends to Jesus, telling Jesus" the words Matthew reports in vv. 8–9. The centurion believed, based on his dealings with the religious class, that a proper Jew would not meet with him (but Jesus would have met with him), so he sent people to represent him. Representation is a biblical principle and a culturally accepted way of meeting with others; in the view of Matthew and his readers, the centurion was present through his representatives.

As I have said, the focal point is Jesus meeting with a gentile, even though the meeting occurred representatively. Jesus answered the gentile's plea because of the gentile's faith. The lesson is, God always responds to faith. The Jews, during the 150 years or so prior to the first advent, had developed a principle of exclusion from gentiles, believing contact with a gentile rendered them unclean. How far this belief extended below the ruling and religious classes is difficult to know. Those whose business was tax collecting or selling dried salted fish had direct dealings with gentiles; and that is one reason they were considered sinners by the overly scrupulous scribes, Pharisees, and Sadducees.

The centurion's faith examples the kind of faith required to be a member of the kingdom. He had faith in the ability and authority of Jesus. It would probably be inaccurate to say the centurion's faith was in the omnipotence of Jesus, a quality of deity. The centurion says "I also" am under authority, indicating he recognized Jesus as possessing authority, perhaps not innate authority, but certainly recognition of the authority God had given Jesus to heal others. He believed Jesus was authorized to exercise divine authority in any manner he thought suitable. This may not be explicit faith in Jesus as God, but it is faith in Jesus as messiah, or at the least, as a genuine prophet of the one true God. Up to this point in Matthew, there have been no healings from a distance, so the centurion's faith is without an exemplar, which in Matthew makes it all the more remarkable. The centurion is acting on what he has heard, not what he has seen.

There is some question as to whether or not in v. 7 Jesus is making a statement or asking a question. Jesus' begins with the word "I," *egō*, normally not needed or used in conversation because the respondent to a question is understood as "I." The interpretive question is why did Jesus explicitly refer to himself? Because of the emphatic *egō*, several commentators interpret v. 7 as a question, "I will come and heal him?" or, "You want *me* to come and heal him?" The implication would be, "You want me, a Jew, to enter the house of a gentile?"

In his entire ministry Jesus went to and entered only one house for the specific purpose of healing, the house of Jairus. His normal method was for sick people to come to him, or to heal the sick from a distance. Undoubtedly Jesus did not believe he would become religiously defiled by entering a gentile house, but his followers would have been greatly offended.

In Matthew the centurion responds to the question of defilement by saying, "I am not worthy." Socially this Roman was the superior, but he addresses Jesus as an equal. He may have felt some personal inadequacy on a spiritual level, for Jesus' authority to heal implied a connection to deity. However, the most likely reason, in context, that he declared himself not worthy, was a recognition of the (unbiblical, but the centurion wouldn't know that) Jewish taboo about entering a gentile home. He modified his request to allow for Jewish religious sensibilities, because he saw no reason Jesus could not heal from a distance with just a word.

Jesus is astonished (revealing his humanity) that this gentile can recognize and positively respond to divine authority. The centurion in effect says that whatever Jesus commands must be done. This belief does not determine whether the centurion believed Jesus' authority was delegated from God, or originated in Jesus. But it does recognize Jesus had divine authority to heal.

This level of faith was not present in Israel, a term here referring to the nation as a whole, not individuals. Though many came to Jesus to be healed, they did not consider his ability to heal as his personal authority. Apparently the centurion did, thus having faith not merely in healing power, but in the one who exercised that power. Faith in the person, not faith in the power, is the kind of faith required to be a kingdom member.

In v. 10b Jesus begins with "truly," marking out his next words as requiring close attention. The "sons of the kingdom" is a reference to the people national ethnic Israel in their relationship with God as Abraham's heirs and Jacob's children. They expected to have a part in the messianic kingdom because of this physical relationship. Jesus tells his disciples that the only relationship that counts for kingdom membership is the one based on faith and commitment exercised toward him. Because of their lack of that kind of faith, some of national ethnic Israel will not be part of the kingdom (but many will, Romans 11:26-27); but those who are not Jews (gentiles) will by their faith be part of the kingdom. Those without faith will end up enduring eternal punishment. Jesus, v. 13, responds directly to the centurion's faith and heals the servant. When Jesus said, "As you have believed, be it to you," he didn't mean the healing would be in proportion to the centurion's faith, but that the servant would be healed because the centurion had faith. The faith of the sick person is not mentioned, because it is the faith of the one praying to Jesus—the faith of the believer—that is important.

Translation Matthew 8:14–17

14 And Jesus, having come to Peter's house, saw his mother-in-law lying sick and running a fever. 15 And he touched her hand, and the fever left her; and she arose and served them. 16 Now evening having come, they brought to him many inhabited by demons, and he cast out the spirits with a word, and he healed all those being sick, 17 so that might be fulfilled having been spoken through Isaiah the prophet, saying: "Himself our sicknesses took, and our diseases bore."

EXPOSITION

Matthew selects two other healing events, one private the other public, to show Jesus is the messiah. Jesus has come from the Capernaum synagogue, Mark 1:21. When told, Mark 1:30, that Peter's mother-in-law was ill, he went and healed her. The healing was instantaneous, and she immediately got up and began to serve them the post-Sabbath meal. Rising to serve was cultural, but one may make a spiritual application: service after salvation is the response of faith.

In the evening people came to the house and Jesus healed them appropriate to their condition. Mark tells us, 1:21–34, that the daylight hours had been during a Sabbath. Since the Jewish day began at sunset, then at the evening the Sabbath was over and people could come to be healed without violating Jewish tradition. There was no prohibition in the Mosaic Law concerning good works on the Sabbath, as Jesus demonstrated many times in his ministry. The prohibition was based on a rabbinical interpretation.

Casting out demons with a word and healing diseases, presumably also with a word, reveals Jesus' authority over more than the human condition. That the demons (fallen angels) obeyed him reveals authority over the spirit domain. This authority would have confirmed popular opinion: Jesus of Nazareth was anointed a prophet and perhaps was messiah. It would not have led them to understand Jesus as deity incarnate. After all, in Daniel 10:13, holy angels had been given authority over fallen angels. It was a small step to believing God had granted such authority to a prophet or the messiah. Demons are mentioned in the Old Testament, Leviticus 17:7; Deuteronomy 32:17, 2 Chronicles 11:15; Psalm 106:37 (all occurrences), but nothing is said about casting them out of a human souls they have inhabited.

Matthew relates this work to another messianic prophecy, Isaiah 53:4, "Surely he has borne our sicknesses (*hŏlî*) and carried our sorrows (*mak'ôb²*)." Matthew presents a view of the whole of Jesus ministry as one of healing, contrary to the usual Christian view of Isaiah 53 (that his healing ministry was the crucifixion).

Translation Matthew 8:18–22

18 Now Jesus, having seen a great crowd around him, he

---

[1] Harris et al, *TWOT*, s. v. "655a."

[2] Ibid., s. v. "940b."

commanded to depart to the other side. 19 And one scribe came to him said to him, "Teacher, I will follow you wherever you may go." 20 And Jesus says to him, "Foxes have holes, and the birds of the air nests, but the son of man has no place where he might lay his head." 21 Now another of his disciples said to him, "Master, allow me first to go and to bury my father." 22 But Jesus said to him, "Follow me, and leave the dead to bury their own dead."

EXPOSITION

As was explained in the Introduction, Matthew's Gospel is not in chronological order. Here he jumps over a great deal of material (which he will write in later chapters) from Jesus in Peter's house to a point in time when Jesus was preaching by the Sea of Galilee. Chronologically this part of Matthew 8 follows the parables in Matthew 13,

Jesus is already in the boat, 13:1–2. Before he leaves for the other side of the Sea (13:52; 8:18), he has a brief conversation with two would-be disciples, 8:19–20.

The teaching is that to be a disciple of Jesus one must put loyalty and commitment to Jesus ahead of earthly possessions and family relationships. The problem with the first man is that he sees Jesus as a great Rabbi (teacher) and wants to attach himself to Jesus as a disciple, in the manner of discipleship practiced by the Jews. Jesus requires more than a commitment for the sake of learning. Jesus didn't even have a home; would the man follow Jesus under those conditions?

The problem with the second man was an attachment to earthly relationships that interfered with following Jesus. To "bury my father" may mean his father was dead. Burying one's father took priority over all religious duties and even some ceremonial restrictions (one could touch the dead body of one's parent). However, burial normally took place on the day of death, so it is much more likely this disciple wanted to attend to his father's needs until his father died. The more likely reason he would not follow Jesus right away was his inheritance. He was saying, "Jesus, I want to follow you, but I have a greater need to attend to my father, so that when he dies, I may receive my inheritance. Then I will follow you."

Whichever view is correct, the man was saying he needed to put off following Jesus until a more convenient time. Jesus says he must be first; if your family objects to Jesus, will you continue to follow?

The true cost of discipleship is demonstrated in these two conversations. Those preoccupied with the things of this world are not occupied with the kingdom, vv. 19–20. The "dead burying their dead" is a reference to being spiritually dead: the soul's sense of spiritual perception is grossly dulled by sin, and the soul is separated from God because of sin. The spiritually dead are also preoccupied with the things of this world, and therefore unsuited to the kingdom.

Translating Matthew 8:23–27

23 And having entered the boat, his disciples followed him. 24 And look, a violent windstorm arose on the sea, so that the boat was being swamped by the waves. But he was asleep. 25 And having come to him, they awoke him, saying, "Master, save us, we are perishing." 26 And he says to them, "Why are you fearful, you of little faith?" Then, having arisen, he restrained the winds and the sea, and there was great calm. 27 But the men wondered, saying, "What kind of man is this, that even the winds and the sea obey him?"

TRANSLATION NOTES

In v. 26 I have translated the word *epitimáō*, "to punish, rebuke, charge" with "restrain." Other versions translate "rebuke." Zodhiates, says, "followed by the dative of thing ["winds," noun dative masculine plural] and implying a desire to restrain, e.g., spoken of winds and waves (Matthew 8:26)."[1]

EXPOSITION

Jesus and the twelve ("his" disciples is possessive, indicating the twelve he had chosen) get into a boat and cross the Sea of Galilee. The Sea was 6–7 miles east to west and 13–14 miles north to south. The goal of the journey is south, to the country of the Gadarenes. The location was the old tribal territory of Gad, who with the tribes of Reuben and half of Manasseh, settled on the east side of the Jordan River.

The focus of the trip across the lake is in v. 27. On the one

---

[1] Zodhiates, *WSDNT*, s. v. "2008."

hand we see Jesus' humanity displayed in the fact he was tired and slept (physically overcome by the demands of the day), resting in the supreme confidence he had in God's care for him and his disciples. On the other hand, we see his divine authority and omnipotence restraining wind and sea.

One cannot expect the disciples to have recognized his deity. To do so would have been too much for them to bear mentally and emotionally. A simple question proves the point: could they have acted and reacted normally to him as his disciples if they had truly grasped that the person with them was God in the flesh? Faith in his mission, faith in God who sent him, personal faith in him as the messiah, was possible. But they understandably fell short in grasping the full content of such faith. The spiritual perception necessary to recognize Jesus as the God-man was withheld from them by the Holy Spirit. Even his parents had not grasped that their son was God incarnate, Luke 2:48–51.

Most of them were fishermen and sailors so had probably sailed during such a storm and prayed for deliverance during such a storm—violent windstorms were common on the lake. In their previous experience God had not stopped the storm but he had seen them safely home. The fact those experienced men now turned to the carpenter indicates how violent the storm had become. Obviously they believed he might be able to save them, perhaps by prayer better than theirs, perhaps by God granting power to see them safely to their destination. As with most of us, they believed he could do something, but they did not know what that something might be.

Without prayer, but with a word of command, wind and wave were calmed. "Just who was this man," they asked themselves. They might also have asked, "Who are we to follow such a man?" Accepting who Jesus is requires understanding of who we are as his followers.

The point of the story is discipleship. The disciples were following, but they were still in the process of understanding exactly what it meant to be a disciple of Jesus. At the risk of sounding clichéd, it wasn't always going to be smooth sailing. Looking ahead post-ascension, following Jesus often leads to trials and persecution. The little faith they had on the sea was not enough to see them through those future trials and persecutions. But here they begin to learn just who Jesus is, and that he has the power to protect them.

As with everything Jesus commanded, his word resulted in an immediate effect. The winds were normal, the waves of the sea were normal. The only evidence of a storm was the water in the ship. That is the way life is. After God has calmed the storms of life, the effects of the circumstances remain for us to deal with, still trusting, still by faith.

Translation Matthew 8:28–34

28 And having come to the other side, to the country of the Gadarenes, two met him, inhabited by demons, coming out of the tombs. They were very violent, so that no one was able to pass by that way. 29 And look, they cried out, saying, "What to us and to you, son of God? Are you come here before the time to torment us?" 30 Now there was far away from them a herd of many pigs, feeding. 31 Now the demons begged him, saying, "If you cast us out, send us away into the herd of pigs." 32 And he said to them, "Go." Now having gone out, they went away into the pigs, and look, all the herd rushed down the steep bank into the sea, and died in the waters. 33 Now those feeding them fled, and having gone away into the city, told everything, even about the men inhabited by demons. 34 And look, all the city went out to meet Jesus; and having seen him, they begged him that he would go away from their country.

TRANSLATION NOTE

There is a text variation in v. 28 as to the place where Jesus and the disciples landed. We know they left from Capernaum on the north beach of the Sea of Galilee and went to the other side. That makes the other side the south beach. The south beach was anciently occupied by the tribes of Gad and Manasseh, though now these were mostly gentile lands. Different manuscripts have different place names: Gadarenes, Geresenes, Gergasenes. "There was a settlement there with a name that could be corrupted into "Gergesa" and perhaps "Gerasa" (cf. the modern Khersa), so that all three names entered the tradition."[1] The better manuscripts read Gadarenes in all three gospels (Matthew 8:25; Mark 5:1; Luke 8:26). I have chosen to use the word Gadarenes as indicative of

---

[1] Morris, *Matthew*, 208.

the ancient tribal area of Gad that Jesus is visiting as part of his mission to all of Israel.

EXPOSITION

The territory of Gadara was said to have extended to the Sea of Galilee, and there is evidence of this in that coins of the period bearing the name Gadara often show a ship. In manuscripts of Matthew, "Gadara" has the best textual evidence.[1] This event took place at or near the southern shore of the Sea of Galilee, in the old tribal territory of Gad. That it took place in a cemetery speaks to the closeness of the city.

Matthew says there were two demonized men. Mark and Luke focus on the man who did the speaking. The men ran out of the tombs, meaning either the area of the tombs (the cemetery in modern terms), or perhaps they were living in abandoned tombs, or in some ante-chamber at the front of one or more tombs. They were exceedingly violent, confronting all who tried to pass by.

The question the demonized men asked Jesus is literally "What to us and to you." In less colloquial terms, they asked,

> Why have you come here and what does it mean in regard to us, son of God? Are you come here before the time to torment us?

Fallen angels, like human beings, have no knowledge other than what they can see, read, and figure out for themselves. They are intelligent, but have no spiritual perception. They didn't know Jesus came to Gadara because it was the old tribal territory of Gad. They didn't know God sent Jesus to expel the demons in the men. If they had known they might have stayed hidden, but their sin nature compelled them to confront this representative of God, this son of God. They didn't know why he was there, but they were afraid of him.

Their ability to identify Jesus as "son of God" does not necessarily mean they knew Jesus of Nazareth was God the Son incarnate in Jesus of Nazareth. That knowledge can be known only through the Holy Spirit. It is a matter of Spirit-given spiritual perception, of which they had none. The Holy Spirit doesn't give spiritual perception to sinners, unless God is saving them. Fallen

---

[1] Metzger, *Textual*, 18.

angels cannot be saved (their doom is sealed, see Revelation 20:10, compare Matthew 25:41. Wherever Satan goes the other fallen angels, bound to him by their mutual sin, go with him.)

Calling Jesus the son of God means nothing more than they heard God call him that at his baptism. Fearing him means nothing more than they knew he had previously cast out other fallen angels, Matthew 8:16. Their question, "Are you come here before the time to torment us?" meant they knew that he cast out their kind by the power of God, and by that same power their kind were sent to the abyss when cast out, to await their final disposition in the lake of fire, Matthew 25:41, Revelation 20:1.

At the most they believed him to be the messiah based on the works he performed, and the words he said, and God naming Jesus his son, see Psalm 2:7. The demons believed and trembled (James 2:19; he knew this incident) because they paid attention to what scripture said, and what Jesus did.

No, they did not know he was God the Son incarnate. God the Son left behind every outward manifestation of his deity when he became incarnate, Philippians 2:7–8. The word Paul uses is very specific. Jesus left behind any visible manifestation of his deity, 2:7, "he emptied himself," *kenóō*.[1] No person, human or fallen angel, knew he was deity incarnate, until the Holy Spirit chose to reveal it to them.

The demons ask to be allowed to inhabit the bodies of a nearby herd of pigs. Not all demons desire to inhabit a material body, but apparently, at least for this legion of demons (Luke 8:30), the desire to remain within the material world in a material body was irresistible.

Jesus tells the demons to "Go," a command to leave the bodies of the two men. This one word command is not a command to inhabit the pigs; at most it was permission to go into the pigs. Unclean animals (so declared by the Law of Moses) seem fitting for unclean angels. The pigs are apparently driven insane by the demonic habitation; it is unrealistic to assume the demons deliberately caused the death of the very animals they desired to inhabit. See Excursus for an opinion on where the demons went after the pigs died.

---

[1] Zodhiates, *WSDNT*, s. v. "2758."

The swineherds fled and informed the inhabitants of the city of these events. The whole city responded and went to meet Jesus. Upon meeting him "they begged him that he would go away from their country." One would suppose they had been grateful that this plague on their region had been relieved. Apparently they were concerned that the economic loss might be repeated.

Perhaps they thought since Jesus could command the demons that he did so as the ruler of demons. From an observer's point of view they heard Jesus tell the demons to leave the men (Luke 8:29), heard them beg to go into the pigs, heard Jesus command them to "Go," and apparently assumed that he had commanded them to go into the pigs. Jesus did not command the demons to enter the pigs, nor to destroy them, but it may have looked that way to the swineherds. An interesting thought is that some of these people may have been descendants of the tribe of Gad (at this time Gadara was a gentile territory) who were raising an animal declared unclean by the law. It seems probable that Jesus had come to the region because the people were descended from that tribe; but they rejected their messiah.

Excursus: Demonic Habitation

In Luke's telling of this event, the demons begged Jesus that he "not command them to go into the abyss." What is the abyss? An answer is found in Peter's second letter. At 2 Peter 2:4 Peter uses the word *tártaróō*, to describe the place where certain fallen angels are imprisoned. Some versions translate *tártaróō* as "hell," but it is not hell. Jude describes the same place but does not name it, Jude 6.

Many define Tartarus the same as the Old Testament *sh^{e}ôl*, but that Old Testament word means the grave, it does not describe a place in the spirit domain, see the discussion of *sh^{e}ôl* in my book *Dispensational Eschatology*. Others define *tártaróō* as the New Testament *hádēs*. *Hádēs* is the place where unsaved human souls go after physical death, Luke 16:19–31. In an illustration, *hádēs* is the equivalent of the county jail, where convicted and sentenced criminals are held pending execution of their sentence. The lake of fire is the eternal prison where the unsaved souls in *hádēs* go to spend an eternity of punishment, Revelation 20:11–15. There are no angels in *hádēs*.

What, then, is Tartarus? In Greek mythology Tartarus was the lowest, darkest pit of *hádēs*. Tartarus was described as a dank and gloomy pit surrounded by a wall of bronze and three layers of night. In early Greek mythology it was the prison for defeated gods. In later myths it was a place of punishment for sinners.

Peter has taken this pagan concept of a place worse than and separate from *hádēs*, and redefined it to teach Christian theology concerning certain fallen angels. Tartarus is the prison for certain fallen angels, not unsaved human beings. Human beings are in *hádēs*; certain fallen angels are in *tártaros*; both locations are within the spirit domain.

There are three parallels to Peter's *tártaroō*. In Luke 8:30, 31, the "legion," of fallen angels inhabiting the two men begged Jesus that he would not command them to go out into the abyss. A second view of the abyss and imprisoned fallen angels is the bottomless pit of Revelation 9:1–3, 11. The third is the bottomless pit where Satan and the angels are imprisoned for 1,000 years, Revelation 20:1–3.

Peter's *tártaroō* is the abyss of Luke and the bottomless pit of Revelation. An abyss is by definition a place so vast and deep it is bottomless, which conforms to the Greek description of Tartarus as the lowest, darkest place in the Greek's view of hell in which their fallen gods were imprisoned. Peter uses Tartarus to refer to a prison in the spirit domain in which certain fallen angels are imprisoned. Peter is using a Greek word familiar to his readers raised on Greek mythology, yet distinct from the *hádēs* of Christianity.

If all the fallen angels were chained in Tartarus the world would be a much better place. But the scriptures teach the fallen angels are busy in the world wreaking havoc in the lives of men. Not all are chained in Tartarus. However, some are in chains of darkness—imprisoned—in the abyss of Tartarus according to Peter, Jude, and Revelation.

The question to answer is, what sin did a particular group of fallen angels commit that they should be imprisoned? To answer we must assume there are commandments angels must obey—including the fallen angels—just as there are commandments human beings must obey, whether they are saved or unsaved. When a commandment is broken there are consequences.

The "Legion" infesting the demonized man of Gadara begged Jesus not to send them into the abyss. Surely this is the key to understanding. Jesus cast out every demon he found inhabiting a human being. Jesus would not have cast them out if inhabiting human beings was not a crime. We know what happened to one group that was cast out: the Legion was cast into the abyss. We know the abyss is filled with fallen angels, Revelation 9:1–11. We know Satan (and his angels) will be imprisoned in the abyss for one thousand years when Christ returns, Revelation 20:1–3. Therefore, it is reasonable to believe Peter's Tartarus and Jude's "in everlasting chains in darkness" is the same as the abyss in Luke and Revelation: a prison for certain fallen angels as punishment for certain crimes, one of which is inhabiting a human soul.

France writes, "according to Matthew 12:43–45 demons do not like to be homeless."[1] This is much too broad an interpretation. Angels were created suitable for life in the spirit domain, and that is their natural home. Inhabiting the souls of human beings is unnatural to the angels. When demons inhabiting human beings are cast out they are imprisoned in the abyss, Luke 8:31, 2 Peter 2:4, Jude 6, Revelation 9:1–3; 20:1–3.

---

[1] France, *Matthew*, NICNT, 341.

Matthew Nine

Translation Matthew 9:1–8

1 And having entered into a boat, he crossed over and came to his own city. 2 And look, they brought to him a paralytic lying on a bed; and Jesus having seen their faith, he said to the paralytic, "Have courage, my son, your sins are forgiven." 3 And look, some of the scribes said to themselves, "This man blasphemes!" 4 And Jesus, having known their thoughts, he said, "Why are you thinking evil in your hearts? 5 For which is easier, to say, 'Your sins are forgiven,' or to say, 'Get up and walk'? 6 But in order that you might know that the son of man has authority on the earth to forgive sins" (then he says to the paralytic), "Get up, take up your bed, and go to your house." 7 And he got up and went away to his house. 8 Now having seen, the crowds were awed, and glorified God who had given such authority to men.

TRANSLATION NOTE

Verse 3 in the NKJV provides a clear example why users of that version must be careful not to let the version's grammar conventions influence understanding and interpretation. In the NKJV the scribes at v. 3 say to themselves, "This Man blasphemes." The capitalization of "man" is completely inappropriate in the mouth and thoughts of Jesus' enemies. So, too, the version's constant capitalization of every pronoun referring to Jesus. An historical-grammatical interpretation of the Four Gospels requires translators and interpreters think of Jesus the same way his friends and enemies thought of Jesus, which was not in capital letters.

EXPOSITION

In v. 1, "his own city," means Capernaum, not Nazareth, see v. 13 and compare Mark 2:1. Jesus had moved to Capernaum a few months earlier, Matthew 4:13. To cross over the lake from Gadara to Capernaum was about twelve miles rowing or sailing, depending on prevailing winds.

This story corresponds to that in Mark and Luke where the paralytic man is lowered through the roof. In Matthew's view of the sequence of events, Jesus left the southern shore of the lake, where he had healed the demonized men, and crossed over the lake to Capernaum, the city where Jesus lived during his time of public ministry. Capernaum became the center of his Galilean ministry.

The point of this story is that Jesus has the authority to forgive sin. It is easy for a person to say, "I can forgive sins." How does that person prove he (or she) has the authority to forgive sin? This is not merely an academic question. The Roman Catholic Church claims their priests have been given authority by God to forgive sins: "*egō te absolve*," "I absolve you," says the priest, and the penalty due sin is (supposedly) forgiven. But that denomination cannot prove their claim by the standard Jesus used.

By healing the man, Jesus proved he had the authority to forgive sin. Jesus, it should be noted, in any act of healing, never makes a direct connection between sin and illness. However, his audience would have been convinced by their miss-taught beliefs that the man was paralyzed because of some heinous sin: that is what the Rabbis taught. Therefore Jesus' act of healing demonstrated to them the power to forgive sin. Do you claim to forgive sin? Go to the hospital and heal sinners with the same voice and by the same power you have claimed to forgive sin.

The scribes believed that as experts in the law they were the ones to pronounce when sin existed and how it could be forgiven. The phrase, "said within themselves," is a mental action, not spoken words. Interestingly, the phrase, "Jesus, having known their thoughts," is in the perfect tense, indicating Jesus had known and continued to know their thoughts.

In the scribes' view, Jesus' statement was blasphemy because in that statement Jesus assumed the prerogative of God. They viewed Jesus as a man; for Jesus to bestow forgiveness was blasphemy. The crowd also viewed Jesus as a man, but their focus was on the healing, not the claim to forgive sin, v. 8. Neither the scribes nor the common man could accept what Jesus had said: "the son of man has authority on the earth to forgive sins," meaning Jesus was not exercising a delegated authority, but his own authority.

In reality, to pronounce healing is the easier thing to say, as the many false healers throughout the church age can testify. And if the healer truly is empowered by God, then healing is easier than forgiving sins. Forgiving sins is harder, because only deity can forgive sins, and God will forgive sins only on the basis of the death of a suitable substitute for the sinner. When Jesus said, "I have the authority to forgive sins," he was showing an awareness of the ultimate goal of his earthly mission: suffering death to propitiate God, 1 John 2:2; suffering death to destroy the power death has through sin (cf. Hebrews 2:9–15).

Jesus did not state he had been given authority to forgive sins, but that he had the authority; it was innate to his essential being. Jesus is not denying his humanity, nor is he denying the scribe's premise that only God can forgive sin. He is giving the scribes and crowd the opportunity to recognize him as God come to earth to forgive sin. Matthew does not tell us whether any person made the connection. The crowd's reaction, which was to the healing not the forgiveness, was to glorify God; but not God in the Person of Jesus the God-man.

Translation Matthew 9:9–13

9 And from there, Jesus saw a man sitting at the tax office, named Matthew, and says to him, "Follow me." And getting up, he followed him. 10 And it happened, reclining at his table in the house, that behold, many tax-collectors and sinners, having come, were reclining at the table with Jesus and his disciples. 11 And having seen it, the Pharisees said to his disciples, "Why is it your teacher is eating with tax-collectors and sinners?" 12 Now having heard, he said, "The strong have no need of a physician, but rather those being ill. 13 But go, learn what is 'Mercy I desire, and not sacrifice.' For I did not come to call the righteous, but sinners."

TRANSLATION NOTE

The Byzantine text (KJV/NKV) ends v. 13 with the words "to repentance."

EXPOSITION

Some time after healing the paralytic, Jesus passes by Matthew the tax-collector; the Matthew who wrote this gospel account. Matthew may have been sitting at a booth on or near the dock to exact a tax on the weight of the night's catch from the Lake. The fish were dried and salted for sale throughout the Roman Empire, so Matthew may have collecting export duties from the wholesaler on fish sold to merchants; or perhaps on merchants for fish bought; probably both. Regardless, Matthew was working, not just sitting.

Matthew the gospel writer does not reveal any previous contact he may have had with Jesus. He may have heard Jesus teach, or seen him heal, or he may have heard others speaking of Jesus teaching and healing. The call assumes the Holy Spirit had somehow made Matthew aware of Jesus and promoted an interest in Jesus. Jesus, the Holy Spirit, and the man cooperated to make Matthew a disciple.

Implied in the call is full-time discipleship that forsakes the old way of life. Although he was probably wealthy—many tax-collectors had gained wealth through excessive fees tacked onto taxes—he had now forsaken his government post, permanently leaving that way of life. No regrets are mentioned. In fact, Matthew gives an expensive party to celebrate his new vocation.

It is noteworthy Matthew invited his old friends from his old way of life, giving them an opportunity to meet Jesus. Apparently some Pharisees were also present, or nearby. In the historical-cultural circumstances of the times, to eat with someone was to have fellowship with them. Thus, to eat with sinners and tax-collectors was to refrain from condemning them.

In the view of the Pharisees a religious man could not eat with these people (why were the Pharisees there?). One must bear in mind that the religious purity practiced by the Pharisees was such that no ordinary person could achieve it in the course of their daily lives, or in the course of making a living. Those of the Pharisees who were not religious professionals hired others to run their businesses so they themselves could avoid any action that might make them "unclean" or have contact with something, or someone, deemed to be unclean. Tax-collectors had contact with gentiles, or the people they employed had such contact, and therefore they were unclean. (To be made religiously unclean by contact with a gentile was not in the Mosaic law, but was a rabbinical tradition added to the law.)

Of course, what these people needed was the very religious instruction the Pharisees could give, but were reluctant to give, at least in a positive way, as leading to righteousness; they only used their knowledge of the law to condemn others.

Jesus' response is simple: the sick need a physician. If the Pharisees saw themselves as strong (*ischúō*, physically strong, thus well), and all others as sick, then why weren't they helping others to get well? Jesus' reply subtly includes the Pharisees as having the same need as the sinners and tax-collectors, if only they were willing to admit their need—Jesus came to save them also, if they would believe on him.

To "go and learn what is" means to make a wholehearted effort to understand the verse Jesus quotes. The quotation comes from Hosea 6:6. Sacrifices were used to atone for sin. A person living a righteous life did not make sacrifices for sin. Mercy relieves suffering; in context the suffering caused by sin. If the Pharisees had practiced mercy by teaching the people the way of righteousness—not the rabbinical way but the biblical way—they all would be strong, not sick. But they did not, so Jesus has come to make well all who are ill—all who are willing to admit they need a physician for their sin-sick soul. He will teach the way of righteousness, beginning with saving faith in him.

Translation Matthew 9:14–17

14 Then came to him John's disciples, saying, "Why do we and the Pharisees fast often, but your disciples do not fast?" 15 And Jesus said to them, "The sons of the bride-chamber cannot mourn as long as the bridegroom is with them, can they? But days will come when the bridegroom will have been taken away from them, and then they will fast. 16 But no one puts a piece of unshrunk cloth on old clothing; for the patch tears away from the cloth, and a worse tear is made. 17 Nor do they pour new wine into old wineskins; but if it is the wineskins burst and the wine is spilled and the wineskins destroyed. But rather they pour new wine into new wineskins, and both are preserved."

TRANSLATION NOTE

In v. 15 Jesus uses the word *numphōn*, "the bridal chamber in which the marriage bed was prepared, usually in the house of the bridegroom where the bride was brought in procession."[1] He uses the word *huiós*, "son" in the phrase "sons of." Together these form the phrase "sons of the bride-chamber." Other versions translate *huiós numphōn* as: wedding guests (HCSB, ESV, NLT); guests of the bridegroom (NIV); friends of the bridegroom (NKJV). So little is known about first century wedding customs—we do know they varied within Palestine and the Roman Empire—that an exact culturally appropriate translation may be impossible. Biblically, the phrase "sons of" is gender neutral. Sons of God are holy angels and human beings in a faith-based relationship with God. Sons of Belial worship idols. Sons of lawlessness are lawless. Thus, "sons of the

---

[1] Zodhiates, *WSDNT*, s. v. "3567."

bride-chamber" may be men or women, or both, who prepare the bridal chamber for the bride and groom. A fair assumption would be "sons of the bride-chamber" are, in modern terms, bridesmaids and groomsmen.

EXPOSITION

Fasting was a regular religious practice by strict Jews of the period, although the only fast required by the law was on the Day of Atonement. The disciples of John Baptist stated they and the Pharisees "fast often," which probably meant twice a week and on special occasions, such as a religious holiday.

Jesus' disciples did not fast, and I have to wonder if John Baptist prescribed a fast for his disciples, or if they simply copied the Pharisees in an effort to seem religious. For that matter, why hadn't all John's disciples become Jesus' disciples? Loyalty to a teacher has natural limits, but for some the cult of personality knows no limits (John Baptist would not have approved, John 3:30).

Jesus had not prescribed fasting for his disciples, and they did not practice fasting. On the one hand this speaks to Jesus as not the typical Jewish religious leader or teacher, and on the other it presents his disciples as more interested in Jesus, not in some outwardly religious program. His inner core, the twelve, were not religious professionals, leading to the conclusion they seldom fasted.

Jesus' response, a question, looks for a negative answer. Now is not the time for Jesus' disciples to fast; but the time is coming when fasting would be appropriate (though never mandated by Jesus or the apostles). The wedding-bridegroom theme may be a rebuke to the Baptist's disciples, for he spoke of Jesus as the bridegroom, John 3:29.

The word "mourn" must have been particularly pointed, because one mourns at funerals not weddings. These disciples of John had rejected the bridegroom John had pointed them to and were in mourning for the loss of their teacher.

There is coming a time when the bridegroom will be taken away, by which Jesus means his death. Fasting in the context of Jesus' death means mourning, but Jesus is not recommending or commanding his disciples to fast when he is dead. He resurrected, he is alive, and he is returning, so fasting for Jesus has little to commend it.

Matthew Nine

The custom Jesus referred to was the end result of the betrothal, i.e., it was the wedding and sexual consummation. In a figure, Jesus and the New Testament church are betrothed, Jesus has departed to prepare his home for the church (John 14:2), and is coming again to being her into his home (John 14:3). Therefore the church does not sorrow that he is gone, but rejoices in the assurance of his return. Moreover, through the Holy Spirit Jesus is always present.

In the historical context of the moment, the illustrations of a patch and wineskin make a point concerning Judaism and messiah's kingdom. In the larger historical context of the coming New Testament church age, the spiritual kingdom, Christianity, is in view. The point is that Judaism is the old, worn garment and the kingdom is the new piece of cloth, out of which a new garment must be made. If the new was attached to the old the new cloth is stronger and would cause strain on the old garment, tearing it further. In other words, Judaism and Christianity are incompatible forms of worship. The former denies Jesus the Christ, the latter worships him.

In Scripture a garment often symbolizes some aspect of moral character, and here it is probably righteousness. Jesus did not come to fix Judaism, whose righteousness had become a matter of strict adherence to man's traditions: the self-righteousness of legalism. What is *not* in view is that which God had begun with Moses. The Jews had so disfigured God's law with their traditions and interpretations that the original Law was no longer of real service to the people. A new garment of righteousness was being offered, the messianic kingdom in Jesus the Messiah. (The Mosaic Law was not only an "administration of condemnation," 2 Corinthians 3:9, but also the moral guide that taught the people how to lead a righteous life, Galatians 3:23–24, and serves the same purpose for Christians, Romans 6:16; 1 Timothy 6:11; 2 Timothy 3:16; 1 John 2:29; 3:7.)

This same truth is communicated by the wineskin illustration. A wineskin was a bottle made of animal hide (sheep or goat) to hold the juice. The residue of old juice left in old wineskins would undergo some degree of decay. If new juice was then put into the old wineskin the new would undergo fermentation, producing gasses which would burst the wineskin and spill the juice. What the kingdom was bringing was new wine, a symbol of the new birth and new joy in the kingdom. Jesus did not come to revise or update Judaism. The new wineskins represent the new life kingdom members have by faith on Jesus as Savior.

Translation Matthew 9:18–22

18 As he was saying these things to them, look, one of the leaders came and knelt before him, saying, "My daughter has just now died, but come and lay your hand upon her and she will live." 19 And Jesus got up and followed him and his disciples. 20 And look, a woman having a flow of blood twelve years, having come behind him, touched the fringe of his garment. 21 For she said in herself, "If only I might touch his garment, I will be delivered." 22 But Jesus, having turned and having seen her, said, "Have courage, daughter; your faith has delivered you." And the woman was delivered from that very hour.

TRANSLATION NOTE

In v. 20 the word translated "fringe" indicates the border of the garment, i.e., the bottom edge at the ankles. What the Greek word is describing is found at Numbers 15:38–39. The Hebrews were to attach a *sîsît* on the *kānāp* of their garment. The word *sîsît* means either a tassel or a fringe. The word *kānāp* means either border or corner.[1] Harris et al states, "It is debated whether *sîsît* indicates the fringe around the edges of a garment or a tassel at each corner. Snaith suggests the threads were twisted in groups to form 'a fringe of tassels.' "[2] The outer garment of every law-abiding Jew had a *sîsît* on the *kānāp*. The woman touched the *sîsît*.

EXPOSITION

According to Mark and Luke, the leader's daughter is not yet dead but dying, and will die before Jesus can reach the house. As he did at 8:5–13, Matthew abbreviates the incident, eliminating the messengers and focusing on faith, healing, and resurrection. "One of the leaders," is ambiguous, but looking to Mark 5:22 and Luke 8:41 Matthew meant a leader at the local synagogue.

In all three accounts the man expresses his faith in Jesus' ability to heal his daughter. Even after his servants report her death (Mark, Luke), when Jesus says "Don't be afraid, believe," the man

---

[1] Harris et al, *TWOT*, s. v. "103a."

[2] Ibid., s. v. "1912."

conquered his fears and believed Jesus was able to heal his daughter even from death.

On the way to the house a woman who had a hemorrhage twelve years in duration came up behind Jesus in the crowd and touched the fringe on the bottom of his outer garment. The faith of the leader and the faith of the woman are the main point of the story.

The details in Mark and Luke, such as the child being twelve years old and the woman's condition resulting in virtual death for twelve years (continuously unclean, thus always separated from others) are meant to be seen as supporting the ruler's faith. The woman's faith is highlighted by the mention of the fringe on the border of the garment. The crowd was huge, Mark 5:31, and everyone was pressed together, so Jesus and his disciples and the man had to push their way through the crowd. The woman would be in danger of being trampled if she fell while reaching for the bottom of the garment. Moreover, as an unclean person, she was in danger of the crowd's wrath for touching a holy man and making him unclean.

Her faith accepted and overcame these obstacles. Her flow of blood made her society treat her as if she was dead, ostracizing her from every human contact. Her faith delivered her, a metaphorical resurrection. Matthew presents a fully-grown faith in those who come to Jesus for healing—not specifically faith in his person, but certainly faith in his authority.

The woman's faith makes her whole, and Matthew pauses long enough in the story for Jesus to commend her faith. Matthew, like Mark and Luke, reveals Jesus addresses the woman as daughter, the only time in the gospels he so addressed a woman. The implication is clear: Jesus healed this daughter, so the ruler should have faith Jesus can heal his daughter.

Translation Matthew 9:23–26

23 And Jesus, having come into the ruler's house, and seeing the flute players and the crowd lamenting the dead, 24 says, "Go away, for the girl is not dead, but sleeps." And they laughed at him. 25 But when the crowd had been put outside, having entered, he took her hand, and the girl sat up. 26 And this report went out into all that land.

EXPOSITION

In due time Jesus comes to the house. Only Matthew notes the flute players. The phrase "the girl is not dead, but sleeps" is not meant to diagnose her condition, nor indicate she was not truly dead. To Jesus death was not permanent, nor was it frightening. The term "sleep" is used throughout the New Testament to communicate a view of death as temporary. The body ceases to function because the soul, which contains the animating principle "life," leaves the body. The saved soul goes to heaven; the unsaved soul to hades. At a future time the body will be recreated—resurrected—and the soul rejoined to the body. An unanswered question in the Bible is, "Where was the soul of those whom Jesus revived, between physical death and restoration to life?"

The crowd laughed at Jesus for saying the girl was sleeping, shifting easily from loud wailing to loud laughter (the loud wailing by mourners, sometimes hired for the occasion, was culturally conditioned not emotionally driven). Death usually occurred in the home, with exceptions for war, or accidents away from the home, and executions. Every person, adult and child, saw and recognized death. Their laughter meant they knew she was dead.

Jesus sent the hired mourners out of the house. Matthew does not mention the parents or three disciples present at the healing, nor what Jesus said to the girl. Jesus took her hand (he was never afraid of uncleanness, in this instance a dead body), and the girl was called back from the state of death. The incident made an impression so the story was widely repeated.

Translation Matthew 9:27–31

27 And Jesus, passing on from there, two blind men followed him, crying out and saying, "Son of David, have mercy on us!" 28 Now having come into the house, the blind men came to him, and Jesus says to them, "Do you believe that I am able to do this?" They say to him, "Yes, Lord." 29 Then he touched their eyes, saying, "According to your faith be it to you." 30 And their eyes were opened. And Jesus sternly warned them, saying, "See that no one knows." 31 But, having departed, they made him known in all that land.

TRANSLATION NOTE

In v. 28 the two blind men answer Jesus' question with "Yes, *kúrios*," the Greek word for sir, master, or lord, which I have decided to translate sir or master, unless context indicates lord is appropriate. This case demands *kúrios* be translated "lord." Not as recognition of Jesus' deity, but because they recognized Jesus as heir to the throne of David, and therefore a king. They may have heard (or heard of) John Baptist proclaiming the Kingdom of the Heavens, Matthew 3:2. A kingdom has a king, and Jesus repeated John's message, 4:17. Jesus is a king, therefore the Son of David and lord.

The blind men likely called Jesus by the title "Son of David," based on the prophecy of 2 Samuel 7:12, for nowhere is the messiah so titled. The Rabbis, however, had connected messianic prophecy to the son of David prophecy. So the blind men believed Jesus Son of David was the messiah who could heal them. These men probably knew Isaiah 42:7, the servant of YHWH would open the eyes of the blind. However, it is unlikely they connected these verses with Psalm 2:7, the messiah is God's son, or Psalm 146:8, "YHWH opens the eyes of the blind." Their actions do not indicate any recognition Jesus was deity.

Because the blind men recognized Jesus as their king and messiah, I have translated *kúrios* as "Lord," in the sense of respect to earthly, royal authority.

EXPOSITION

Healing the blind is unique to the gospels (Paul's blindness was not the same), and this alone marked out Jesus as of a different order than the Old Testament prophets and others who performed miracles. The details indicate this healing is not the same as the one paralleled in Mark 10:46–52; Luke 18:35–43; Matthew 20:29–34. The blind men followed Jesus (how is not stated, although the simplest solution is that sighted friends guided them), crying out his royal title as a reason for their blindness to be healed. Morris suggests the reason Jesus apparently ignored them until he was in the house was, "such a term might well have led many of the passers-by to think that he was claiming to be a political messiah"[1] ("Son of David" being taught by the Rabbis as a militant messianic title).

Jesus went into "the house," perhaps his house (although cf. 8:20), but more likely some house where he had been given temporary room and board. The two men followed. Jesus asks them

---

[1] Morris, *Matthew*, 233.

about their faith. Their positive response "Yes, Lord" indicates their belief Jesus is king and messiah; they may also understand he is the servant of Isaiah 42:7.

Jesus commands they be healed "according to your faith" and so it was. The meaning is not "in proportion to your faith," but "because you have faith." Jesus "sternly" warned them not to reveal this event, a word indicating he was quite serious. They ignored the warning. The word translated "made him known" means "to advertise, to spread one's fame abroad."[1]

Translation Matthew 9:32–34

32 Now, as they were going out, look, they brought to him a mute man, inhabited by a demon. 33 And the demon having been cast out, the mute spoke. And the multitudes were astonished, saying, "Never was it seen like this in Israel!" 34 But the Pharisees said, "By the ruler of the demons he casts out demons."

EXPOSITION

Matthew records the incident and the Pharisees' criticism without comment. The man's friends brought him to Jesus. Matthew makes no comment on the man's faith—although his friends had faith—or the method/words of Jesus, just the result. The crowds were astonished. The Pharisees acknowledged the miraculous, but deliberately explained it wrongly. Because Jesus was not on their side he must be on the wrong side. They could not accept Jesus wielding the power of God, so he must be a servant of Satan.

Translation Matthew 9:35–38

35 And Jesus went to all the towns and the villages, teaching in their synagogues, and proclaiming the good news of the kingdom, and healing every disease and every infirmity. 36 But having seen the crowds he was moved with compassion for them, because they were wearied and scattered, as sheep not having a shepherd. 37 Then he says to his disciples, "Truly the harvest truly is plentiful, but the workers few. 38 Pray therefore the master of the harvest, that he might send workmen into his harvest."

TRANSLATION NOTE

---

[1] Zodhiates, *WSDNT*, s. v. "1310."

The Byzantine texts end v. 35 with *én tó laós*, "in the people," giving the sense "healing every disease and every infirmity in the people." In my view "in the people" is a redundancy inserted by a scribe with the intent to clarify what did not need clarification. Without the insertion the reader understands Jesus was healing people, not dogs or cats or chickens.

In v. 38 I have translated *kúrios* as "master" in keeping with the agrarian culture. Those listening would have understood *kúrios* as the owner of the field or the hired manager supervising the reapers. To translate *kúrios* here as "lord" would be an interpretation, something best left to the exposition.

EXPOSITION

Matthew summarizes Jesus teaching, preaching and healing ministry as an introduction to the second major discourse, which runs from 9:35–10:42. Although the wording is similar to 4:23, it would seem that Matthew uses these summaries individually to introduce a new section, not as brackets for the preceding section.

What the reader is to understand from v. 35 is that Jesus went on a third preaching/teaching tour of Galilee. As he sees the crowds following him, his compassion for the needs of the people is balanced by his action to send out laborers, 10:1.

The word translated "moved-with-compassion," in v. 36 is *splagchnízomai*. Outside of three gospel parables (Matthew 18:27; Luke 10:33; 15:20) there is no instance (in biblical or other literature) of the word being used of men; it is always used of Jesus (Matthew 9:36; 14:14; 15:32; 20:34; Mark 1:41; 6:34; 8:2; Luke 7:13) and characterizes the divine nature of his acts.[1] This is the mercy of the messiah, his divine compassion active in the world.

Sheep without a shepherd are defenseless and vulnerable to predators. They are poor at foraging and therefore need a shepherd to take them to good pasture and good water. "Sheep without a shepherd points to people who are in great danger and without the resources to escape from it."[2]

The harvest refers to the souls waiting to hear the message of the kingdom, presumably those who are "ripe" for entry into the

---

[1] Bromiley, *TDNT*, 7:553.
[2] Morris, *Matthew*, 239.

kingdom. One wonders how far to extend the sheep and crop analogies. Sheep cannot shepherd themselves, and a crop cannot harvest itself; laborers are needed for both. But sheep and crop represent people, who bear some responsibility for themselves. Bringing the analogy into real conditions, a "shepherd" can only tell people where to find spiritual food and water (the Word of God) and workers can only tell people the Gospel of Salvation. People are responsible to read the Word and believe unto salvation.

The harvest in this particular context is the lost sheep of the house of Israel. The master of the harvest cannot be everywhere, so he will appoint and send out workers into his harvest, 10:1ff. The need for laborers is to be met with prayer on the part of the disciples. God is the master of the harvest, because souls belong to him, and he decides when to reap the harvest; but God uses workers to preach the good news used to reap souls to salvation.

The term "harvest" may also be used in the sense of judgment, e.g., Matthew 13:39, 41, 49; Revelation 14:17–20, in which case the workers are angels acting on the orders of the Lord to reap the earth for judgment. However, the context indicates the workers are Christ's saved people giving the good news to the unsaved: evangelization. People do not reap others for salvation or judgment; that is God's work. The prayer for workers is for men and women to "preach the Word," that through their (Holy Spirit directed) labor God may reap a harvest of souls for heaven.

Matthew Ten

Translation Matthew 10:1-4

1 And having called twelve of his disciples, he gave them authority over unclean spirits, so as to cast them out, and to heal all kinds of disease and all kinds of infirmity. 2 Now the names of the twelve apostles are these: first, Simon, the one called Peter, and Andrew his brother; and James the son of Zebedee, and John his brother; 3 Philip and Bartholomew; Thomas, and Matthew the tax-collector; James the one of Alphaeus, and Thaddaeus; 4 Simon the Zealot; and Judas Iscariot, who also betrayed him.

EXPOSITION

Matthew summarily deals with the selection of twelve disciples to be special messengers (the meaning of apostle), simply noting that Jesus called them to him and empowered them with the sign gifts that he himself was using to validate the message of the kingdom. The repetitious "all" kinds of disease and "all" kinds of infirmity is meant to indicate their authority extended over any organic disease or demonically caused condition.

This is the only time Matthew uses the word "apostle." Peter is "first," in the sense of preeminence. Peter's preeminence was his office as announcer: he proclaimed Jesus as the Christ, Matthew 16:16; he introduced the gospel to the Jews, Samaritans, and gentiles, Acts 2:14ff.; 8:14, 17, 20; 10:34ff; he turned the Hebrew Christians away from imposing the Mosaic Law on saved gentile Christians, Acts 15:7-11. He was not first in coming to Jesus (Andrew brought him, John 1:40-42). He was not the ruling authority over the apostles, 1 Peter 5:1; cf. Acts 15:6 ff., the council of Jerusalem, where James (the brother of Jesus) led the council.

James and John were from Galilee, as presumably was Matthew, who identifies himself as "the tax-collector" (one would presume he was collecting in the place where he was living, Capernaum). Peter and Andrew were from Bethsaida-Galilee (John 1:44), as was Philip. (Bethsaida-Galilee was on the west side of the Sea of Galilee in the territory of Herod Antipas; the other Bethsaida was Bethsaida-Julius in the territory of Herod Philip, where the 5,000 were fed, on the northeast side of the lake).

The other Simon is called "the Zealot" (also Luke 6:15, Acts 1:13), a translation of the Aramaic word "Canaanite." In later history, at the time of the Jewish War[1] (AD 66–73), "Zealot" became the technical name for the revolutionary religious party, so use of this title circa AD 30 may have been a reference to religious zeal, or to revolutionary/political zeal, or to his Canaanite heritage.

Thaddaeus, also known as Lebbaeus, is called Judas son of James in Luke's list, 6:16 (see also John 14:22). The last person listed is Judas Iscariot, who is always identified as the one who betrayed him. Judas Iscariot was the only apostle who was not from Galilee.

These were ordinary men, not marked out by any special accomplishments or abilities. Faithfulness to Jesus is what made them able to do extraordinary works.

Translation Matthew 10:5–8

5 These twelve Jesus sent out, having instructed them, saying, "Do not go into the way of the gentiles, and do not enter any city of the Samaritans. 6 But go rather to the lost sheep of the house of Israel. 7 Now going proclaim, saying, 'The kingdom of the heavens has drawn near.' 8 Infirm be healing, dead be raising, lepers be cleansing, demons be casting out. You freely received; freely give."

EXPOSITION

Matthew focuses on the instructions, not the mission, for he doesn't show them going out or coming in (cf. 11:1). The instruction concerning the gentiles is sensible, because messiah's mission during his first advent mission was to Israel. Jesus himself never left the original boundaries of the land as given to the twelve tribes by Moses and Joshua. Therefore his special messengers would also minister within the land. Jewish prejudice would have hindered their work if they were known to consort with gentiles.

The instruction "do not enter any city of the Samaritans" may be based on similar Jewish prejudice toward Samaritans. The Jews considered Samaritans unclean because gentiles had lived in the area for centuries and intermarried with Jews, thus they were not of strictly Jewish descent. Since Galilee was surrounded on three sides by gentile territory and on the fourth by Samaria, their mission is in practical terms restricted to Galilee.

However, the specifics of the restriction, the "way [road] of the

---

[1] France, *Matthew*, NICNT, 378.

gentiles," or a "city of the Samaritans," did not exclude contact with individual gentiles or Samaritans. The apostles were to remain out of areas-regions-cities known as being gentile or Samaritan.

Again, for the purposes of his first advent, Jesus was sent to minister to Israel as their prophesied messiah. gentiles were always looking for some kind of deliverer, and the Samaritan messiah was of a different nature (The *Taheb*, the one who would reveal the truth as the ultimate prophet of God.[1]). Toward other people groups Jesus would soon become the Savior, but during the ministry of the first advent Jesus was the messiah of national ethnic Israel. The twelve were not restricted from visiting Jewish territories besides Galilee.

Their mission was to preach the kingdom. The validation that their message was messiah's message was their authority to heal the sick, cleanse the lepers, raise the dead, and cast out demons. The verbs (healing, raising, cleansing, casting) are present imperative active voice, which means "these are your works." But words sick, lepers, dead, and demons are not identified with the definite article, indicating the apostle's main message was not the miraculous but the kingdom. With the article, the sick/lepers/dead/demonized would each have been viewed as a class, thus the apostolic mission would have been to the sick, to the lepers, etc. Without the article they have authority to heal those individuals whose quality or characteristic of life is that of being sick, being a leper, being dead, being possessed by a demon.

Therefore the mission was the proclamation of the kingdom. The works, when and if they occurred, were intended to validate the proclamation of the kingdom and its king. Given the fraud perpetrated by so-called healers since apostolic times, it is important to understand the written account of these miraculous events is itself the only validation required for the gospel message, because the account is an authentic, credible, and accurate history of what Jesus and the apostles did.

Certain Old Testament events serve as the exemplar. For example, God parted the Red Sea once, but only once. Scripture refers to this incident time and again as validation of God's love for Israel and his mighty power to accomplish his will. So, too, with miraculous gifts. They were done during a particular period of time

---

[1] Quiggle, *John 1–12*, 138.

as validation of the gospel message, then recorded in the Scripture for all time. They need not be repeated.

The apostles were to preach the present reality of the kingdom and do the miraculous as a supplementary part of the message. They were to treat others in the same manner God had treated them. They received blessings from God without cost to themselves and were to dispense these blessings in the same manner.

Translation Matthew 10:9–15

9 "Do not take gold, nor silver, nor copper in your belts, 10 nor food-bag for the journey, nor two tunics, nor sandals, nor a staff: for the worker is worthy of his hire. 11 Now into whatever city or town you may enter, ask who in it is worthy, and there remain until you may leave. 12 Now entering into the house, greet the family. 13 And if the house be worthy, let your peace come upon it; but if it not be worthy, let your peace return to you. 14 And whoever may not receive you, nor will hear your words, when going out of that house or the city, shake off the dust of your feet. 15 Truly I say to you, it will be more tolerable for the land of Sodom and of Gomorrah in the day of judgment than for that city."

EXPOSITION

In the ancient world there was a tradition of traveling teachers and evangelists. Itinerant teachers promoting various philosophies traveled from city to city exchanging knowledge for money. Meeks speaks of "the Cynic preacher appearing in public, always identifiable by his rough cloak, long, unkempt hair and beard, staff, and begging pouch."[1] Though this activity was more in Greek and Roman parts of the Roman Empire, the Jews would have been familiar with the tradition. The ancient Jewish prophets had also walked the land on preaching tours. John Baptist had come in this tradition. Jesus practiced the tradition and sent his apostles in that tradition.

Just as they were to go with Jesus' message, and validate that message by Jesus' authority (delegated to them by Jesus), they were to go in the same manner in which Jesus traveled: in complete dependence on God to supply their needs through the kindness of others. They would thus be seen as true messengers of the

---

[1] Meeks, *Moral World*, 52.

messiah, not prophets themselves, or miracle workers, but heralds of the messiah (even in those days so-called miracle workers lived off the gullibility and naivety of others).

They were not to make additional provision (elaborate preparations?) for their own needs. They were to go as they were. They were not to take money (more than they might have had on their person at the start of the mission) to meet their personal needs while on their mission. Gold, silver, and copper means coins of all denominations, with copper coins having the least monetary value. They were not to take any money, not even (in modern terms) a penny. The belt (or sash) worn around the waist often had a pocket to serve as a purse for money.

They were not to take the customary bag (woven basket) in which Jewish travelers kept food and extra clothing. They were not to take extra clothes, sandals, or a staff.

The "sandal" is *hupódēma*, shoe or sandal, not *sandálion*, sandal (Mark 6:9; Acts 12:8, all uses). Jesus may have meant they were not to wear a shoe but a sandal. A shoe was made out of soft leather, had a heel attached, and enclosed the foot. A sandal was made out of hard leather and used straps to attach to the foot. Poorer people wore sandals. Jesus may have meant they were to go barefoot, as did the poorest people. However, he probably meant they were not to take a second pair of shoes/sandals in addition to the ones they were wearing. *Hupódēma* is used at Matthew 3:11; 10:10; Mark 1:7; Luke 3:16; 10:4; 15:22; 22:35; John 1:27; Acts 7:33; 13:25.

By "do not take a staff," Jesus may mean no extra staff, he may mean take no staff at all, or he may have meant do not get a staff if you do not have a staff. With a staff they would be seen as protecting themselves; Jesus may have wanted them to be seen as protected by God. The most likely intent was either no extra staff or no staff at all: whatever they had, or did not have, when they went out. A staff was used as support when walking and to fend off wild animals.

The apostles were to depend on those to whom they ministered to supply their daily needs. The comment "the worker is worthy of his hire," is probably based on Deuteronomy 25:4, and reminds one of 1 Corinthians 9:9; 1 Timothy 5:18. The word translated "hire," is *trophḗ*, "food, nourishment, sustenance," but the context requires "stipend, hire, wages."[1]

This is not a prescription for today. The cultural circumstances of Israel and the ancient world made dependence on strangers possible. The culture's view of hospitality extended to providing a few days free room and board to strangers, and more so to prophets. Jesus himself depended on this cultural custom and viewed the custom as God providing. As God's workman God would provide them wages for their labor; their faith, not their means, was what was important.

When they came to a village, they were to look for a household in which to stay. The modern concept of a hotel or inn in every city should be abandoned. A small inn, such as the one at which the Good Samaritan left the man he helped (Luke 10:34), might be a guest-chamber in a house, rented out to weary travelers, and thus there was an "inn-keeper," i.e., the owner/occupant of the house. For larger groups of travelers, the "inn" could be a cave, or simply a safe place where people gathered and pitched their tents. At the most, an "inn" was an open courtyard surrounded on four sides with walls, into which niches were built where people might be sheltered from the weather. Animals would remain in the courtyard, in front of the niche where the traveler was staying, so they would be secure from thieves.[2] (Apply this information to Luke 2:7.)

Jesus did not tell them to stay at an inn, but as guests in private homes. The apostles were to be discriminating in their choices, drawing a measure of respectability in the eyes of a city's inhabitants from the people with whom they stayed. The criteria for "worthy" was undoubtedly known to the disciples and original readers since it is not stated. Perhaps, thinking of the greeting of v. 12 (the traditional "Peace to you"), the criteria for "worthy" would be both willingness to provide hospitality and receptivity to the kingdom message The admonition to "remain until you may leave," that is, until your mission in that city was finished, assumes the custom of limiting one's stay as a guest (some sources suggest three days) in a particular house.

They were not to stay long in any one city by being a guest from house to house, but to get on with the mission of visiting many cities. If, v. 13, the house proved not to be worthy of the kingdom

---

[1] Zodhiates, *WSDNT*, s. v. "5160."
[2] Wight, *Manners*, 272–274.

message, or perhaps more simply of the peace implied in the greeting, then God's peace would not be given to that household (the Greek word translated "house" means the structure, not the people, but by a metonymy it means the people in the house). The phrase "let your peace return to you" probably means to leave in peace even if you did not find God's peace in that household.

If the case is that the household, or the people of the city, did not receive the message, then the apostle was to "shake off the dust of your feet" as a witness against them. Two interpretations, not mutually exclusive, are possible. One, when a Jew returned from gentile lands, which were considered unclean, he would shake the defiling gentile dust off his shoes. In this view, Jesus is saying the people of that household or city are to be treated as one would treat gentiles.

The second view comes from Exodus 3:5. Moses, at the burning bush theophany, is told to remove his shoes because the ground is holy. Shoes, in both a physical and a religious sense, were used to keep the feet from getting dirty or defiled. Moses was to remove his shoes because the ground had been made (temporarily) holy by God's presence. For Moses to have left his shoes on would have been to communicate that God was not holy and the place where God manifested was not made holy by his presence. The opposite seems to be in view in Matthew. When the kingdom message or messenger was rejected the ground was made unclean by that lack of faith. Shaking the dust off left the unclean dust at that place as a testimony to God that it was a place without faith in the kingdom and its king. This second view seems the most likely.

Verse 15 is a hyperbolic illustration. Sodom and Gomorrah were destroyed for their wickedness. The place where the kingdom was rejected was more wicked, because they had rejected the witness of the messianic king concerning himself and his kingdom, a witness validated by specific messianic signs (stated in the Old Testament prophecies), and therefore unmistakable. In the final judgment those faithless people would be judged more harshly than Sodom and Gomorrah.

Translation Matthew 10:16-20

16 "Look, I am sending you as sheep among wolves. Therefore you be wise as the serpents and innocent as the doves. 17 But beware of men. For they will deliver you to councils; and in their

synagogues they will whip you; 18 and before governors and kings you will be brought on account of me for a testimony to them and to the gentiles. 19 But when they deliver you, do not be anxious how or what you might say. For it will be given you in that hour what you should say; 20 for you are not the ones speaking, but the Spirit of your Father is speaking through you."

EXPOSITION

The gospel records do not mention the apostles being persecuted during this particular mission in Galilee. Jesus' instructions in vv. 16–39 (and some application of vv. 40–42) seem to reach beyond the immediate mission of the twelve to Israel, to the later Christian mission, the persecution of the New Testament church, and perhaps believing Israel during the Tribulation. Certainly what follows shows the deep division that will come to exist between those with genuine faith in Jesus as Messiah-Savior and all other people. The division between the present and future is marked by the change in instructions: from being received in peace and giving peace in return, to being sheep among wolves, being scourged by religious officials, and suffering government sanctioned persecution.

In v. 16 Jesus uses *egō*, "I," to refer to himself. The sentence can be read the same without *egō*, as "I" is implied by the first person singular form of the verb "sending you." Therefore the *egō* is emphatic: "Look, I (Jesus), I am sending you," etc. He sends them out as sheep in the midst of wolves. The metaphor communicates their danger, but not necessarily their defenselessness, because it is Jesus who sends, and he has foreseen the danger.

In view of the danger they are to be as wise, smart, wary, cunning, and shrewd as serpents. A serpent will get out of the way of danger. Serpents were thought of as clever (and hostile, but hostility is not the emphasis). His disciples are also to be as innocent as doves. The Greek word translated "innocent" means "without any mixture of deceit, without any defiling material."[1] Doves do not threaten any creature.

Jesus' disciples are not to be helpless, clueless, naive, or lack common sense. Nor are they to be deceitful, immoral, or unethical.

---

[1] Zodhiates, *WSDNT*, s. v. "185."

They are to be thoughtful, careful, and cautious so as to avoid or mitigate the danger imposed by the nature of their mission. They are not to give offense; the gospel by its nature gives offense to the unbelieving, but Jesus' disciples are not to be personally offensive. Jesus' disciples are not to be hostile, malicious, or angry (unrighteously angry). They "need the cunning of snakes without the venom."[1] They are to be gentle, without guile, and faithful. Believers are to exercise common sense and wisdom; to be smart sheep who can recognize both danger and opportunity, and act accordingly.

The metaphors are set aside and Jesus speaks directly. "Men," here used as a generic term for "persons," and by which Jesus must mean unbelievers, will oppose the gospel testimony and its messengers. There seems to be an historical progression that corresponds to the history of the gospel in the world, beginning with the first testimony in the book of Acts.

The word "councils" is used in the New Testament only for the Sanhedrin. A synagogue is the Jewish worship assembly, but they were also places of religious instruction and judgment, where courts could sit in judgment on Jewish religious and civil matters.

Governors and kings relate to later New Testament history as the gospel and the church spread out among the gentile nations. When believers were brought to religious or civil trials because of their faith and testimony, they were not to be anxious about what they might say, because the Holy Spirit would give them an appropriate testimony in those circumstances. This does not exclude careful preparation in less hostile circumstances. The warning is applicable then, now, and into the future.

Translation Matthew 10:21–26

21 "Now brother will deliver brother to death, and father child; and children will rise up against parents and will put them to death. 22 And you will be hated by all on account of my name. But the one having endured to the end, he will be delivered. 23 But whenever they persecute you in the one city, flee to the next. For truly, I say to you, by no means will you have completed the cities of Israel till the son of man may come. 24 A disciple is not above the teacher, nor a servant above his master. 25 Sufficient for the disciple that he

---

[1] France, *Matthew*, NICNT, 391. Cf. Romans 12:17-21; 16:19.

be as the teacher, and the servant as his master. If they called the master of the house Beelzebul, how much more the members of his household! 26 Therefore you should not fear them"; [continued]

TRANSLATION NOTE

In v. 22 the word translated "will be delivered," is *sōzō*, "to save, deliver, make whole, preserve safe from danger, loss, destruction."[1] Much too often this word is translated "saved," when delivered or rescued would be appropriate. (Of the major versions, only the HCSB translates *sōzō* "delivered" in v. 22.)

In v. 25 the word Beelzebul is a Jewish title for Satan. The word is usually misspelled Beelzebub.

EXPOSITION

In v. 21, the word translated "will deliver" is *paradídōmi*, to deliver someone into the power of another. The gospel will cause divisions even among family members, and these divisions will occur throughout society, so that believers will be hated just because they believe in Jesus as Savior, and delivered to the authorities for punishment on account of their faith. In v. 22 the word "hated," *miséō*, is the opposite of friendship and love. *Miséō* is active ill will that seeks the worst possible outcome for another. To "endure to the end" must be seen in its theological context of perseverance in the faith by faith throughout life and through death into eternal life with Jesus.

In v. 23, the flight from one city to the next may have an eschatological meaning, as the reference to the coming of the son of man indicates. There is no shame in fleeing from persecution, if God provides a way of escape. Christians are to endure persecution and death if it captures them, but are not required to remain and suffer.

In vv. 24–25 Jesus provides a proverbial statement and example. The Savior is hated by men because of his message of grace and true faith in one God and one Savior, Jesus the Christ. Those who believe in and proclaim this message will be hated because their master, Christ, is hated. The goal in Christian discipleship is to be like Jesus. A believer may suffer persecution and death just like Jesus, who was called Beelzebul. So, too, those

---

[1] Zodhiates, *WSDNT*, s. v. "4982."

who follow Jesus will be maligned and persecuted.

Jesus' word to his disciples when persecuted is, "Do not be afraid of those who would persecute you." Believers belong to Jesus, who did not fear his enemies, even knowing how they would treat him and what they would do to him. Believers belong to Jesus, who will see them safely home through all manner of persecution and death.

Translation Matthew 10:26–31

26 [continued] "For nothing is concealed which will not be revealed, and hidden which will not be known. 27 What I tell you in the dark, speak in the light; and what you hear in the ear, proclaim upon the housetops. 28 And do not be afraid of those killing the body, but are not able to kill the soul; but fear rather the one being able to destroy both soul and body in Gehenna. 29 Two sparrows are sold for a brass coin, aren't they? And not one of them will fall to the ground apart from your Father. 30 But even the hairs of your head are all numbered. 31 Fear not, therefore; you are worth more than many sparrows."

TRANSLATION NOTE

In v. 29 two sparrows are sold (for food) for a brass coin. The Greek word is *assárion*, a brass coin equal to the tenth part of a drachma. The Roman word is *as*. A Roman denarius was worth sixteen *as* (*assárion*). One loaf of bread, which was enough for one person, cost one *assárion* (a loaf of bread in Jesus' time was much a smaller than a modern loaf). A day's wage was normally 10–12 *assárion*. In Matthew 20 the point of paying a denarius for a day's wage is that it was extravagant. At Revelation 6:6 the point of bread for a denarius is that it will be expensive.

EXPOSITION

The evil men do will be revealed and the proclamation the disciples will make cannot be hidden. The good news of the kingdom is to be openly proclaimed, unlike evil men trying to hide their deeds. Only evil attempts to hide its works, believers proclaim their works openly.

Reflecting on the subject of "Do not fear," men should fear, i.e., all human beings should reverence-respect-worship God, v. 28, because he can "destroy" the soul and the body in hell, i.e., eternal punishment in the lake of fire. "Destroy" is not annihilation (a concept foreign to Scripture) but eternal separation from God. Unbelievers are eternally separated from God at their physical death, and therefore should reverence God in the here and now (by believing on Christ as their Savior). Believers should not fear physical death because they are in an eternal salvific relationship with God in Christ, and therefore should always reverence God and not fear what man may do.

Verses 29–31 reiterate the principle that God knows and cares for his people. If sparrows matter to God, how much more human beings? So much more that even the tiniest detail is important and of continuing interest to the believer's heavenly Father. Our God is not too small. He takes an interest in everything concerning his people.

Translation Matthew 10:32–39

32 "Anyone therefore who will confess in me before men, I also will confess in him in the presence of my Father who is in the heavens. 33 But whoever may deny me before men, I also him in the presence of my Father who is in the heavens. 34 Think not that I came to bring peace to the earth. I came not to bring peace, but a sword. 35 For I came to incite a man against his father; and a daughter against her mother; and a daughter-in-law against her mother-in-law; 36 and the man's enemies his household. 37 The person loving father or mother more than me is not worthy of me; and the person loving son or daughter more than me is not worthy of me; 38 and he who does not take his cross and follow after me is not worthy of me. 39 He who having found his life will lose it; and he having lost his life on account of me will find it."

TRANSLATION NOTE

The Greek text of the sentence fragment identified as v. 36 does not have a verb. The grammar is conjunction, adjective, definite article, noun, definite article, noun, pronoun: "and enemies of the man the household of him." The article-noun phrase "of the man" is a genitive, indicating possession, thus, "the man's." The pronoun "of him" is also genitive, thus, "his household." These facts account for the translation. The verse division is unfortunate: "For I came to incite a man against his father; and a daughter against her mother; and a daughter-in-law against her mother-in-law; and the man's enemies his household." Other versions add a verb" "will be his household."

EXPOSITION

The "therefore," in v. 32, makes the point priorities matter. Who should the believer fear? The ones who can kill the body? Or the One who imprisons body and soul in hell? Should the believer fear the ones who plan in secret to persecute the gospel messenger? Or should he/she love and reverence the One who values his people so much that he knows the tiniest detail of their life? Who should the believer follow? The worldling who cares only for him/herself? Or God who has an avid and continuing interest in the welfare of each believer? Jesus confesses (acknowledges) to his Father those who confess having have a faith-based relationship with him. Conversely, v. 33, he must deny those without a faith-based relationship.

Jesus speaks of the division faith causes, vv. 34–36. Jesus is a source of division, not by means of some malicious act, but because sinners reject faith in Jesus, and therefore act out against those who have faith in Jesus. Rejecting Jesus is the same as rejecting God, John 5:23. Sinners reject Jesus for the same reasons they reject God.

The "for" of v. 35 presents an explanation of v. 34. The household relationships are used to illustrate the conflict because these are the closest of human relationships. Jesus is not disrespecting family relationships, but using them as a comparative and a test to prove faith. Comparatively, love for Jesus must be greater than familial love. The reason is a family member who rejects Jesus as Savior will persecute the father, mother, son, daughter, or in-law who does accept Jesus. When facing rejection and persecution from a family member because Jesus has become more important, how will you stand, and who will you stand with?

Faith in Jesus as Savior is about a relationship with God who is in the heavens. If, as is the case, vv. 35–36 are true, then a believer must love Jesus more than he loves his earthly relationships. This is not the love of affection or sentiment, but the action of the will in deciding who to obey and follow. One must always choose to obey and follow Jesus first and foremost in all of life's possible choices.

Verses 37–38 strengthen the point: following Jesus means the denial of the worldly life and taking up a life lived for the sake of and glory of Jesus. The cross is a symbol of death. Here it is the death of the sins of the old life, which must be put away, even if that means being hated by one's family. The Christian does not hate or cause conflict; his faith becomes the source of conflict and hatred on the part of others. In losing the old life the believer finds the new life Jesus has promised and delivers.

Translation Matthew 10:40–42

40 "The person receiving you receives me; and the person receiving me receives the one having sent me. 41 The person receiving a prophet in the name of a prophet will receive the reward of a prophet; and the person receiving a righteous man in the name of a righteous man will receive the reward of a righteous man; 42 and whoever might give one of the little ones of these a cup of cold water, only in the name of a disciple, truly I say to you he shall by no means lose his reward."

EXPOSITION

Here is an important principle in testimony. When the sinner believes the testimony about Jesus he hears from a believer, he is not just accepting another's word, or adopting his philosophy, or deciding to follow his life principles: he is believing on Jesus. This is the power believers have, to bring sinners to the Savior by means of proclaiming the gospel of "Jesus saved me a sinner. If you have faith in him he will save you too."

To receive a prophet was to believe in the prophet's message, and there was a spiritual result. To receive a righteous man was to accept the testimony of his life, and there was a spiritual result. To receive a disciple of Jesus is to receive his testimony concerning Christ, and there is a spiritual result. To receive a prophet, a righteous man, or a disciple, is to recognize not merely their testimony about Jesus, but to respond positively to their testimony with a life-changing decision made by and through personal faith Jesus who sent the prophet, the righteous, and the disciple. The "cup of cold" water is not a perfunctory act of small kindness to a small person, but is to recognize that person as belonging to Jesus. Those who do the good works the Father has prepared for them to do (Ephesians 2:10) will receive a reward. Worldly values have no meaning for the disciple, only the values of the Father and Son (and Spirit) have meaning.

Matthew Eleven

Translation Matthew 11:1–6

1 And so it was when Jesus finished instructing his twelve disciples, he left there to teach and to preach in their cities. 2 Now John, having heard in the prison the works of the Christ, sent two of his disciples, 3 said to him, "Are you the Coming One, or are we to look for another?" 4 And answering Jesus said to them, "Go and tell to John what you hear and see: 5 blind see, and lame walk, lepers are cleansed, and deaf hear, and dead are raised, and poor have good news proclaimed. 6 And blessed is he who may not be offended in me."

EXPOSITION

Matthew says nothing about the apostles' evangelistic mission, and only a notice of Christ's independent tour of Galilee. This is probably because the current evangelistic tour duplicated past teaching, preaching, and healing tours in Galilee. The important view for Matthew is the work of the Christ, not the work of his followers.

When John Baptist heard about these works he sent two of his disciples to question Jesus. John had proclaimed a King who would judge the people and establish his kingdom according to certain Old Testament messianic prophecies. Although we cannot fully know John's thoughts, apparently he wondered why this process had not begun.

Jesus responds by pointing John to the messianic signs he had performed, v. 5, implicitly referring to Isaiah 35:5–6; 61:1. John had preached that the messiah would judge sinners—burn up the chaff. When John heard that Jesus was consorting with prostitutes, tax-collectors, lepers, etc., this seemed to be very un-messianic behavior. In answer Jesus pointed John to Isaiah's prophecies of messiah preaching of the good news to the poor. What Jesus was doing was exactly what Isaiah said the messiah would do.

In v. 6 the word "offended" indicates the difference between faith and no-faith. In context, Jesus is saying, "Blessed the person who does not allow his preconceptions to cause him doubt I am the messiah." These same works should have informed the religious leaders who opposed Jesus. They also were offended.

Matthew Eleven

Translation Matthew 11:7-10

7 Now as they were going away, Jesus began to speak to the crowds about John. "What went you out into the wilderness to see? A reed waving in the wind? 8 But what did you go out to see? A man in soft clothing? Look, those wearing soft clothing are in the houses of kings. 9 But what did you go out to see? A prophet? Yes, I say to you, and more than a prophet. 10 For this is he of whom it has been written: 'Look, I send my messenger before your face, who will prepare your way before you.' "

EXPOSITION

Jesus asks a series of questions that define who John was and asks his listeners why they had responded to John and his message. Was John a popular preacher whose message could be swayed by popular opinion? No, he was not; his style and message were consistent and his manner of life demonstrated the faith required by his words. Did John represent himself as an ordinary man or a prophet? John presented himself as a prophet of God. The word "soft" refers to fabric, versus the camel hair clothes and hard leather belt John wore. The idea is cultural sophistication versus plain speaking. John was not the "yes-man" of a king's house but forcefully proclaimed the truth.

Was John a prophet? Yes, and more than a prophet. John was the herald prophesied by God (YHWH) at Malachi 3:1.

> "Look, I send my messenger, and he will prepare the way before me. And YHWH, whom you seek, will suddenly come to his temple, even the messenger of the covenant, in whom you delight. Behold, he is coming," says YHWH Sabaoth.

YHWH is the one speaking in this passage (Malachi is the medium through whom the message was communicated). The word "messenger" identifies two persons.

When YHWH says "Look, I send my messenger and he will prepare the way before me," the reference is to the yet-future coming of John Baptist, whom YHWH designates as the herald (the one preparing the way) of "Me," i.e., the Baptist is the messenger of YHWH preparing the way before YHWH.

When YHWH says, "And the Lord ('$ādôn$), whom you seek, will suddenly come to his temple, even the messenger of the covenant, in whom you delight," the reference is to the yet-future messiah.

Messiah is the messenger of the covenant, and messiah will be coming to his temple, the Jerusalem temple, which was dedicated to YHWH and belonged to YHWH. The Lord (*'ādôn*) whom you seek is the messenger of the covenant, who is the messiah, who is coming to his, YHWH's, temple.

The Jews didn't understand. YHWH is declaring the messiah is YHWH and the Baptist is his herald. Here in Matthew Jesus is declaring John Baptist is the herald of YHWH preparing the way before the messenger of the covenant, who is their messiah, who is YHWH.

The Baptist understood he was messiah's herald. He had initially believed his relative Jesus of Nazareth was the messiah. His imprisonment had depressed him. Jesus' actions were not what he had expected the messiah would do. He had, with the rest of his generation, blended messiah's first and second advents (the New Testament dispensation was a mystery God had yet to reveal). Jesus assured John that he was the messiah, by referring John to scriptures about the messiah. Jesus chastised the crowd for not supporting his herald.

Translation Matthew 11:11-15

11 "Truly I say to you, there has not risen among those born of women any person greater than John the Baptist. But the least in the kingdom of the heavens is greater than he. 12 Now from the days of John the Baptist until now, the kingdom of the heavens is sought with haste, and the forceful seize it. 13 For all the prophets and the law prophesied until John. 14 And if you are willing to receive it, he is Elijah who must come. 15 The person having ears, let him hear!"

EXPOSITION

Positionally before God, no person born before John had been of more importance or had a mission greater than John (which does not mean there were not others with an equally important mission). The phrase "born of women" seems intended to mean the entire human race. John was at that time in prison, and he had not been respected by all during his ministry, so this was a great avowal of John's importance to the kingdom, and of John himself as a great servant of God. John, however, belonged to the Old Testament order of things. Who is greater? The herald; or the one the herald proclaims? Those who by the new birth become part of the kingdom will be positionally greater than John. They will have believed in the messiah John was sent to proclaim, and will be permanent members of Messiah's kingdom.

The "days of John the Baptist" do not indicate his entire lifetime but the days of his ministry as the herald of YHWH/Messiah. The meaning is, "from those days when John began his ministry to the present days."

The meaning of the last part of v. 12 is developed from three words. The first is *biázō*, a verb, meaning "to overpower, impel, but also to rush into."

> In Matthew 11:12 . . . with the middle meaning . . . the kingdom of God is sought with eagerness, haste . . . In the middle voice, meaning that one presses into the kingdom with his own energy as if the kingdom could be had as something to be grasped . . . to "accept Christ" without having experienced repentance of sin."[1]

The second word is *biastḗs*, a noun, from *biázō*. This word means "a violent person, one who uses force."

> In Matthew 11:12 it refers to those who heard the preaching of John the Baptist and came to him to be baptized without truly repenting of their sins, They must have said to themselves, 'Let's hurry to be baptized; let's accept the advantages by the mere physical act of baptism.' But they never repented and believed in Christ. They were rushing into the kingdom and as such they were *biastḗs*, those who speedily pushed their way in."[2]

The third word is *hárpazō*. In 1 Thessalonians 4:17 it means "to snatch away." Here in Matthew 11:12 the meaning is "seize upon with force . . . an open act of violence."[3]

Those who wanted to be known as messiah's followers for some religious or social advantage had identified themselves with John's message, but they had taken by force what could be had only by repentance and faith.

The NIV and others misunderstand the verse as "the kingdom is entered with burning zeal, 'the kingdom has been forcefully

---

[1] Ibid., s. v. "971."
[2] Ibid., s. v. "973."
[3] Ibid., s. v. "726."

advancing, and forceful men lay hold on it.'" However, the three words explained above must guide an interpretation.

People can only rightly enter the kingdom by having the humility and lowliness that confesses and repents of their sin of unbelief, and receiving by faith Jesus as the one who—without their help, apart from their works—brings them into the kingdom through their faith. "It is much more likely in such a context that Matthew understood the words of the opposition of evil rather than the progress of the good."[1]

In vv. 13–15 Jesus makes a distinction between the old covenant and the new covenant. The old covenant, given and explained by the law and the prophets, was the content of faith until the days of John Baptist. John announced the coming of the messenger of the covenant, Malachi 3:1. The covenant YHWH refers to in Malachi is the Davidic Kingdom. The old covenant of the Law is to be fulfilled and then superseded by the New covenant (the law and the prophets remain to inform our faith and remind us of our moral duty). The Old Testament period and its revelation was preliminary (and preparatory, Galatians 3:19–25) to the coming of Messiah. Since, as is the case, John the Baptist is the prophesied Elijah—coming in the spirit and power of Elijah, Luke 1:17—then the time for the kingdom is at hand. All those with spiritual perception ("the person having ears, let him hear") must pay attention to and understand this change in God's means of interacting with the world.

Translation Matthew 11:16–19

16 "But to what will I compare this generation? It is like little children sitting in the markets and calling out to others, 17 saying, we piped for you and you did not dance; we wailed and you did not beat your breast. 18 For John came neither eating nor drinking, and they say, 'He has a demon.' 19 The son of man came eating and drinking, and they say, 'Look, a glutton and a wine-drinker, a friend of tax-collectors and of sinners!' But wisdom is justified by her works."

TRANSLATION NOTE

In v. 17 the word *koptō*, is usually translated mourn or lament.

---

[1] Morris, *Matthew*, 282; France, *Matthew*, NICNT, 430.

But the word, when used in the middle voice as it is here, indicates the physical actions that accompany mourning or lamenting: "to strike or beat one's body, particularly the breast, with the hands in lamentation."[1]

EXPOSITION

In v. 15 Jesus calls for spiritual perception. The illustration of vv. 16–17 is intended to reveal the lack of spiritual perception, as seen in the fickleness of little children as they are at play. Perhaps their play is pretending to weddings and funerals?[2]

The illustration models two extremes to make the point. John came as a serious man who lived an ascetic lifestyle, with a serious message calling for a complete change in spiritual life and daily practice. They said he was demonized; they ridiculed the man and his message "as the meanderings of a maniac."[3]

Jesus was not ascetic like John, and he associated with all sorts of people, so they accused him of being a sinner. They ridiculed the man and his message by demeaning his social habits.

Thus, they would not repent with John nor enjoy the kingdom with Jesus. The proverb shows there is a difference between those who believed on Jesus and those who rejected him. Unbelievers lack faith because they have no spiritual perception.

Translation Matthew 11:20–24

20 Then he began to reproach the cities in which his most mighty works had been done, because they did not repent: 21 "Woe to you, Chorazin! Woe to you, Bethsaida! Because if the mighty works having taken place in you had been done in Tyre and Sidon, then long ago they would have repented in sackcloth and ashes. 22 But I say to you, it will be more tolerable for Tyre and Sidon in the day of judgment than for you. 23 And you, Capernaum, who will be lifted up to heaven will be brought down to hades. Because if the mighty works taking place in you had been done in Sodom, it would have remained until this day. 24 But I say to you, that it will be more tolerable for the land of Sodom in the day of judgment than for you."

---

[1] Zodhiates, *WSDNT*, s. v. "2875."
[2] France, *Matthew*, NICNT, 433.
[3] Morris, *Matthew*, 285.

TRANSLATION NOTE

In v. 23 the text could be rendered as a statement, e.g., NKJV, "who are exalted to heaven, will be brought down to hades"; or as a question, HCSB, "will you be exalted to heaven? You will go down to hades." The literal word order is, "And you Capernaum who to heaven will be lifted up to hades will be brought down." The "who" is an adverb, so I moved it to modify the verb "will be lifted up" and reordered the words and added punctuation to make better sense in English.

EXPOSITION

There is equity in God's justice that punishes according to the nature of the crime. Jesus has come to these cities and performed mighty works (by a metonymy: miracles) and proclaimed Scripture in a way that clearly identified him as the messiah. Yet their response ranged from apathy to rejection. Miracles and a positive message of salvation were not performed in Tyre, Sidon, or Sodom, cities noted for evil and destroyed by God (directly, as with Sodom, or by means, as with Tyre and Sidon). When the people of those ancient cities come to their final judgment, they will receive a lesser degree of punishment because they had a lesser witness of God to be held accountable for than Chorazin, Bethsaida, and Capernaum.

To some extent this is hyperbole to communicate the greater privilege, and thus the greater sin, of all the people to whom Jesus ministered, of which Chorazin, Bethsaida, and Capernaum are the examples.

Translation Matthew 11:25–30

25 In response to these things Jesus then said, "I glorify you Father, Lord of the heaven and the earth, that you did hide these things from the wise and discerning, and did reveal then to the unlearned. 26 Yes Father, because doing so was good in your sight. 27 All things have been delivered to me by my Father. And no one knows the Son except the Father. Nor does anyone know the Father except the Son, and to whom the Son may choose to reveal him. 28 Come to me, all those laboring and being burdened, and I will give you rest. 29 Take my yoke upon you and learn from me, for I am gentle and humble in heart, and you will find rest for your souls. 30 For my yoke is easy and my burden is light."

EXPOSITION

Matthew Eleven

The text opening v. 25 literally reads, "At that time answering Jesus said." The word that may be translated "answering" means to make a response related to things previously said. I chose to translate the sense of the words.

Matthew lets us read a prayer Jesus said, vv. 25–26. The phrase "Lord of heaven and earth" is found only here in the New Testament in Matthew, the parallel passage of Luke 10:21, and Paul's sermon to the Athenians in Acts 17:24. The equivalent is found in Genesis 14:19, God Most High, possessor of heaven and earth. (Compare Genesis 24:3; Deuteronomy 4:39; 10:14; Joshua 2:11, 1 Chronicles 29:11; Psalm 115:15; Isaiah 66:1; Jeremiah 23:24.)

Jesus addresses God as Father, not in a general sense, but as his personal Father and God. To pray is to worship, so it is most appropriate for Jesus to address the Father as he worships in prayer.

The phrase "you did hide" means God withheld spiritual discernment from the world's wise ones. God chose to give spiritual discernment to the "unlearned." The word translated "unlearned" is literally infants, babies. A figurative meaning is required because of the comparison with "wise and discerning." "Unlearned" does not mean ignorant or stupid, but means those whose faith led them to seek understanding from God, cf. 1 Corinthians 1:18–19; 2:6–8.

The key to understanding God is spiritual perception, and the key to spiritual perception is a faith-based relationship with God in Christ. The Holy Spirit gives spiritual understanding, 1 Corinthians 2:11–13.

Jesus agreed with the Father's actions. God responds positively to faith, negatively to no-faith. God restricts understanding to those with no-faith. God intended—he planned it out according to what seemed good to him—that understanding the kingdom and the way it is entered was not given to the wise or discerning, but revealed to the lowliest and least capable. The point is, the clever must find the kingdom by the same means the lowly find the kingdom: by faith.

This does not mean a person is to suspend his or her rational or critical thinking. God convicts men about the state of their soul and men reason about the state of their soul. God gives the sinner personal understanding and infallible conviction that the facts concerning his spiritual state are true. The sinner's part is to exercise his rational faculties in the certainty of spiritual truth and respond with saving faith.

In v. 27 Jesus addresses his disciples. The term "all things" probably relates to the knowledge of the kingdom. In Jesus' mouth "all things" could mean everything-it-is-possible-to-know, but we know Jesus self-limited his knowledge of some things, e.g., Matthew 24:36; "all things" may mean all the power and dominion that Jesus possesses. The context is spiritual apprehension of the kingdom, and limiting "all things" to this context is appropriate to the immediate audience, even though the other views are true.

When Jesus says that no one knows the Son except the Father, he is not referring to his essential being, but that no one comprehends the Son as the Son of the Father. The Jews had rejected him as the Son, and the disciples had an inadequate understanding of his deity-human person and his relationship with the Father as the God-man.

In the same sense no one knows the Father. Jesus is not speaking of God's essential nature, but of knowing him in a salvific way, which includes that knowledge of God which follows salvation and leads to perseverance in the knowledge and ways of God. Revelation concerning God comes to us as authorized by Jesus. In his first advent he was the revealer of the Father. In a Trinitarian view, Jesus is the divinely appointed intermediary between God and man, apart from whom no man can know God, and he sends his Spirit to give this knowledge.

God the Father has given Jesus the authority and the power to accomplish his (the Father's) will on earth. Jesus alone has the knowledge necessary for sinners to enter the kingdom. No one else has the relationship to the Father that Jesus has—thus no one else has power and authority concerning the kingdom.

Jesus himself is the only way, because to him alone has the Father committed the power and authority to actualize the kingdom and populate it with saved people. More than this, the Father remains spiritually unknown until Jesus reveals him to the soul. People know there is a God, and some things about God (seen in his works of creation), but to "know the Father" means to have a spiritual relationship with him through faith in Jesus Christ. The Father has decided that it is only through Jesus Christ that one may gain a relationship with himself. Thus, Jesus is claiming that he alone has an original relationship with the Father, and he alone can bring others into a similar relationship.

In vv. 28–29 Jesus addresses all listening. This is an invitation consistent with his position as the Revealer of the Father. The invitation is addressed to "all" those laboring and burdened. In this use "all" seems to be without limitation, because all who are sinners are "laboring" and "burdened" by their lost-ness. The word translated "laboring" means to work until weary, thus to be worn out, fatigued. The term "burdened" means to overburden, like a ship overloaded with freight.

The illustrative "yoke" indicates laboring and burdened are to be understood in a figurative sense. Jesus does not place a literal yoke on his people, therefore a figurative use must be in view. Jesus is speaking of service toward himself as God and Savior.

Serving Jesus the Savior is unlike the religious service the people were performing. They had been given a heavy burden by rabbinical traditions and interpretations of the things they must do in order to be righteous. They were worn out by serving the Mosaic Law, a harsh taskmaster demanding perfection. Moreover, indwelling sin in their human nature created burdens in daily life: the constant struggle against temptation, the recurring need for repentance and sacrifices.

The people needed rest from the Mosaic Law, rabbinical traditions, and the temptations of sin, and this was what Jesus was offering in himself. To all who were wearied and burdened by sin and religion Jesus was inviting them to come to him and be refreshed. Jesus himself will give them rest.

He will give them rest because he will save them from the criminal accusations of the Mosaic Law, the unreasonable burdens of Jewish traditions, and the persuasive power of sin tempting them to commit crimes against God. He will give them rest because he will establish a faith-based relationship with himself, and give them the Holy Spirit, and a new spiritual birth. He will put no burdens on them that he does not empower them to bear, if they will accept his yoke. If they will believe on Jesus as their Savior and then as their master, he will give them no burdens beyond what they are able to bear with his help.

Matthew Twelve

Translation Matthew 12:1-8

1 At that time Jesus went through the grainfields on the Sabbath. And his disciples were hungry, and began to pull off heads of grain and to eat. 2 And the Pharisees having seen said to him, "Look, your disciples are doing what is not lawful to do on the Sabbath." 3 But he said to them, "Have you not read what David did when he was hungry, and those with him? 4 How he entered into the house of God, and he ate the bread of the Presence, which it was not lawful for him to eat, nor for those with him, but for the priests only? 5 Or have you not read in the law, that on the Sabbath the priests in the temple profane the Sabbath, and are guiltless? 6 I say to you that a greater than the temple is here. 7 But if you had known what is 'I desire mercy and not sacrifice,' you would not have condemned the guiltless. 8 For the son of man is Lord of the Sabbath."

EXPOSITION

In Luke this scene is set with the phrase, "the second first Sabbath," indicating the second Sabbath after a Passover, counting from Passover to Pentecost, Leviticus 23:15. That would make the Passover preceding this event the second of Jesus' ministry, marking the end of his first year public ministry (Passover AD 30–31) and beginning his second.

Gleaning grain from the fields was permissible under the Mosaic Law, Deuteronomy 23:25. The issue was not the law, but the rabbinical traditions and interpretations of the law. Under these interpretations plucking grain was reaping, shucking husk off the grain was threshing, and the whole could be understood as food preparation. Rabbinical interpretation made this sequence of events "work" under Exodus 31:15. Under these interpretations it was "illegal" to reap and grind corn greater in bulk that a lamb's mouthful or a dried fig's bulk (m. *Shabbath*, 7.2; 7.4.) Of course, this destroyed the intent of the law because it prevented a person from satisfying his hunger per Deuteronomy 23:25. But Jesus did not make his defense from Deuteronomy 23:25. Instead, he used the occasion to teach something about himself and about the intent of the Law.

Jesus refers to two Old Testament events, one from history,

the other from the Law, to illustrate that the Sabbath Law did not prevent acts of mercy and required people to serve the Lord on the Sabbath. In vv. 3–4, David, 1 Samuel 21:1–6, claimed to be in the service of the Lord (not a wrong statement, as he was the Lord's anointed and was fleeing Saul), and the bread in question had previously been removed from the table (in the holy place) and replaced with new bread; so David was given and did eat the old bread removed from the presence of the Lord. The ceremonial obligations relating to the bread, Leviticus 24:9, were superseded by the moral obligation to provide for David and his men. If David as God's anointed was allowed to eat the bread, how much more Jesus who was greater than David?

The second example, vv. 5–6, shows that the priests "break" the Sabbath by working in the temple on the Sabbath, Numbers 28:9–10; service to the Lord took precedence over the Sabbath. If the priests were obligated to perform necessary works on the Sabbath, how much more Jesus who was anointed to serve God, and whose Person and work was greater than the temple, seeing that he was the messenger of the covenant, Malachi 3:1?

In v. 7 Jesus again refers to Hosea 6:6 (cf. Matthew 9:13). God's desire isn't for ritual and ceremony, his desire is for mercy for the good of the people. Sacrifices are for those who have sinned. Those showing mercy on the Sabbath and those who worship and serve God on the Sabbath have not sinned.

Finally, Jesus declares himself Lord of the Sabbath. He had complete authority over the Sabbath, i.e., he is the one who can authoritatively declare the rules for Sabbath observance.

Translation Matthew 12:9–13

9 And having left from there, he went into their synagogue. 10 And look, a man having a withered hand. And they asked him, saying, "If it is lawful to heal on the Sabbath?" that they might accuse him. 11 But he says to them, "What man will there be among you, who will have one sheep, and if it falls on the Sabbath into a pit, will he not lay hold of it and lift it up? 12 How much, then, is a man more valuable than a sheep? Therefore it is lawful to do good on the Sabbath." 13 Then he says to the man, "Stretch out your hand." And he stretched it out, and it was restored whole as the other.

EXPOSITION

Matthew follows the declaration of v. 8 with an example of Jesus' authority on the Sabbath. Jesus' enemies confront him and he does not refuse the challenge. The propriety of rescuing a sheep on the Sabbath would have been admitted, but the conclusion, that healing a person on the Sabbath was also doing good, was rejected.

The rabbi's permitted acts of mercy and healing on the Sabbath if a life was in danger, and Jesus' example of the sheep in a pit shows their rule was somewhat broad and self-serving. However, the withered hand was not life-threatening, so in their view there were six other days for healing.

A man, however, is worth much more than a sheep. The right conclusion is that it is much more right to heal a man than to rescue a sheep. More than that, it was lawful to heal, the very point his enemies were contesting. There was no legal or moral reason this man should continue to suffer.

Jesus heals this man with a command. The hand was healed when the man exercised faith through obedience to the command. The man acted to stretch out the hand that could not be stretched out, and the hand was restored (Luke says it was his right hand). As for the rulers of the synagogue, Mark says Jesus was angry and deeply distressed at the hardness of their hearts.

Translation Matthew 12:14–21

14 Now, having gone out, the Pharisees held a counsel against him, how they might put him to death. 15 But when Jesus knew, he withdrew from there. And great crowds followed him, and he healed them all, 16 (and warned them that they should not make him known), 17 so that it might be fulfilled that having been spoken by Isaiah the prophet, saying: 18 "Look, my servant whom I have chosen, my beloved in whom my soul is well pleased. I will put my Spirit upon him, and he will declare justice to the gentiles. 19 He will not quarrel nor will he cry out; nor will anyone hear his voice in the streets. 20 A bruised reed he shall not break, and a smoking wick he will not quench, until he has led justice to victory; 21 and in his name gentiles will hope."

EXPOSITION

The religious leaders decided Jesus must die for breaking the Sabbath. They could not accept his reasoning, because it required them to change their doctrine, making Jesus a distinct threat to

Matthew Twelve

their faith and practice. In their view he was a Sabbath-breaker and thus was worthy of death. So they rationalized their hatred and plotted to murder him.

Jesus avoids further confrontation, but does not stop his preaching, teaching, and healing ministry. As he healed people he cautioned them not to make his actions known. Matthew takes this opportunity to give a reason as to why Jesus chose to remain out of the spotlight of public opinion. Jesus is not afraid of his enemies, he is following messianic prophecy. The messiah would not strive against others. He will work his works and preach his message without directly confronting those who oppose him, and pay the cost for his faith and service toward God. Matthew quotes from Isaiah 42:1–4.

> Behold! My Servant whom I uphold, my elect One in whom my soul delights! I have put my Spirit upon Him; he will bring forth justice to the gentiles. He will not cry out, nor raise his voice, nor cause His voice to be heard in the street. A bruised reed he will not break, and smoking flax he will not quench; he will bring forth justice for truth. He will not fail nor be discouraged, Till he has established justice in the earth; and the coastlands shall wait for His law. (NKJV)

This prophecy is directly opposite the popular messianic expectation. But the Old Testament presents Messiah as the Servant of YHWH. YHWH has put his Holy Spirit on him. The implication is that Jesus is empowered by God's Spirit and therefore is acting in accordance to God's will. The messiah will "lead justice to victory." Isaiah has a great deal to say about justice (twenty-nine occurrences of the word). Messiah will bring the people back to the righteous practices God requires.

How will messiah do this if he is gentle and patient? Because, as Isaiah indicates elsewhere, he will be a suffering messiah. Justice will be led to victory through messiah suffering God's justice against the sins of the people. Messiah will heal the people of their sins and bring them into the kingdom. He will do this for Jews and gentiles alike. This is contrary to the popular view, wherein gentiles were despised and Israel was specially favored, but it is consistent with messianic and kingdom prophecies.

The messiah will not engage in confrontation and he will not promote himself. The messiah will help the helpless—bruised reeds—and heal the broken—smoking wicks. The reference is to a wick floating in the oil-filled lampstand. A smoldering (smoking) wick is not burning and giving out light, thus it is broken.

Jesus heals, not destroys. He takes the broken and with patience and compassion makes broken people useful. God's servant will persist in these things until justice triumphs. The injustices of this world that cause people to become hopeless and helpless will be conquered. This will be done in a different manner than expected. Jesus changes people and circumstances by being gentle, merciful, and compassionate. Thus, the broken, helpless, and hopeless of the world (the probable intent of "nations"), including Israel, will come to place their trust in this lowly and effective Servant of God.

Translation Matthew 12:22–28

22 Then was brought to him a person inhabited by a demon, blind and mute, and he healed him, so that the mute man spoke and saw. 23 And all the crowds were amazed, and said, "This is not the son of David, is he?" 24 Now the Pharisees having heard, said, "This person does not cast out the demons if not by Beelzebul, the ruler of the demons." 25 But having known their thoughts, he said to them, "Every kingdom having divided against itself is brought to desolation, and every city or house having divided against itself will not stand. 26 And if Satan casts out Satan, he is divided against himself. How then will his kingdom stand? 27 And if I by Beelzebul cast out demons, by whom do your sons cast out? On account of this they will be your judges. 28 But if by the Spirit of God I cast out demons, then the kingdom of God has come upon you."

EXPOSITION

Matthew has a number of healings of the blind. Healing the blind is unique to the Four Gospels, and a sure sign that the person doing the healing does so by the power of God. Here, Jesus casts out a demon to restore sight and speech. The populace rightly interprets this action as a sign of the messiah, but they have doubts about Jesus, because Jesus meets some, but not all, their messianic expectations. This event is apparently placed here by Matthew to introduce yet another example of the religious leader's unreasoning rejection of Jesus.

The accusation by the Pharisees is that the spiritual power by which Jesus causes demons to leave the demonized is the power of Beelzebul the master of the demons. The view they are promoting

Matthew Twelve

is that Jesus is himself demonized.

Jesus always knew their thoughts (Matthew uses the perfect tense, indicating an ongoing action). In this particular instance Jesus refutes them with a simply analogy. If an earthly kingdom has internal divisions and strife, it will destroy itself or be susceptible to destruction from without. The result of disunity is dissolution. Satan is surely aware of this very principle. Why would he cast out himself, meaning cast out his demon followers who are doing evil works that promote his agenda?

If Satan is empowering Jesus, then he is enabling Jesus to deliver people from Satan's power. Demon would be fighting against demon, desolating Satan's kingdom, destroying his influence over mankind. Satan might do this a few times in order to deceive, but Jesus casts out every demon he meets, thus destroying Satan's kingdom and influence. BY this simple logic Jesus proves the Pharisees are wrong.

Jesus then examples the Pharisees themselves, who cast out demons (or claimed to). Consistency requires that the power be the same in both instances. The power by which Jesus casts out demons is God's power, the power of the Holy Spirit. Since this is true, then they should recognize that Jesus is the Messiah and the messianic kingdom is at hand.

Translation Matthew 12:29–32

29 "Or how is anyone able to enter into the house of the strong and plunder his goods, if not first he bind the strong? And then he will plunder his house. 30 The person not being with me is against me, and the person not gathering with me scatters. 31 Because of this I say to you, every sin and blasphemy will be forgiven men, but blasphemy against the Spirit will not be forgiven. 32 And whoever speaks a word against the son of man, it will be forgiven him; but whoever may speak against the Holy Spirit, it will not be forgiven him, neither in this age nor in the one coming."

EXPOSITION

A second illustration to make the point, Jesus is the one who binds Satan and plunders his house. Then, a principle: one is either for Jesus or against him; works with Jesus or against him. The Pharisees were against Jesus. See Excursus, below, for a discussion of vv. 31–32

Excursus: 12:31–32, What is the unpardonable sin?

First, if you are a believer who is concerned you may have committed this sin, then you haven't. A person who commits this sin against the Holy Spirit feels no need for repentance. One of the distinguishing marks of a Christian is that he or she knows sin is wrong. Whenever a Christian commits a sin, he or she feels remorse and godly sorrow, and comes to the Lord in repentance and confession, to be forgiven and restored to fellowship with God. A believer has accepted by faith everything this sin denies: Christ as Savior and the work of the Holy Spirit in his or her life. A believer will not commit this sin: the Holy Spirit will not let him.

If you are an unbeliever worried about this sin, then the fact that you worried, seeking to understand sin, the Savior, and salvation, indicates you have not committed this sin. People who have committed the unpardonable sin don't worry about it. They have made up their mind to reject the salvation God offers them in Jesus Christ. You would not be here if you had committed this sin.

What is the unpardonable sin? First, let's read the Scripture.

> Matthew 12:31–32 Because of this I say to you, every sin and blasphemy will be forgiven men, but blasphemy against the Spirit will not be forgiven. 32 And whoever speaks a word against the son of man, it will be forgiven him; but whoever may speak against the Holy Spirit, it will not be forgiven him, neither in this age nor in the one coming.
>
> Mark 3:29 But whoever may blasphemes against the Holy Spirit never has forgiveness to the eternity, but is guilty of eternal sin.
>
> Luke 12:10 And every person who will say a saying against the son of man, it will be forgiven him; but the person having blasphemed against the Holy Spirit will not be forgiven.

If we look at the context of Matthew, Mark, and Luke, and the larger context of the Holy Spirit's operations in the gospels, we can find several defining characteristics that will help us understand this sin.

> The Scribes and Pharisees kept on accusing Jesus of casting out demons by the power of Satan. They did not make this accusation once; the Greek verb tense is, "they kept on saying." They were hardened in their opposition to Jesus,

and made an accusation deliberately intended to slander him and the Holy Spirit, in order to turn people away from faith in Jesus. Their slander was a habitual act that indicated an underlying unrepentant attitude of unbelief and opposition toward God.

The Scribes and Pharisees knew, from Scripture, that the power by which Jesus performed these miracles was in fact the power of the Holy Spirit.

The Old Testament Scriptures said the messiah would come in the power of the Spirit of the Lord to heal people, Isaiah 11:12, 49:8.

John the Baptist had told Israel that messiah was immediately coming and would baptize with the Holy Spirit.

Jesus quoted Isaiah 61:1, 2 as validating his ministry, therefore the authority and power by which he cast out demons was the Holy Spirit.

The Pharisees understood that they were slandering the Holy Spirit. To blaspheme is to slander or defame. They recognized that the Holy Spirit was the source of the power by which Jesus performed miracles, but they said that the source of Jesus' power to cast out demons was demonic, satanic. This slander, said Jesus, cannot be forgiven.

Returning to the exposition

Can the "unpardonable sin" occur today?

The people who originally committed this sin were religious people who knew the Scriptures, saw Christ and the Spirit working in the world, and made a decision to slander the Holy Spirit and reject Christ as their messiah. They were unbelievers.

However, this sin is not simply disbelief or rejection of Jesus as Savior. That sin of unbelief is always forgivable, up to the moment of death. Remember, Jesus said, "every sin and blasphemy will be forgiven men," except slander against the Holy Spirit. The unpardonable sin is slander against the Holy Spirit. Slander is not accidental, it is knowing and deliberate.

It is possible to commit this sin today under two circumstances.

One way is to agree with the Scribes and Pharisees that the work of the Holy Spirit is really the work of Satan. Satan is actively at work in the religions of the world, even where the name

"Christian" is over the door. But, Satan cannot be the power behind Christian worship, fellowship, obedience, and serving God. Satan does not produce morality, ministry, unity, and fellowship according to the scriptures. Satan does not forgive sin and change people's lives from sinner to saved. To see these particular things at work in the lives of sinners being saved and believers living like Christ, and then to reject it as evil or demonic or satanic, is to agree with the Scribes and Pharisees that the power of the Holy Spirit is the power of Satan. It is appropriate to recognize Satan at work, even when he is doing a bad imitation of God; it is inappropriate to recognize the Holy Spirit at work and knowingly slander him.

The second way to commit this sin is to reject the Spirit by rejecting his work to save sinners. I am not speaking of the temporary rejection—often more than one time—that can be part of the process used by the Spirit to convict a sinner and bring him/her to faith and salvation. I am speaking of rejection throughout all of life into physical death. The power of physical death is to seal the soul into its spiritual state at the time of death. A lifetime of rejecting the Spirit's work to convict and save results in a soul never convicted and never saved.

The Holy Spirit is the divine Person who applies the truth of God to the sinner's soul. The Holy Spirit is the One who applies the grace of God that brings salvation. Any unbeliever truly seeking to understand sin, the Savior, and salvation will in some measure participate in the external benefits the Holy Spirit brings to his people: the morality, ministry, unity, and fellowship of Christianity. But if, after experiencing the external benefits of work of the Spirit, the unbeliever then rejects the Spirit's testimony, and permanently (throughout his/her lifetime) turns away from faith in Christ, the unrepentant attitude toward the things of God is a sin against the Spirit. This person is not repentant, and without repentance there is no forgiveness.

Finally, why can't this sin be forgiven? It is less a matter of God forgiving, than the sinner repenting. Remember, the unbelieving Jews unrepentantly rejected Christ and the Spirit's witness. Their unrepentant attitude is seen in their slander of the Spirit. This same attitude is seen in the book of Acts, where time and again they rejected the works of the Spirit as being God's works. The works of the Spirit make this statement to every sinner: "Here is Jesus the Savior who will save you from your sins." That testimony requires a choice. A person either repents of his sin, or he rejects the Spirit's witness. To reject Jesus out of ignorance is forgivable. To reject the Holy Spirit is to be knowingly unrepentant; if one does not repent, then he or she cannot be forgiven.

Anyone who is truly repentant, no matter how shameful or serious his or her sin might be, can be saved. But, the person who rejects the Spirit's witness of their sin, and their need for repentance and forgiveness, that person's sin is unpardonable, because he or she refuses to walk the path that leads to salvation.

Translation Matthew 12:33–37

33 "Either make the tree good and its fruit good, or make the tree bad and its fruit bad; for by its fruit the tree is known. 34 Generation of vipers! How are you, being evil, able to speak good things? For out of the abundance of the heart the mouth speaks. 35 The good man out of his good treasure puts forth good things, and the evil man out of his evil treasure puts forth evil things. 36 Now I say to you, that every insincere word that men will speak, they will give an account of it in a day of judgment. 37 For by your words you will be justified, and by your words you will be condemned."

TRANSLATION NOTE

In v. 36, the word I have translated "insincere" is *argós*, "not at work, idle, not employed, inactive."[1] At "Matthew 12:26, insincere language of a person who speaks one thing and means another."[2] Most versions translate "idle," or "careless."

EXPOSITION

A simple illustration that teaches what is on the inside comes out for all to see. People will be judged by the spiritual condition of their souls. The "insincere" word is not the cause of judgment, it is the symptom of a sin-filled soul. This point is made clear by v. 35. This saying is aimed squarely at the Pharisees who are accusing Jesus of collaboration with Satan. The words they have spoken will judge them, because the words reveal what is in their hearts. Notice Jesus' authority, v. 36: "Now I say to you."

Translation Matthew 12:38–42

---

[1] Zodhiates, *WSDNT*, s. v. "692."
[2] Ibid.

Matthew Twelve

38 Then some of the scribes and Pharisees responded, saying, "Teacher, we want to see a sign from you." 39 But answering he said to them, "A generation evil and adulterous seek for a sign, and a sign will not be given to it, except the sign of Jonah the prophet. 40 For just as Jonah was in the belly of the great fish three days and three nights, so will be the son of man in the heart of the earth three days and three nights. 41 The men of Nineveh will stand up in the judgment with this generation and will condemn it, because they repented at the preaching of Jonah, and look, greater than Jonah is here. 42 The queen of the South will stand up in the judgment with this generation and condemn it, for she came from the ends of the earth to hear the wisdom of Solomon, and look, greater than Solomon is here."

EXPOSITION

The request for a sign is asked with the same insincerity as all other opposition. Matthew has made it clear the scribes and Pharisees do not believe Jesus is a prophet sent from God and do not believe he is the messiah. They are looking for a way to justify their unbelief and prove Jesus false in the eyes of the crowd. The healing, preaching, and teaching were sufficient signs of the messiah, because they conformed to prophecy concerning the messiah. If they rejected those signs, which they did, they would reject any sign.

Jesus doesn't intend to stop doing the biblical actions that testify he is the messiah. But none of those signs will change those already convinced he is a fraud. So Jesus announces one final sign (knowing they will reject that sign also). Jesus says he will give them the sign of the prophet Jonah.

The sign of Jonah is described here as being three days and three nights in the heart of the earth just as Jonah was three days and three nights in the belly of the great fish. Jonah described his experience as like death, Jonah 2:2; thus being vomited out of the fish, 2:6, was like resurrection: "you [YHWH] have brought up my life from the pit." So Jesus in the heart of the earth is his death and Jesus will come out of the earth in resurrection. The comparison with Nineveh and the Queen of the South is the same kind as at 11:20–24, the greater testimony provided by the greater person will result in greater condemnation.

Translation Matthew 12:43–45

Matthew Twelve

43 "Now when the unclean spirit is gone out from the person, it goes through barren places, seeking rest, and finds none. 44 Then it says, 'I will return to my house from where I came out.' And having come, it finds it empty, and swept, and put in order. 45 Then it goes and takes with itself seven other spirits more evil than itself, and having entered in they dwell there; and the last of that person is worse than the first. So it will also be unto this evil generation."

TRANSLATION NOTE

In v. 43 I have translated *ánudros tópos*, as "barren places." The words mean a place that is without water, dry, barren, desert. Zodhiates states "The Jews supposed that the abode of evil spirits was in deserts."[1] Jesus was undoubtedly tying his lesson into their belief. However, the point is not the lack of water or what the Jews misbelieved. In the story the unclean spirit (fallen angel) searches for a new dwelling in uninhabitable places. Where do fallen angels naturally live? In the spirit domain, identified as the second of the three heavens (heavens: sky, spirit domain, heaven proper, the last seen at Revelation 4, 5). So the unclean spirit/fallen angel had a place in which he could—if he wanted to, and was supposed to—dwell. Some fallen angels desire to inhabit human souls. Such was the case here. In order to stay connected with the meaning of *ánudros tópos* but communicate the lesson I translated "barren" versus dry (NKJV), waterless (HCSB), arid (NIV), or desert (NLT).

EXPOSITION

Jesus sums up his accusations against the unbelief of "this generation" to whom he has come as the messiah. The generation that has rejected Jesus is like a man who was once upon a time freed from an indwelling demon (fallen angel), but took no action (saving faith) to secure his soul from being re-inhabited. The demon looked for another soul to inhabit, but could not find a suitable soul. He returned to the soul from which he was cast out, and discovers it is still suitable; so much so he finds seven other demons to join him. The number seven indicates the completeness of the person's degradation and "lost-ness."

The point of the lesson is that self-reformation is not salvation. In fine, committing one's self to perform every biblical

---

[1] Zodhiates, *WSDNT*, s. v. "504."

commandment perfectly, as the Pharisees did, does not earn the merit necessary to be saved. Good works cannot make a person righteous to salvation. Only the merit of Jesus saves the lost soul, and that merit can be gained only by faith in the salvation given by Jesus: "believe on the Lord Jesus Christ and you will be saved."

What makes a soul suitable for demonic habitation is anyone's guess, but perhaps it is willingness to give oneself over to gross sins; or surrendering moral authority to the demon. The demon searched uninhabitable places, meaning human souls not suitable for demonic habitation. Uninhabitable souls are not necessarily saved souls, simply souls not suitable (not yet suitable?) to demonic habitation. (Saved souls cannot be inhabited by any spirit being other than the Holy Spirit.)

The point of the story is in v. 44. The person, upon being rescued from demonic control, made a moral reformation, but did not exercise the faith required for his soul to be regenerated by faith. Jesus came to Israel healing demonic habitations, but the people rejected him. Their resultant spiritual state was worse than before Jesus came.

Morris relates this illustration to v. 30: one cannot be neutral toward Jesus, else he ends up in a condition worse than before.[1] France relates it to exorcism, meaning individuals set free must become disciples, else they will relapse into a condition worse than before.[2] Carson combines these two views, "those who through the kingdom power of God experience exorcisms must beware of neutrality toward Jesus the Messiah, for neutrality opens the door to seven demons worse than the one driven out."[3] The lesson for Carson is, "the wicked and adulterous generation" is so neutral toward Jesus that they require a sign.

These opinions undoubtedly strike the proper note about neutrality and discipleship, but we must be careful not to try and put some meaning into every detail in the story. The story is not about neutrality or exorcism. The story is about rejecting Jesus. There is no neutrality toward Jesus, and in that sense the story connects with v. 30, "The person not being with me is against me."

---

[1] Morris, *Matthew*, 330.
[2] France, *Matthew*, NICNT, 494.
[3] Carson, *John*, 298.

To be neutral toward Jesus is to positively reject Jesus.

Therefore the story is not about becoming a disciple, but about being saved. The word "disciple" is used in two senses in the Four Gospels. One is the cultural sense: a person attaches himself to a teacher, follows him about the country, and learns his teachings. In this sense many whom Jesus healed or cast out demons became disciples.

The other sense is the spiritual sense. A disciple is a person who has exercised saving faith in Jesus Christ, resulting in the person being born-again: made a disciple of Christ by the regenerating work of the Holy Spirit. Being now born-again, the person is able to learn how to be a disciple and put learning into practice to live like Christ, because his/her born-again soul is capable of being like Christ. The story of the wandering unclean spirit is about the failure of sinners to exercise saving faith in Jesus Christ. Jesus freed many persons from demonic habitation, but they didn't take the next step of saving faith. When the opportunity to be saved is rejected, the state of the person's soul is worse than before.

Translation Matthew 12:46–50

46 While he was speaking to the crowds, look, his mother and brothers were standing outside seeking to speak with him. 47 Then someone said to him, "Look, your mother and your brothers are standing outside, seeking to speak with you." 48 But answering, he said to the person telling him, "Who is my mother? and who are my brothers?" 49 And having stretched out his hand to his disciples, he said, "Look, my mother and my brothers. 50 For whoever shall do the will of my Father who is in the heavens, he is my brother and sister and mother."

EXPOSITION

Jesus is not disparaging family relationships. He is saying that the salvation relationship is the most important (and the longer lasting). Doing the will of God is more important than family relationships. The life of the believer should be focused on worship, fellowship, service, and obedience toward God, for these are the four pillars of the Christian life. All other relationships must take second place to one's relationship with God in Christ.

Matthew Thirteen

Translation Matthew 13:1-2

1 On that day, Jesus having left the house, he sat by the sea. 2 And great crowds were gathered together to him, so that he entered a boat to sit down; and all the crowd stood on the shore.

EXPOSITION

Chapter twelve apparently ends in the house where Jesus lived when he visited Capernaum. After he confronted the scribes and Pharisees, Jesus left the house to teach on the shore of the lake. Sitting was the position Jewish teachers assumed when teaching. Sitting in the boat would force the crowds to spread out along the shoreline, limiting the depth of the crowd, thus allowing everyone to be close enough to hear. Sitting in the boat also prevented Jesus from being mobbed by the crowd.

From this point forward in his ministry, Jesus teaches less in the synagogues and more outdoors. He now uses stories—parables—to teach, versus the plainer method of his previous evangelistic tours. The previous encounter reveals the opposition and unbelief that led Jesus to change his method of teaching. Israel's rejection had reached a certain stage, indicating the lack of faith that refused to seek understanding. Parables are understandable only through the discernment given by the Spirit. Because God has chosen to respond to faith and leave those with no-faith in their ignorance, only those who exercised faith, or had the desire to believe, were given the spiritual discernment necessary to understand the parables, 13:10-17. The same remains true to this day.

Although there are parables in the Old Testament, Jesus uses more parables more frequently and more effectively than any other biblical person. A parable is often defined as an earthly story with a heavenly message. Certainly the elements of a parable are drawn from life, and they are intended to teach spiritual truth.

A parable is a story using an extended simile to draw a verbal picture that teaches spiritual truth. In most instances, a parable is like an arrow in that it is aimed at one target, that is, it is intended to communicate one specific spiritual truth. The earthy elements of a parable are the cart that carries the message. The earthly elements are real, not fabulous as in a fable, i.e., inanimate things do not act as though alive; animals do not act sentient, etc.

The parables explain the nature of messiah's kingdom as a consequence of the first advent. The religious leaders had led their disciples and the common man and woman to expect a militant messianic king conquering the world. Jesus explains the messiah is not out to conquer the world, but to make sinners members of his kingdom. Toward the Christian in this New Testament church age, the kingdom parables are intended to explain the state and progress of the spiritual kingdom between Christ's two advents.

Translation Matthew 13:3–9

3 And he spoke many things to them in parables, saying, "Look, the one sowing went out to sow, 4 And in his sowing, some indeed fell along the road; and the birds having come devoured them. 5 Now others fell upon rocky places, where they did not have much soil, and immediately they sprang up, on account of not having depth of soil. 6 But the sun having risen, they were scorched, and through not having root, were dried up. 7 Now others fell upon thorns, and the thorns came up and choked them. 8 But others fell upon good soil and yielded fruit, some indeed a hundredfold, but some sixty, but some thirty. 9 The person having ears, let him hear!"

EXPOSITION

The basic story is drawn from the agrarian lifestyle dominant in the ancient world and familiar to city dwellers. The dispersal of the seed is true to life, as are the results of that dispersal. The call in v. 9 is to spiritual perception. The parable is explained at vv. 18–23, so I will withhold specific comments until then.

Translation Matthew 13:10–17

10 And the disciples, having come to him, said to him, "Why do you speak to them in parables?" 11 Now answering he said to them, "Because it has been given to you to know the mysteries of the kingdom of the heavens, but to them it has not been given. 12 For whoever has, to him will be given, and he will have abundance; but whoever does not have, even what he has will be taken away from him. 13 On account of this I speak to them in parables, because seeing they see not, and hearing they hear not, nor do they understand. 14 And in them the prophecy of Isaiah is fulfilled, the one saying, 'In hearing you will hear and by no means understand, and seeing you will see and by no means perceive; 15 For the heart

of this people has grown callous, and with the ears they heard dully, and their eyes they have closed, lest they should see with the eyes, and with the ears they should hear, and with the heart they should understand and return and I will heal them.' 16 But blessed are your eyes because they see, and your ears because they hear. 17 For truly I say to you, that many prophets and righteous desired to see what you see, and did not see, and to hear what you hear, and did not hear."

EXPOSITION

At first reading Jesus seems callous toward those who came to hear him. He quotes from Isaiah that the people cannot understand because their spiritual condition prevents them from understanding—and God has decided to leave them in this condition as a judgment for their lack of belief. Jesus is not uncaring but knows the heart of this people. He knows they hear and see the signs of the messiah but do not believe on him. They might believe he is the messiah of Rabbinical interpretation: the warrior come to defeat the Romans, restore Jewish independence, and rule the gentiles. But they will not believe he is the messiah sent by God to rescue sinners from their enslavement to sin. His every miracle demonstrates the truth: he rescues people from sickness and demons; he does not oppose worldly authority.

So what Jesus is teaching is that rejecting the kind of messiah God sent leads to continued spiritual dullness. In Isaiah's day there was continuing idolatry and immorality. In this environment Isaiah would preach the word of repentance toward sin, of return to faith in YHWH, and of covenant keeping as the practice of that faith. The heart that had grown dull, the ears that did not hear, and the eyes that did not see reflected the spiritual state of the whole person: one of spiritual inability and a lack of spiritual perception due to sin. Speaking through the prophet Isaiah, God says he will allow this spiritual condition to continue. It continues because the faculty of spiritual perception is already grossly dulled by the indwelling sin nature, and the lack of faith causes that condition to continue and worsen. What is in view in Isaiah is judgment because of their refusal to repent and believe. God responds to even the tiniest amount of faith; this people had no-faith.

The same is becoming true of Israel's response to Jesus. Jesus has been ministering for about two years. He has clearly identified himself as the messiah through the prophesied messianic signs and through his teaching the messianic good news. Those who have some confidence in him as, at the least, a prophet sent from God, at best, the messiah, have their faith enlarged with greater spiritual perception. Those who continue to reject him will lose whatever spiritual perception they may have had, or had been given, when Jesus first began to minister. Jesus' response to Israel's continued lack of faith is to teach the truth about the kingdom through parables, which the faithful will understand, and those without faith will fail to understand.

The modern application is that continued rejection of gospel testimony will lead to increasing inability to understand the gospel. God respects a person's choices, because he respects what he created: the authority and power to make a moral choice. God will always respond to any measure of faith by giving increased understanding. He will always respond to no faith by not giving increased understanding.

Translation Matthew 13:18–23

18 "You therefore, hear the parable of the one having sown. 19 Everyone hearing the word of the kingdom and not understanding, the evil one comes and snatches away that having been sown in his heart. This is that having been sown on the road. 20 But that having been sown upon the rocky places, this is the person hearing the word, and immediately receives it with joy. 21 But he has no root in himself, but is temporary; but tribulation or persecution having come on account of the word, immediately he falls. 22 Now that having been sown among the thorns, this is the person hearing the word, and the anxiety of this present age and the deceit of riches choke the word, and it becomes unfruitful. 23 But that having been sown on the good soil, this is the person hearing the word and understanding, who indeed brings forth fruit, and indeed produces a hundredfold, but some sixty, but some thirty."

EXPOSITION

The explanation of the parable of the sower is that the seed being sown is the "word of the kingdom" (in Luke the seed is the word of God). The word of the kingdom is more than a reference to the kingdom "at hand," it is the total kingdom message Jesus has been preaching and teaching; ultimately it is the gospel of salvation.

Matthew Thirteen

Jesus has been sowing the "good news" of the kingdom, 4:23; 9:35, in the field of Israel. The good news is received in four ways. One, it is not understood. Because of sin there is no spiritual perception of the message. When this happens, Satan (the evil one) acts to separate the hearer from the gospel, lest some interest develop.

Two, the message is received with joy, but the soil of faith is not present. The rocky path is a figure of the heart, i.e., the person who rejects spiritual things and therefore the word of the kingdom has no meaning. The joy was due to the promise of hope, or a moral reformation, or some promise of relief from worldly circumstances, but the person receiving the word falls when faced with the trouble or persecution that comes with professing faith in Christ. In my view this indicates this person does not continue on to faith in Christ, and there is no salvation. (An alternative view understands receiving the word with joy as salvation, and fall as indicating some sin committed as a Christian.)

The third type of person hears but becomes unfruitful due to the cares of the world and the deceitfulness of riches. This may mean unfruitful as to the seed bearing the fruit of salvation, or unfruitful in the Christian life. I believe the first view is the one most true to the parable and to Scripture. The cares of this world and riches can occupy the mind and heart to the exclusion of faith.

The fourth type of hearer receives the gospel on good ground, indicating faith, and therefore he understands, indicating salvation. In this case the word believed brings forth the fruit of a saved life lived for Christ. The varying yield of the seed in this soil has to do with spiritual ability, spiritual gifts, and perseverance in the faith: some believers mature at a greater pace than others; some are used for greater things than others. This parable also explains the reception accorded to the gospel of salvation in this New Testament church age.

The four soils describe in a figure the typical reaction of any one sinner hearing the gospel of salvation. Some reject it right away; some assent to it but don't let it change their life; to some it is just another program in a life full of activities; and some receive it, are changed by it, and live because of it. Because salvation is by grace through faith, and grace-faith-salvation is a gift God, any of the first three kinds of soil may become a fourth soil. But God respects what he created. He allows people to make a choice. Most choose not to believe; some choose to believe.

Translation Matthew 13:24–30

24 Another parable he put before them, saying:

"The kingdom of the heavens has become like a man having sown good seed in his field, 25 but while the men are sleeping, his enemy came and sowed darnel among the wheat, and went away. 26 But when the grass sprouted and produced fruit, then the darnel also appeared."

27 "Now the servants of the master of the house, having come to him, said to him,

'Sir, you sowed good seed, didn't you? How then has it darnel?'

28 "Now he said to them,

'A man, an enemy, did this.'

'So the servants said to him,

'Then do you want that we should go and gather them?'

29 "But he said,

'No, lest gathering the darnel you might uproot the wheat with them. 30 Allow both to grow together until the harvest; and in the time of harvest I will say to the harvesters,

"First gather the darnel and bind them into bundles in order to burn them; but the wheat gather together into my barn." ' "

TRANSLATION NOTE

In v. 26 Jesus uses the word *chórtos*, "the grass or herbage of the field,"[1] translated "darnel." Both wheat and darnel are classified among the grasses.

EXPOSITION

This parable explains why the visible church is composed of believers and false professors. Christ fills his kingdom with his saved people, but Satan sows the unsaved into the kingdom. Telling the difference can be difficult. Let us bear in mind a parable teaches one point. Here that point is, Christ's Kingdom in the current age seems to be composed of good and bad believers, when in reality it is composed of the saved and the unsaved. The unsaved are making a false profession concerning their salvation. Some know

---

[1] Zodhiates, *WSDNT*, s. v. "5528."

they are unsaved; some may believe they are saved. The church is not prevented from protecting itself against false professors, especially those who want to change or corrupt the doctrine, see, e.g., Jude. But violence (uprooting the darnel) is never justified. The Word preached either convicts and converts, or convicts and causes the unsaved to leave.

The farmer sowed wheat. The enemy sowed darnel. "Darnel" is a grass that continues to grow today in the wheat fields of Palestine. "The Arabs still give the name *zirwan* to a noxious grass (which is only too common in the cornfields of Palestine) simulating the wheat when undeveloped, though easily distinguishable at 'harvest' time."[1] The grain of the darnel plant produces effects similar to intoxication, and in large quantities may be poisonous. Hence it was an enemy that sowed the darnel among the wheat.

This parable has an eschatological theme: judgment occurs at the end of the kingdom age, i.e., when messiah inaugurates his kingdom at the second advent. The wheat will be gathered into the barn and the darnel will be burned. If the parable is viewed as the course of Christian history, i.e., until Christ returns and inaugurates his kingdom rule on earth, then wheat and darnel grow together during the church age, and only death can permanently separate them. Death seals a soul in its spiritual state as wheat, i.e., saved, or darnel, i.e., unsaved.

One cannot press the details too far, for in one sense wheat is a darnel that got saved. The point is that the righteous (saved) and unrighteous (unsaved) are mixed during the New Testament church phase of the kingdom (the Mystery Kingdom), but when the messiah inaugurates his Davidic-Messianic-Millennial kingdom at his second advent, only the righteous will enter in.

Translation Matthew 13:31–33

31 Another parable he put before them, saying: "The kingdom of the heavens is like a seed of mustard, which a man having taken sowed in his field, 32 which indeed is smallest of all the seeds; but when it is grown it is greater than the garden plants and becomes a tree, so that the birds of the air come and nest in its branches." 33 Another parable he spoke to them: "The kingdom of the heavens is like leaven, which a woman having taken hid in three measures

---

[1] [http://www.botanical.com/botanical/mgmh/g/grasse34.html#dar].

of flour until all of it was leavened."

EXPOSITION

Skeptics point out that the mustard is not the smallest of all seeds. Those with faith understand Jesus is speaking phenomenally, not scientifically. The mustard seed was the smallest seed planted and harvested by the agrarian population.

The point of the two stories is the growth of the kingdom. Some commentators view the kingdom in the stories as the messianic kingdom to be established on earth after the second advent. Others view the kingdom in the stories as the spiritual kingdom of the present age, which is the New Testament church between the two advents. The latter view is my view. The meaning of the growth of the kingdom is expressed in the details of two stories.

In one view the New Testament church (kingdom) begins small, grows to visible prominence, and becomes influential in the world. In a contrary view the New Testament church begins small, grows to visible prominence, but its size is due to many false professors, so that its influence is hampered by worldliness, carnality, schismatics, heretics, and apostates.

If we remember the parables of the soils and the parable of the wheat and darnel we will remember that the kingdom is a mixed multitude of believers and unbelievers. A mustard bush could grow to as large as ten feet, thus looking like a tree in height and breadth. But, the fruit it produced was still the tiny seed. The visible church looks big and prosperous, but its life is in the seed, not the bushy branches. The church grows, but only part of it is the true kingdom.

The same is true of the leaven. Some translations have "yeast," but what was used to cause fermentation in new dough was a small piece of old dough which had yeast in it from previous bread making. The old lump of dough was the leavening agent for the new dough. The action of leaven (yeast) is to introduce gas (carbon dioxide) into the dough by breaking down the sugar in the wheat, making the dough rise, giving it flavor and airy texture, with the result the lump of dough look bigger and taste better. But the amount of dough never changes. The church looks bigger and seems better than at its beginning, but it is a mixed multitude of genuine believers and false professors. The church spreads over the whole world, but is composed of wheat and darnel. The church has stony soil, poor soil, thorny bushes, and good soil. The church looks big and prosperous but only a small part is the true church. Only the good soil, wheat, seeds, and flour are the true believers with the gospel message in the visible church. The false professors are the gas and worldly flavor that makes the church palatable to the world.

The meaning of the birds of the air nesting in the mustard "tree" has been disputed for centuries. Interpreters assign a meaning consistent with their view of the church's growth (although France makes an odd connection to Daniel 4:12, 21.[1]) Most likely the birds are meant to fill out the picture of the seed becoming large, i.e., birds cannot nest in a garden herb, but they can nest in a large bush/tree. In that view the birds represent worldliness.

Translation Matthew 13:34–35

34 All these things Jesus spoke in parables to the crowds; and without a parable he did not speak to them, 35 so that might be fulfilled that having been spoken by the prophet, saying, "I will open my mouth in parables; I will utter things secret from the foundation of the world."

EXPOSITION

The prophecy referred to is Psalm 78:2. In its original setting this was not a prophecy, but Matthew broadly views the Old Testament as a prophetic utterance which pertains to messiah. The psalm was created by Asaph, who was said to be a prophet, 1 Chronicles 25:2; 2 Chronicles 29:30, so there is scriptural justification to understand Psalm 78:2 as pertaining to messiah teaching Israel in parables. Through parables Jesus revealed truth and wisdom hidden from human ability to discern, but now made known to those who are spiritually enabled to understand. In the psalm Asaph reveals how God made salvation known, and judged unbelievers.

Translation Matthew 13:36–43

36 Then having dismissed the crowds, he went into the house. And his disciples came to him, saying, "Explain to us the parable of the darnel of the field." 37 Now answering he said, "The one sowing the good seed is the son of man, 38 and the field is the world. Now the good seed, these are the sons of the kingdom; but the darnel

---

[1] France, *Matthew*, NICNT, 526–527.

Matthew Thirteen

are the sons of the evil one. 39 Now the enemy having sown them is the devil, and the harvest is the consummation of the age, and the harvesters are angels. 40 As therefore the darnel is gathered and consumed in fire, so it will be at the consummation of the age. 41 The son of man will send his angels, and they will gather out of his kingdom all that offends and those practicing lawlessness, 42 and they will cast them into the fire of the furnace. There will be the wailing and the gnashing of teeth. 43 Then the righteous will shine forth as the sun in the kingdom of their Father. The one having ears, let him hear."

EXPOSITION

This is Jesus' explanation to his disciples of the wheat and darnel. To the first explanation, vv. 24–30, Jesus adds additional information.

> Jesus is the sower
>
> The field represents the world
>
> The wheat represents the sons of the kingdom
>
> The sons are righteous (the saved)
>
> The darnel represents the sons of the evil one
>
> The sons of the evil one are those who offend and practice lawlessness (the unsaved)
>
> The harvesters are angels
>
> The harvest is at the consummation of the age
>
> The kingdom is the Father's

There is information that points to the consummation of the age being the kingdom on earth to be inaugurated at the second advent. And there is information pointing to the consummation of the age being the Great White Throne judgment (GWT) followed by the Eternal Kingdom in a new heaven and earth. And there is information that could occur in either period of time.

For example, saved and unsaved are mixed during the present form of the kingdom (the Mystery Kingdom), the New Testament church age, until the judgments of the second advent, Ezekiel 20:33–38 (Israel); Matthew 25:31–46 (gentiles), that determine who will enter the Davidic Messianic Kingdom. But, the saved and unsaved are also mixed during the Davidic Messianic Kingdom, until God destroys the present heaven and earth,

Revelation 20:7–11, leading to the GWT and the Eternal Kingdom. Another example, the righteous will shine, v. 43, which coordinates with Daniel 12:3, which is at the beginning of the Davidic Messianic Kingdom. But Jesus says the Kingdom is the Father's, Matthew 13:43, which coordinates with 1 Corinthians 15:28, which is the Eternal Kingdom.

At the beginning of the Davidic Messianic Kingdom, Christ sends his angels to gather national ethnic Israel out of the gentile nations and bring them to the land of Israel, Matthew 25:31. This is preparatory to the judgment of Israel, Ezekiel 20:23–38, which determines who of national ethnic Israel will enter the Davidic Messianic Kingdom. But the gathering by angels in the parable of the sower, vv. 30 and 41, is of those who offend and practice lawlessness—the unsaved; and these will be burned and experience wailing and gnashing of teeth, things associated with sinners in Gehenna, i.e., the lake of fire, as a result of the GWT judgment.

To make things more difficult, only the unsaved dead (those who died physically in an unsaved state) appear at the GWT. Those dead are resurrected just prior to their appearing. So when do the angels reap the unsaved dead? Christ reaps the unsaved prior to the Davidic Messianic Kingdom, Revelation 14:14–16. This agrees with Matthew 25:46; Ezekiel 20:38. The angels might assist in this undertaking.

Finally, Christ is not addressing the church, but Jewish men seeking to understand the messianic kingdom. In their mind Christ is explaining the Davidic Messianic Kingdom to be established after messiah's advent.

So the question is, is the consummation of the age the second advent, ending the New Testament church age and beginning the Davidic Messianic Kingdom? Or is the consummation of the age the Eternal Kingdom after the Davidic Messianic Kingdom and the GWT?

I think in this instance Christ is using an Old Testament prophetic point of view that ignores elapsed time between two events. For example, the Old Testament prophets saw the two advents without seeing the intervening church age. More precisely, they saw the two advents of Christ as one advent. Christ would come and suffer and then the Davidic Messianic Kingdom would happen. James said something similar at Acts 15:16 when he quoted Amos 9:11–12, as did Peter on the day of Pentecost when he quoted Joel 2:28–32. I believe this is what Jesus is doing:

blending the judgment before the Davidic Messianic Kingdom and the judgment after the Davidic Messianic Kingdom (at the GWT) into one prophetic view, without showing the elapsed time (the thousand years of the Davidic Messianic Kingdom) between the two events.

Translation Matthew 13:44–46

44 "The kingdom of the heavens is like a treasure having been hidden in the field, which having found, a man hid, and for joy of it goes and sells all that he has and buys that field. 45 "Again, the kingdom of the heavens is like a man, a merchant, seeking quality pearls, 46 and having found one valuable pearl went away and sold all, as much as he had, and bought it."

EXPOSITION

These two parables explain faith's positive reaction to the kingdom message. Some will see in the offer of salvation a great treasure to be attained at any cost. One cannot press the details, because salvation cannot be purchased in the sense of money or works. The "cost" of salvation to the individual is repentance of sins and trusting the eternal destiny of his/her soul to Jesus.

The man in the parable does not buy the treasure he buys the field the treasure is in. The background is ancient law. There were no banks (although pagan temples served in a similar capacity), so people having a great treasure, or in some cases expecting war or invasion, would bury their treasure in a field. If the person died before retrieving his treasure it remained for another to find, not necessarily by deliberate effort, but found nonetheless.

The only legal way to ensure that the found treasure went to the finder was to purchase the field in which it was found. Remember, the details are carrying the message, they are not the message. The kingdom is in the world, but the point is not the kingdom in the world; the point is the extreme value of being part of the kingdom. The same is true of the pearl. The value of the one pearl is salvation through a personal relationship with Jesus Savior and King. That is worth giving up all that one has in the world.

The sinner obtains salvation through repentance of his/her sin of unbelief and placing faith in the Savior. Jesus the Savior, the one and only, is the true treasure. In some ways Jesus is hidden in the world, of great value to those who find him. The other point in these two parables is the necessity to take immediate action to seize the opportunity. Jesus offers membership in the kingdom. One must immediately count all else as loss and become a member. The day of salvation is always today.

Translation Matthew 13:47-50

47 "Again, the kingdom of the heavens is like a dragnet having been cast into the sea and having gathered of every kind, 48 which, when it was filled, having drawn it to shore, and having sat down, they gathered the good into vessels, but the bad they cast out. 49 So it will be in the consummation of the age. The angels will go out and will separate the evil from among the righteous, 50 and will cast them into the furnace of the fire. There will be the wailing and gnashing of the teeth."

EXPOSITION

This parable may be combining the judgments as before. At the beginning of the Davidic Messianic Kingdom gentiles and national ethnic Israel will be judged to determine who will enter the Kingdom. Those failing the judgment (those having the mark of the beast, Revelation 14:9-11) will go into hades to await the GWT. During the Davidic Messianic Kingdom there will be saved and unsaved throughout the Kingdom, with the unsaved going into hades upon their physical death. At the end of the Davidic Messianic Kingdom, Revelation 20:7-10, those living sinners who rebel against Christ will be killed and go into hades. Then the GWT will be conducted, the result of which is all the unsaved souls will be taken out of hades, rejoined with their resurrected (but corruptible) bodies,, and imprisoned in the lake of fire for eternity. Apparently the angels have some duties at the GWT, "The angels will go out and will separate the evil from among the righteous, and will cast them into the furnace of the fire."

Translation Matthew 13:51-58

51 Jesus said to them, "Have you understood all these things?" They said to him, "Yes, sir." 52 And he said to them, "Because of this, every scribe having been discipled into the kingdom of the heavens is like a man, a master of a house, who brings out of his treasure things new and old." 53 And so it was when Jesus had finished these parables, he withdrew from there.

54 And having come into his native city, he taught them in their

Matthew Thirteen

synagogue, so that they are astonished and are saying, "From what place to this man the wisdom and the ability? 55 Is not this the son of the carpenter? Is not his mother called Mary? and his brothers James and Joses and Simon and Judas? 56 and his sisters; are not all with us? From what place then to this man all these things?" 57 And they were offended at him. But Jesus said to them, "A prophet is not without honor except in his native city, and in his household." 58 And he did not many mighty works there because of their unbelief.

EXPOSITION

The disciples may not have understood all the details, but they understood the main points. Verse 52 describes the well-instructed disciple who not merely knows, but understands and applies these truths.

Jesus' native city is Nazareth, versus his own city, 9:1, which is Capernaum. This is his second rejection at Nazareth (the first is Luke 4:16–30). They would not accept Jesus as the Messiah because their past experience with him as child and man had been unremarkable. They and their children were taught in the same Nazareth synagogue school Jesus attended, so where did Jesus get all this learning, and from where this ability over sickness and demons and death?

Here we have confirmation that Joseph was a carpenter and that Mary and Joseph had a normal marriage producing children; and that Jesus grew from child to adult through a normal and mundane life.

The villagers in his hometown were offended at him. The term "the son of the carpenter" gives us their view of Jesus' place in society. In their view Jesus had left his proper place and was associating with people and powers no simple villager should associate with. They compared him to themselves, and they would not involve themselves in such things. The proverbial saying too often proves true, as people sort out others in terms of their personal limitations. In Nazareth Jesus did only a limited number of works (Mark 6:5), because there was little faith among the villagers.

Matthew Fourteen

Translation Matthew 14:1–12

1 At that time Herod the tetrarch heard the report about Jesus 2 and said to his servants, "This is John the Baptist. He is risen from the dead, and on account of this mighty power works in him." 3 Because Herod having arrested John, he bound him, and put him in prison, on account of Herodias, the wife of Philip his brother. 4 For John had been saying to him, "It is not lawful for you to have her." 5 And wanting to kill him, he feared the crowd, because they regarded him as a prophet.

6 But when Herod's birthday had come, the daughter of Herodias danced in the midst and pleased Herod. 7 Whereupon with an oath he promised to give to her whatever she might ask. 8 Now having been urged by her mother, she says, "Give me here upon a platter the head of John the Baptist." 9 And the king, though grieved, on account of the oaths and those reclining with him, he commanded it to be given. 10 And having sent he beheaded John in the prison. 11 And his head was brought on a platter and was given to the girl and she brought it to her mother. 12 Then his disciples having come took the body and buried it; and having come they told it to Jesus.

EXPOSITION

John Baptist's death is told here in a flashback. Verses 1–2 are contemporary with or a little after the Nazareth rejection. Matthew uses this event to example the confusion regarding Jesus. When Jesus at a later time asks his apostles who people say he is, they reply John Baptist, Elijah, Jeremiah, or some other Old Testament prophet. The beliefs of the crowds show the popular understanding of Micah 4:5.

Although we know John and Jesus ministered concurrently for a little while, it is likely Herod did not know. There was no reason for Herod to pay attention to an obscure Galilean prophet. John caught Herod's attention only because the crowds had gathered to him, posing the risk of an insurrection. As John had predicted, Jesus' popularity grew, and it was this growing popularity that brought Jesus to Herod's attention.

Herod had wanted to kill John, but he feared arousing the people. Herod believed John was a "righteous and holy man," Mark

6:20, but when John began to denounce Herod's marriage to his brother Philip's wife, he was just as willing to kill him as he had been to listen to him. Herod had imprisoned John, says Matthew (Mark 6:17–18; Luke 3:19–20) because John had denounced Herod's marriage to Herodias as illegal.[1] Herodias was the granddaughter of Herod the Great by his son Aristobulus. She had married her uncle Herod Philip (not the Tetrarch Philip, Luke 3:1). Herod Philip was Herod Antipas's half-brother. She divorced Herod Philip and married Herod Antipas. Leviticus 18:16; 20:21 made this intra-family marriage illegal.

Salome was the daughter of Herodias and Herod Philip. She later married Philip the Tetrarch, half-brother to Herod Philip, thus becoming both aunt and sister-in-law to her own mother. The Herodians had little regard for God's law.

Herodias, angry and heedless of the consequences, engineered John's death through her daughter Salome (Mark 6:24). We need not assume Salome danced a sexually suggestive dance, merely that her dancing in celebration of Herod's birthday greatly pleased him and his guests. Pride (and drunkenness?) caused him to utter his promise; pride made him keep it. Possibly six months had passed from John's imprisonment to his death, so his influence had waned and he had faded from the memory of the general populace. His disciples recovered the body and informed Jesus of the death.

Translation Matthew 14:13–18

13 Now Jesus, having heard, left from there by boat to a deserted place to be alone. And the crowds having heard followed him on foot from the villages. 14 And having gone out, he saw a great crowd, and was moved with compassion toward them, and healed their sick. 15 Now evening having come, the disciples came to him, saying, "This place is desolate, and the time already passing. Dismiss the crowds, that having gone into the villages they might buy for themselves food." 16 But Jesus said to them, "They have no need to go away. You give to them to eat." 17 But they say to him, "We have here only five loaves and two fish." 18 Then he said, "Bring them here to me."

EXPOSITION

---

[1] Morris, *Matthew*, 370, n. 12.

Matthew Fourteen

Matthew says when Jesus heard of John's death he withdrew away from the city and crowds to a deserted place. Matthew says he went to be alone, but the presence of the disciples indicates Jesus went to be alone with his disciples.

The deserted place was on the northeast shore of the lake, close to Bethsaida-Julius (Luke 9:10). The location was not a desert or desolate, but uncultivated land used as pasture for sheep. Today the place where Jesus went, the hills above the delta where the Jordan River enters the lake, is known as the Golan Heights.

As Jesus traveled by boat across the lake from Capernaum, people from Capernaum and other villages saw or heard he was going and followed his course overland to the same place. From Capernaum the walking distance was about four to five miles—a little less than a two hour walk. Jesus and the disciples got there first, the people soon after.

Jesus always had compassion, and though he had come to rest, he set aside his own needs and ministered to the crowd. The disciples probably managed the crowd, keeping order, setting appointments, and bringing people to Jesus. By the end of the day they also were hungry and tired. The five loaves of bread and two fish were probably leftovers from an earlier lunch. I wonder if they had shared with Jesus?

The multitudes had come without much thought for tomorrow. They had probably brought some food in their baskets (an almost universal accessory in those times), but that would have been eaten earlier in the day. When evening came (Mark: late in the day; Luke: late in the afternoon), the crowd had nothing to eat, except some few may have had a leftover here and there.

When Jesus asked the disciples to give the crowds something to eat, it was to see if they would turn to him for a miracle. They did not, telling him of their lack, not of their faith in him to provide. That is the point of the miracle: Jesus provides for all the necessities of life, specifically spiritual necessities, but not ignoring material needs.

The fish were the dried and salted fish caught in the lake. Five loaves and two fish would have been sufficient lunch for one person but have left two still hungry. The loaves were probably unleavened; something like pita bread.

Bread was the most important food item in the ancient world.

The Old Testament Scripture used this importance to express certain conditions of life, e.g., the bread of affliction, of tears, of sorrows, of wickedness, of idleness, of adversity, of the increase of the earth, of a miser, of mourners, of God, of sincerity. To give bread was a blessing. When Jesus miraculously provided bread it was considered a messianic sign, similar to God giving manna. See John 6 which tells the aftermath of the feeding of the five thousand. Without bread there was no life, a fact of ancient life Jesus used to his advantage when he declared himself the bread of life, John 6:35.

Translation Matthew 14:19–21

19 And having commanded the crowds to recline upon the grass, taking the five loaves and the two fish, looking up to heaven, he spoke a blessing; and having broken the loaves he gave to the disciples, and the disciples to the crowds. 20 And all ate and were satisfied; and they took up the excess, twelve hand-baskets full of the fragments. 21 Now those eating were about five thousand men, besides women and children.

EXPOSITION

Order is God's rule. John says Jesus told the disciples to "make the people sit down," but with his usual economy of words and focus on Jesus, Matthew ignores the disciples. For the skeptics: Jesus told the disciples who told the crowd what Jesus said. The people would have done what people everywhere have always done: arranged themselves alongside others they knew, i.e., by family and village.

The five loaves would each have been about the size of a bun, similar to modern pita bread. John says they were "barley loaves," the bread of the poor, supposed by the ancient world to be less nutritious than wheat, and sold for about half the cost of wheat. Actually barley is only slightly less nutritious than wheat.[1] Barley has slightly more calories (due to a slightly greater amount of carbohydrates and saturated fatty acids), but has slightly less amounts of the same minerals, vitamins, and amino acids. As noted above, the two fish were the small dried and salted fish from the Sea of Galilee, exported all over the ancient world.

---

[1] [http://fnic.nal.usda.gov/].

When Jesus multiplied bread and fish, a creative act was taking place in his hands. Jesus gave the pieces to the disciples, who distributed them to the people. The people ate and were completely full. There was so much food left over twelve hand-baskets full of pieces of bread and fish were gathered. Travelers often carried their belongings in a basket (the word translated hand-basket was used in a Latin form by Juvenal—a Roman poet of the late first century and early second century—as the usual baggage of the Jews when traveling[1]). The twelve disciples would have hand-baskets, and thus Jesus had provided food for them also. Matthew (and the other gospels) estimated the size of the crowd at five thousand men, plus women and children.

Translation Matthew 14:22–31

22 And immediately he made the disciples enter into the boat and to go before him to the other side, while he dismissed the crowds. 23 And having dismissed the crowds, he went up on the mountain by himself to pray. Now when evening having come, he was there alone. 24 But the boat, in the midst of the sea, about three miles from land, was being tossed by the waves, for the wind was contrary. 25 Now in the fourth watch of the night, he went to them, walking on the sea. 26 And the disciples, having seen him walking on the sea, were fearful, saying, "It is a ghost!" And they cried out from fear. 27 But immediately Jesus spoke to them, saying, "Have courage, it is I, fear not." 28 Now Peter answering him said, "Master, if it is you, command me to come to you on the waters." 29 And he said, "Come." And having descended from the boat, Peter walked upon the water and came to Jesus. 30 But seeing the wind boisterous, he was afraid. And having begun to sink, he cried out, saying, "Master, save me!" 31 Now immediately Jesus, having stretched out his hand, took hold of him, and says to him, "You of little faith, why did you doubt?"

TRANSLATION NOTE

In v. 24 one set of Matthew texts has "and the boat was now amidst the sea." Other Matthew texts have "and the boat was many *stádion* from the land." At John 6:19 the disciples had rowed about "twenty-five or thirty *stádion*." Mark 6:47 reads, "the boat was in the midst of the sea." Which Matthew text is the most accurate is

---

[1] Alexander, *Matthew*, 397.

uncertain.[1] I decided to combine the Matthew texts and use the information in John to tell how far the men had rowed, as an indication of the strength of the contrary winds.

The word *stádion* indicates a measure of distance equal to about 605 English feet. John 6:19 says they were twenty-five or thirty *stádion* from the shore, which is about three English miles, or about halfway between Bethsaida Julius, close to where they began, and Bethsaida-Galilee, about where they landed.

EXPOSITION

Matthew does not tell us why Jesus immediately sent the disciples away before he sent the crowds away. John 6:14–15 says the crowd wanted to make Jesus their king. The disciples, whatever their political aspirations, should not be involved in that error, for Jesus' kingdom was not of this world at this time, and their continuing mission would be to proclaim him as Savior, not king. How Jesus sent the crowds away is not important. Afterward, he used the solitude, which he had been seeking, v. 13, to pray.

They were rowing toward Capernaum, John 6:17, and were about half-way between where they had been and where they were going. During the storm, as they toiled at the oars, they saw a figure—it was Jesus—walking on the water toward them. It was in the fourth watch. The Romans divided the time between 6:00 p.m. and 6:00 a.m. into four watches (the Jews used three watches). The fourth watch was between three and six a.m. We don't know exactly when they boarded the boat—between 6:00 p.m. and midnight would be probable—but the winds must have been blowing quite hard for them to have went only half way across the Lake.

When the twelve saw Jesus walking on the sea (if close to 6 a.m. the horizon was glowing behind him with the coming dawn) their collective experience told them that such an act was impossible for a living person. Their cry "It is a ghost" was not theology but superstition uttered in a moment of great fear: the Jews believed disembodied souls of the drowned haunted the sea and lakes.

Jesus' reply is calm and calming, reassuring in its ordinariness. Peter's reply is courageous but reckless; what if it had been a

---

[1] Metzger, *Textual*, 30.

ghost? Peter's "if" is in a grammatical construction known as the condition of the first class, meaning Peter assumed the figure was Jesus, but he sought to confirm by asking Jesus to "command" him to come to him on the water. If the figure really was Jesus, as Peter supposed, then he will make his servant able to walk on water. Peter has either become confident that Jesus has authority to exercise the power of God, or he is testing his hypothesis that Jesus has such authority. The successful outcome contributed to their declaration at v. 32.

Jesus' one word answer is sufficient for Peter, so he climbs down out of the boat and begins to walk on the water toward Jesus. One wishes for more detail (did he walk up and down with the waves, or was the surface smooth and flat?), but what is reported must suffice.

The reference to the wind being boisterous indicates Peter felt the force of the wind, and it may be the waves on which he was walking (or that he could see in front of him?) were kicked up by the wind. Peter takes his eyes off Jesus and looks at the circumstances.

Note the mercy of the Lord. Peter only begins to sink. Peter's faith to walk on water was overcome by worldly circumstances, but he did not doubt that Jesus could rescue him. Jesus is immediately present and supports Peter until he is able to reenter the boat. Jesus did not have to grab Peter to save him; Peter needed the reassurance of a strong hand. Jesus compassionately condescends to our needs.

Jesus and Peter walking on the water has become a favorite story for ridicule by skeptics and entertainment media. One either accepts by faith that Jesus had the authority to change the principles regulating the operation of the universe—the laws of physics—or he did not. If he did, then he exercised the omnipotent authority of God. Because omnipotence is an incommunicable attribute of deity, the exercise of omnipotent power by sovereign authority means Jesus was God.

This miracle was similar to an earlier miracle: making an iron axe head float, 2 Kings 6:4. Surely no one believes sympathetic magic—Elisha threw a stick into the water and the axe head floated—was involved with the iron axe head? The use of means was to show that God made the iron axe head float at the prophet's request, not that Elisha made it float.

Something similar is seen at Exodus 14:16, 21. God told Moses, v. 16, "lift up your rod and stretch out your hand over the sea and divide it," (NKJV), but it was God who divided the sea, v. 21, "Moses stretch out his hand over the sea and YHWH caused the sea to go back" (NKJV). God parted the Red Sea and God made the axe head float.

To the observer these were miracles; so also Jesus and Peter walking on water. A miracle is an exceptional activity of God in the material realm, not explainable by man's understanding of the physical laws governing the universe, brought about by the immediate efficiency or simple volition of God. A miracle is something which no one but God himself can perform, which is why the world rejects the truthfulness of the gospel reports of the miracles Jesus did. If, as is the case, Jesus did what only God can do, then Jesus was/is the God-man.

Translation Matthew 14:32–36

32 And they having entered into the boat, the wind ceased. 33 Then those in the boat bowed to him, saying, "Truly you are God's son." 34 And having crossed over, they came to the land of Gennesaret. 35 And the men of that place having recognized him, sent to all that surrounding region and brought to him all those being sick, 36 and begged him that they might only touch the fringe of his garment. And as many as touched were healed.

EXPOSITION

When they got into the boat the wind stopped, and Matthew is probably implying Jesus caused the wind to cease. The reference to "those who were in the boat" is almost certainly the twelve only, considering the size of the boat. In 1986 a Galilean fishing boat was discovered. The boat was 26.5 feet long, 7.5 feet wide, 4.5 feet high. It could hold about fifteen people.[1] If this was one of the fishing boats owned by the Zebedee Fishing Company (Matthew 4:18–22), which is very likely, then the boat would be carrying nets as well as people, so twelve plus Jesus seems right.

Bowing to Jesus was not worship, as most versions translate. The basic meaning of the word *proskunéō* is "do obeisance, show respect, fall or prostrate before, literally to throw a kiss in token of

---

[1] [http://www.christiananswers.net/q-abr/abr-a003.html].

respect of homage."[1] Let us think clearly. If the twelve believed God was literally in their presence in the person of Jesus of Nazareth, then they would not have been able to function as his companions. They would have fallen flat on their faces and remained prostrate before him in reverent awe. They would have feared for their lives, because God had said to Moses, "No person shall see my face and live," Exodus 33:20 (NKJV). They were in awe of him, but not reverent, worshiping "you are God" kind of awe. No prophet had ever done what Jesus had just done. So they had continued to ask themselves, "Who is this man?" Here they come to a conclusion.

What, then, did they mean when they said, "Truly you are God's son"? Three meanings are available.

> One, they understood he was God incarnate in Jesus of Nazareth. This is unlikely. They were completely discouraged following the crucifixion, e.g., Luke 24:21, "we were hoping that it was he who was going to redeem Israel." They didn't understand he would resurrect, and didn't believe when they were told he had resurrected. The Holy Spirit withheld spiritual perception of Jesus as deity incarnate until after the resurrection, and possibly until after the ascension.
>
> Two, they could have been declaring him a true son of God. The Jews believed they were sons of God. If this was the disciples' meaning, then they were giving respect to a prophet who had shown that he truly was a son of God, i.e., one to whom God had given great authority and power.
>
> Three, they bowed to him and called him, "God's son" in the sense of what Psalm 2:7 said concerning the messiah: "I will declare the decree: YHWH has said to me, 'You are my son.' " If this was the case, it was a moment when they began to believe he was the messiah—not merely a prophet in the Old Testament mold, but the Deliverer and King promised by the prophets.

My view is that they saw him through the lens of options two and three.

After Jesus and Peter entered the boat, and the wind calmed,

---

[1] Zodhiates, *WSDNT*, s. v. "4352."

Matthew Fourteen

they finished rowing the boat across the lake, and they landed on the shore near the village of Gennesaret. John's Gospel says the disciples had sailed "toward Capernaum." Mark's account, 6:45, says the disciples were rowing toward Bethsaida, i.e., to Bethsaida-Galilee on the west side of the Lake, identified by John as the city of Philip, Andrew, and Peter (1:44; 12:21). The disciples had been rowing the boat in the direction of Capernaum, but the wind blew them off course, so, Mark 6:45, they landed between Gennesaret and Bethsaida-Galilee.

The village of Gennesaret was about three miles south of Capernaum, which gives us some idea of the location of Bethsaida-Galilee, as between Gennesaret and Capernaum. In Matthew's Gospel, 14:35, Jesus healed people in the land of Gennesaret. John says the next day (the day after the miraculous feeding) the crowd from Bethsaida-Julius came seeking Jesus in Capernaum, John 6:24, and found him, John 6:25, "on the other side of the sea." Jesus healed the sick in Gennesaret (Matthew), and then Jesus and the disciples walked the three miles or so from Gennesaret to Capernaum, which is where those seeking him found him (John 6:59).

Matthew Fifteen

Translation Matthew 15:1–6

1 Then Pharisees and scribes came from Jerusalem to Jesus, saying, 2 "Why is it your disciples transgress the tradition of the elders? For they do not wash their hands when they eat bread." 3 Now answering he said to them, "And why is it you transgress the commandment of God on account of your tradition? 4 For God commanded, 'Honor the father and the mother' and 'the person speaking evil of father or mother, let him die the death.' 5 But you say, 'Whoever may say to the father or the mother, "Whatever it may be by me you might profit, it is a gift," 6 by no means will he honor his father or his mother, and you made God's word of no effect on account of your tradition.

EXPOSITION

This is another example of opposition by the religious leaders. These scribes and Pharisees (many scribes were Pharisees but not all Pharisees were scribes) had expressly come from the great city of Jerusalem to rural Galilee for the purpose of confronting Jesus.

The Pharisees and scribes confront Jesus on a matter of their washing tradition, which had nothing to do with hygiene. In the law the priests must wash their hands (sometimes feet) before performing Mosaic rituals. The elders' washing tradition extended this to the common man in an effort to keep everyone ceremonially clean during the events of daily life.

Over time the growing body of traditions had determined that many things in daily life were unclean, thus making the person unclean. To be unclean meant the person must wash with running water (poured out, thus running) to remove ceremonial defilement. This was to be done by everyone before ordinary meals. That a religious teacher would not require his disciples to wash was in their view apostasy from the Mosaic Law, because they had given their traditions equality with God's law.

Their actions are a warning to Christians. The Pharisees had extended a commandment to its logical conclusion, but in so doing had applied the commandment far beyond God's intent in giving the Law. This particular commandment was for the priests, and was intended to teach the necessity of a righteous life when approaching God for worship. Hands symbolize work, feet one's

Matthew Fifteen

path in life. Together they symbolize one's manner of living, which is supposed to be righteous. But the Pharisees' concern wasn't for a righteous life but ritual, ceremonial cleanliness. The Law did not require ritually cleanliness when eating. Christians should beware how they apply God's commandments in the New Testament. As one example, the commandment to confess to one another your sins (James 6:16) has become the auricular confession of Roman Catholicism, required by that church in order to be in communion with the church, with Christ, and to go to heaven when dead.

Examples of unbiblical traditions abound. For example, there was a time when the only hymns to be sung in church must be from the book of Psalms. Isaac Watts (AD 1674–1748) introduced hymns he had written into congregational worship. Many believed he had blasphemed Christ by singing songs written by man instead of God. Again, there was a time when the only musical instrument allowed in church services was the organ; the piano was considered worldly. The same has been true in modern times of drums and guitars (although percussion and stringed instruments were used for worship in the Old Testament, 1 Samuel 10:5; Psalm 33:1; 81:1; 92:3). Another example, in some denominations only the pastor or priest can perform baptism, or distribute the elements of the Lord's Supper (Communion, Eucharist). When deacons, and later ordinary church members, began performing those functions, many believed those churches had broken God's law. Traditions are useful friends but when they are believed equal to God's commandments they become terrible masters.

The "traditions of the elders" was a body of written and oral rabbinical interpretations concerning the Mosaic Law and how to keep it. The traditions were said to be a fence around the Law to protect the Law from being broken. If the traditions were kept then no one would come near to breaking the Law. Over time these traditions came to be viewed as equally important and binding as the Law. In practice many of the traditions broke the Law, as Jesus illustrates.

By accusing his disciples of breaking their traditions they are accusing Jesus of teaching false doctrine. In vv. 3–5 Jesus counters their washing tradition by citing another. One of their traditions allowed an adult child to dedicate some or all of his possessions to the temple, and in so doing he was relieved of his obligation to use his worldly means to support his aged parents. According to the elders, such a gift did not have to be actually given to the temple. The person could retain use of the gift as long as it was not given to the person(s) specified in the vow.[1]

In a society where the adult child's home was the live-in care facility for the aged, this practice was socially and morally wrong, as well disobeying God's command to honor mother and father. In fact, said Jesus, it was the same as cursing one's parents, a crime punishable by execution.

In v. 4 Jesus is referencing Exodus 21:17, "Whoever curses his father or his mother must be put to death" (HCSB). In the Greek text the Hebrew phrase, "must be put to death," becomes "let him die the death." Because God's Law was broken, the person was worthy of execution. Jesus says their tradition violated God's Word. He is saying those following their tradition, and by implication those teaching the tradition, were not honoring father or mother, and were worthy of execution for their crime.

The reason for the Exodus commandment is that parents represent God to their children. The parent that follows God's commandments represents God's authority. To reject the parent is to reject God, a matter of blasphemy, for which the penalty is death.

Translation Matthew 15:7–14

7 "Hypocrites! Justly Isaiah prophesied about you, saying: 8 "This people draw near with their mouth and with the lips honor me, but their heart is far from me. 9 Moreover in vain they worship me, teaching as doctrines the precepts of men.' " 10 And having called the crowd, he said to them, "Hear and understand: 11 not that entering into the mouth defiles the man, but that coming out of the mouth, this defiles the man." 12 Then the disciples having come to him said to him, "Do you know that the Pharisees were offended when they heard this saying?" 13 But answering he said, "Every plant that my heavenly Father has not planted will be uprooted. 14 Leave them; they are blind leaders of the blind; but if blind lead blind both will fall into a pit."

EXPOSITION

To sum up, Jesus says that the words Isaiah spoke about his

---

[1] Morris, *Matthew*, 392, n. 11.

own generation are applicable to the current generation. These scribes and Pharisees professed concern for obedience to God's word, yet by their traditions they annulled God's word. They said the right things but believed in and did the wrong things. Their worship was not acceptable to God.

The sin nature is what defiles a person. Even when a person engages in some act which is by its own nature defiling, the decision to engage in that act came from within. Therefore what defiles a person is the source of theirs words and actions (the evil principle sin resident in their human nature) not the words and actions themselves.

The disciples may or may not have been concerned that the Pharisees were offended; regardless they reported the matter to Jesus. Jesus responds that unrepentant sinners will not be saved. When people believe in things that God did not reveal or require, then they cannot prosper here or in the hereafter. The scribes and Pharisees were blinded by their self-righteousness and blindly led other sinners into their error.

Translation Matthew 15:15–20

15 Then Peter answered and said to him, "Explain to us this parable." 16 And he said, "Are you also still without understanding? 17 Do you not yet understand that everything entering into the mouth goes into the stomach and is cast out to the toilet? 18 But the things going out of the mouth come out of the heart, and these defile the man. 19 For out of the heart go forth evil thoughts, murders, adulteries, sexual immorality, thefts, false witness, verbal abuse. 20 These are the things defiling the man; but to eat with unwashed hands does not defile the man."

TRANSLATION NOTE

In v. 17 the word I translated "toilet" is *aphedrōn*, "a privy, a separate or private place where people sit to relieve themselves or empty their bowels."[1]

EXPOSITION

Peter is usually the unofficial spokesperson for the group of twelve. Here Jesus explains that it is the sin nature that causes

---

[1] Zodhiates, *WSDNT*, s. v. "856."

defilement, see comments vv. 10–11. The defilement spoken of here originates in the soul, and by actions coming out of the defiled soul the person commits wrongful, unrighteous acts.

Jesus speaks of these actions as coming from the heart. The heart is a term in Scripture that refers to the personality: the seat of moral reflection, choice of the will, and pattern of behavior. The term includes all the mental processes, feelings, affections, and emotions, along with the internal motivations, leading to one's decisions and responses to life situations.

An application may be made to the things that enter the eyes or the ears. "These things are what defile," says the skeptic. Even in Peter's world there would have been skeptics saying alcohol or drugs or fatty/sugary foods entering the mouth defile the man. But, Titus 1:15, "All things are pure to the pure. But to those defiled and unbelieving, nothing is pure, but both mind and conscience are defiled." What the eyes see and the ears hear may not be the choice of the person, but reaction to those things is a choice, just as what one eats and drinks and injects is the result of choice. The defilement within determines the state of one's soul.

Translation Matthew 15:21–28

21 And having gone from there, Jesus withdrew to the area of Tyre and Sidon. 22 And look, a Canaanite woman from the same area, having come out, cried out, saying, "Have mercy on me, lord, son of David. My daughter is grievously inhabited by a demon." 23 But not a word did he answer her. And his disciples having come to him entreated him, saying, "Dismiss her, for she cries out after us." 24 But answering he said, "I was not sent except to the lost sheep of the house of Israel." 25 Now having come she bowed to him, saying, "Sir, help me!" 26 But answering he said, "It is not right to take the children's bread and throw it to the little dogs." 27 But she said, "Yes, sir, yet even the little dogs eat the crumbs that fall from their masters' table." 28 Then answering Jesus said to her, "O woman, great is your faith! Be to you as you desire." And her daughter was healed from that very hour.

TRANSLATION NOTES

In v. 22 the woman cries out "*kúrios* (sir, master, lord), son of David." This gentile woman had heard someone else use the words—Jesus' reputation having spread (Mark 7:25)—and she repeated the words to catch his attention. It is doubtful she understood the full meaning of the terms. Therefore I did not capitalize *kúrios*, lord, in the first use. If "*kúrios*, son of David," had been spoken here by a Hebrew, I would have capitalized "lord" and "son" as I did at 9:27–28. A Hebrew would have used "*kúrios*, son of David" to indicate his faith that Jesus was the prophesied Davidic king, possibly the messiah. He would have intended *kúrios* to mean "Lord" in respect of the royal status of the son of David, as the blind men did in chapter 9. In vv. 25 and 27 I have translated *kúrios* as "sir." When Jesus didn't respond to the Jewish title she switched to polite discourse.

In v. 25 the NKJV, NLT, and older versions translate *proskunéō* as "worship," but this gentile was not worshiping, she was being respectful. She knelt or bowed. Because the pronoun is in the dative case, "she bowed to him" seemed more natural than "she knelt to him."

The translation "little dogs," in v. 26, 27 is from *kunárion*, the diminutive of *kúōn*, a dog, thus a puppy or little dog.

EXPOSITION

Jesus leaves Galilee and travels west to Tyre and Sidon. They were predominantly gentile areas, but in the past had been the tribal territory of Asher, according to the division of the land by Moses and Joshua. Tyre and Sidon were gentile cities on the Mediterranean coast but controlled an inland region to the east. Tyre was about forty miles northwest of Capernaum. Sidon was about twenty-five miles north of Tyre. Remember that walking was the only mode of public transportation, averaging about twenty-five miles in a day. In the Gospels events that seem to occur one right after another are sometimes many days separated as Jesus walked from one place to another. Such was the case in v. 21 and at v. 29.

Matthew does not say Jesus went to the cities, but that he visited the area. Mark 7:24 says he entered a house. Looking to Jesus' instructions to the twelve at 10:5, the house was probably in a small village, not in one of the cities. Mark's Gospel has the only parallel, and neither Matthew nor Mark indicates the time was spent in a preaching/healing tour of the area. In both Matthew and Mark Jesus leaves the area after this one healing. In a similar manner to his journey through Samaria to meet the woman at the well, Jesus went to the area of Tyre and Sidon to meet this gentile woman.

The Canaanite woman came and asked him to heal her

daughter from demonic habitation. The term "Canaanite" in Jesus' time probably meant a woman from the Phoenician territories, which was the region of Tyre and Sidon, although Matthew may have used the word in order to clearly indicate a gentile.

This gentile woman calls upon Jesus by the title "son of David," which he rightly ignored. No gentile had a right to call upon him by that name, for it was in that name that he had come, as he says, v. 24, to the lost sheep of the house of Israel. Evidently she heard Jesus make that comment, for she dropped the Jewish title, came closer, bowed to him, and respectfully called him "sir." That was how Jesus wanted her to view him, and how he wanted his disciples to view his relationship to the gentiles. To the gentiles Jesus is Savior, not son of David.

The statement about "little dogs" need not have been said harshly, and must in fact have been said with an encouraging look and tone of voice. A dog was not usually a household pet among the Jews, but in this statement must be seen as a pet. The proverbial-form of the saying is that families have priorities, and children come before pets.

The Jews spoke of gentiles as dogs because in the eyes of the Mosaic Law they were hopelessly unclean and did unclean and abominable things. However, this gentile is not being called a dog in that pejorative sense, but is being told she is part of the family and must be dealt with according to family priorities. The woman seizes on this hope and reveals an understanding of her place in the family. Yes, the children must be fed first, but even the family pet eats the crumbs the children drop. This is faith: even for a "little dog" there is a crumb. Jesus responds to her faith and heals her daughter, from a distance. The woman's faith does not fail at this word. She leaves the house with the inward assurance of faith that her daughter has been healed.

Translation Matthew 15:29–31

29 And having left there, Jesus went along the Sea of Galilee; and having gone up on the mountain, he was sitting there. 30 And great crowds came to him, having with them lame, crippled, blind, mute, and many others, and they placed them at Jesus' feet and he healed them, 31 so that the crowd marveled, seeing the mute speaking, the crippled made healthy, the lame walking, and the blind seeing; and they glorified the God of Israel.

Matthew Fifteen

EXPOSITION

Jesus returned to Galilee from the regions of Tyre and Sidon. According to Mark 7:31 he returned to Galilee, then went into the region known as the Decapolis, meaning the ten-cities, another gentile region. The Decapolis was on the east side of the Lake. In ancient times it had been the territory of East Manasseh.

Looking to Mark 7:31, Jesus left Tyre and traveled north along the Mediterranean coastline to Sidon. From there he turned southeast, traveling through Phoenicia (Tyre and Sidon were in the country of Phoenicia), then through northern Galilee to the lake. Where he might have arrived along the lake's shore is a guess, but I will guess at the northern entrance of the Jordan River into the lake, not far from where he had fed the 5,000. From there he turned south along the east shore of the lake, through the country of Gaulanitis until he came into the Decapolis, probably a little north of Hippos. The area is the far southern part of what is now known as the Golan Heights. The city of Magdala, v. 39, on the opposite, west, shore, lying halfway between Tiberius and Capernaum, gives us some idea of where he was on the east side. Matthew says he went up on the mountain. There are several high hills that would serve the purpose.

Jesus probably sat down to teach, but healing always accompanied his teaching ministry. The effect of his healing ministry was that the crowds glorified the God of Israel. They continued to view Jesus as a prophet whom God has given authority and power over their many diseases. The crowds were with him three days, v. 32.

Translation Matthew 15:32–39

32 Now Jesus, having called his disciples, said, "I have compassion toward the crowd, because already they continue with me three days, and have nothing that they might eat. And I am not willing to send them away hungry, lest they faint on the way." 33 And the disciples say to him, "From where to us in this wilderness so many loaves as to satisfy so great a crowd?" 34 And he says to them, "How many loaves have you?" And they said, "Seven, and a few small fish." 35 And having told the crowds to recline on the ground, 36 having taken the seven loaves and the fish, and having given thanks, he broke and gave to the disciples, and the disciples to the crowd. 37 And all ate and were satisfied; and they took up

seven baskets full of the fragments that were left. 38 Now those eating were four thousand men, besides women and children. 39 And having dismissed the crowds, he got into the boat, and came to the area of Magdala.

EXPOSITION

This feeding proceeds similar to that of the five thousand. We know it is a different event: after three days the food they brought with them had been consumed. Also, the number fed is less, the amount of food available to be multiplied is different, the number of baskets full of leftovers is less, the baskets were larger, and the four thousand did not try to make Jesus their king.

How much time had passed between feeding the five thousand and the four thousand is unknown, but one may guess. After feeding the five thousand Jesus went across the lake and healed at Gennesaret. Then he walked the short distance to Capernaum where John 6:22–71 took place. Then he had the confrontation with the scribes and Pharisees over the tradition of the elders. After that he walked to the region of Tyre, taking perhaps two days, and healed the gentile woman's daughter. Then he went to the region of Sidon, a full day with time for rest and meals, and then turned east and walked three or four days to where he fed the four thousand. We may put in a few days here and there for resting, eating, sleeping, and other necessities of daily living. So a week passed, more likely two, perhaps three. The disciples should have remembered the five thousand.

The disciples focused on the problem, not the solution, which had been shown to them when the five thousand had been fed. It is not wrong to understand a problem, but understanding is not the end of the process, it is the beginning of a solution. Jesus created food in the same manner as before. People were filled full as before. Fragments of leftovers were taken up as before. I emphasize the similarities in anticipation of 16:5–12. After this the disciples and Jesus took a boat to Magdala on the west shore of the lake.

Matthew Sixteen

Translation Matthew 16:1–4

1 And having come, the Pharisees and Sadducees tempting asked him to show them a sign from heaven. 2 Now answering he said to them, "Evening having come you say, 'Fair weather, for the sky is red'; 3 and in the morning, 'Today a storm, for the sky is red being overcast.' Indeed you know how to discern the appearance of the sky, but signs of the times you are not able. 4 A generation evil and adulterous seeks a sign, and no sign will be given to it, except the sign of Jonah." And having left them he went away.

EXPOSITION

In v. 1 Matthew uses a definite article to grammatically unite the Pharisees and Sadducees to represent official Judaism. These were the two primary religious-political parties of the day, and they were seldom united on anything. The Pharisees followed the traditions of the elders, which often contracted the Bible, and the Sadducees would accept only what was specifically stated in the Bible. For example, the Sadducees didn't believe in resurrection because their Bible, the Old Testament, doesn't use the word (but see, e.g., Job 19:25–27).

In practical terms, the Sadducees were the secularists of the day, looking for political independence, while the Pharisees were the religionists of the day, who would accept any rule as long as their own practices were not disturbed. In Jesus they found a common enemy. Matthew mentions them the most. This is the only time they are seen in the gospels outside the region of Judea.

They came to tempt him, *peirázō*, the word meaning test to destroy, not test to approve (which is *peirasmós*). They wanted to find some fault they could use to discredit him. A sign from heaven meant some divine act they would accept as indisputably certifying him as YHWH's Messiah. They were looking for a burning bush, but many signs from heaven had already been given: the blind, the leper, the lame, and the mute were healed, and demons cast out. Many of them had witnessed these things.

To his opponents these miracles had other explanations. One wonders if even a burning bush, a divided sea, or fire from heaven would have been sufficient to convince them that God was with Jesus?

Jesus uses a common saying to show their deliberate ignorance. They could tell the weather by observing the sky. Yet, they would not observe current events and understand the meaning. By "signs of the times" Jesus meant that the events of his ministry were the sign from heaven they were seeking; they lacked the faith necessary to have the spiritual perception to understand that he and his works were God's sign from heaven.

A "generation" refers to the people living at that time. Jesus describes the Pharisees, Sadducees, and all those living at that time and following their lead in terms of great moral evil. The accusation "adulterous" is used in spiritual sense. Adultery, when not referring to the sexual act, was used in the Old Testament to indicate religious infidelity: worshiping idols and false gods. The false gods these Sadducees and Pharisees worshiped were their traditions and their personal political and religious agendas.

As before, Jesus tells them the sign they will be given is his resurrection. This reference to Jonah must have confused them, for there are many things which might be interpreted as the sign of the prophet Jonah: God pursuing him, his symbolic death and recovery, a gentile nation responding with repentance to his message of destruction. Jonah was sent to a gentile nation, so they must have wondered how Jonah could be a sign to Israel respecting the messiah?

Translation Matthew 16:5–12

5 And the disciples having come to the other side, they had forgotten to take bread. 6 But Jesus said to them, "Take heed and beware of the leaven of the Pharisees and the Sadducees." 7 Now they reasoned among themselves, saying, "Because we took no bread." 8 But having known, Jesus, said, "Why reason you in yourselves, O you of little faith? Because you took no bread? 9 Do you not yet understand or remember the five loaves for the five thousand and how many hand-baskets you took away? 10 Nor the seven loaves for the four thousand, and how many baskets you took away? 11 How do you not understand that I did not speak to you about bread, but to beware of the leaven of the Pharisees and Sadducees?" 12 Then they understood that he had not said beware of the leaven of bread, but of the teaching of the Pharisees and Sadducees.

EXPOSITION

Jesus uses a simple circumstance to teach a spiritual lesson, but the disciples at first understood Jesus' words literally, not as metaphor. Leaven in Scripture is a symbol of sin, but to their minds it was used for making bread and fermenting juice. Leaven was something they removed from their houses for the Passover-Feast of Unleavened bread, and used in the offering at the Feast of Pentecost. The spiritual meaning of these actions, although known, was not obvious; it was simply the ritual to be performed.

Leaven is removed at Passover because, to use a later New Testament phrase, "Christ our Passover was sacrificed for us" (1 Corinthians 5:7). Leaven represents sin, but the long-ago Passover in Egypt, and Christ as the believer's Passover, has no sin. In the Feast of Pentecost the offering was leavened loaves of bread. They were leavened because the loaves represented the church body formed out of individuals. In the church there is sin: still resident in the saved, and in the visible church a mixed multitude of saved and unsaved.

Jesus corrects the disciples' misunderstanding about literal leaven and bread by referencing the feedings of the five and four thousands. Obviously Jesus could provide them food at any time. Then they understood. The teaching of the Pharisees and Sadducees—their doctrine—corrupted all that it touched. The action of the leaven of the Pharisees and Sadducees was to make their evil look better and useful, but the core of sin, hidden in the subtleties of their teaching, remained and defiled all that it touched.

Translation Matthew 16:13–20

13 Now Jesus having come into the area of Caesarea Philippi, he questioned his disciples, saying, "Who do men say the son of man to be?" 14 Now some said, "Indeed some John the Baptist"; and others, "Elijah," and others, "Jeremiah or one of the prophets." 15 He says to them, "But you, who do you say me to be?" 16 Now Simon Peter answering said, "You are the Christ, the son of the living God." 17 And Jesus in reply said to him, "Blessed are you, Simon son of Jonah. Because flesh and blood revealed this not to you, but my Father who is in the heavens. 18 Now I also say to you, that you are Peter, and on this the rock I will build my church, and the gates of hades will not prevail against it. 19 And I will give you the keys of the kingdom of the heavens; and whatever if you might bind on earth will be bound in the heavens, and whatever if you

might loose on earth will be loosed in the heavens." 20 Then he commanded the disciples that to no one should they say that he is the Christ.

EXPOSITION

Jesus now travels away from Galilee and further confrontation with the scribes, Sadducees, and Pharisees, to about 25 miles north of the lake to the city of Caesarea Philippi, which lay at the foothills of Mount Hermon. His ultimate goal is Mount Hermon, 17:1ff. This was gentile territory at the time of Jesus. thus limiting his chances of contact with the scribes, Sadducees, and Pharisees. Caesarea Philippi was close to the location of the ancient city of Dan in the old tribal territory of Naphtali, and Mount Hermon was in the far northern reaches of what had been the tribal territory of East Manasseh.

In this place of relative quiet Jesus asked his disciples what the general populace of Israel thought about him, that is, how did the people describe Jesus in relation to his preaching, teaching, and healing. The answer is that the populace thought he was one of the great prophets resurrected, or enough of a prophet to be counted among the prophets. The answer, "John the Baptist," reveals some were confused about John and his ministry. Elijah was thought of in relation to Malachi 4:5. Past Jewish rabbis had taught that Jeremiah would come at the end of the age. Apparently popular opinion had not yet embraced him as the messiah.

Peter answers for the group: You are the Anointed (messiah, christ) of God, the son of the living God. Peter's ability to answer immediate indicates they had discussed this very issue more than once, and made a decision that kept them at Jesus' side.

The Greek word "Christ" is a reference to a few Old Testament passages, notably Psalm 2:2, where the Hebrew word for "anointed" is *māshîah*, which is transliterated into English as "messiah." God's Anointed would rule the earth, Psalm 2:8, 9.

Their use of the phrase, "son of the living God," does not reflect an understanding of Jesus as God the Son incarnate, but reflects Psalm 2:7, where YHWH says of the Anointed, "You are my son, today I have begotten you." The word "begotten" could be used in the Old Testament both literally of physical descent, or metaphorically, e.g., God begot the rain, or one's sins beget sorrow. The twelve could have understood "son" other than literal, that is, in a spiritual, non-incarnate way. Everyone who worshiped YHWH was a son of God in the sense of a faith-based relationship.

There is no indication the disciples knew the circumstances of Jesus' birth before the crucifixion, resurrection, and ascension. That information was locked away in Mary, to be revealed at an appropriate time. As God's anointed/messiah/christ, the disciples could certainly consider Jesus as the messiah-son of the living God per Psalm 2:7. Nor was there need to understand him as the God-man in order to believe he was the one whom God had appointed, empowered, and sent as the promised messiah. As interpreters we must take care not to read later revelation and theological understanding into the understanding of the twelve during the time of Jesus' earthly ministry.

Jesus says Peter's confession of him as the Christ was the result of divine revelation. This is the reason others, v. 14, didn't get it. Jesus said, Matthew 11:27, that no one knows the son except the Father. A person could know the son if God had revealed Jesus of Nazareth as Jesus the Christ, 16:20. Knowing that Jesus of Nazareth is Jesus the Christ could not be known by man's ability to collect, collate, analyze, synthesize, and draw conclusions from the facts of the case. One might conclude Jesus was displaying all the Old Testament signs of messiah—which the scribes, Pharisees, and Sadducees did—without being convicted that Jesus was the Christ to whom they must give allegiance and in whom they must rest their faith.

Matthew 16:18 has caused considerable discussion and disagreement in the church. But the verse reduces to a play on words. The word "peter" is *pétros*, a small stone, but the word "rock" is *pétra*, a massive rock or cliff.[1] The definite article is used with *pétra*, the massive rock, indicating a specific rock. A *pétra* cannot come from the *pétros*. Just the opposite: a small stone comes from the massive rock

Peter *pétros* is a small stone from Jesus *pétra*, the massive rock. It is upon the massive rock of himself that Jesus will build his church. Paul understood this, 1 Corinthian 3:11, the foundation of the church and the individual believer is Christ alone.

There is a view of the verse that states "the rock (*pétra*)" is

---

[1] Ibid., s. v. "4074, 4073" (respectively).

Peter's confession, "You are the Christ." That is to say, not the words, but the knowledge that Jesus is God's anointed to bring in salvation and the kingdom. The mass of rock on which the church is to be built, says this view, is the knowledge of Jesus as the Christ, the Son of the Living God. But versions old and modern don't correctly translate the text. Jesus said upon "this the rock" I will build my church, using the definite article to identify a specific rock, which is Jesus the Christ. The confession is not the rock. Jesus is the rock, as comparison with other scriptures reveals.

> Then [Israel] abandoned God who made him and rejected the rock of his salvation. Deuteronomy 32:15.
>
> You are forgetful of the rock who begot you, God who fathered you. Deuteronomy 32:18.
>
> In God is my salvation and glory; the rock of my strength and refuge is in God. Psalm 62:7
>
> He shall cry to me, 'You are my Father, my God, and the rock of my salvation.' Psalm 89:26
>
> For they drank from the spiritual rock that followed them; that rock was Christ. 1 Corinthians 10:4.

The Bible knows the rock, *pétra*, is Christ.

Verse 19 has also proved troubling for many believers, and troubling throughout the history of the church. The verse consists of two parts. The "keys to the kingdom of the heavens" is one part. A key symbolizes authority, not power: a key opens and shuts. The power of the key is not the key itself but the authority of the one who holds, or in this case gives, the key.

If Peter has been given the keys by Christ, then we should see Peter using the keys according to Christ's Word. What we do not see is Peter exercising authority over the New Testament church. At Acts 15, the first church council, Peter has his say, 15:7–11, but it is James (Jesus' half-brother) who leads the council, 15:13–21. At 1 Peter 5:1 Peter exhorts as an elder and a witness, not as the person in charge of the church.

Peter uses the authority symbolized by the keys three times.

> At Acts 2:37–41 Peter opened the kingdom of heaven to the Jews.
>
> At Acts 8:14–25 Peter opened the kingdom to the Samaritans.

At Acts 10:34–43 Peter opened the kingdom to the gentiles.

After those three uses Peter never uses the authority of the keys again. He has opened the door to salvation to the three groups of human kind, as per Jesus' command, in Jerusalem, in all Judea, and Samaria, and to the end of the earth, Acts 1:8.

After using the authority of the keys, Peter's ministry, as far as the record in God's Word is concerned, required three additional acts, which were not the use of the keys: he testified at the council in Jerusalem, Acts 15; he wrote two letters. The Bible gives no record, no basis for supposition or assumption, no hint or inference, that Peter was the spiritual leader of the entire New Testament church, as the Roman Catholic Church has claimed.

Peter opened the Gospel of salvation to the Jews at Pentecost. Then the Gospel of Salvation was preached to the Ethiopian proselyte by Philip after Peter had earlier used the keys to open the kingdom to the Samaritans. Then Barnabus and Saul (Paul) preached the Gospel of Salvation to the gentiles after Peter brought the Gospel of Salvation to the gentile Cornelius.

The Ethiopian was either a Jew of the *diaspora* or a proselyte. Cornelius the Centurion was a God-fearer. They keys, then, are the authority to open the doors of salvation to the people groups of the world, Jew and gentile, and those considered part Jew-part gentile (Samaritans). Peter was authorized by Christ to use the authority the keys represented in a manner consistent with doctrines, principles, values, and precepts of the king and his kingdom. He preached Christ and him crucified to people needing the Savior. Paul takes up this authority in his capacity as apostle to the gentiles. Peter opened the door to the gentiles, and then Paul used the open door to bring more gentiles into the house of the Lord.

The other part of the verse appears to convey on Peter the authority to confirm people in salvation or in their sins: "whatever if you might bind on earth will be bound in the heavens, and whatever if you might loose on earth will be loosed in the heavens." In deciding on an interpretation we must begin with clear and unambiguous doctrine. God is the one who decides guilt or innocence and executes the divine sentence. God is the One who forgives or retains sins.

Believers are authorized to declare the divine standards and proclaim the divine judgments for faith or no-faith. Peter is given the power of declaration, but not of absolution or damnation (not just Peter but others also, John 20:23, indicating the whole church by reference to its first representatives). Believers are empowered to authoritatively declare whose sins will be forgiven: those who believe on Jesus as Savior will have their sins forgiven. Jesus promises that God will act savingly toward anyone who believes the church's testimony that salvation is in Jesus Christ alone. The believer's power is great: to proclaim the means to eternal life. But that power is not terrible: to decide who lives or who dies eternally.

God has said he will support the believer's testimony about Jesus Christ. When, by the power of the Holy Spirit, a believer declares the Gospel of Salvation, God has promised that he will forgive all who have faith in Christ through that testimony. The testifying believer is a divinely appointed representative of the gospel, with the authority to proclaim the way to life. That's what Jesus meant.

We see a similar act by Jesus in John 20:23, empowering his disciples to conduct their mission. "If of any you may forgive the sins, they are forgiven them; if any you may retain, they are retained." Forgiven by whom or retained by whom? God is the person either retaining or forgiving sins. The question is, does God merely ratify (so-to-speak) a decision made by a disciple; or is the disciple declaring the works of God?

> The disciples were empowered by the Holy Spirit and therefore acting under the control of the Holy Spirit. The apostles and other disciples had received delegated authority from Jesus: "I also send you . . . you will receive power when the Holy Spirit has come." Their pronouncements concerning sin, the Savior, and salvation were authoritative precisely because they were caused by and empowered by God the Holy Spirit. Put a little more simply, forgiveness of sins or retention of sin is the result of preaching the gospel. This is the power God gives his Word. Those who proclaim his Word declare on the authority of God that faith in God's testimony concerning Jesus the Christ causes forgiveness of sins, but no-faith causes retention of sins. This is the true continuation of Jesus' mission in the world, even as he has called all his saved people throughout the church age to it and empowered them to do it. Put another way, this declarative power

wasn't given to individuals, but to the New Testament church. Wherever the Gospel of Salvation is preached the remission or retention of sins is declared, and the declaration made effective by the faith or no-faith of the hearer.

This authority to "preach the Word," then, was not given to the eleven apostles only, but to the church . . . . . The apostles and other disciples could neither remit nor retain sins on their own authority; what they could do was authoritatively declare what God was doing—to say what Jesus through the Holy Spirit had revealed to them, and do the works the Holy Spirit was doing through them. God forgives sins upon faith in his testimony that salvation is in Christ alone, and he retains sins when such faith is absent. That is what the apostles and other disciples—what every believer preaching the gospel—declares with divine authority; it is what Christ's disciples have declared from apostolic days. The believer can say with authority, "Unless you believe you cannot be saved." Verse 23 is of the same order as 13:20, "the one receiving whomever I may send receives me." The one receiving the message of salvation is saved; the one not receiving is not saved.[1]

Jesus commanded the twelve who were with him, v. 20, not to disclose to others what God had disclosed to them concerning him. Their understanding that Jesus of Nazareth was the Christ was not to be their testimony at this time. That was because the true doctrine of the messiah was corrupted in Israel, because people were looking for a political or military hero, not a Savior. The true testimony at this time would have been misunderstood. Later, after the ascension, Christ's saved people would testify, until he comes again, that Jesus of Nazareth is the Christ.

Translation Matthew 16:21–23

21 From that time Jesus began to show to his disciples that it is necessary for him to go away to Jerusalem, and to suffer many things from the elders and chief priests and scribes, and be killed, and on the third day to be raised. 22 And having taken him aside, Peter began to rebuke him, saying, "Far be it from you, master; no,

---

[1] Quiggle, *John 13–21*, 239–240.

Matthew Sixteen

this will never be to you." 23 But having turned he said to Peter, "Get behind me, Satan! You are an offense to me, because your thoughts are not of the things of God, but the things of men."

TRANSLATION NOTES

In v. 22 "master" is *kúrios*. The choices are, does Peter call Jesus the formal "sir," or does he call him "lord" in the sense of ruling over him, or does he call him "master," a term used by a disciple toward his teacher? Other versions translate "Lord" as though Peter knew Jesus was God incarnate. Undoubtedly Peter believes his teacher is the messiah, so "lord," or even "Lord" in the sense of ruling over him—the messiah being of royal lineage—is a valid choice. But to translate "Lord," or even "lord," would imply Peter knew Jesus was God incarnate; it would be anachronistic to make Peter know here the revelation given later by the Holy Spirit at Pentecost, Acts 2:36–39, that Jesus is God incarnate. That particular spiritual perception was withheld during his first advent, for reasons I have previously explained. My choice was to translate *kúrios* as "master," which fits Peter speaking respectfully as a disciple to his teacher, and acknowledging Jesus the messiah as the Davidic King and his ruler.

In v. 23 Jesus says "You are an offense," *skándelon*, "to me" etc. The word *skándelon* literally refers to the trigger of a trap on which the bait is placed, which, when touched by an animal, causes it to close, entrapping the animal.[1] Jesus uses this word several times in Matthew's Gospel. *Skándelon* is used in a moral sense in the New Testament, and may be translated offend, offending, offences, stumbling, stumbling block, scandal, temptation.

EXPOSITION

As explained at 4:17, the phrase "from that time Jesus began," *apó tóte árchomai ho Iēsoús* (vocabulary forms), at 4:17 and 16:21 is a structural marker dividing Matthew's Gospel into three sections, 1:1–4:16; 4:17–16:20; 16:21–28:20. The evangelistic tours began at 4:17 and end at 16:20. From 16:21 forward Jesus focuses on preparing the twelve to continue the mission after his death, resurrection, v. 21, and ascension. This does not mean Jesus stopped evangelizing, healing, and confronting his enemies, but

---

[1] Zodhiates, *WSDNT*, s. v. "4625."

that the focus is on training the twelve.

As Peter in v. 22 reveals, by his denial of the crucifixion, this new focus was completely contrary to their notions of the messiah. An integral part of their acceptance of Jesus as the messiah was their anticipation of positions of authority in his kingdom and an Israel free from and independent of gentile control. How could these things be accomplished if Jesus was dead?

When the disciples heard "be killed" they stopped hearing. To be fair to them, "to be raised" was incomprehensible after "to be killed." They believed in a general resurrection and judgment at the end of the age, e.g., Daniel 12:1–3, but the individual and personal resurrection of Jesus immediately following his death was beyond the scope of their experience, doctrine, and comprehension.

Nothing in their understanding of the Old Testament prepared them for messiah's death and resurrection. Their understanding of messiah was all of Psalm 2, the conquering messiah, and none of Psalm 22, the crucified messiah, or Isaiah 53, the propitiating messiah who redeems sinners. The raising of Samuel's soul, 1 Samuel 28:7, was not a resurrection, so that incident was of no help. The dead man reviving when his corpse contacted Elisha's bones, 2 Kings 13:20, could not be correlated with the Christ. The spiritual perception necessary to apply Psalm 16:10 to the Christ waited for the Holy Spirit at Pentecost, Acts 2:25–31. Neither did their experience with Jesus give them understanding. Prior to Matthew 16:21 Jesus had returned two people to life, Luke 7:11–17; Matthew 9:24–25, but Jesus had not connected those events with his death and resurrection. In their view, those two revivals were the power of God working through Jesus. God's power raising a dead Jesus was far from their minds.

Jesus' statement that he would be raised the "third" day was utterly incomprehensible to them. There was nothing in the Old Testament to connect "three days" with the messiah, except the sign of Jonah, Matthew 15:4, which the disciples did not understand. But Jesus wasn't asking them to understand his death and resurrection. He wanted them to accept his death and resurrection by faith.

Peter is not, of course, Satan, but he is speaking discouraging words as Satan would. The *skándelon* Jesus speaks of is the temptation to avoid the crucifixion necessary to the salvific mission. Peter heard that Jesus would die and he rejected that death. This is the strategy of Satan, now, after the resurrection, who would deny sinners salvation through Christ's propitiating death for their sins. Living in the here and now is the focus of Satan—he knows his future—and he discourages any from living with eternity in view. Peter was speaking in the manner of Satan and unsaved men.

Translation Matthew 16:24–28

24 Then Jesus said to his disciples, "If anyone desires to come after me, let him deny himself, and take up his cross, and follow me. 25 For whoever may desire to save his life, will lose it, and whoever may lose his life on account of me will find it. 26 For what will it profit a man, if the whole world he gains, and his soul loses? Or what will a man give as an exchange for his soul? 27 For the son of man is about to come in the glory of his Father, with his angels, and then he will give to each according to his conduct. 28 Truly I say to you, there are some of those standing here who shall not taste of death, until they might see the son of man coming in his kingdom."

EXPOSITION

This is the new message replacing the "repent for the kingdom of heaven is at hand" message of 4:17. The new message concerns those who believe on Jesus as Messiah, a belief that will lead them to receive Jesus as Savior. The new message is salvation and discipleship.

When Jesus speaks of saving or losing one's life, he is not speaking in terms of physical death, but of spiritual life and death. He has acknowledged himself to them as the messiah. He has told them of his impending death and resurrection. Now he brings them into the new dispensation by telling them just what it will mean to be a disciple of the messiah. Those who follow the suffering messiah must themselves expect to suffer. To "come after me" means a life-time commitment to Jesus. To "deny himself" means to renounce self-interest and seek the glory of God and the best spiritual good of others.

To "take up his cross" is equivalent to "deny himself" but more so. It is to leave behind worldly attachments and desires where these compete with discipleship. The cross is always a symbol of death, and here it means the death of the old sin nature, not in the sense of denial, but in the biblical sense of death as separation. The believing soul has been separated from the world and sin by being born-again. The new spiritual life is incompatible with the old sinful life, thus the believer must constantly separate him/herself from sinful desires and temptations.

The born-again believer may occasionally sin, but does not habitually sin. He/she lives a life of habitual righteousness (1 John 3:6–7; see my commentary, *John's Epistles*). The believer has the obligation to say "No" to temptation to commit an act of sinning. The believer has the spiritual authority and power—given by Christ and the Holy Spirit—to enforce that decision. One must deny self-interest, self-seeking, self-promotion, and the motions of the sin in the soul in complete dependence on Jesus, first as Savior and then as Lord. Jesus is Savior by grace through faith, Ephesians 2:8–9, and then Jesus is Lord in worship, fellowship, obedience, and service, Ephesians 2:10.

In vv. 25–26, Jesus explains and illustrates that to continue on in the present way of life, a sinner needing salvation, is to lose one's life in the eternal sense. To receive Jesus as one's Savior is to gain eternal life by losing the old life of a spiritually dead sinner. The eternal destiny of the soul in a salvific relationship with God is worth more than the entire world.

Verse 27 makes reference to judgment. As the messiah speaking to Jews expecting the Davidic Messianic kingdom, the reference is to the second coming, when Jesus will separate believers from unbelievers and inaugurate his kingdom on earth. Believers will enter the Davidic-Millennial Kingdom; unbelievers will go to hades to await the Great White Throne judgment.

In v. 28 Jesus makes a prediction which has been the subject of much discussion. The phrase, "some of those standing here," refers to some of those physically present at the moment of this prediction. The term "his kingdom" refers to the kingdom which belongs to and is ruled by the messiah. Some of those present would not "taste death" until they saw Jesus entering into his kingdom. To "taste death" means to die physically (Matthew 16:28; Mark 9:1; Luke 9:27; John 8:52; Hebrews 2:9). The key phrase is "coming into his kingdom," and the key question is, "What kind of coming?" A physical coming of Jesus as the Davidic King of the messianic kingdom of Old Testament prophecy cannot be meant, because it did not happen. This leaves either a representative coming or a spiritual coming. Seven interpretations have been

proposed:[1]
- The transfiguration
- The resurrection and ascension
- Pentecost
- The spread of Christianity
- The internal development of the Gospel
- The destruction of Jerusalem
- The second advent

Of these, the transfiguration seems correct in the immediate context. The New Testament church is not yet in view, so Jesus cannot mean the mystery form of the kingdom as explained in the parables of Matthew 13.

---

[1] Morris, *Matthew*, 434.

Matthew Seventeen

Translation Matthew 17:1–8

1 And after six days Jesus takes with him Peter and James, and John his brother, and brings them into a high mountain by themselves. 2 And his form was changed before them, and his face shone as the sun, and his clothes became white as the light. 3 And look, Moses and Elijah appeared to them, talking with him. 4 Now Peter responding said to Jesus, "Master, it is good for us to be here. If you so desire, we will make here three tabernacles: one for you, and one for Moses, and one for Elijah." 5 While he was still speaking, look, a bright cloud overshadowed them; and look, a voice out of the cloud, saying, "This is my son, the beloved, in whom I am well pleased. You listen to him." 6 And having heard it, the disciples fell upon their faces, and were greatly afraid. 7 And Jesus having come to them and touched them, said, "Get up, and be not afraid." 8 Now having lifted up their eyes, they saw no one except Jesus himself alone.

TRANSLATION NOTE

In v. 2 I have translated the word *metamorphóō* as "his form was changed." The word is a compound of *metá*, change of place or condition, and *morphóō*, to form.[1] Most versions translate "transfigure." The HCSB and NLT translate "transform." Transform and transfigure are synonyms that mean "to change in outward form or appearance." I choose to give the direct translation of *metamorphóō*.

EXPOSITION

The notice of "after six days" is the only such specific time reference in Matthew, and the effect is to link the final verses of the preceding chapter with the opening verses of chapter 17. (Mark says "after six days," Mark 9:2, and Luke says "about eight days after," Luke 9:28. This would make the trip up the mountain seven days after 16:28. There is probably no significance to the number of days.)

Jesus takes his inner circle with him to the mountain. Although Mount Tabor in Galilee is the traditional site for the transfiguration,

---

[1] Zodhiates, *WSDNT*, s. v. "3339."

Matthew Seventeen

the better place is Mount Hermon, north of Caesarea Philippi. Jesus was in Caesarea Philippi, 16:13, and from the transfiguration they returned to Galilee and Capernaum, 17:22, 24; Mark 9:30, 33.

The story is told from the disciples' point of view. Matthew presents the event in his usual succinct style. He leaves out Luke's details: Jesus was praying; Moses and Elijah were speaking with Jesus about his death; the disciples were in a deep sleep and awoke to see Jesus transfigured and speaking to Moses and Elijah. Matthew wrote his gospel after James had been killed (Acts 12:2), so he learned of the events from Peter or John. Peter seems the likely source, compare 2 Peter 1:17–18.

What is important to Matthew is the glory of the Christ, his preeminence with the Father, and his messianic mission. Jesus was *metamorphoō*, changed in form. Exactly what happened cannot be known. Jesus remained identifiable, but his face "shone as the sun," and his clothes became "white as the light."

My understanding is that the essential glory of the God-man was allowed to shine through the veil of his flesh. Glory is a manifestation of the being and attributes of God. The glory of the messiah was hidden in his first advent, Philippians 2:6–8, but on the mountain his glory was momentarily revealed. This is how the Son of Man will appear when he comes into his kingdom, 16:28. Compare Ezekiel 1:4, 27–28; Habakkuk 3:4; 2 Thessalonians 2:8, "the brightness of his coming," at his second advent, and Hebrews 1:3. This is God, as the Scripture teaches us to expect the appearance of God, seen here in the person of Jesus the Messiah, the son of God, the God-man. This is the "son of man coming in his kingdom" he spoke of in 16:28.

Moses represents the Law. Elijah represents the prophets. Together they represent the Old Testament testimony of the messiah. Moses may be said to represent the deliverance of Israel from slavery. In the light of Malachi 4:5, 6 Elijah specifically represents the messianic advent. Moses may represent his prophecy in Deuteronomy 18:15, "The Lord your God will raise up for you another prophet like me from your midst, from your brethren. Him you shall hear" (NKJV), cf. John 1:21.

Peter and the others are mentally and emotionally overcome by this scene. How they recognized Moses and Elijah is unknown (perhaps Jesus called them by name?). Peter makes a suggestion, deferring to Jesus' decision ("if you so desire"), to make three "tabernacles," a covered or shaded place. This is not a temple but a structure like a lean-to (used at the Feast of Tabernacles), a tent, or some more permanent type of shelter. Peter seems to be thinking that all the important people in Jewish theology are present, including Jesus the Messiah (16:16), therefore it was good to be there with them. He may have desired to prolong the moment for as long as possible; he may have desired to reverence (not worship) these three. Luke (9:33) says Peter did not know what he was saying. Peter did not understand his suggestion. To put Moses and Elijah on equal terms with Jesus was wrong.

God's pronouncement puts everything into perspective. This is the same as at the baptism with an addition: "You listen to him." The change in Jesus' appearance and the presence of Moses and Elijah is a messianic declaration. Jesus is the prophet Moses foretold: "Hear him"; Jesus is the messiah the prophets foretold: "Hear him." Moses and Elijah have done their job; the messiah is here, so turn from the proclaimers to the one they proclaimed. The display of glory is like to that which will occur when Jesus inaugurates his Davidic Messianic kingdom.

The disciples "fell on their faces" in fear at the voice. Jesus came and reassured them with a comforting touch and encouraging words. Moses and Elijah had disappeared, Jesus' appearance was normal. They leave the mountain. The time has come for Jesus to move steadily toward Jerusalem and the propitiation he will make on the cross.

Translation Matthew 17:9-13

9 And as they came down from the mountain, Jesus commanded them, saying, "Tell no one the vision until that the son of man is risen from among the dead." 10 And the disciples asked him, saying, "Why then the scribes say that it is necessary that Elijah come first?" 11 And answering he said, "Elijah indeed comes and will restore all things. 12 But I say to you that Elijah is already come, and they knew him not, but did to him whatever they desired. Thus also, the son of man is about to suffer from them." 13 Then the disciples understood that he spoke to them about John the Baptist.

EXPOSITION

As they left the mountain Jesus tells them not to reveal what they had seen or heard, until after his resurrection. Mark says they discussed what "risen from the dead" might mean; Mark means they did not understand. They had just seen the messiah in his essential glory, as though coming into his Davidic Messianic kingdom. How then could he die and what does he mean by risen from among the dead?

Peter says that the power and coming of the Lord Jesus Christ was seen on the mountain, 2 Peter 1:16–18. There God the Father gave Jesus honor and glory when he spoke from the cloud. In the political and religious climate of the day, this would have been the indisputable sign the religious leaders had been seeking. Certainly the crowds would have acclaimed Jesus as the warrior-messiah of their hopes. That was what Jesus wanted to avoid, because his mission in this first advent was to be the propitiation for sins. He must be killed by the religious leaders with the crowds assenting to his death; and then rise from among the dead. This was not fate on the part of those who killed him, Jews or gentiles, Acts 2:23, but choice of the wicked.

In Matthew it may seem the three disciples understood the "risen from among the dead" statement. However, we know from Mark they did not understand. They had been given an indisputable sign from heaven that Jesus was the Messiah. But, they wondered, where was Elijah?

> Malachi 4:5, 6, Behold, I will send you Elijah the prophet before the coming of the great and dreadful day of the Lord. And he will turn the hearts of the fathers to the children, and the hearts of the children to their fathers, lest I come and strike the earth with a curse. (NKJV)

They knew this Scripture, which seemed to conflict with their recent experience. But close attention reveals Elijah is to come before "the great and dreadful day of the Lord," which Christians know as the Tribulation. And so he does, Revelation 11:3–4. In the same way John Baptist fulfilled the Elijah prophecy for the first advent, so another will be like Elijah for the second advent. God doesn't resurrect (nor reincarnate) his saved people in heaven to come and suffer again on earth. The Malachi prophecy is that type of prophecy with a near or partial fulfillment and a far or ultimate fulfillment. The near fulfillment was John Baptist. The far fulfillment is Revelation 11:3–6.

We should not take the disciples to task for forgetting Matthew 11:14, "he [John Baptist] is Elijah who must come," without some prompting from Jesus, for our memory is as unreliable as theirs. Jesus' answer should be understood as this: the prophecy remains valid. Elijah is coming before that great and terrible day. But for this advent John Baptist came in the spirit and power of Elijah to prepare the way for messiah, as prophesied by Malachi. That these three "understood that he spoke to them about John the Baptist" reveals why they were privileged to see Jesus revealed on the mountain. They had the quality of faith necessary to receive greater spiritual perception from the Holy Spirit.

Someone will come in the future, in the spirit and power of Moses and Elijah, to "restore all things" by denouncing sin and announcing the coming of messiah at his imminent second advent. John Baptist came in the spirit and power of Elijah to restore all things. By proclaiming the necessity to be prepared for the messiah, John anticipated the atonement which would deliver human kind from the penalty, power, pleasure, and presence of sin.

Translation Matthew 17:14–21

14 And they having come to the crowd, a man came to him, kneeling down to him, 15 and saying, "Sir, have mercy on my son, because he is an epileptic and miserably suffers. For often he falls into the fire, and often into the water, 16 and I brought him to your disciples, and they were not able to heal him." 17 Now Jesus answering said, "O generation without faith and perverse, how long will I be with you? How long will I bear with you? Bring him here to me." 18 And Jesus rebuked the demon and the demon went out from the boy and the boy was healed from that hour. 19 Then the disciples, having come to Jesus in private, they said, "What is the reason we not able to cast it out?" 20 Now he said to them, "On account of your little faith. For truly I say to you, if you have faith as a mustard seed, you will say to this mountain, 'Move from here to there,' and it will move; and nothing will be impossible for you. 21 But this kind does not go out except but by prayer and fasting."

TRANSLATION NOTE

In v. 18 the Greek text reads (word order) "and rebuked him Jesus and went out from him the demon." The word *daimónion*, demon, is in the neuter gender. The first "him" is a third person singular personal pronoun in the dative case, *autō*, which may be either masculine or neuter. If masculine, the translation is, "Jesus rebuked the boy and the demon went out from the boy and the boy was healed." If neuter, "Jesus rebuked the demon and the demon went out from the boy and the boy was healed." Either is as likely as the other, and various commentators have good reasons for both. In my translation I have replaced the pronouns with nouns and given what I believe to be the best sense.

EXPOSITION

The boy's father, and probably some of the crowd, see Jesus approaching and come to him. The father respectfully asks Jesus to heal his son. At 4:24 I discussed that the word *selēniázomai* describes what we now know to be epilepsy (although it may also indicate a different mental disease with the same symptoms).

Mark says the demon made the boy unable to speak, fall down, foam at the mouth, grind his teeth, and become rigid. Luke says that when the demon seizes the boy he (the boy) shrieks, and the demon throws the boy into convulsions until he foams at the mouth. Luke speaks of the demon wounding the boy, and this is what the father means in Matthew when he speaks of his son falling into water and fire. The disciples were unable to cure the boy.

Referencing the boy's symptoms to demonic habitation conforms to the Bible's distinction between an organic disease and a demonically-caused condition. While the distinction is more prominent in Luke's Gospel, we see it here also. The father is speaking phenomenally: the boy is *selēniázomai*. Matthew and Jesus reveal the truth: the boy does not have an organic disease but a condition caused by demonic habitation. That is why Jesus did not heal the boy, but rather he casts out the demon.

Jesus' response to the father seems out of character, but it is not directed at the man. The "generation without faith and perverse," is the subject of 11:16; 12:39; 16:4. A generation is all the people living at about the same time, so it refers to Israel in this time of the first advent.

These appear to be a rhetorical questions, thus they are in the nature of a comment. Jesus has been in public ministry for almost three years. When will the nation begin to have faith? The word translated "perverse," means to turn away from the right way, Luke 9:41; 23:2; Acts 13:8; 20:30; Philippians 2:15. The people continue to turn away from faith in Jesus.

Jesus' comment to his disciples about "your little faith" is not a matter of quantity but quality. Faith is an intangible, faith has no physical measurement. The disciples certainly would not have tried to cast out the demon if they did not believe they had the authority to cast it out. However, the validity of belief begins with the Person in whom one believes. Do I believe in the power to cast out demons, or do I believe in Jesus who can give the authority and power to cast out demons? The authority and power to cast out demons belongs to Jesus. When Jesus gives his people the authority, then the power is present to do the work. God in Christ must be the focus of faith in order to be given the authority and receive the power.

Based on past experience the disciples believed they had the power to cast out the demon. But did they have the authority? The disciples were trying to use the power and authority they had been previously given, 10:8, for a specific set of circumstances. However, the delegation of divine authority is specific to each need, not given generally, nor remaining after the need is met. Delegated power must be renewed, the believer must constantly come to God for a "recharge," if that be God's will.

Delegated power must be used according to God's will, if the exercise of power is to be effective. The point of vv. 20, 21 is not some ritual or formula for getting God to give authority or answer prayer. The point is to focus on God who has the authority and the power to cast out a demon. God's will was to free this boy from the demon, but God would have Jesus get the glory. Therefore, the disciples needed prayer, because by prayer we humble ourselves as dependent on God alone; and the disciples needed fasting, because fasting focuses on God, not self.

Any amount of faith in Jesus is adequate, v. 20, because Jesus is the one who has the power to move mountains, a proverbial saying for resolving seemingly insurmountable problems. The apostles should have known the origin of their power and authority was faith in and dependence upon Jesus. Thus, in relation to the seemingly unlimited promise in v. 20, we can understand that one needs knowledge as well as power: knowledge to know God's will, then God's power and authority to accomplish his will. The mountain only moves when we have faith and knowledge, power and authority. God is always sovereign; nothing will be impossible when God's will and God's power is brought to bear through the believer's faith.

Translation Matthew 17:22–23

22 Now as they were together in Galilee, Jesus said to them, "The son of man is about to be betrayed into the hands of men, 23 and they will kill him; and on the third day he will be raised up." And they were deeply distressed.

EXPOSITION

They, i.e., the twelve, pay attention to the part about death, because they do not understand the part about Jesus' resurrection. Why did Jesus say this here and now? Perhaps Matthew intends his readers to connect the sorrow of the apostles with their need for faith as small as a mustard seed. Instead of having faith they were exceedingly sorrowful. Note the expression, "will be raised up," words that highlight the work of the Father. In the fuller expression given by later revelation we know this must indicate Jesus' confidence that his propitiation will be an acceptable sacrifice.

Translation Matthew 17:24–27

24 Now they having come to Capernaum, those receiving the double-drachma tax came to Peter and said, "Your teacher, does he not pay the double-drachma tax?" 25 He says, "Yes." And having entered into the house, Jesus anticipated him, saying, "What do you think, Simon? The kings of the earth, from whom do they receive customs or tax, from their sons or from strangers?" 26 Now he having said, "From the strangers," Jesus said to him, "Then the sons are free. 27 But in order that we might not offend them, having gone to the sea, cast a hook, and the first fish having come up take, and having opened its mouth, you will find a four drachma coin; that having taken, give to them for me and yourself."

EXPOSITION

The double-drachma tax was paid annually by adult Jewish males for the upkeep of the temple. The tax was of recent origin, but was based on Exodus 30:11–16. Why the collector did not approach Jesus is unknown, but perhaps the custom was to ask a teacher's disciples for the tax.

The collector assumed a positive response. Some commentators have suggested the collector was asking if Peter's teacher paid this tax, because priests and others in God's service could claim an exemption.[1] This view cannot be conclusively

---

[1] Brown, *Dictionary*, 3:752.

supported.

Jesus answered Peter's question before he could ask. Morris's comment is on the mark. This paragraph "indicates Jesus' view that in the light of his relationship to the heavenly Father he was under no obligation to pay the temple tax, but also the fact that while he was here on earth he submitted to the regulations that people in general were bound to observe."[1] The coin in the fish was God's provision. Perhaps one can see here a reference to Peter's earthly vocation—God provides for our obligations through our labor.

The temple tax issue was a matter of controversy. Some rabbis supported it, some did not. If Jesus used money that had been voluntarily donated to support him it might have divided his supporters. If Jesus had refused, the matter would have to be decided at Jerusalem. This would put the collectors in an awkward position. To avoid controversy, and to avoid offense to the collectors and others, Jesus sends Peter to find some money, by fishing, with a hook in a fish's mouth (elsewhere it is a net, so a hook to catch the fish, a net to bring it into the boat). Found money belongs to the finder, so Jesus is not involving himself in any way with the temple tax controversy. The "four drachma" coin was known as a *statēr*.

---

[1] Morris, *Matthew*, 451.

Matthew Eighteen

Translation Matthew 18:1–6

1 In that hour the disciples came to Jesus, saying, "Who then is greatest in the kingdom of the heavens?" 2 And having called to a child, he set it in the midst of them, 3 and said, "Truly I say to you, if you are not converted and become as the little children, you will by no means enter the kingdom of the heavens. 4 Whoever therefore will humble himself as this little child, he is the greatest in the kingdom of the heavens. 5 And whoever may receive one such little child, in my name, receives me. 6 But whoever may cause offense to one of these little ones believing in me, it is better for him that a heavy millstone should be hung around his neck, and he be drowned in the depth of the sea.

TRANSLATION NOTE

In v. 3 the word translated "converted" is *stréphō*, "to turn, to turn about."[1] When used figuratively, as it is here, *stréphō* means to become another kind of person. The disciples were seeking personal preeminence in messiah's kingdom. They needed to adjust their values, i.e., they needed to turn from worldly values to godly values. That change begins with salvation. In this context *stréphō* is equivalent to born-again.

EXPOSITION

The greatest in the kingdom of the heavens is not the one who seeks greatness, but the one who is humble. Humility means having an accurate opinion of yourself in relation to God and in relation to others. The humble person knows his worth as a person comes from his relationship with God in Christ. A person with more skills and abilities than another is not worth more than other people, rather he is more responsible and accountable to God to further the interests of the kingdom, to bring glory to God, and to use his/her skills and abilities to help others. Appropriate pride comes from doing a job correctly: in Christ's name, for his glory. Appropriate pride comes from being a neighbor to others. True humility views others as equal or better than self. True humility recognizes that I am a valuable part of the whole, but I am a single part, not the

---

[1] Zodhiates, *WSDNT*, s. v. "4762."

whole.

One must carefully note what Jesus *does* say in v. 3. He says conversion is first. Without salvation one cannot enter the kingdom. The word *stréphō* is in the passive voice, indicating the change is not something that can be brought about by the person himself, but by something or someone acting on the person: the new birth of John 3:3–6. When the new birth happens the sinner becomes humble, dependent, believing. He/she becomes "poor in the spirit," 5:3, i.e., able to be filled with the righteousness of Christ, adopting God's values as his/her own. In comparing believers to little children, Jesus isn't speaking of the attitude of a little child, but a child's social status.

In the ancient world little children had zero social status. The ancient world valued people for their ability to contribute to society. Children were not valued for the potential contribution they might make as an adult. Little children had no contribution to make to society, and therefore had little value. They knew nothing, influenced nothing, gained nothing, and could not be used for anything that could create value. They were little in size, thus in ability, maturity, influence, and profit. Whatever value they might gain would come from serving others as they matured.

Jesus is not saying leaders have little value, or no contribution to make. He is taking the perceived social value of a little child and saying Christian leaders are to have an attitude toward self and others that resembles the social status of a little child. The Christian leader is not more valuable than others, he/she has more responsibility than those he leads, and therefore more accountability. The Christian leader is to serve, not be served.

Jesus is not saying innocence and trust are a contest to see who becomes greatest in the kingdom. Such a view is contrary to the humble status of a child. Jesus is saying that whoever humbles himself until he/she becomes lowly, like a little child, has become greatest in the kingdom. Jesus is saying that greatness in the kingdom is becoming like a little child in the practice of one's faith, and humility is the specific quality in view. The first step is being born-again; then comes being like a little child: negatively in pride, malice, envy, etc.; positively in trust, prayer, relationships, etc.

Using a little child as an example, Jesus calls his saved people little children. Whoever receives a saved person in Jesus name receives Jesus. Whoever harms a saved person it would be better to be drowned than to have harmed a saved person. In v. 5, whoever receives the person believing on Christ as Savior receives the Savior in the person of this saved sinner. Whoever rejects a believer rejects Christ. Later revelation shows that the basis for v. 5 is the unity between Christ and his people. Believers are "in Christ," i.e., they are incorporated into a vital, indissoluble spiritual union with him, so any rejection of the person who is in Christ is a rejection of Christ.

The spiritual lowliness in view is the same as at 5:3, "blessed are the poor in spirit." Spiritual lowliness—humility—consists of knowing one must depend on God for every need. The spiritually lowly are destitute of their own righteousness, thus prepared to be filled full by the grace and righteousness of Christ. The spiritually lowly endure the trials and persecutions of the world through dependence on God. The humble person does not aggressively insist on his or her rights.

In these circumstances the world, which views aggressive self-assertion as a positive moral characteristic, is all too ready to take advantage of or otherwise mistreat the humble person. Whoever acts against the best interests of Christ's saved people, it would be better for him if he had drowned instead of acting against a believer. The millstone around his neck and being drowned in the depth of the sea is a figurative statement meant to communicate the consequences of offending a believer: punishment may be delayed but it cannot be escaped. The works men do will be judged. The punishment for offending a believer—through persecution for faith, temptations to sin—will be added to the eternal punishment due the unsaved for their unbelief in Jesus as Savior. Of course, one who offends a believer may still be saved by personal faith in Jesus the Savior. Salvation is always possible in this mortal life, but if rejected, there remains only judgment after death.

Translation Matthew 18:7–10

7 "Woe to the world because of the offenses. For it is inevitable the offenses come; but woe to the person by whom the offense comes. 8 But if your hand or your foot causes you to sin, cut them off and cast them from you. It is better for you to enter into life crippled or lame, than having two hands or two feet, to be cast into the eternal fire. 9 And if your eye causes you to sin, take it out and cast it from you. It is better for you to enter into life one-eyed, than

having two eyes to be cast into the fire of Gehenna. 10 See to it you not despise one of these little ones. For I say to you, that their angels in the heavens continually see the face of my Father who is in the heavens."

EXPOSITION

The word translated offenses is *skándelon*. Here it means a temptation or other action that would lead to sinning or weaken faith. Sinners will cause offenses; the consequences are severe: to be cast into the lake of fire (Gehenna). To cause a *skándelon* does not prevent salvation. Unforgiven sin through no faith in Christ the Savior is the only cause of eternal separation from God in the lake of fire.

Verses 8–9 are not to be taken literally, as though literally cutting off a hand or foot or literally plucking out an eye will cause a person to go to heaven. Jesus is using hyperbole for effect, see comments at 5:27–30. Hand, foot, and eye are being used in a figurative way to illustrate spiritual truth. With their hands sinners shed innocent blood. With their feet sinners run to evil, they make haste to shed blood. What one sees can be the occasion or opportunity for sin. Evil actions are not caused by hands, feet, or eyes but by a sinner's choice to do evil things, prompted by the evil principle sin in their human nature. The will, persuasively influenced by the evil principle sin, makes a choice to commit an act of sinning. The hands, feet, and eyes are the instruments that carry out the choice of the will. The only way to overcome sin is to repent and have saving faith in Jesus.

The unrepentant, unsaved unbeliever will be punished for his unbelief in Jesus, and for the way in which he/she treats believers. In these sayings about the hand, foot, and eye Jesus is saying one must get rid of the occasion for sin, the opportunity—the *skándelon*—to sin. If a person is engaged in an activity, an attitude, a philosophy of life that could lead to an act or habit of sinning, then that activity or attitude or philosophy must be cut out from their life. For the unbeliever true spiritual change is accomplished only by salvation. To be "cast into the everlasting fire" might be viewed by some as metaphorical for being eternally lost, but the scriptures tell us that the lake of fire is the eternal prison for all who do not repent and believe, Revelation 20:15.

The message of v. 10 is simple enough: do not be the occasion or opportunity for sinning in one of Christ's saved people; deliberate action is implied in "not despise." There is an emphasis on the individual, "one of these little ones." God cares deeply for each and every believer; each believer has God's full attention.

The term "their angels" does not mean a specific "guardian angel," but refers to angels as those who minister to the saved, Hebrews 1:14. There is no Scripture support for the idea that one angel is assigned to protect each believer. The divine charge to the angels is to minister to the church at large and individuals in particular as the need arises, Psalm 91; Hebrews 1:14. The significance of these angels seeing the Father's face is the watch-care and love the Father has for Christ's saved people: angels care for the church at the direction of the Father; his love and wrath are what is in view.

Translation Matthew 18:11

<11 For the son of man has come to save that which has been lost.>

EXPOSITION

Metzger says on v. 11, "There can be little doubt that the words are spurious here, being absent from the earliest witnesses representing several textual types (Alexandrian, Egyptian, Antiochian), and manifestly borrowed by copyists from Luke 19:10."[2]

Mark has part of this particular discourse (Mark 9:42–47, corresponds to Matthew 18:6–9) but does not have the story of the lost sheep nor a statement corresponding to Matthew 18:11 or Luke 19:10. John does not have this discourse. In Luke's Gospel the story of the lost sheep is at 15:4–7, not 19:1–10. The context of Luke 19:10 does not correspond to the context of Matthew 18:11. The statement in Luke 19:10 occurs as the conclusion of the story of Zacchaeus: "10 Salvation has come to the house of Zacchaeus because he also is a son of Abraham: 11 because the son of man has come to seek and to save that which has been lost."

Some person transcribing Matthew's Gospel did not understand the context and used Luke 19:10 to give the verses an evangelistic outlook. But the context of Matthew 18:1–14 is the saved. The saved are Christ's little children. The flock in Matthew 16: 12 is one

---

[2] Metzger, *Textual*, 36.

hundred sheep belonging to the shepherd and one of the one hundred goes astray. In Matthew the straying sheep is not an unsaved person, but a saved person who has wandered into sin, whom the shepherd recovers.

The lost sheep story at Luke 15:4–7 is not parallel to the lost sheep story at Matthew 18:12–14. In the Luke passage Christ tells the lost sheep story with an evangelistic intent. In Matthew the intent is recovering a sinning believer.

We should not stumble at Jesus telling a story more than once but using the same story in more than one way. In Matthew the story is told to the disciples in partial answer to their question about who is the greatest in the kingdom. In Luke the context is Christ receiving and eating with sinners. In Matthew one sheep "wanders off." In Luke the shepherd "loses one of them." In Matthew the shepherd goes "to the hills" to find the wandering sheep. In Luke the shepherd searches the wilderness for the lost sheep. In Matthew the shepherd rejoices when he finds the wandering sheep. In Luke the shepherd calls his friends to rejoice with him. In Matthew the story ends with "it is not the will of your Father who is in heaven that one of these little ones should perish." Jesus has previously established that his "little ones" refers to the saved, 18:3, 10. In Luke the story ends with "there will be more joy in heaven over one sinner who repents." The Matthew and Luke stories are similar in some ways, but have significant differences in context and intent. My decision is Matthew 18:11 is not part of the original Matthew text.

Translation Matthew 18:12–14

12 "What do you think? If some person has a hundred sheep, and one of them has wandered, will he not leave the ninety-nine on the hills, and having gone, seek the one wandering? 13 And if he should find it, truly I say to you, that he rejoices over it more than over the ninety-nine not wandering. 14 So it is not the will of your Father who is in the heavens that one of these little ones should be lost."

EXPOSITION

The connection between v. 10 and vv. 12–14 is the love of the Father for the saved, v. 10, which results in his protection of the saved. In v. 10 they are protected by angels, and in vv. 12–14 they are protected by the will of the Father in recovering those who have been led into temptation and sin, vv. 6–9. The man in the story has 100 sheep. He is not seeking to gain 100 sheep, he already possesses 100 sheep. The sheep in this story are the "little ones" of vv. 10, 14,i.e., those who are saved. What happens if a saved person wanders, i.e., he/she sins? The ones who are not sinning (at least at this point in time), the ninety-nine, do not need rescuing. The one who has sinned is sought and recovered. Each believer is precious and important.

In the light afforded by later revelation, we can say the Holy Spirit brings conviction leading to repentance, confession, cleansing, and restoration. There is rejoicing when that wandering sheep is recovered from his/her act of sinning and restored to fellowship. The action of the shepherd in the story illustrates the love the Father has for believers. The eternal security of the believer in Christ is clearly stated.

Translation Matthew 18:15–18

15 "Moreover if your brother sins against you, go and rebuke him, between you and him alone. If he will hear you, you have gained your brother. 16 But if he will not hear, take with you more, one or two, that on the mouth of two witnesses or of three, every word may stand. 17 But if he disregards them, tell it to the assembly. But if he disregards also the assembly, let him be to you as the pagan and the tax collector. 18 Truly I say to you, whatever you may bind on the earth will be bound in heaven, and whatever you may loose on earth will be loosed in heaven. 19 Amen." [continued]

EXPOSITION

Jesus has been speaking of the one who gives offense, now he addresses the attitude and action of the one who has been offended. The one who has been offended is to take the initiative to resolve the matter. The offended brother is the shepherd seeking the wandering sheep, who is the brother who gave offense. The offended brother seeks offending brother in order to bring him back to fellowship.

A private matter is to be dealt with privately. The offending brother may reject this attempt at recovery. Recovering an offending brother is so important the offended brother is to try again. In v. 16 "on the mouth of two witnesses or of three" is an Old Testament rule to establish the truth of a matter (Deuteronomy 19:15). This does not mean the witnesses have direct knowledge

Matthew Eighteen

of the offense, or that they find the offended brother's report of the incident compellingly credible. What the witnesses are witnessing is the offended brother's effort to resolve the issue and reconcile. The words "if he disregards" means the offending brother will not listen to reason, or will not allow reconciliation, or otherwise ignores or rejects his brother's love. If such is the case then let two or three witnesses observe so as to report the exact words used, to be able to testify that reconciliation was attempted but rejected.

If he refuses to hear "them" means the witnesses; they are now also engaged in recovering this offending brother. They are present to add their voices to persuade this sinning brother to repent and reconcile. If he refuses to hear them then the matter is to be taken to the *ekklēsía*, the assembly.

Ekklēsía is used in the Gospels only here and 16:18. The word indicates a specific group of people who may be identified in some way as a group separate from the general populace or other groups. In Acts 19:41 the city clerk at Ephesus dismisses the "assembly," the *ekklēsía*, which was a group of citizens out of the larger population of Ephesians, who had been making an unlawful public protest. Those hearing Jesus might have thought of the *ekklēsía* as the synagogue (cf. Morris, a part of Israel assembled or not assembled.[1])

In the Acts and epistles the *ekklēsía* is usually the New Testament church, and almost always a local church. We can make an application of this story to the New Testament church, but in this context the word is properly translated "assembly."

To "tell it to the assembly" probably means to rehearse the entire incident to all the brethren, from the offense to the several attempts at reconciliation. The initial purpose is not judgment. The offending brothers response in this story has been to disregard everyone trying to recover him to fellowship. All the brethren oppose his behavior and all the brethren want him to be recovered from his sin. This should be effective. However, if he continues to sin, by denying the witnesses, and an appeal from his brothers and sisters in Christ, then the assembly is to treat him as they would treat a pagan or tax collector: like an unsaved sinner. (Jesus is not politically correct. Although he mingles with tax collectors to give them the gospel, he does not hesitate to use them as a symbol of

---

[1] Morris, *Matthew*, 468.

sin.)

Verse 18 should be compared with comments at 16:19, to wit, that binding and losing was the power of proclamation. The power of the gospel proclaimed is to loose sinners from sin or to confirm sinners in sin. However, at 16:19 the subject was the gospel, "Jesus is the Christ." Here in 18:18 the subject is Christian conduct, "if your brother sins against you." The authority of the assembly, for Jesus uses the plural "you," is the declaration of the assembly unified in their decision of right and wrong behavior. Obviously all such declarations must be in accordance with Scripture, and therefore the assembled "you" are evaluating the offending brother's behavior in the light of Scripture.

This statement is also applicable in matters of Christian liberty, for it is the authority of the assembly that is in view. I once belonged to a church whose members believed attending a movie theater was sinful. Although that was not my personal belief, I conformed to that "binding" authority and did not attend a movie while a member of that assembly.

Translation Matthew 18:19–20

[19 continued] "I say again to you, that if two of you may agree on the earth, about any matter to be done, that if they might ask, it will be done for them, by my Father, who is in the heavens. 20 For where two or three are gathered together to my name, there am I in the midst of them."

EXPOSITION

The promise in v. 19 can be misunderstood and misused. God is always sovereign. Prayer is a divinely decreed means to his ends, not a lever to move him to our will. The agreement of two in prayer cannot bind God and so must be understood as agreement according to his will.

The circumstance supposed is two or more believers uniting in prayer over some particular matter. The unity of two agreeing in prayer indicates God is guiding those praying, thus it is God's will and shall be done. God will always hear his people united in prayer and will answer as he sovereignly wills. The unity of the body of Christ, not an answer to some prayer, is the point. The Lord's will has usually been revealed when there is unity among the brethren.

The promise "in the midst of them," v. 20, in the first instance indicates Jesus guiding the church in its binding and loosing proclamations, and in the second a warning to do all things according to his will (expressed in Scripture). In the smallest group, for even the lowliest reasons, if Jesus is the reason for his people assembling, then he is present. This is why so much prayer fails: Jesus was not the reason we assembled to pray. When believers come together in the name of Jesus, consideration must be given to worshiping the Person and expressing prayers that conform to the works and character of Jesus. When that happens Jesus is there in the midst.

Translation Matthew 18:21–22

21 Then, having come, Peter said to him, "Master, how often will my brother sin against me, and I will forgive him? Up to seven times?" 22 Jesus says to him, "I do not say to you, up to seven times, but up to seventy times seven."

EXPOSITION

The previous conversation probably prompted this question. The rabbis said one should forgive three times, and then retribution was allowed. In asking "up to seven times" Peter shows he has grasped the idea of the fuller forgiveness expected of a disciple, but not the full spirit of Jesus' teaching. The sinner owes God a huge sin debt. Believers commit acts of sinning every day. When should God stop forgiving? Jesus tells Peter he should forgive "seventy times seven," although some manuscripts read seventy-seven times. Either way it is a lot of forgiveness. The idea is that forgiveness is always the appropriate response to repentance. The intent is not to count the number of times forgiveness has been extended, but always be ready to forgive and in fact to forgive.

God's forgiveness toward his saved is based on repentance and faith, and that is a good rule in one's relations with others. Compare Luke 17:3–4"Pay attention to yourselves. If your brother may sin, rebuke him. And if he may repent, forgive him. 4 And if seven times in the day he may sin against you, and seven times may return to you saying, 'I repent,' you will forgive him."

The believer must not forget God's longsuffering, mercy, and grace overlooks sin, at least temporarily, when there has been no repentance, and must him/herself be willing to act in longsuffering, mercy, etc. To forgive is not the same as to trust, but it is to act without resentment, malice, or revenge toward the one forgiven.

God acts in kindness even toward those who reject him, and the final action due unrepentant sin belongs to God, not the believer. Thinking ahead to v. 35, the believer must practice forgiveness just because he himself has been forgiven, therefore the forgiveness one extends toward others should not count or consider the number of offenses when forgiveness is required, or requested.

Translation Matthew 18:23-35

23 "On account of this, the kingdom of the heavens is like a man, a king, who desired to settle accounts with his servants. 24 Now, he having begun to settle, one was brought to him, a debtor of ten thousand talents. 25 But he not having means to pay, the master commanded him to be sold, and the wife and the children, and as much as he had, and payment to be made. 26 Therefore the servant, having fallen down to him, was on his knees, saying, 'Have patience with me, and I will pay all to you.' 27 Now having compassion, the master of that servant released him, and forgave him the debt. 28 But having gone out, the servant found one of his fellow servants, who owed him a hundred denarii, and having taken hold of him, he choked him, saying, 'Pay what you owe!' 29 Having therefore fallen down, his fellow servant begged him, saying, 'Have patience with me, and I will pay you.' 30 But he was not willing, and having went away, he cast him into prison until when he should pay that which was owing. 31 Therefore having seen the things that occurred, his fellow servants were deeply grieved, and having gone, made known to their master all that had occurred. 32 Then having called to him, his master says to him, 'Evil servant. I forgave you all the debt because you begged me. 33 Should you not also have compassion on your fellow servant, as I had compassion on you?' 34 And being angry, his master delivered him to the torturers, until that he should pay all being owed to him. 35 Thus also my heavenly Father will do to you, if each of you does not forgive his brother from your heart."

EXPOSITION

This is a parable to illustrate forgiveness. A king conducts an audit and discovers that a servant—in the cultural setting probably a government official or a tax collector—owes him a huge debt. Like all ancient systems of monetary value, a talent was a measurement of weight. He could have owed 10,000 talents of gold, silver, or copper. The monetary value of one talent is today estimated at 1,000.00 USD. The value of 10,000 talents in today's money was 10 million dollars.

In ancient times 10,000 talents of money was an enormous amount. Think of the buying power of governments and billionaires. Josephus estimates taxes collected from Palestine at 8,000 talents (*Ant.* 12.175). The amount of money this servant owed was more than he could repay in a lifetime, and that is the point. The king had complete authority over the servant's life. The king's response to the servant's inability to pay was to sell all his assets and sell him and his wife and children as slaves. His wife and children are to be sold because they were viewed by the ancient world as the man's property.

The servant offers to "pay all" which probably is not possible. The man's begging and pleading catch the king's compassion and he forgives the servant the entire debt. This is grace from the king: blessing in the face of positive demerit.

One talent was worth about 6,000 denarii; the 10,000 talents the man owed was equivalent to 60,000,000 denarii. A denarii was worth 16 *as*, and a day's wage for a laborer was 10–12 *as*. If it is assumed he made 12 *as* per day, and every *as* earned every day was devoted to paying the 60,000,000 denarii debt, leaving nothing for himself and his family, it would take him 5,000,000 days, or 13,689 years to pay the debt; but one must provide for family. Even if he was a tax-collector and grossly overcharged the tax-payers he could not pay off the debt. Even if we assumed the man earned one talent yearly (6,000 denarii per year), an enormous sum, it would take him more than a lifetime to pay the debt. That is the point of the story: the man owed an unpayable debt.

The man goes to a fellow servant who owed him one hundred denarii, a trivial amount compared to the 10,000 talent debt the man owed. In first century AD Rome a secretary made fifteen denarii a month; a messenger nine denarii a month; a private in the army twenty denarii a month; a centurion about 300 denarii a month.[1] Obviously the one hundred denarii debt could have been paid within a reasonable time. A male slave (for general domestic labor) sold for 500–1500 denarii, so if the servant owing 100 denarii

---

[1] [http://www.ancientcoins.biz/pages/economy].

had slaves, he might have sold one and paid the debt.

That the unforgiving servant would not forgive speaks to his character, and probably his extravagant lifestyle—every little bit was counted as necessary. Debtors were put in jail to encourage relatives or business partners to pay the debt.

The fellow servants saw that the man had put his own debtor into prison, and were greatly distressed. When the king hears, he rescinds his previous forgiveness and puts the unforgiving servant into prison to be tortured until the 10,000 talent debt was paid; but the debt was so huge it could never be paid.

The parable of the unpayable debt was told to teach one point: believers are to forgive because they have been forgiven. The believer was a sinner with an unforgiveable debt owed to God, the debt of the crime of sin. God in grace paid the sinner's debt—Jesus' propitiation of God for sin—and in grace God accepted the sinner's faith in Christ as Savior and forgave the debt and saved the sinner. The sins one person might commit against another are significantly lesser debts than the one that was owed to God. Just as God forgave the believer his/her unpayable debt, the believer is to forgive those who sin against him, or her.

Having explained the point of the parable, an application made be made. Every unsaved sinner owes God an unpayable debt. No sinner can earn sufficient merit to pay the debt. Only Christ's merit, applied by faith, accepted by grace, can forgive the debt. If the debt is not paid in this lifetime, then the sinner will suffer an eternity of separation from God, because the unsaved sinner has no merit and can earn no merit to pay the unpayable debt of sin. Suffering does not accrue merit, because it is just punishment due the crime of sin. Only Christ paid the debt for the crime of sin. Only his merit is sufficient to forgive the sinner's debt. The sinner must be saved during this mortal life from the penalty due sin by God's grace through the sinner's faith in Christ the Savior. After physical death the unsaved suffer the second death: eternal separation from God.

The followers of Jesus forgive because they have been forgiven; they have experienced forgiveness of their unpayable debt owed to God for their sins. They have been extended grace so they extend grace to others.

Matthew Nineteen

Translation Matthew 19:1–2

1 And so it was when Jesus had finished these sayings, he left Galilee and came to the area of Judea beyond the Jordan. 2 And great crowds followed him, and he healed them there.

EXPOSITION

The date is mid-March, AD 32. The new year of AD 33 will begin March 20, with Passover fourteen days later on the evening of April 2, AD 33. Jesus has raised Lazarus from the dead, John 11:1–44, at the village of Bethany, just east of Jerusalem. From there Jesus went to Ephraim, John 11:54, a village about twelve miles north of Jerusalem, on the main road going to Galilee and the Lake. From Ephraim he traveled to Sychar, but then turned northwest into west Galilee. In Galilee he gathered all the disciples not with him when Lazarus was raised.[1] Here Matthew 19:1 picks up the story. Jesus went east along the Galilee-Samaria border into Perea, then south to Jericho. Jesus is on his way to Jerusalem for the AD 33 Passover, where he will be crucified, buried, and resurrected. He will return to Galilee after his resurrection.

On this final trip to Jerusalem, there is some question as to the route Jesus took. Did he travel down the path on the west bank of the Jordan River to Jericho, or down the path on the east bank, through Perea, and across the Jordan to Jericho?

The question is resolved when we know there were two cities named Jericho. There was the original Old Jericho near the Jordan River, and there was New Jericho about two miles west of Old Jericho. There was a road running south from Scythopolis along the west bank of the Jordan which passed through Samaria into Judea and terminated at New Jericho. Then there was a footpath running east out of Scythopolis, to the Jordan River, where it crossed into Perea, and ran south along the east back of the Jordan to a crossing opposite Old Jericho. Matthew 20:29; Mark 10:46; and Luke 18:35; 19:1 tell us Jesus passed through Old Jericho and then New Jericho, which means he came out of Perea into Judea at the Jordan River crossing a few miles west of Old Jericho.

---

[1] See my commentary *John 1–12*.

Matthew Nineteen

So, after leaving Galilee, Jesus went through Scythopolis, crossed the Jordan east of Scythopolis into Perea, traveled south through Perea, then entered Judea by crossing the Jordan east of Old Jericho. The scriptures below are in this order of travel, with explanatory comments in brackets.

Luke 17:11, And it happened in the going up to Jerusalem, that he was passing through the midst of Samaria and Galilee. [That is, he traveled along the border running between Samaria and Galilee.]

Matthew 19:1, And so it was when Jesus had finished these sayings [Luke 18:1–14], he left Galilee and [went to Scythopolis and] came to the area of Judea [east of Scythopolis] beyond the Jordan [into Perea]. (Parallel passage: Mark 10:1, "And he left there [Galilee] and came [to Scythopolis and into] into the region of Judea [east of Scythopolis], and beyond the Jordan [into Perea]. And, again, crowds came together to him. And as he was accustomed, again he taught them."

Mark 10:32, Now they were on the way [into Perea, going south], ascending to Jerusalem [Jerusalem is at 2500 ft. above sea level and the Jordan River valley is below sea level.], and Jesus was leading them.

Mark 10:46, And they came to [Old] Jericho [by crossing the Jordan into Judea.]

Luke 18:35, Then it happened as he drew near to [old] Jericho, a certain blind person was sitting beside the road, begging. [Jesus healed him].

Matthew 20:29, As they were leaving [Old] Jericho, a large crowd followed Him. Mark 10:46, And as He was leaving [Old] Jericho with His disciples and a large crowd, Bartimaeus (the son of Timaeus), a blind beggar [Matthew says 2 blind men; Mark mentions only one], was sitting by the road. [Jesus healed them.]

Luke 19:1, And having entered [New Jericho], he was passing through [new] Jericho [about two miles west of Old Jericho and he met Zacchaeus].

Matthew 19:1 continues the story of Jesus as he and his disciples are leaving Galilee and traveling through Perea, to 20:29 where they are leaving Old Jericho.

Translation Matthew 19:3–6

3 And Pharisees came to him, putting him to the test, and saying, "Is it lawful for a man to divorce his wife on any grounds?" 4 Now answering he said, "Have you not read, that he who created them, from the beginning made them male and female, 5 and said, 'On account of this, a man will leave the father and the mother and will be joined with his wife, and the two will become one flesh'? 6 So that, no longer are they two, but one flesh. What therefore God united let not man separate."

EXPOSITION

Why a man might divorce his wife was a contested issue in Israel. According to the then-contemporary standards, a man was expected to remain with his first wife—the wife of his youth—and the majority did. But the right of a man to divorce his wife was unquestioned. The cause for which divorce was allowed was the issue, and the people were divided.

The ground of the debate was Deuteronomy 24:1, where Moses recognizes divorce will happen and states a reason for which a man might want to divorce his wife: "[if] it happens that she finds no favor in his eyes because he has found some uncleanness in her." The debate centered in a definition of "no favor" and "uncleanness."

The form of the Pharisees' question, "on any grounds" expressed the dominant view, in which a bad meal, or because a man saw someone he liked better, or some other trivial reason, could be used as grounds for divorce. The opposing view restricted divorce to real cases of ritual or physical uncleanness. The Pharisees reasoned that whatever Jesus might answer he would offend many people.

I discussed this issue in depth at Matthew 5:31–32, and please review that discussion. Perhaps the Pharisees had been waiting for an opportunity since hearing that "Sermon on the Mount" teaching.

Jesus' answer here is that God had made human kind as a race of two genders: male and female. Jesus is paraphrasing Genesis 1:27, "in the image of God created he him; male and female created he them" (KJV). God created human kind in the person of Adam. Adam the male had everything required for God to make the female gender. God took "one from his side" (usually translated "rib") and from those cells created the female gender, body and soul.

Marriage joined together what God had created: the union of one male with one female in a heterosexual relationship.

Jesus' statement in v. 5 must be carefully read. The reason God "made them male and female" was for marriage: "a man will leave the father and the mother and will be joined with his wife." This doesn't mean everyone must be married, but that marriage is a two gender-based relationship intended by God as part of the usual course of human life.

God made human beings as a two gender race to be fit for one another, and the outworking of that "comparable helper" (Genesis 2:20) relationship between the two genders is the basis for all other societal relationships. One might add that marriage as a two gender relationship is normal and expected, since the vast majority of men and women are in a male-and-female marriage relationship. This state is so normal and expected that one of the Hebrew words for man, *'îsh*, is the word for husband, and the feminine equivalent, *'ishshā* is the word for wife. These words, *'îsh* and *'ishshā*, man and woman, husband and wife, are the words used in Genesis 2:24, which Jesus quotes in v. 5.

The result of marriage is that one male and one female unite in marriage to become "one flesh." Ancient interpretations viewed the one flesh relationship as the sexual union of husband and wife. France points out "in the Genesis context the 'one flesh' image derives from the creation of the woman out of man's side to be 'bone of my bones and flesh of my flesh'; in marriage that original unity is restored."[1] The view makes "one flesh" the permanent joining of a man and a woman in marriage, v. 6.

I have an alternate view, based on the description of marriage. The one-flesh relationship refers to an exclusive loyalty covenant between the one man-one woman. The man exercised his authority to change his loyalty from his father and mother, Genesis 2:24; Matthew 19:5, to his wife. He joined with his wife in a covenant, and it was that covenant that made them one-flesh. It is the covenant marriage relationship between a man and a woman that makes them "one flesh," not specifically the sexual component of that relationship.

The exclusive loyalty of the one-flesh covenant is exercised in

---

[1] France, *Matthew*, NICNT, 717.

the moral, spiritual, intellectual, emotional, and physical aspects of the marriage. Morally the two are committed for a lifetime to one another and no one else. Spiritually they are committed to practicing righteousness in their daily lives. Intellectually they are partners in the marriage, sharing the decision-making process and carrying out the decisions made. Emotionally they are committed to supporting and sharing their innermost thoughts and feelings with each other and no one else. Physically they are intimate with one another and no one else.

What, then, it a biblical marriage?

> The union of one male with one female in a permanent, monogamous, heterosexual relationship, male and female being joined together by an exclusive loyalty covenant that commits them to each other and none else, solemnized by a culturally suitable public declaration of that exclusive loyalty commitment.

What is the exclusive loyalty covenant of a biblical marriage?

> A biblical marriage is an exclusive loyalty covenant between one man and one woman—what the Bible describes as a one-flesh relationship. The terms and conditions of the exclusive loyalty covenant require the man and woman commit their physical, emotional, and spiritual being to the benefit and enjoyment of one another and none else. The marriage covenant does not exclude friendly relationships with others, but it does exclude commitments, especially sexual and emotional commitments, that are of the same order as those composing the marriage relationship.

When a man and woman marry they become two individuals joined together in what God intended to be a permanent union. Since this is what God intended, according to Jesus, divorce is not to be permitted under any circumstances, except the breaking of the one flesh union by breaking the exclusive loyalty covenant through a sexual union with another. Divorce, says Jesus, could happen, but in view of God's will for his creation of man as male and female, it should not happen.

Translation Matthew 19:7–9

7 They say to him, "Why then did Moses command to give a certificate of divorce, and to send her away?" 8 He says to them, "For the hardness of your heart, Moses permitted you to divorce

your wives, but from the beginning it was not this way. 9 Now I say to you, whoever shall divorce his wife, except for sexual immorality, and shall marry another, commits adultery; and he who marries her that is put away, commits adultery."

EXPOSITION

Jesus corrects their point of view. Moses did not command, he permitted. As discussed in chapter 5, Moses is regulating an existing practice for the benefit of the woman, to give her legal protection when she is unwanted and forced from her home by the divorcing husband.

An unwillingness to live godly lives and work out problems with righteous solutions is the cause of divorce. In fairness to those who are being divorced but want to continue in marriage, I must point out that sometimes one party is so determined to dissolve the marriage that the other party becomes an unwilling victim of this social violence. In all cases a writ of divorce is the protection that frees the divorced person from certain legal consequences of that act of violence.

A divorce for any cause but sexual immorality causes the divorcing spouse to commit adultery, and the one who marries the divorced spouse commits adultery. The onus is on the man who divorces his wife for any other cause. The "sexual immorality" clause recognizes that a sexual union apart from the marriage sexual union breaks the original one flesh relationship. Can it be fixed? Of course. Conviction of wrong doing, confession, repentance, and forgiveness are part of the Christian life. However, if one spouse defiles and breaks the one flesh relationship by establishing a one flesh relation with another person, the other spouse is freed from that marriage.

What about the case when one spouse commits the act of divorce against the spouse who is unwilling to divorce? My opinion is that the victim of divorce is not guilty and is free to remarry. I consider this circumstance to be the same as when an unbelieving spouse leaves his/her believing spouse: the believer is "not under bondage," i.e., not bound to the marriage, in such cases, 1 Corinthians 7:15.

Another consideration is this. In ancient culture, especially in Jewish culture, only the man could initiate divorce, but the woman could go to court and force her husband to divorce her. This is the point of view of "whoever marries her who is divorced commits adultery," meaning the woman who forces a divorce is guilty. This agrees with Mark 10:11–12, "whoever divorces his wife" and "if a woman divorces her husband." In Mark Jesus teaches the one who commits the act of divorce, or forces the act of divorce, is the party who commits adultery in remarriage. If this is the case, then the spouse who has suffered the social violence of divorce against himself or herself is free to marry without the new marriage being considered adultery.

Translation Matthew 19:10–12

10 His disciples say to him, "If this is the case of the man with the wife, it is better not to marry." 11 But he said to them, "Not all receive this saying, but only to whom it has been given. 12 For there are eunuchs who were born thus from their mother's womb, and there are eunuchs who were made eunuchs by men, and there are eunuchs who made eunuchs of themselves on account of the kingdom of the heavens. The one being able to receive it, let him receive it."

EXPOSITION

The disciples expressed anxiety over Jesus' ruling on divorce. I doubt they were thinking of divorce their spouses. They were probably thinking that in cases of gross incompatibility divorce might be desirable, perhaps even needful. In this sense, v. 10 is practically an advertisement for 2 Corinthians 6:14, "Do not be unequally yoked with unbelievers," as it is with 1 Corinthians 7:12–13, 15, "If any brother has a wife who does not believe, and she is willing to live with him, let him not divorce her. And a woman who has a husband who does not believe, if he is willing to live with her, let her not divorce him. But if the unbeliever departs, let him depart; a brother or a sister is not under bondage in such cases." However, the 1 Corinthians passage is the same as in Moses: it is by permission, for God desires the unbeliever to be saved.

Jesus' answer in v. 11 may be understood in three ways. In view one, Jesus may be saying that not everyone in the kingdom is capable of meeting this standard of behavior. This kingdom rule sets a high ethical standard. Christians are saved sinners with varying levels of spiritual maturity. Some may not be able to maintain the standard, though all should. This does not mean some are a spiritual elite, just that this standard requires a certain level of spiritual maturity in order to maintain the rule.

In view two, Jesus' answer responds to the disciples' comment "it is better not to marry." Some people, says this view, are not spiritually equipped to marry. The discussion of "eunuchs" makes sense in this view. However, this means when Jesus says, "All cannot accept this saying, but only those to whom it has been given" he is referring to what the disciples said, not what he has said.

The better view (three) is that Jesus is referring to v. 6, "What therefore God united let not man separate." Some men can accept this saying and not marry, making themselves eunuchs for the sake of the kingdom of heaven. Let him who is able to live in an unmarried state, that he may devote himself to the kingdom, accept this saying. Although view one is true, and proven true in Christian experience, interpretively the third view seems to be the better view.

Translation Matthew 19:13-15

13 Then little children were brought to him, that he might lay hands on them, and pray, but the disciples rebuked them. 14 But Jesus said, "Let the little children come to me and do not forbid them; for of such kind is the kingdom of the heavens." 15 And having laid hands on them, he departed from there.

EXPOSITION

"Then" changes the scene away from the confrontation with the Pharisees, linking it in time to the next thing that happened Unlike the religious teachers of Jesus' day, or the religious teachers of other times and places—even today—Jesus liked little children, expressing a great interest in them. The word "little" can mean very small, but it was also used of older children.

The disciples stopped the parents, because they believed a religious teacher should not be bothered by children (see comments 18:4). Jesus corrected them (Mark says Jesus was displeased with this action by his disciples). Two thoughts seem evident. One, the "be converted and become as a little child" view of salvation seems appropriate here. Two, literal little children were of value to Jesus, are of value to the kingdom, and can be saved. Jesus did as the parents requested. From there he left for somewhere else.

Translation Matthew 19:16-22

16 And look, one having come to him, said, "Teacher, what good shall I do that I might have eternal life?" 17 But he said to him, "Why are you asking me about what is good? Only one is good. Now, if you desire to enter into life, keep the commandments." 18 He says to him, "Which?" And Jesus said, "you will not murder; you will not commit adultery; you will not steal; you will not bear false witness; 19 honor the father and the mother; and, you will love your neighbor as yourself." 20 The young man says to him, "All these things I have kept. What yet lack I?" 21 Jesus said to him, "If you desire to be perfect, go, sell your possessions, and give to the poor, and you will have treasure in the heavens; and come follow me." 22 But the young man having heard this saying, he went away grieving, for he was a person having many possessions.

TRANSLATION NOTE

The Byzantine texts of v. 16 have the word "good" as an adjective modifying "teacher." The word is absent from most Alexandrian and Western texts.[1] The word would seem to have been brought in from the parallel accounts of Mark 10:17 and Luke 18:18. The scribe importing "good teacher" into Matthew from Mark and Luke must also change v. 17. We have seen this kind of scribal "improvement" before at 18:11. The Matthew text is understandable without importing "good."

EXPOSITION

The question seems genuine. This person genuinely wanted to know if he was on the path to eternal life. By "eternal life" he meant that after physical death his soul would continue forever in heaven in the company of YHWH and the patriarchs.

The man isn't looking for a prophet, still less a messiah. He calls on Jesus as a teacher of the Law, as he would any scribe or Pharisee. He had probably asked this question many times of many teachers, and received a variety of answers. Yet the man did not have the assurance he was seeking.

The young man asks "what good shall I do." The word "good" is the Greek *agathós*, and in this context might be translated benevolent: "what benevolent thing shall I do to merit eternal life." In the theology of the day, the rich were supposed to earn merit

---

[1] Metzger, *Textual*, 39.

for heaven by using their wealth to benefit the poor. Undoubtedly this man had used some of his wealth for the poor, but he wanted to know if he needed to do more. That is the problem with earning salvation through good works. How many good works are necessary to merit eternal life? The biblical answer is "none," because only the merit of Jesus Christ saves the sinner.

In reply, Jesus asks the man a question: "Why are you asking me about what is good?" The primary emphasis is on the word "why" with a lesser emphasis on the word "me." "*Why* are you asking me about what is good?" If the man was seeking a true answer, an answer that would cause him to have eternal life, then the source of the answer must be considered. If eternal life is something to be merited on the basis of doing good, then the definition of the good that merits eternal life must come from the person who can give eternal life. What are God's rules, what are God's values, concerning "good?" That is the point of Jesus' question. To put it another way, Jesus is asking, "Do you recognize me as the person who decides why someone should merit eternal life?" It was because no one whom he had previously asked the question had the authority to give a definitive answer that he kept seeking an answer.

Jesus tries to help the man come to the understanding that only God could provide the answer. "Only one is good." Without doubt the young man would have understood "only one is good" to mean YHWH. We may infer Jesus is saying, "You must recognize my answer is an answer from YHWH." Otherwise Jesus is just another teacher with another answer. It is, perhaps, too much for Jesus to require the man to recognize Jesus as YHWH incarnate, but the man should acknowledge that Jesus is informed by YHWH in order to give the right answer. Jesus is not merely a teacher; he is, at the least, a prophet sent by YWHW to reveal YWHW, or he is the one anointed by YWHW (the messiah) to authoritatively give the word of YHWH.

Jesus tells the man to keep the commandments. If one might keep the commandments perfectly throughout life, then he/she merits eternal life. Jesus is not saying works merit salvation. Jesus knows "there is none righteous, no not one," Psalm 14:1 (Romans 3:10). Jesus knows no person is capable of keeping the law perfectly (except himself). The question has the same design as the previous question: to make the man think about his condition. If only one is good, then the man cannot do any good thing to merit eternal life. If meriting eternal life requires keeping the commandments—not merely habitually but continuously, perfectly—then no one can merit eternal life. If the man can gain that spiritual perception, then he will find the answer. What is required is faith in the only one who can give the merit required to gain eternal life.

But the man is certain he has already kept the commandments, so he asks, "Which?" in order to justify himself. Jesus lists five of the Ten Words, Exodus 19:12–16, and summarizes the sixth (shall not covet) by using Leviticus 19:18. The man replies, "I have kept these; what else." No reply from Moses' Law would give the man the assurance he sought. The Law cannot give righteousness—not because of a fault in the Law, but because man the sinner cannot perfectly keep the law. But the man lacked the spiritual perception required to know this truth. Jesus could have listed all 613 commandments[1] and the man would have replied the same, with the same lack of assurance of eternal life.

In v. 21 Jesus is not saying that impoverishing one's self is the way to merit eternal life. Jesus is answering one person's question, "What yet lack I?" Good works and keeping the law gave the man no assurance of meriting eternal life. Jesus cuts to the heart of the man's problem: a lack of faith. The man's riches are the symptom, not the problem. A superficial reading of the Old Testament will lead one to believe that being rich is a sign that you are pleasing God. But the same Bible that says "the blessings of YHWH makes one rich" (Proverbs 10:22) also says "there is none righteous, no not one."

The young man trusted in his riches as a sign God was blessing him for his righteousness, the righteousness he had established by keeping the commandments. To rid himself of his riches was contrary to his religious beliefs, beliefs that then and still guides Judaism and many other religions (including such as the false "Prosperity Gospel" of apostate Christianity). "Faith" in these belief systems is that material blessing means I am alright with God, for look how he is blessing me materially. God allows men to be rich that they might use their wealth for the good of others. That was the rich man's problem at Luke 12:16–21, and at 16:19–25. They

---

[1] Chill, *The Mitzvot.*

didn't use their wealth in righteous ways. That was the young man's problem.

When Jesus uses the word "perfect" he means that in order to have the true righteousness which results in eternal life, then the man must stop trusting in his old faith, his riches, and put all his faith in God, without the prop of material success. The perfection the man will obtain is spiritual maturity in the faith he is seeking: to trust God alone in this life and for eternal life. A necessary part of that necessary faith is following Jesus, who, although a "good" teacher, was obviously an impoverished teacher, meaning that (in general) those who were following Jesus during his public ministry were themselves poor in material possessions.

Trusting in wealth, or parents, or heritage, or some good or religious work or works is not trusting in God. We have to get rid of our trust in those things—sometimes we must rid ourselves of those things themselves—and follow Jesus. In v. 22 we see the heart of this young man. He was seeking to be justified in what he thought was a correct faith: doing righteous works to attain a level of righteousness that merited eternal life. His riches were a sign to him he was succeeding. To rid himself of his riches was to acknowledge that his faith, his works, and his riches did not merit eternal life, as he had believed. "Treasure in heaven" was the goal he was seeking, but the way to attain that treasure was foreign to his presuppositions. So, he went away sorrowful.

Translation Matthew 19:23–26

23 Then Jesus said to His disciples, "Truly, I say to you, that a rich man with difficulty will enter the kingdom of the heavens. 24 And again I say to you, it is easier for a camel to pass through the eye of a needle, than a rich man to enter into the kingdom of God." 25 Now having heard this, the disciples were greatly astonished, saying, "Who then is able to be saved?" 26 But having looked on them, Jesus said to them, "With men this is impossible, but with God all things are possible."

EXPOSITION

In the religious view of the day material success was a sign God was blessing your life and faith. Jesus says, v. 23, that when one has riches one tends to trust in riches in order to make his way in the world, keep him safe from trials and persecutions, and help him do good works in order to merit heaven. Jesus' point is that faith in one's self creates self-righteousness, which keeps the sinner from the spiritual poverty Jesus can fill with his own righteousness (blessed the poor in spirit, 5:3). Trust in one's self is not merely the opposite of trust in God, it is antithetical to trust in God.

Verse 24 is an illustration only. In the Middle Ages (9th century) someone invented a gate in the wall, colloquially named the "eye of the needle," to explain the verse. But v. 24 is only an illustration of the spiritual poverty needed for salvation. There was no "eye of the needle" gate which was so low and narrow one had to remove all baggage from the camel for it to walk on its knees and squeeze through. If there was such a gate, why not use one of the many larger gates?

Jesus is repeating a saying, similar to others then current, to describe an impossible circumstance. The disciple's understood the illustration to mean that it is impossible for a rich person to enter the kingdom (whereas, if there was such a gate, then pointing to it would indicate poverty was the key to entering heaven, which it isn't). As long as a person trusts in his riches, versus trusting in God, he cannot enter the kingdom.

That Jesus "looked on them," v. 26, was unusual. The phrase occurs in two circumstances: this parable (here and Mark 10:27), and the (different) parable of Luke 20:9–19. Jesus looked on the disciples to focus them on what he would next say, to impress them to listen. (Whereas at Luke 20:17 he is evaluating his opponents.) The disciples' view of God was too small. They thought if riches could keep a person out of the kingdom, then who could be saved. Without doubt Peter, his brother Andrew, and their business partners James and John, were among the rich. They were rich enough to walk about Israel with Jesus for months, leaving their business in the hands of employees, returning only occasionally to make sure all was well. If riches kept one out of the kingdom, then how could they enter? A rich man entering the kingdom is possible with God, because God's work of grace will put riches and faith in proper perspective. Most of us are rich because we have enough to meet our needs and satisfy some of our desires. That is something to keep in mind as we read this passage. In whom, or in what, do you have faith?

Translation Matthew 19:27–30

27 Then Peter answering said to him, "Look, we left all and

followed you; what then will be to us?" 28 Now Jesus said to them, "Truly I say to you, that you having followed me, in the restoration, when the son of man will sit down upon his throne of glory, you also will sit on twelve thrones, judging the twelve tribes of Israel. 29 And everyone who has left houses, or brothers or sisters, or father or mother, or wife, or children, or lands, for my name's sake, a hundredfold will receive, and will inherit eternal life." [v. 30 moved to chapter 20]

EXPOSITION

Of course, Peter, and the others, had not left all to follow Jesus. Peter's fishing business was still at work supporting the business's many families, and probably also contributing to the welfare of the twelve, and Jesus, as they went about the country preaching the kingdom.

But one of their motivations for "leaving all" was the expected reward for joining with the messiah in his kingdom. Even as late as the day of the ascension, Acts 1:6, they were thinking about their place in the kingdom. Pentecost put an end to that point of view, as the Holy Spirit refocused them to their evangelistic and ecclesiastical missions. But at the time of Matthew 18:27 their mind was on their possible future with the one they had begun to believe was the messiah.

That is why they were always discussing which of them would have the superior position in the kingdom. That is why Peter asks his question: what will they gain the by following Jesus? Jesus' answer is far reaching. They will receive the kingdom and share equally in it with all other members. Paul answered this question for all believers by saying that we are joint-heirs with Christ. An answer had already been given in the Sermon on the Mount: the meek, those who follow Jesus as Savior, inherit the earth.

The twelve have a special place of honor: judging the tribes of Israel. This probably refers to the judgment immediately following the second advent: who among national ethnic Israel will enter into Messiah's Davidic Kingdom? That judgment is spoken of at Ezekiel 20:33–38.

The chapter break is unfortunate, for the parable of 20:1–16 is explanatory of 19:30, which I have moved to the next chapter.

Matthew Twenty

Translation Matthew 19:30—20:7

19:30 "But many first will be last, and last first. 20:1 For the kingdom of the heavens is like a man, the master of a house, who went out at dawn to hire workers for his vineyard. 2 Now having agreed with the workers for a denarius a day, he sent them into his vineyard. 3 And having gone out about nine o'clock, and seeing others standing unemployed in the marketplace, 4 and he said to them, 'You also go into the vineyard, and whatever is right I will give you.' 5 And they went. Now again having gone out about noon and three o'clock, he did likewise. 6 And about six o'clock, having gone out, he found others standing, and says to them, 'Why stand you here unemployed all the day?' 7 They say to him, 'Because no one hired us.' He says to them, 'You also go into the vineyard, and whatever is right you will receive.' "

TRANSLATION NOTES

In vv. 3, 5, and 6, I have changed the expression of the time of day to modern time equivalents. The third, sixth, ninth, and eleventh hours of the day are 9:00 a.m., 12:00 p.m., 3:00 p.m., and 6:00 p.m., respectively. These are approximations, because people told time by looking at the position of the sun in the sky. For example, when the sun was halfway between dawn and its zenith, it was halfway between dawn and noon, thus the third hour of the day, or 9:00 a.m.

In v. 1, modern versions (NKJV, HCSB, NIV, NLT) interpret *oikodespótēs* as "landowner" because of the context. However, the word is a compound of *oíkos*, house, and *despótēs*, a lord, despot, master. The translation is "master of a house."[1]

In v. 1 the translation "at dawn" is from *prōí* is "an adverb of time."[2] The word means early in the morning, at dawn.

In vv. 3 and 6 I have translated *argós*, "not at work, idle, not employed, inactive," as "unemployed."[3] Other versions translate "idle" or "doing nothing." They weren't lazy (idle, doing nothing),

---

[1] Zodhiates, *WSDNT*, s. v. "3617."

[2] Ibid., s. v. "4404."

[3] Ibid., s. v. "692."

they were waiting for someone to employ them, and concerned enough about working to wait all day for any kind of work.

In v. 7 the phrase, "and whatever is right you will receive" is not in some manuscripts.

EXPOSITION

The parable of the workers begins with 19:30, "But many first will be last, and last first." The parable of the workers is an illustration of 19:30 and intended to explain the truth expressed to Peter in 19:28–29, in response to his question in 19:27. The point of the parable is seen in 20:8–16, which is that all the sons of the kingdom have an equal share in the blessings of the kingdom.

One must not think of a "share" in the kingdom as a portion of the whole. Each member of the kingdom shares in the whole equally with all other members. The entire kingdom and its material and spiritual benefits belong in whole to each member.

We could consider this parable an illustration of how God acts in grace, giving to all an equal reward for labor in the kingdom, whether or not they were members at the beginning or came into the kingdom at a later time. The point would be that Peter and the others did not have an advantage, i.e., they would not receive a larger share of the benefits.

One might also see this parable in an eschatological sense, that all kingdom members, regardless of their experiences in the world—when they were saved, how long they labored and under what conditions—receive the same measure of grace and reward. The person saved moments before Jesus returns to reign will receive the same reward as those who bore trials and persecutions and martyrdom in the years intervening between the first and second advents. Is it not lawful for God to do what he chooses to do with that which is his?

In the parable the vineyard owner goes out at dawn to hire workers to work in his vineyard. He agrees to pay them a denarius as a day's wage. A denarius was a Roman coin equal in value to sixteen *assárion* (the Greek name; the Roman name was *as*). Think of the denarius as a dime, which is equal in value to 10 pennies, whereas one denarius equals sixteen *as*.

Later, at 9:00 a.m., 12:00 p.m., 3:00 p.m., and 6:00 p.m., the master of the house hires more laborers, promising to pay what was right for their labor. The laborers' hired at these later hours probably expected a fair proportion of a denarius for their labor. The point in hiring throughout the day is that the owner continued to need workmen, even at the latest hour. If viewed eschatologically, the owner of the vineyard, Jesus the messianic king, continues to bring people into his vineyard, the kingdom, right up to the last opportunity.

Translation Matthew 20:8–16

8 "Now evening having come, the owner of the vineyard said to his manager, 'Call the workmen, and give them the wages, beginning from the last unto the first.' 9 And those hired about 6:00 p.m., having come, they received a denarius each. 10 And the first having come, they thought they would receive more, and they received, they also, a denarius each. 11 But having received, they complained against the master of the house, 12 saying, 'These the last have worked one hour, and you have made them equal to us, those having borne the burden of the day and the scorching heat.' 13 But answering to one of them he said, 'Friend, I do not wrong you. Did you not agree with me for a denarius? 14 Take what is yours and go. For I have chosen to give to this last as also to you. 15 Is it not lawful for me to do what I will with that which is mine? Or is your eye evil because I am good?' 16 So the last will be first, and the first last."

TRANSLATION NOTE

In v. 8 the word translated "owner" is *kúrios*, "lord, master, sir." The lord or master of the vineyard is the owner.

In v. 16 the ending phrase in some manuscripts, "for many are called, but few chosen" was most likely imported by a scribe from 22:14, so as to summarize this parable. The phrase is not needed, and if removed the ending repeats the beginning, 19:30. I chose not to include the phrase.

EXPOSITION

The fulcrum on which the parable turns to make its point is the amount paid to the workers. Day laborers earned between ten to twelve *as* for a day's work. The owner was paying a denarius, equal to sixteen *as*. The amount was extravagant for those who had worked all day, more so for those who worked less than a full day.

The sovereign God does with his own as he chooses. He gives the same promises to all who believe and are faithful, regardless of their circumstances. The lesson here is quite simple: God rewards faithfulness. In the parable every worker was faithful to the work, so every worker was equally rewarded.

Verse 16 *does not* establish a priority system for members of the kingdom. That view is contrary to the lesson of the parable. The point of v. 16 is that all are treated according to God's valuation. In the world the last is always last and the first is always first. Some felt they should be first in rank, such as Peter and the apostles (at this particular moment in their life). God rewards faithfulness, not worldly priorities of rank and privilege.

In the kingdom everyone is ranked according to faithfulness in worship, fellowship, obedience, and service toward God in Christ. In application, there are many who are viewed as of great importance to the kingdom by others, but in heaven we may find the faithful church janitor lauded more than the pastor others see as greater because of his position, but who was not as faithful to his charge as the janitor. If viewed eschatologically those last saved are soon to experience the second advent kingdom, while those first saved bear the "heat" of contrary worldly circumstances while waiting a long time for the second advent and the inauguration of the kingdom on earth. They first are in a sense last.

Translation Matthew 20:17–19

17 As Jesus was going up to Jerusalem, he took the twelve disciples aside, and on the way said to them, 18 "Look, we go up to Jerusalem, and the son of man will be betrayed to the chief priests and scribes; and they will condemn him to death, 19 and they will deliver him to the gentiles to mock and to scourge and to crucify; and the third day he will rise again."

EXPOSITION

In vv. 17–28 Jesus and the twelve are in Perea, walking south to the ford that crosses the Jordan River near Old Jericho.

This is the fourth time in Matthew's Gospel that Jesus predicts his crucifixion and resurrection (16:21; 17:12, 22–23). The reason Jesus takes the twelve aside is because the road is filled with people going to Jerusalem for the AD 33 Passover. The prediction is for the disciples alone.

Jesus has mentioned the betrayal before. The joint mention of chief priests and scribes under one definite article probably indicates Jesus has in mind an official condemnation by the religious leaders, i.e., by the ruling council, the Sanhedrin.

The detail concerning the gentiles is mentioned here for the first time. The reason the gentiles will become involved is because the Roman government reserved the right of execution to itself. The Jews could, and did, condemn people to death, but were required to turn them over to the Romans for execution. The local Roman government official, at this time Pontius Pilate, would conduct a brief examination, and if the death penalty was justified under Roman law he would carry out the execution.

Mocking was sometimes part of the execution process. Scourging was always part of the execution process, both as part of the punishment and to hasten death through blood loss, physical stress, and exhaustion. Execution could be by many means, but crucifixion was reserved for slaves, criminals and other undesirables—usually the worst offenders against the state. Roman citizens could not be crucified. Jesus says he will resurrect out from among the dead on the third day after the crucifixion was completed.

Translation Matthew 20:20–28

20 Then came to him the mother of the sons of Zebedee, with her sons, kneeling, and asking something from him. 21 Now he said to her, "What do you desire?" She says to him, "Say that these two sons of mine might sit, one on your right hand, one on your left hand, in your kingdom." 22 But Jesus answering said, "You know not what you ask. Are you able to drink the cup that I am about to drink?" They said to him, "We are able." 23 He says to them, "Indeed my cup you will drink. But to sit on my right hand and on the left, this is not mine to give, but to those for whom it has been prepared by my Father." 24 And having heard, the ten were indignant about the two brothers. 25 But Jesus, having called them, said, "You know that the rulers of the gentiles exercise dominion over them, and the great exercise authority over them. 26 It will not be so among you; but whoever among you may desire to become great, he will be your servant; 27 and whoever among you may desire to be first, he will be your servant; 28 even as the son of man came not to be served, but to serve, and to give his life a ransom for many."

TRANSLATION NOTE

The phrase "be baptized with the baptism that I am baptized with" in vv. 22 and 23 is "absent from early and good witnesses [manuscripts] representing several types of text [i.e., from several different sources].[1] In the Byzantine texts (used by the KJV/NKJV) the phrase appears to have been imported into Matthew from the parallel account in Mark 10:38, 39. Mark wrote for gentiles, but Matthew wrote for the Jews, to prove Jesus of Nazareth was their messiah. Baptism is a symbolic act representing different things depending on its historical-cultural context. For example, to Christians, baptism represents death and resurrection: the death of the old nature and birth of the new, born-again nature, Romans 6:4. To first century Jews baptism was a ritual used for symbolic cleansing from religious defilement. John's baptism was to symbolize genuine spiritual repentance, a use the religious leaders' didn't understand. The symbolic use of baptism to represent crucifixion and death in this passage would be confusing to the Jews. Considering these things, it seemed best not to include the phrase as part of Matthew's original text.

EXPOSITION

A comparison of the women said to be at the cross (Matthew 27:56; Mark 15:40; John 19:25) suggests the mother of Zebedee's sons, James and John, may have been Jesus' aunt, i.e., his mother's sister. See comments at Matthew 27:55–56.

In v. 20 the mother of Zebedee's sons comes to Jesus, bringing her sons with her, and assumes a respectful position. Her request need not be located chronologically after Jesus' prediction, vv. 18–19, but only sometime on the way to Jerusalem. Within the culture it would be natural for a parent, usually the father (he is in Galilee running the family business) but in this case the mother, to ask a favor for her sons. She believes in the Davidic Messianic kingdom and Jesus as the messianic king. She is trying to position her sons advantageously in the coming kingdom. If she was Jesus' aunt, then her request was very natural to the culture: the king's aunt asking a favor for the king's cousins.

To sit on the right and the left are the places of the highest honor. It may mean to be placed as second and third rulers of the kingdom. This is no little thing she is asking. We can applaud the

---

[1] Metzger, *Textual*, 42.

conviction concerning Jesus and the kingdom, and not judge too harshly their desire to occupy a prominent place in that kingdom.

Jesus asks if they are able to drink the cup. The term "cup" is used in several ways in the New Testament, but the most likely meaning agrees with both Old and New Testament uses as the cup of the wrath of God. In relationship to his messianic mission, the cup Jesus speaks of is his suffering and temporary spiritual separation from the father: his propitiation for sin when he becomes the sin-bearer, ending in his physical death. The cup of propitiation they could not suffer, but they could and did suffer persecution and death at the hands of those persecuting them for Jesus' sake. James was the first of the twelve to be martyred, Acts 12:1–2. John suffered torture (if the traditional accounts are accurate) and then exile on the island of Patmos. Indeed, they did not know what they were asking.

Their positive response is not so much arrogance as ignorance. They are so filled with anticipation of the glory of the kingdom that they cannot see the suffering Jesus continues to predict. They sincerely believed that they were ready to endure the immediate future, whatever that might be, in order to achieve their ultimate goal.

As to places at Jesus' right and left hand in the Davidic Messianic kingdom, Jesus says he cannot give those places, because his Father has already assigned them to others. Who those "others" might be is not explained in the New Testament. However, looking at John 17:24; Ephesians 2:19–22; 1 Peter 2:5, 9; Revelation 1:6; 5:10 the church, considered as a whole, would fit the description. Perhaps it is the New Testament church on one hand and national ethnic Israel on the other. Or perhaps all the Old Testament saints from Adam forward on one hand, all the New Testament saints from Pentecost to the second advent on the other.

Their fellow disciples, the ten, were indignant, though why is not stated. They would have accepted the right and propriety of the mother asking for her sons. Perhaps they were upset because James and John had been the first to try and gain what the others also wanted. Jesus uses the occasion to instruct all in the true spirit of the kingdom, that of lowliness and service. He uses himself as the quintessential example. Servant leadership is to help others achieve the best they are capable of in order to meet the goals you, as the leader, have set. The servant labors for others without inquiring into their merit for such aid, and without seeking recognition for his efforts, indicating the kind of lowliness and humility appropriate to a Christian leader.

Translation Matthew 20:29–34

29 And as they were going out from Jericho, a great crowd followed him. 30 And look, two blind men sitting beside the road, having heard that Jesus is passing by, cried out, saying, "Lord! Have mercy on us Son of David!" 31 Now the crowd rebuked them, that they should be silent; but all the more they cried, saying, "Lord! Have mercy on us Son of David!" 32 And having stopped, Jesus called them, and said, "What do you want I should do unto you?" 33 They said to him, "Lord, that our eyes may be opened." 34 Now having been moved with compassion, Jesus touched their eyes; and immediately they received sight, and they followed him.

EXPOSITION

Jesus is leaving Old Jericho on his way to New Jericho, which was about two miles further west, where several roads converged. As they are leaving Old Jericho two blind men hear that Jesus is passing by. Because they call out to Jesus by his royal title, "Son of David," I have translated *kúrios* "Lord," as befitting one calling out to a king.

The crowd tells the men to be quiet, but they cry out all the more. Jesus stops and calls them to himself. When they are brought to him he asks what they want. The request is straightforward, to be able to see. Jesus has compassion for their condition, touches them, and they are immediately healed. Jesus doesn't mention their faith, because their faith is evident in calling him by a messianic title, and their assurance that he can heal them.

They choose to follow him. No reason is stated, but their faith in him as messiah is the likely reason. When Jesus makes people see him for who he is, they want to follow him.

Matthew speaks of two men. Mark and Luke speak of one man, named Bartimaeus, because one man was the more vocal of the two, making him the one whom Mark and Luke write about. Matthew does not relate the story of Zacchaeus which occurs in New Jericho, but picks up the story as Jesus is nearing the Mount of Olives at Jerusalem.

Matthew Twenty-One

Translation Matthew 21:1–7

1 And when they drew near to Jerusalem and came to Bethphage at the Mount of Olives, then Jesus sent two disciples, 2 saying to them, "Go into the village, that is ahead of you, and immediately you will find a donkey having been tied, and a colt with her; having untied them, bring them to me. 3 And if anyone says anything to you, you will say, 'The Lord has need of them.' Now immediately he will send them." 4 Now this came to be that might be fulfilled that having been spoken by the prophet, saying, 5 "Tell the daughter of Zion, 'Behold, your King comes to you, meek, and mounted on a donkey, even upon a colt, the foal of a beast of burden.' " 6 Now the disciples having gone, and having done as Jesus commanded them, 7 they brought the donkey and the colt, lay their clothes upon them, and he sat on them.

TRANSLATION NOTE

The word *kúrios*, "sir, master, lord," is used in v. 3, "And if anyone says anything to you, you will say, 'The *kúrios* has need of them.' Now immediately he will send them." What is the correct translation of *kúrios* in the mouth of Jesus referring to himself? Not "sir," but "lord" or "master." To have his disciples say "The master has need of them" is plausible. Four reasons argue for "Lord." One, the word *kúrios* when spoken by Jesus most often refers to YHWH, in which case the proper translation would be "Lord." Two, it is plausible the person receiving this message could interpret *kúrios* as referring to YHWH: "You will say, 'The Lord [i.e., YHWH] has need of them.' " Three, the owner could have understood "Lord" as a reference to the messiah. Four, because Jesus is entering Jerusalem as the Davidic King and YHWH's Messiah, Zechariah 9:9, quoted in v. 5, then Jesus using *kúrios* in the sense of "Lord" to refer to himself is plausible. The best translation of *kúrios* here is "Lord."

EXPOSITION

The location of Bethphage, other than as described here, is not precisely known. Apparently Bethphage was on the road running from Bethany to Jerusalem to the Eastern gate, Bethphage being between Bethany and Jerusalem. The geographic description fits the location of Bethany. The village of Bethany was about "fifteen stadia" from Jerusalem (John 11:18). The Roman *stadion* was equivalent to a modern measurement of about 604.5 feet,[1] thus fifteen *stadia* was about 1.7 miles. Bethphage, then, if between Bethany and Jerusalem, was very close to Jerusalem. The Mount of Olives was a "Sabbath day's journey," Acts 1:12, from Jerusalem, about 3,000 feet (a mile is 5,280 feet).[2]

Jesus intends to fulfill the messianic prediction made by Zechariah 9:9, "Rejoice greatly, O daughter of Zion! Shout, O daughter of Jerusalem! Behold, your King is coming to you; he is just and having salvation, lowly and riding on a donkey, a colt, the foal of a donkey" (NKJV). A king on a horse signified war, a king on a donkey signified peace. This is the moment when Jesus publicly declares himself to be the messiah. If the crowd had understood the prophecy—not a warrior (cf. Zechariah 9:10) but a savior—they would not have rejected him a few days later.

Jesus prepares the two disciples beforehand to answer a challenge to a seeming theft of property. Some commentators believe this was prearranged and the response "The Lord has need of them," was the password to the owners to release the donkeys.[3] One question is sufficient to eliminate this issue: was Jesus the God-man a deceitful person? It is better to honor God and believe the Holy Spirit had prepared the owners for this moment, than that Jesus has prearranged the moment to imitate prophetic fulfillment. The disciples understood the moment, for they knew the prophecy, v. 7.

Verse 6 is what I call the narrative connective, seen often in the Bible. The disciples were told to go and get the animals, so they went as they were told and got the animals.

All the other Passover pilgrims are on foot, so by riding into Jerusalem Jesus is making a very noticeable statement. Matthew mentions, v. 7, the colt and the adult donkey, two animals. Zechariah was probably referring to the one animal on which messiah would ride, using Hebrew parallelism to refer to the animal twice. Matthew has not made a mistake and introduced a second animal, for the messiah can ride only one, and it is the colt, per

---

[1] Zodhiates, *WSDNT*, s. v. "4712."
[2] Bromiley, *ISBE*, s. v. "Sabbath Day's Journey."
[3] France, *Matthew*, NICNT, 776; Morris, *Matthew*, 520.

Zechariah. The foal's mother was brought along to calm the younger animal, which had never been ridden.

Translation Matthew 21:8–11

8 Now the very large crowd spread their clothes on the road; but others were cutting branches from the trees, and were spreading them on the road. 9 Then the crowds going before him, and those following, were crying out, saying, "Hosanna to the Son of David! Blessed the one coming in the name of the Lord! Hosanna in the highest!" 10 And he having come into Jerusalem, all the city was agitated, saying, "Who is this?" 11 Now the crowds said, "This is the prophet, Jesus, the one from Nazareth of Galilee."

EXPOSITION

The pilgrims on the way into the city for Passover also grasped the moment, laying out their clothes (cf. 2 Kings 9:13) and palm branches to pave the way for "the prophet, Jesus, the one from Nazareth of Galilee." Their hope was that Jesus was the messiah. Entering the city in accordance with Zechariah's prophecy was not proof, to them, that he was messiah, but a sign he might be messiah. The proof they were looking for was delivering them from Roman oppression. If Jesus disappointed that expectation, as he did, then they would turn against him, as they did.

Palm branches were signs of celebration, and there is some historical evidence palm branches were signs of victory.[1] People waved palm branches during the recitation of the *Hallel* psalms, Psalms 113–118, during major Jewish holidays, including Passover.[2] If this latter is correct, the intent was to welcome a militant messiah who would give them victory over the Romans occupying their land.

The word "hosanna" means "save now." The original meaning was lost and it had come to mean something corresponding to the modern "hurrah." This view of hosanna as verbal applause fits the ending sentence, "Hosanna in the highest," meaning "we are giving the highest praise to the Son of David," or, "praise the Son of David everywhere, even to the highest heaven."

The sentence "Blessed the one coming in the name of the Lord." is from Psalm 118:26, which has clear messianic notes. Jesus

---

[1] Morris, *Matthew*, 522, n. 2, citing 1 Maccabees 13:51; 1 Maccabees 10:7.
[2] Bock, *Context*, 147.

Matthew Twenty-one

is proclaimed as the one who comes representing YHWH. However, none of the gospels records the crowd directly acclaiming him as the messiah.

Their true understanding is seen in v. 11. Until Jesus performs some act or sign that the people will accept as distinctly messianic, then he remains the prophet Jesus from Nazareth. Of course, he had given every meaningful messianic sign for three years, but they had rejected him. That is to say, their leaders rejected him, so the people did also. In fairness to the people, they knew only what their leaders had told them about the messiah, because they did not have a personal copy of those scriptures; what excuse does the world have today, when the scriptures are available in print, eBook, and on the internet, in every language except a few remaining remote people groups, and carried by every missionary and Christian in the world.

Translation Matthew 21:12–17

12 And Jesus went into the temple court and cast out all those selling and buying in the temple, and overturned the tables of the money changers, and the seats of those selling the doves. 13 And he says to them, "It has been written, 'My house will be called a house of prayer,' but you have made it a den of robbers." 14 And blind and lame came to him in the temple, and he healed them. 15 But the chief priests and the scribes having seen the wonderful things that he did, and the children crying out in the temple court and saying, "Hosanna to the Son of David!" they were indignant, 16 and said to him, "Hear you what these say?" But Jesus says to them, "Yes. Did you never read, 'Out of the mouth of babes and sucklings you have prepared praise'?" 17 And having left them, he went out of the city to Bethany, and lodged there.

EXPOSITION

Matthew is more interested in the messianic implications of the events than a chronology, so he has compressed the story. Other Gospels tell us that after his entry into Jerusalem, Jesus left Jerusalem and went to Bethany. The next day he returned to Jerusalem and cleansed the temple.

This is the second time Jesus has cleansed the temple. He cleansed the temple at the beginning of his ministry, the AD 30 Passover. The first cleansing, John 2:14–17, was a warning. Three years later Jesus found the same conditions, but what had been a

Matthew Twenty-one

"market house," John 2:16, has become "a den of thieves." The nation had turned aside from true righteousness and worship, and had not changed their spiritual course, despite the clear word of God from their Messiah. After the first cleansing Jesus' authority was challenged; after this second cleansing the Jewish leaders actively sought an opportunity to kill him.

Selling animals and foreign money exchange was for the benefit of those Jews living outside Jerusalem and Palestine. Having traveled far, they arrived with no animals for sacrifice. Those living outside Palestine brought foreign currency. The temple tax, which all males twenty years old and upward must pay, was a half-*shekel* per person. The required coin was a Tyrian *stater* or a *tetradrachma*, which was worth two *shekels* (a *shekel* was a unit of weight), thus coins other than a *tetradrachma* needed to be exchanged. The money-changers performed this service, charging a small percentage as a fee. There is no indication in this narrative that the money changers or the animal sellers were charging inflated prices. (Compare Mark 11:15–17. See also Jeremiah 7:11.) Why, then, did this valuable service provoke Jesus to action?

The word translated "temple" is not *naós*, the temple proper, but *hierón*, the outer courts surrounding the *naós*. One *hierón* was reserved for males, another was reserved for women, and a third was reserved for gentiles. gentile proselytes were not allowed into the *naós*, so the *hierón* was the only place they could worship. By selling sacrificial animals and exchanging currency in the courts, gentile believers were prevented from their worship. In relation to Jewish worshipers, to get inside the temple they must pass through the noise, confusion, and commerce of the animal sellers and money changers. One can understand Jesus' view that these activities were in the wrong place.

The lesson given in AD 30 wasn't learned, so now, near the end of his ministry, Jesus gives a different message. He is calling the temple "his house," citing Isaiah 56:7, "My house [says YHWH] will be called a house of prayer for all nations." "Den of robbers" probably comes from Jeremiah 7:11, a condemnation of idolatry and immorality.

Jesus' works and the response of the crowds threatened the religious leaders. Jesus now appears to be in charge, and there is always the danger of Roman military intervention should the crowds get out of hand. The word Matthew uses to describe the religious leaders is "indignant." The indignity of throwing businessmen out of the temple, the unbridled enthusiasm of the crowds, and most certainly the children unthinkingly repeating their parent's acclamation—children running about in the temple!—was grossly inappropriate, in their opinion, for this obscure prophet from Galilee. At the least Jesus should stop the children. In response Jesus refers them to Psalm 8:2, citing from the LXX version, "which indicates that the praise of God from little children is perfect praise."[1] Jesus then leaves Jerusalem and returns to Bethany.

Translation Matthew 21:18-22

18 Now in the morning, having come back into the city, he became hungry. 19 And having seen one fig tree beside the road, he came to it and found nothing on it except leaves only. And he says to it, "Let there be no more fruit from you for the age." And the tree immediately withered. 20 And having seen it the disciples marveled, saying, "How did the fig wither so quickly?" 21 Now Jesus answering said to them, "Truly I say to you, if you have faith and do not doubt, not only will you do what was done to the fig tree, but also, if to this mountain you might say, 'Be removed and be you cast into the sea,' it will be done. 22 And all things, as many as you might ask in prayer, believing, you will receive."

EXPOSITION

In Mark, Jesus returns to Bethany after the triumphal entry the first day, sees the fig tree the morning of the second day, curses the tree, and in the evening of the second day, as they are returning again to Bethany, the tree is dead from the roots. Matthew compresses this account. He says the tree withered away as soon as it was cursed, indicating the curse took immediate effect, and Matthew says no more about the tree. By the evening the tree was completely dead, as Mark's account reveals.

Matthew's concern is always to show Jesus is the Messiah. Therefore he compresses the account to tell his readers that the word of the messiah is accomplished as soon as it is spoken. The curse took immediate effect, and as the tree began to wither the disciples noticed and asked their question. This is one of the few times a miracle takes place as a process—the tree took from

---

[1] Morris, *Matthew*, 529.

morning to evening to die. Because the fig tree represents Israel, the process of withering probably indicates the three years Jesus tried, in vain, to minister successfully to Israel.

The event is used as an occasion to teach, again, the necessity of faith. The Bible's full revelation on prayer lets us understand that the belief necessary to receive the things asked for in prayer, v. 22, is the result of God-given conviction pertaining to his will, see comments at 7:11; 18:19–20. The mountain—a Jewish figure of speech for difficult problems—is removed only when one has both faith and knowledge: knowledge of God's will, faith in his promises. God is always sovereign. Therefore nothing will be impossible when God's will and God's power are brought to bear through faith. The stress is on faith, "have faith and do not doubt," not miracles. Genuine faith is always the result of the Holy Spirit giving conviction concerning God's will. Faith is not what we want, but is always in God, through his word, to accomplish his will.

The leaves indicated the tree should have had some fruit. The season was early, but when leaves appear, even early in the season, there should be a few figs. Jesus is not acting out of anger or malice toward the tree because it "lied." The tree is a metaphor for Israel, which gives every outward evidence of being spiritual, therefore receptive to Jesus as messiah. But the appearance was deceptive. National ethnic Israel rejected Jesus, an irrevocable decision for the nation (but, Romans 11:1, 26); however, individuals Hebrews would be saved, Acts 2:41; Romans 11:5, and become part of the New Testament church.

Looking past the crucifixion, God will temporarily stop interacting with the world through the nation ethnic Israel—the people of the Abrahamic, Mosaic, Palestinian, and Davidic covenants—and interact with the world, including the people of Israel, through the New Testament church, a people saved under the New covenant (Hebrews 8:7–13; 10:11–18). God will save and bring individual Jews into the New Covenant as they believe in Christ as Savior. Then, during the Tribulation period and the Davidic Messianic Kingdom following the Tribulation and second advent, God will resume interaction with the world through national ethnic Israel, bringing the Abrahamic, Palestinian, Davidic, and the New covenant (Jeremiah 31:31–34) to their fulfillment at Christ's second advent. (See my book *Dispensational Eschatology.*)

Translation Matthew 21:23–27

Matthew Twenty-one

23 And he having come into the temple court, the chief priests and the elders of the people approached him as he was teaching, saying, "By what authority are you doing these things? And who gave to you this authority?" 24 But Jesus answering said to them, "I also will ask you one thing, which if you tell me, I also will say to you by what authority I do these things. 25 The baptism of John, from where was it? From heaven or from men?" Now they were reasoning with themselves, saying, "If we might say, 'From heaven,' he will say to us, 'Why then did you not believe him?' 26 But if we might say, 'From men,' we fear the crowd, for all hold John as a prophet." 27 And answering Jesus they said, "We know not." And he said to them, "Neither do I tell you by what authority I do these things."

EXPOSITION

Jesus is in Jerusalem, in the temple court—probably the court of the men—so the religious leaders have the opportunity they have waited for: to confront Jesus on their turf in their areas of expertise; or so they believe. They go to the heart of the matter. What is his authority to fulfill the Zechariah prophecy, to heal and cast out demons, to teach the people an interpretation of the Scripture that is contrary to centuries of Jewish interpretation and tradition, to present himself as a prophet of God, and (in their view) have messianic pretensions.

Authority in Judaism came from God, through the Mosaic Law and rabbinical interpretations, and was vested in the priests and the councils. The Sanhedrin council made civil laws and decisions of national importance, and local councils throughout the land handled local concerns. John Baptist and Jesus did not fit into this structure, and to acknowledge them as having authority was to threaten the existing authority. John and Jesus were out of place and could not be accepted, even as some sort of prophets. Yet, the populace did accept them as prophets. The tension could only be resolved if some way was found to expose Jesus as a fraud; or by accepting him, which they would not do.

Perhaps there is a sense of impatience in Jesus. He has, after all, spent three years performing messianic signs, including his teaching which has provided a clear interpretation of the law in its spiritual intent. His authority to heal the blind and lame, raise the dead, and cast out demons is evident from the very nature of the case.

Therefore Jesus forces them to answer their own question, although they do not have sufficient spiritual perception to grasp the point. If John Baptist's baptism was from heaven, then his message of a coming messiah was from heaven, and they should believe in the one that John testified was the Messiah, Jesus of Nazareth. If they accept John's testimony, then Jesus' authority is evident: it is from YHWH; but they do not and cannot believe John was a prophet and Jesus is the Messiah.

Of course, they view Jesus' question in terms of their own religious liability. To believe John's message is to deny all they believe in. To deny John's message is to put themselves in jeopardy with the crowds who, popularly if not critically, accept John and Jesus as prophets sent from God. Faced with, to them, an impossible situation, they answer that they do not know. Jesus refuses to pander to their unbelief and does not answer their question. Do not answer a fool according to his folly, Proverbs 26:4

Translation Matthew 21:28–32

28 "But what do you think? A man had two sons, and having come to the first, he said, 'Son, go today, work in the vineyard.' 29 Now he answering said, 'I will not'; but afterward having repented he went. 30 Now having come to the second he said in the same manner. Now he answering said, "I [go], sir,' and he did not go. 31 Which of the two did the will of the father?" They say, "The first." Jesus says to them, "Truly I say to you, that the tax collectors and the prostitutes go before you into the kingdom of God. 32 For John came to you in the way of righteousness, and you did not believe him; but tax collectors and the prostitutes believed him; but you having seen, did not afterward repent to believe him."

TRANSLATION NOTE

In v. 30 the answer of the second son is "I, sir." The Greek language often left out what was implied. Here it is implied the second son said "I go, sir." Because "go" is implied but not in the text, I have enclosed it in brackets.

EXPOSITION

The setting is simple enough. A man asks his two sons to work in the vineyard. One says no, but later regrets his response and works in the vineyard. The other promises he will work, but did not fulfill his word. Which obeyed the father? The religious leaders correctly answer: the son who at first denied but then did as he was told. The point of the parable is in vv. 31–32.

The religious leaders believed they were doing God's will, but were not. The tax collectors and prostitutes disobeyed, but when John Baptist came they responded to the message, repented, and believed. The ones the religious leaders despised as sinners, because they did not make any effort to keep the traditions of the fathers, and in fact committed great sins, these had turned toward God in faith; the religious leaders were stuck in their disobedience.

More than this, when the religious leaders saw the repentance and faith of tax collectors and prostitutes they despised it, because they despised those people as sinners and themselves as righteous. Therefore, believing themselves to be righteous, they could not have any need for John and his message In their religious beliefs the righteous ministered to the righteous, not to sinners. The chief priests and Pharisees did not understand or accept John's message.

Translation Matthew 21:33–41

33 "Hear another parable. There was a man, a master of a house, who planted a vineyard, and placed a fence around it, dug a winepress in it, and built a tower, and hired it out to vinedressers, and went away into a foreign country. 34 Now when the season of the fruits drew near, he sent his servants to the vinedressers, to receive his fruits. 35 And the vinedressers having taken his servants, one indeed they beat, but one they killed, and one they stoned. 36 Again he sent other servants, more than the first, and they did the same to them. 37 Now afterward he sent to them his son, saying, 'They will respect my son.' 38 But the vinedressers, having seen the son, said among themselves, 'This is the heir. Come, let us kill him, and possess his inheritance.' 39 And having taken him, they cast him out of the vineyard and they killed him. 40 When therefore, the owner of the vineyard shall come, what will he do to those vinedressers? 41 They say to him, "He will destroy miserably those wicked men, and the vineyard he will hire out to other vinedressers who will give to him the fruits in their seasons."

EXPOSITION

The details in v. 33 are true to life. Many Jews lived in foreign countries, and some undoubtedly owned land in Palestine. But this parable is directed against the religious leaders.

God placed Israel in a land, but the land belonged to YHWH, not Israel, Leviticus 25:23. The fruits of the land belonged to the YHWH, of which a tenth was given (to support the tribe of Levi, which had no inheritance in the land) in recognition of this fact, Leviticus 27:30. But beyond these physical circumstances, the nation owed God the fruits of worship, and God had charged the religious leaders with teaching the people their duties toward God.

God had placed the civil and religious leaders in charge of his vineyard, Israel. These leaders had forgotten they were tenants and began to believe they were owners, disregarding their responsibilities toward God and the people. The servants in the parable are the prophets God sent to claim his own place in the nation; but they mistreated the prophets, and killed some of them. They refused to walk in the ways of God and rejected those God sent to return them to the right path. Finally, God sent his son. He too is rejected. The sad fact is that although the religious leaders perceived the parable was aimed at them, vv. 45–46, they did not recognize that Jesus was the son sent by the Father.

The religious leaders understand the story but do not get the spiritual point. They pronounce their doom: God will destroy unbelieving Israel, and replace them with others who will be obedient to and worship God. We can't take the details too far. Israel was destroyed as a nation, but not as a people, for they will continue as a people group separate from all others, and be restored as a nation in the future as God's covenant people and inherit the Davidic kingdom. The new tenants, the New Testament church, do not replace national ethnic Israel, Romans 9–11, but are presumed to be more faithful vinedressers, giving God the fruits of their spiritual labors.

Translation Matthew 21:42–46

42 Jesus says to them, "Did you never read in the scriptures, 'The stone which those building rejected, this has become the chief corner; this was from the Lord, and it is marvelous in our eyes'? 43 On account of this I say to you, that the kingdom of God will be taken from you, and it will be given to a people producing its fruits. 44 And the one having fallen on this stone will be broken; but on whomever it may fall, it will grind him to powder." 45 And having heard his parables, the chief priests and Pharisees knew that he speaks about them. 46 And seeking to lay hold of him, they feared

the crowds, because they held him as a prophet.

EXPOSITION

Jesus interprets the right answers to the two parables. Because the religious leaders have rejected Jesus, God has rejected them. The reference in v. 42 is Psalm 118:22. Building foundations were made up of large flat stones set on the ground. The structure was built upon the foundation stones. To begin building the structure, a "cornerstone" was the first stone laid upon the foundation. All the other stones were set in place based on the position of the cornerstone. The cornerstone of a building had to be set square, level, and plumb in order for the entire building to be square, level, and plumb. The term "cornerstone" did not mean it was at the corner of a building—it could have been in the middle of the foundation—but that it was the most important stone in the building.

All stones were hand cut out of native rock and hand shaped for their specific purpose. In the case of the cornerstone the size and shape influenced the whole building. In the Psalm, the cornerstone for a certain building (perhaps the temple Solomon built) was rejected for unknown reasons; perhaps it had an odd shape, or otherwise appeared unsuitable. The stone rejected by the builders was the stone God designated the chief cornerstone, and it is marvelous in our eyes. (Verse 42 in Matthew ends in a question mark because it is the end of the question asked by Jesus. In the Psalm this is a statement, not a question.)

Because the Jews rejected Jesus, God will give the kingdom to others. By reason of later revelation we know the "others" are the New Testament church. This is not the Davidic Messianic Kingdom following the second advent, but the Spiritual Kingdom during the New Testament church age. The promises God made to national ethnic Israel concerning their position in the Davidic Messianic Kingdom cannot be broken.

Jesus concludes with a warning. To fall on the stone is to be broken, i.e., in spiritual terms to repent of sin and have faith in Jesus the Christ. If the stone should fall on a person it will destroy him: in spiritual terms to reject Jesus as Savior, be forever lost, and suffer eternally in the Lake of Fire. The broken person can be healed; the person ground into powder cannot. The stone imagery in v. 44 calls Daniel 2:34, 44–45 to mind.

Matthew Twenty-one

They understood Jesus was opposing and condemning them. They wanted to arrest and imprison him, but feared the reaction of the crowds.

Matthew Twenty-Two

Translation Matthew 22:1-7

1 And answering Jesus again spoke to them in parables, saying, 2 "The kingdom of heaven may be likened to a man, a king, who made a wedding feast for his son, 3 and sent his servants to call those having been invited to the wedding feast; and they were not willing to come. 4 Again, he sent out other servants, saying, 'Tell those having been invited, "Look, I prepared my dinner; my oxen and the fatlings have been killed, and all things are ready. Come to the wedding feast."' 5 But not caring they went away, one indeed to his own field, but one to his business, 6 and the rest having laid hold of his servants mistreated and killed them. 7 Now the king was furious, and having sent his armies he destroyed those murderers, and burnt their city."

EXPOSITION

This is the third of three parables aimed at the religious leaders. God is the king, Jesus is the son, the unnamed bride is the kingdom, the servants are the Old Testament prophets. Israel was invited to the kingdom but refused to come when called.

A second invitation to a banquet was normal to the times. The responses were abnormal. After the people had rejected the second invitation, the king sent his armies to the city, which was not the same location as the banquet, indicating some time and some events passed before the murderers were executed and the city burned.

The point: Israel has rejected the offer of the kingdom. The people invited to the wedding represent the Israel to whom Jesus has presented himself for three years. Israel rejected their messiah. God will destroy those who murdered his servants the prophets and rejected his son. He will burn their city. God did destroy Israel as a nation in AD 70, and the city, Jerusalem, was burned. Yet, God has not abandoned national ethnic Israel. There will be salvation for individual Israelites in the present Spiritual form of the kingdom. Then, people group national ethnic Israel will receive the Davidic Messianic kingdom with Christ their Messiah at his second advent.

Translation Matthew 22:8-14

8 "Then he says to his servants, 'The wedding feast is ready,

but those having been invited were not worthy. 9 Go therefore into the highways, and as many as you may find, invite to the wedding feast.' 10 And those servants having gone out into the highways brought together all, as many as they found, both evil and good. And the wedding hall became full of those reclining. 11 But the king having come in to see those reclining, he saw there a man not dressed in wedding clothes. 12 And he says to him, 'Friend, how did you come in here not having wedding clothes?' And he was speechless. 13 Then the king said to the servants, 'Having bound him, feet and hands, cast him into the outer darkness; there will be weeping and gnashing of teeth.' 14 "For many are called, but few chosen."

EXPOSITION

A parable is aimed at one point, so it is best not to assign meaning to every detail. In broad terms, the Israel which had the covenant relation with God through Abraham and Moses and David, was invited into messiah's kingdom. They rejected the invitation. So the invitation became more general, inviting all the people of the world to the wedding feast (including those of Israel who will respond). In this general invitation, persons both good and bad respond. Many are given a wedding garment, which represents salvation. The parable is unusual in that it has two sub-points and one main spiritual point. The first sub-point is that the Jews have rejected their messiah and his kingdom.

Even if the Jews had accepted Jesus, he still would have been crucified.

> The Messianic Kingdom always required a crucified Savior. The salvation and kingdom in Isaiah 54–66 are the ordained consequence of the crucifixion-resurrection in Isaiah 52:13–53:12. The prophesied rejection of messiah in Psalm 118:22 is followed by prophesied salvation, prosperity, and blessing. The suffering in Psalm 22 is followed by the kingdom, 22:28. In Psalm 2:1–3 the gentile nations conspire and plot against God's anointed. What would be the outcome? After the suffering comes the kingdom, 2:6–9. There was not and never would have been a Davidic-Messianic kingdom for Israel without a suffering, crucified, resurrected, and ascended Savior.

Was the Davidic Kingdom postponed by Israel's rejection?

No. God's plan was always the crucifixion, then the church age, then the Davidic-Messianic-Millennial Kingdom. Just because God chose not to reveal the New Testament church age to the Old Testament prophets does not mean it was not always part of the plan. The church age was always part of the plan, as Paul reveals in Ephesians 2:11–3:13. Abraham's seed was always physical and spiritual—the sand of the sea; the stars in the heavens. Christ blessing all nations, tribes, peoples, and tongues was always the plan, Genesis 12:3. The Messianic Kingdom promised to national ethnic Israel was proclaimed to be at hand, a genuine offer whose rejection was known and prophesied, and it is at present where it was always planned to be by the foreordaining choices of God: yet-future.

The plans and processes of God concerning the rejection of Messiah and the intervening church age may be seen in a subtle change in Matthew's Gospel. In Matthew 4:17 Jesus proclaimed the Davidic-Messianic Kingdom: "from that time" Jesus proclaimed the kingdom to be at hand. The phrase, "from that time" gives structure to Matthew's Gospel, and it reoccurs in Matthew 16:21, where it indicates a shift in the focus. The kingdom and its Messiah had been rejected. "From that time" forward Jesus focused on preparing the twelve for his death and resurrection. This does not mean he stopped evangelizing, healing, and confronting his enemies, but that the focus from Matthew 16:21 forward was the training of the twelve to assume the gospel proclamation after Jesus' death, resurrection, and ascension. When the Kingdom was rejected Jesus initiated the next step in God's plan: to prepare his apostles for the New Testament church.[1]

Although there is one wedding feast in the parable, an explanation is made easier by identifying them as two feasts: the first which wasn't held because the invited guests declined, and the second to which both evil and good persons were invited. The first wedding feast was the offer of the Davidic-Messianic kingdom to Israel, which was rejected. The second wedding feast is the kingdom in its spiritual form, which is the New Testament church

---

[1] Quiggle, *Dispensational*, 210–211.

age.

The second sub-point of the parable is made at the second wedding feast. One person does not have a wedding garment. He is not reclining at the table with the others. He is not, in fact, a wedding guest. He was invited, but he came without the appropriate attire, the wedding garment. The wedding garment represents righteousness gained through salvation. The person improperly dressed is representative of all like him: the ones who are unsaved.

The second feast represents the kingdom in its present spiritual and mystery forms, the New Testament church, which is a mixed multitude of saved and unsaved. The unsaved are invited into the spiritual kingdom, but because they do not have the garment of righteousness they cannot attend the feast. Eschatologically the outcome looks to the wedding feast in heaven, Revelation 19:1–10, where only those who are saved will be present.

The king addresses the unsaved man as "friend" simply as a socially polite form of address. The man has nothing to say, perhaps because his inappropriate clothing is obvious to him and he knows he is guilty. The inappropriate clothing is meant represent some aspect of character. This man is wrongly at the wedding feast, because he does not have the qualification required to be a guest: he is unsaved. The punishment is that which waits all who reject Jesus as Savior.

The implication is that this wrongly clothed man represents the religious leaders who opposed Jesus. That is how the Pharisees understood the point of the story, see v. 15.

Verse 14 gives the main spiritual point of the parable. A call is not the same as a response. Many hear the call to the kingdom. Many respond, for many reasons. Only some respond with saving faith.

The contrast between "called" and "chosen" is the difference between the moral responsibility to believe and be saved, and the actual choice to believe and be saved. God desires all to be saved: all persons have a moral responsibility to repent of their sins and believe in Jesus as Savior. God will respond savingly to any who do repent and believe. But God's hasn't willed all to be saved. God has chosen some persons, Ephesians 1:4, to whom he gives the gift of grace-faith-salvation, Ephesians 2:8–9. Compare 2 Thessalonians

2:13, chosen for salvation, through sanctification of the Holy Spirit, and belief in the truth. Those who receive God's gift of grace-faith-salvation will by faith repent of their sin, believe on Christ the Savior, and are be saved. All others have the moral responsibility to believe, and the moral authority to choose to believe, but will remain unsaved because effectively persuaded by the evil sin principle in their human nature to reject God. But God will act savingly should they chose to repent and believe.

These truths can be expressed in a figure. The river of life carrying all human kind flows swiftly to the waterfall of death emptying into the lake of fire. God reaches into the river and saves some; he does not prevent any from coming to the shore of salvation. He acts savingly toward any who will believe on Christ. He places his saved people on the shore to invite all needing salvation to come, believe on Jesus, and be saved.

Translation Matthew 22:15–22

15 Then having gone, the Pharisees took counsel how they might trap him in his words. 16 And they send to him their disciples with the Herodians, saying, "Teacher, we know that you are true, and teach the way of God in truth; and you do not care about anyone, for you do not look on the person of men. 17 Tell us, therefore, what do you think? Is it right to give tax to Caesar, or not?" 18 But Jesus having known their malice, said, "Why do you test me, hypocrites? 19 Show me the tax money." And they brought to him a denarius. 20 And he says to them, "Whose this image, and whose inscription?" 21 They say to him, "Caesar's." And he says to them, "Give therefore the things of Caesar to Caesar, and the things of God to God." 22 When having heard they marveled; and having left him went away.

EXPOSITION

Rather than repent and accept Jesus, the religious leaders look for ways to discredit him. Matthew's "then" indicates this next event happened some amount of time after Jesus had given the three parables, because time was needed to come up with a new strategy against Jesus.

The leaders decide to send their disciples, who are students, to communicate their question. Students are learners, so their motives might not be suspect. The only thing known about the Herodian party is what might be gleaned from their name:

Matthew Twenty-two

supporters of the Herodian rulers. These two parties, one religious, one political, come to Jesus with a respectful address hiding a devious plot. They say Jesus is sincere and faithful to the truth. In saying Jesus does not care about anyone they mean he is fearless in speaking the truth, regardless of what people might think or how they might act when hearing the truth. Finally, Jesus is no respecter of persons. The same could not be said about the religious leaders. As to teaching "the way of God in truth," if they truly believed Jesus did so, that then they would not have been trying to "trap him in his words." They are using flattery to disarm any suspicions and set him up for a question that will destroy Jesus' credibility by aligning him with one faction or another.

The tax question was another hot button issue in Palestine. The tax in question was the "poll tax." In the USA people pay sales taxes, property taxes, and income taxes, but not a poll tax. A poll tax is the tax a person pays for the privilege of living in a government's territory. Governments can use a poll tax for many purposes. In many countries paying poll tax was, and still is, used as a qualification for the right to vote. In ancient Rome the poll tax was used to generate money. It was a "per person" tax levied because one was under Roman rule. The poll tax was unpopular because it forced the Jews to support a government they viewed as oppressive and unlawful (unlawful because the Jews viewed themselves as self-governing under God's authority). However, they paid it, because the first alternative was forfeiture of all property, and the second was military intervention. To the Romans, paying taxes and keeping the peace were the two most important duties of conquered peoples and Roman administrators (governors, procurators).

Jesus is asked whether or not the poll tax was "right." Was it morally right for Jews to pay taxes to Rome? Does the Law of Moses, does our position as YHWH's covenant people, support this type of taxation? The Jews had an answer from Deuteronomy 17:15, "You will set a king over you whom YHWH chooses." This verse had been interpreted to mean the poll tax was not legal. The interpretation ignores the principle, later expressed in the New Testament, that every authority is appointed by God, Romans 13:1. (Paul didn't pull the principle out of thin air, but from scriptures such as Deuteronomy 17:15).

So the question, if framed honestly, was this: "Jesus, do you think is right for the people of YHWH under the Torah to pay this poll tax?" The question is framed for a yes or no answer. If Jesus answered yes, then he would be seen as supporting the political parties agreeable to Roman rule, alienating most of the Jewish population. If he said no, then he was opposing the Roman government, which might feel obligated to take some action against him. Undoubtedly his opponents congratulated themselves, because with either answer they had outsmarted Jesus.

Their flattery, and the fact they were disciples of his enemies, let Jesus know they were not seeking information or a religious opinion. Jesus asked to see a denarius. They "brought," not gave, him a denarius. A religious leader would not have carried a coin bearing an image when he went into the temple, so they probably did not have a coin on hand, and had to send someone to get a denarius.

Jesus asks whose image and inscription was on the coin. They answer, "Caesar's." The image and inscription made the coin the legal tender for all monetary transactions under Roman rule. They knew quite well the image and inscription, for they had accepted Roman money as the basis of all their economic transactions, the temple excepted.

There is an interplay of different words in the question and reply that helps us understand what Jesus is teaching. The question asked, v. 17, uses the word *dídómi*, is it is right "to give of one's own accord and with good will."[1] Jesus answers, v. 21, using the word *apodídōmi*, it is right "to do something necessary in fulfillment of an obligation or expectation."[2] Paying taxes to Caesar was an obligation: give the things of Caesar to Caesar. Worshiping, serving, and obeying God was an obligation: give the things of God to God.

A citizen—whether of earth or heaven—has obligations to the governing authority. In Calvin's words,

> Outward subjection does not prevent us from having within us a conscience free in the sight of God . . . In short, Christ declares that there is no violation of the authority of God, or any injustice done to his service, if, in respect of outward government, the Jews obey Rome . . . Every man, according

---

[1] Zodhiates, *WSDNT*, s. v. "1325."

[2] Ibid., s. v. "591."

to his calling, ought to perform the duty to which he owes to men . . . provided that God always retains the highest authority.[1]

In this answer Jesus recognizes kingdom members in this New Testament church age have a dual citizenship. They are citizens of an earthly state, and thus have earthly obligations to that state. Kingdom members are also citizens of the kingdom (in a sense expatriates from heaven), and thus have obligations toward God. Both obligations must be met with an appropriate response. More than that, the believer's obligation to God covers all aspects of life, requiring him/her to serve Caesar in a way that is honoring to God.[2] Jesus' wisdom left them speechless, and they went away.

Translation Matthew 22:23–33

23 In that day the Sadducees came to him, saying there is no resurrection, and they questioned him, 24 saying, "Teacher, Moses said that if anyone should die not having children, his brother will marry his wife, and raise up children for his brother. 25 Now there were with us seven brothers; and the first having married, died, and having no children, left his wife to his brother. 26 In the same manner the second also, and the third, even to the seventh. 27 Now the woman died last of all. 28 Therefore, in the resurrection, of which of the seven will she be wife, for all had her." 29 Now answering, Jesus said to them, "You are lead astray, not knowing the scriptures or the power of God. 30 For in the resurrection they do not marry, nor are given in marriage, but they are like the angels of God in heaven. 31 Now concerning the resurrection of the dead, have you not read that having been spoken to you by God, saying, 32 'I am the God of Abraham and the God of Isaac and the God of Jacob'? He is not God of the dead, but of the living." 33 And having heard, the crowds were astonished at his teaching.

EXPOSITION

Most Jews believed in an undefined afterlife in Sheol (*sh$^{e'}$ôl*), followed by a final resurrection of all persons, the righteous to eternal life, the unrighteous to eternal punishment. In this they were mistaken, for *sh$^{e'}$ôl* is a reference to the grave, not to life after

---

[1] Calvin, *Commentary*, 17:44–45.
[2] Morris, *Matthew*, 558.

death (see my book, *Dispensational Eschatology*, pp. 132–134). The unsaved have always gone to *hádēs* to await judgment at the Great White Throne, Revelation 20:13. The saved dead have always gone to heaven to be with God, Luke 23:43 (cf. 2 Corinthians 12:4; Revelation 2:7). In the Old Testament, life after death is defined by passages such as the one quoted by Jesus, Exodus 3:6 (cf. Job 13:15; Daniel 12:2, 13 where the idea of the grave and life after death is presented).

The Sadducees believed the soul died with the body because they saw nothing specific about resurrection in the Law or the rest of the Old Testament Scripture.[1] Because they disbelieved the resurrection they ridiculed the belief by giving it a carnal interpretation. Their test for Jesus is based on Deuteronomy 25:5–6. If the resurrection is real, they ask, which of the brothers will have her as a wife when all are resurrected, because all had her as a wife in the present life?

Jesus answers that the carnal view of the resurrection is the wrong view. Resurrected men and women do not marry (men married) nor are given in marriage (women are given to the man in marriage). In this they are "like the angels," i.e., not becoming angels, but like the angels in that resurrected human beings will not marry, and resurrected human beings will not have male and female genders.

The Scripture universally represents angels as masculine. However, based on this and parallel passages, angels do not have male and female genders. The appearance of masculinity is just that, an appearance. This is the same as God representing himself as masculine. The order God created vests spiritual leadership in the male gender; therefore God represents himself and his messengers (the literal meaning of *ággelos*, angels) as masculine. Angels are not masculine, nor feminine, because they do not marry, which is activity of the male gender, and they are not given in marriage, which is the activity of the female gender. Even so, resurrected human beings will not have male and female genders after the resurrection.

The Sadducees' carnal concept of resurrection is incorrect. The resurrected saved person has everlasting physical and spiritual life. There is no necessity for them to propagate to perpetuate the

---

[1] Josephus, *Antiquities*, 18.1.4; *Wars*, 2.8.14.

species, as there is in this mortal life. There is no such thing as a celestial marriage (Mormonism), or virgins awaiting the faithful man (Islam).

Jesus now proves the doctrine of resurrection is true through the testimony of God in the Old Testament. The argument cannot be said to come from the present tense of the verb in the Old Testament text of Exodus 3:6, because the Hebrew text does not have a verb. Literally the text is, "I God of your father, God of Abraham, God of Isaac, God of Jacob." That Abraham and all Old Testament believers (and unbelievers) are alive in an afterlife is the conclusion Jesus comes to based on the covenant relationship that is the basis for Exodus 3:6.

God has a continuing relationship with those of faith. In Genesis 17:7 God says to Abraham, "And I will establish my covenant between me and you . . . for an everlasting covenant, to be God to you." God is the God of the living, not merely during their earthly lifetime, but everlasting; therefore a person must live on after physical death.

> Our problem is that we force on the text a neoplatonic dualism and demand a choice between immortality and resurrection (cf. Warfield, *Shorter Writings*, 1:339–347). The point is simply "that God will raise the dead because he cannot fail to keep his promises to them that he will be their God" (Marshall, *Luke*, 743), read against the background of biblical anthropology and eschatology.[1]

Jesus probably did not convince the Sadducees (the approving scribes in Luke 20:39 were undoubtedly Pharisees), but the multitudes were astonished at his wisdom and interpretation.

Translation Matthew 22:34–40

34 Now the Pharisees, having heard that he had silenced the Sadducees, came together in the same place. 35 And one of them, a lawyer, questioned him, testing him. 36 "Teacher, which commandment is the greatest in the law?" 37 Now he said to him, "You will love the Lord your God with all your heart, and with all your soul, and with all your mind. 38 This is the great and first commandment. 39 The second is like it: 'You will love your neighbor as yourself.' 40 On these two commandments all the Law stands,

---

[1] Carson, *John*, 462.

and the Prophets."

EXPOSITION

The Pharisees recognized the relative importance of the several commandments and debated as to which were "heavier" and which were "lighter." They also debated which commandment summarized the obligations imposed by the whole. To choose which were most important would involve Jesus in theological argument, which would tend to discredit him with some, perhaps many, people. In their estimation, since they could not decide this question, any answer Jesus gave would alienate almost everyone.

Jesus answers with two precepts that embody a basic biblical principle. The principle is to love, Deuteronomy 6:5; Leviticus 19:18. To love God is to dedicate yourself—your thoughts, actions, attitudes, and words—to his glory. To love God is to be obedient to all the commandments. Then Jesus, unasked, gives the second greatest commandment, because to fail to do the latter is to fail in the former. To love your neighbor as yourself is to act for the neighbor's best, highest good. To love your neighbor is to act out the love God has for you and your neighbor. As John says, 1 John 4:11, 20, since God so loved us we ought to love one another, and how can a man love God whom he has not seen if he cannot love his brother who he has seen.

A believer's relationship with his/her brethren in Christ is essential to their relationship with God. More properly, love toward one's fellow man is the natural outworking of the attribute love God has given to his saved people. In v. 40 Jesus is saying that acting in accordance with these two commandments eliminates the need to argue about the others. In doing the two greatest one does all, and in doing all one works out the two greatest in his life. The result of loving God is obedience to his commandments. Obedience to his commandments engages the believer in love toward others.

Translation Matthew 22:41–46

41 And the Pharisees having been gathered together, Jesus questioned them, 42 saying, "What do you think about the Christ? Whose son is he?" They say to him, "Of David." 43 He says to them, "How then does David in spirit call him 'Lord,' saying, 44 'Said the Lord said to my Lord, "Sit at my right hand, until I may place your enemies as a footstool for your feet"?' 45 If therefore David then calls Him 'Lord,' how is he his son?" 46 And no one was able to

answer him a word, nor dared anyone from that day question him any more.

EXPOSITION

The Pharisees were left speechless by the convincing answer of vv. 37–40. So, Jesus asks them a question, "Whose son is the Christ?" The answer, from 2 Samuel 7:12, 13, is that the Christ is David's son, i.e., a descendant of King David from Israel's past.

Jesus then asks, "If the Christ is David's son, why does David, by the inspiration of the Holy Spirit, call the Christ his Lord?" The reference is to Psalm 110:1, and it is plain from the Psalm that David's Lord is the Christ and that the Christ is greater than David.

> A Psalm of David. "Said YHWH to my Lord [*'ādôn*], 'Sit at my right, until I make your enemies your footstool.' "

In this psalm messiah bears the title *'ādôn*, a word intended by both David and the Holy Spirit to refer to David's descendant. This word was used to refer to men (e.g., Genesis 18:12) and God (e.g., Psalm 8:1). It was a particularly appropriate designation for the one who would be God-man.

David's descendant is his Lord who will sit at the right hand of YHWH, and YHWH will make the enemies of this Lord his footstool (subjugated to him). This view, although plainly stated in the psalm, is opposed to the common Jewish view that the father is always greater than any of his descendants. Thus, if the Christ is David's Lord, how can he also be David's son? David states the Christ is greater than himself, a person to whom David owes homage, his Lord.

The other popular view of the Christ was that as David's son he would be in the same mold as David, a great political and military leader. The psalm does declare messiah's enemies will be subjugated to him, but also states messiah will be a priest, i.e., a person who mediates between God and man. The Christ, as greater than David, is not bound to be like David.

The Pharisees cannot find a good reason as to why King David would give his descendant the title, "Lord," for the Lord of David would be greater than David. Jesus starts with their uninformed and unscriptural view of the Christ. By asking the question and citing Psalm 110:1, Jesus asks them to rethink their understanding.

If they had given Psalm 110 serious consideration, they might have concluded the Christ was the divine Savior, not a human warrior. All the elements are there: to sit at God's right hand is to be equal with God; to make his enemies his footstool is to subject his enemies to divine authority; to be a priest is to be the mediator between God and man. But they would not consider the implications of what Jesus had taught them. Matthew says there were no more questions from the religious leaders, and the remainder of his gospel agrees.

Matthew Twenty-Three

Translation Matthew 23:1–12

1 Then Jesus spoke to the crowds and to his disciples, 2 saying: "The scribes and the Pharisees, having sat down on Moses' seat, 3 all things, therefore, as much as they might tell you to do, that keep; but do not do according to their works, for they say and not do. 4 But they bind heavy burdens [and hard to bear], and lay them on men's shoulders; but themselves with their finger they are not willing to move them. 5 But all their works they do to be seen by men. For they broaden their phylacteries, and enlarge their borders. 6 Now they love the chief place at the feasts, and the chief seats in the synagogues, 7 and the greetings in the marketplaces, and to be called by men, "Rabbi. 8 But you, you may not be called 'Rabbi', for one is your teacher, and you are all brothers. 9 And you may not call anyone on the earth your 'father'; for one is your Father, who is in heaven. 10 Neither be called masters; for one is your master, the Christ. 11 But the greatest among you will be your servant. 12 Now he who will exalt himself will be humbled, and whoever will humble himself will be exalted."

TRANSLATION NOTE

In 23: 4 there is disagreement whether the words in brackets were in the original text. The preponderance of evidence is the words were imported from Luke 11:46.[1]

In 23:8, the words "the Christ" are added after "teacher" in some manuscripts. The words were brought up from v. 10, which see note, below.

In 23:10 the word translated "masters" and "master" is *kathēgētēs*, "a guide in the way, a teacher, leader, equivalent to rabbi, master; a title of respectful address to Jewish teachers."[2] Because the reference is to Christ, who is more than a teacher, and teacher was previously mentioned at 23:8, I decided to follow the ASV and HCSB and translate "master." If *kathēgētēs* is translated "teacher," then 23:10, 8 are similar. This similarity probably prompted some scribe to copy "the Christ" from 23:10 into 23:8.

---

[1] Metzger, *Textual*, 49.
[2] Zodhiates, *WSDNT*, s. v. "2519."

EXPOSITION

Jesus is still in the temple area, so as he speaks to his disciples and the crowds; the religious leaders are also present. The sustained length of these denunciations is unparalleled in the other gospels.

Jesus is not saying all scribes and Pharisees are hypocrites, for history tells us there were good men who were scribes and Pharisees. To be a Pharisee was to follow a religious philosophy dedicated to being obedient to the law and traditions. The scribes were the academics of the day, the Bible students, teachers, and theologians. Not everyone was a hypocrite, but it must have been common enough, or obvious enough, to the average Jew that no one raised any objections to this characterization, either here or in secular documents.

When Jesus said the scribes and Pharisees are sitting in Moses' seat, he meant when they authoritatively taught the meaning of the Law of Moses. When they taught the Law the people were to apply these teachings to their daily lives. Jesus did not say the same about the traditional interpretations of the Law. Verse 4 indicates there were many traditions that did not conform to the Law, or expanded the Law in a manner not consistent with the Law, and therefore were not to be heeded. These were the "heavy burdens." Jesus also said one should listen to what the scribes and Pharisees taught about the Law and those things do, but do not live as the scribes and Pharisees lived.

The phylactery the scribes and Pharisees enlarged was a little box containing a copy of Exodus 13:1–10; Deuteronomy 6:8; 11:13–21, as a literal fulfillment of those verses. Many Jews wore them during prayer. Some wore them in public. Phylacteries discovered at the Qumran community were made to be strapped to the forehead. Others were worn on the wrist. They were rectangular and were of various sizes.

Jesus is not condemning the practice of wearing phylacteries so much as the public demonstration created by making one's phylactery bigger to make it highly visible. This is the same thing as ostentatious public giving, or loud public praying. The intent was to show others that you were religious, full of devotion and piety.

A modern equivalent would be wearing ten gold chains rather than one, so it is obvious the wearer has wealth; or the very rich man buying a larger yacht than his rich friends. The professional Bible student, theologian, college professor must have a better library than others, the professional author the most books sold, and so on. The overly pious Christian must have a bigger Bible, of fine leather, with his name, or a Bible verse, in gold letters pressed into the cover. The bigger the Bible the more devoted the believer; the larger the phylactery the more pious the Pharisee. But God looks upon the heart, not the large Bible; or the phylactery.

The "border" of the garment was a band of blue ribbon sewn to the bottom hem. Tassels were attached to the border. See Numbers 15:38. The purpose of the border and tassel (Jesus wore them) was a reminder to obey God's law, Numbers 15:40. To make the blue ribbon broader was to say, "I am very serious about obeying God's commandments; I pay attention to the Law; I am more obedient than other Jews; I am more pious than you." Taking pride in a job well-done is not the problem. Wanting others to congratulate you by calling attention to yourself and your works is the problem.

In vv. 7–8 Jesus condemns their practice of requiring the respect of others. God respects a proper humility, not an arrogant preeminence. The scribes and Pharisees wanted to be recognized as better Jews than others. They did things that placed them in the public consciousness. In today's world they would be seeking print and electronic media publicity so everyone could see just how religious they were, just how important they were.

The Hebrew word "rabbi" indicated someone who occupied a socially prominent and respected position.[1] In the mouth of a disciple (student) it means "teacher." The one who is addressed as rabbi is higher in rank than the speaker. A student (disciple) would call his mentor rabbi, meaning "my master" or "my teacher." When, after several years, the student reached a certain level of proficiency in the oral law, he was allowed to teach others and assume the title, Rabbi.[2] However, the greeting "Rabbi" in the marketplaces was out of place from a non-student, implying subordination from the one speaking. The relationship between believers is one of equals, therefore only Jesus can be appropriately addressed as Rabbi, or in modern terms, Teacher.

---

[1] Kittle, *Dictionary*, 6:961.

[2] Ibid., 6:962.

There is no indication anyone living was called "father" as a term of respect or submission in Jesus' time, except one's literal father (but see 2 Kings 13:14). The earlier rabbis, on whose interpretations the traditions were based, were collectively known as the fathers.[1] The reference to "one is your Father, who is in heaven," indicates the context refers to those in an ecclesiastical position, or with spiritual authority or influence. We must be aware of 1 Corinthians 4:15 in this regard, for Paul said to the Corinthians, "you do not have many fathers; for in Christ Jesus I have begotten you through the gospel." Paul is speaking of himself as the one who preached the gospel to them, resulting in their salvation. Believers who testify of the way to salvation are like a mid-wife assisting in the birthing process.

What is forbidden by Jesus is using of the term "father" as a title for a superior, just as "teacher," v. 8, and "master," v. 10, are forbidden for the same reason. There is one spiritual Father, God in heaven, and one teacher and master, the Christ.

Translation Matthew 23:13–15

13 "But woe to you, scribes and Pharisees, hypocrites! Because you shut up the kingdom of the heavens against men; for you neither enter, nor even those who are entering do you allow to go in. [14 Woe to you, scribes and Pharisees, hypocrites! Because you devour widows' houses, and as a pretense are praying long prayers. On account of this you will receive greater condemnation.] 15 Woe to you, scribes and Pharisees, hypocrites! Because you traverse the sea and the dry land to make one convert, and when he may become so, you make him a son of hell twofold more than yourselves."

TRANSLATION NOTE

Verse 14 is not in the Alexandrian and Western texts of Matthew's Gospel. In the Textus Receptus (KJV/NKJV) it is after v. 13. In other manuscripts it is before v. 13. The NIV, ESV, and NLT do not include this verse; the HCSB, KJV/NKJV, ASV, YLT do. The verse is considered to have been imported from Mark 12:40 or Luke 20:47.[2]

---

[1] France, *Matthew*, TNTC, 863. Carson, *Matthew*, 475.

[2] Metzger, *Textual*, 50.

As to an interpretation of v. 14, six possibilities have been proposed.

Scribes accepted payment for legal assistance, though such payment was forbidden.

Acting as a lawyer for a widow's estate they cheated the widow out of her inheritance.

Abusing the hospitality and generosity of widows.

Taking money from credulous widows in exchange for intercessory prayer.

Mismanaging estates entrusted to them.

Taking a house as a pledge for a debt that realistically could not be repaid.

However, there is too little information, in Scripture or history, to know exactly what Jesus meant.

EXPOSITION

A woe is a dreadful event. (Luke 11:42–52 has six woes directed at the scribes and Pharisees.) Example: when an adult child suffers the death of an aged parent that is a sad event; when a young parent suffers the death of their little child that is a woe. The judgment on these religious leaders for their hypocrisy will be terrible. They are indicted for keeping others out of the kingdom. They do not know the way themselves, and thus cannot lead others into it, but do lead others into eternal destruction with them. They do not know the way themselves and prevent others from entering by keeping the door to the kingdom shut by their false teachings. A false teacher believes his lies. The scribes and Pharisees are hypocrites just because they believe they are leading the way to heaven, but are not. They are deserving of death, Deuteronomy 13.

Since travel was not easy, the phrase "you travel the sea and the dry land" may be proverbial for extraordinary effort. The scribes and Pharisees gave much energy to make a proselyte (a gentile convert to Judaism), but since they were false teachers their efforts resulted in a lost soul. Put another way, a gentile knew nothing about Judaism, therefore all his knowledge in his new faith came from the scribes and Pharisees. He was sincere and zealous, but sincerely wrong, which made his zeal fanaticism.

Translation Matthew 23:16–22

16 "Woe to you, blind guides, those saying, 'Whoever might swear by the temple, it is nothing; but whoever might swear by the gold of the temple, he is obligated.' 17 Foolish and blind! For which is greater, the gold or the temple that sanctifies the gold? 18 And, 'Whoever might swear by the altar, it is nothing; but whoever might swear by the gift that is on it, he is obligated.' 19 You blind! For which is greater, the gift or the altar sanctifying the gift? 20 Therefore he who having sworn by the altar, swears by it and by all things that are on it. 21 And the one having sworn by the temple, swears by it and by the one dwelling in it. 22 And he who having sworn by heaven, swears by the throne of God and by the one sitting on it."

TRANSLATION NOTE

In some manuscripts v. 19 begins with the words "fools and blind," as is in v. 17, and in other manuscripts v. 19 begins with the word "blind." Because there is no reason to have deleted "fools and" from v. 19 if these words had been in the original text, the words are considered to have been copied from v. 17 into v. 19.

EXPOSITION

Being deeply religious, or spiritual as it is called today, has nothing to do with God if it conforms to the values and practices of the world. The gold was more important to the religious leaders who had made the rule because it had tangible value, and the same was true for the gift on the altar. Materialism was what really mattered to these people. By pointing to tangible things they believed their religion could be measured; and if measured, then compared; and if compared, then by having more they could claim to be deeply religious. The response of the soul toward God—dedication, sanctification, devotion, worship—could not be touched or seen, and therefore had no measurable value.

Jesus spoke against such oaths in the Sermon on the Mount. Here he declares that true values are intangible and center in God. An oath is valid when witnessed by God, who knows the truth of the matter and will judge the oath maker not only by his words but also his actions. How much easier to certify an oath by the gold in the temple, for the gold cannot judge the sincerity of the oath maker, nor take action should the oath not be fulfilled. But God does and will. The religious leaders had substituted the world for an intimate relationship with God.

Translation Matthew 23:23–26

23 "Woe to you, scribes and Pharisees, hypocrites! Because you pay tithes of mint and dill and cummin, and have neglected the weightier matters of the law: justice and mercy and faith. Now it is necessary to do these, and those not to neglect. 24 Blind guides! Those straining out the gnat but swallowing the camel! 25 Woe to you, scribes and Pharisees, hypocrites! Because you cleanse the outside of the cup and of the dish, but inside they are full of robbery and self-indulgence. 26 Blind Pharisee! First cleanse the inside of the cup and of the dish, that the outside of them might also become clean."

EXPOSITION

Here again the logic and worthless value system of the religious leaders is exposed. The scribes and Pharisees took great care to tithe on the spices they used—a man-made tithe not required by the Law—so they may meet the most exacting requirements of their traditions concerning the Law. But they could not be bothered to take an interest in justice, mercy, and faith, which were the heart of the Law.

The various tithes required by the Law are much too complex to explain in full here (see my book, *Why Christians Should Not Tithe*, which has a detailed discussion of the tithe in the Mosaic Law). In brief, only grains, fruits, nuts, herds (cattle, oxen), and flocks (sheep goats) were tithed; some for one tithe, some for another, of the four kinds of tithes.

Jesus is not saying they should have tithed on their spices, but that tithing was appropriate (they were under the Law) and should be done. But—and it is a big objection—doing one part of the Law does not fulfill the whole Law. Tithing, in fact, was of less importance than the weightier matters of justice and mercy and faith.

The word weightier means important not trivial.[1] Jesus was using the terminology of the day; the religious professionals divided the Law into weightier and lighter commandments: some laws were important, some less important, and some trivial. Their worldly value system placed the emphasis on the things that could be seen

---

[1] Zodhiates, *WSDNT*, s. v. "926."

as the measure of piety. The scribes and Pharisees avoided their responsibilities under the Law with a show of religious works.

Verse 24 is a proverbial-type saying. They were careful to avoid the smallest unclean animal, the gnat, Leviticus 11:41, but swallowed the largest unclean animal, the camel, Leviticus 11:4. More plainly, they allowed themselves to sin the greater sins while avoiding the smaller sins. The smaller sins were the most obvious sins, the most public and visible sins. The larger matters, like injustice, cruelty, inequity, and no-faith were internal and easier to hide under the guise of religious affectation.

The cup and dish are metaphors. The outside of the cup is the outward appearance of piety in strict adherence to the elders' traditions and the minutia of the Law. The inside of the cup is the true spiritual condition of the Pharisees. Self-indulgence means they allowed themselves behavior that they condemned in others. Robbery may be literal. Perhaps, since many Pharisees were not religious professionals (were not scribes) but businessmen adhering to a certain religious philosophy, Jesus is saying they unjustly profit from their businesses. To cleanse the inside of the cup is to experience spiritual transformation: confession and repentance of sin because of genuine faith in God as Savior. When the inside is clean then the outside—one's actions—will be clean (righteous) also.

Translation Matthew 23:27–32

27 "Woe to you, scribes and Pharisees, hypocrites! Because you are like tombs having been whitewashed, which indeed outwardly appear beautiful, but inside are full of bones of the dead, and of all uncleanness. 28 Even so you indeed outwardly appear righteous to men, but inwardly you are full of hypocrisy and lawlessness. 29 Woe to you, scribes and Pharisees, hypocrites! Because you build the tombs of the prophets and adorn the monuments of the righteous, 30 and you say, 'If we had been in the days of our fathers, we would not have been partakers with them in killing the prophets.' 31 Thus you bear witness to yourselves that you are sons of those having murdered the prophets, 32 and you fill up the measure of your fathers."

TRANSLATION NOTE

In v. 30 the text reads, in part, "partakers with them in the blood of the prophets." I have given the sense of the text:

"partakers with them in killing the prophets."

EXPOSITION

The simile of tombs is similar to the cup and dish metaphor. Tombs are kept clean on the outside but are full of decay and bones on the inside. This describes the spiritual condition of the scribes and Pharisees. They had an outward appearance of spiritual life, but in their souls they were spiritually dead.

Their outward actions suggested they viewed the great prophets of God as their spiritual ancestors and honored others known for their righteousness. However, their true ancestors were the ones who had rejected God's prophets. They were just like their true ancestors and would act toward Jesus in the same manner their true ancestors had acted toward the prophets.

The demonstration of this fact is their preoccupation with the tombs of the prophets and righteous, versus listening to and following the message of righteousness communicated through these men. Jesus is making a logical syllogism. Since you spend your time decorating the tombs of the prophets, you show you are more interested in prophets as dead heroes rather than their living message. You show you are in agreement with the men who murdered the prophets.

The phrase "sons of" in v. 31 is not literal but figurative. Figuratively, a "son of" possesses the characteristics of the person or thing he or she is a son of. A "son of" those who murdered the prophets shares the same characteristics as the murderers: they will reject God's message and kill the messenger. To "fill up the measure of your fathers" is to complete what their fathers began, i.e., to kill God's final messenger, Jesus the Christ.

Translation Matthew 23:33–39

33 "Serpents, offspring of vipers, how may you escape from the condemnation of Gehenna? 34 Because of this, look, I send to you prophets and wise and scribes. Some of them you will kill and crucify, and some of them you will scourge in your synagogues, and will persecute from city to city, 35 so that upon you may come all the righteous blood being shed upon the earth, from the blood of Abel the righteous, to the blood of Zechariah son of Berekiah, whom you murdered between the temple and the altar. 36 Truly, I say to you, all these things will come upon this generation. 37 Jerusalem,

Jerusalem, killing the prophets and stoning those having been sent to her! How often would I have gathered your children, as a hen gathers her chicks under the wings; and you were not willing! 38 Look! Your house is left to you desolate. 39 For I say to you, no you shall not see me, from now until you say, 'Blessed the one coming in the name of the Lord!' "

EXPOSITION

Two different Greek words are used for "serpents" and "vipers" and the meaning is "snakes and sons of snakes."[1] They are just like their "fathers" who deserve the lake of fire (Gehenna, hell) for killing the prophets. How then can they escape if they reject Jesus?

Over and over again God has sent his messengers, and they are repeatedly rejected and killed. The opening of v. 34, "Because of this," emphasizes their failure. The religious leaders would continue to kill God's messengers. The emphatic "'I' send to you" may refer to YHWH sending prophets and wise and scribes in the Old Testament, or Jesus sending the same in the New Testament. Just as the unrighteous killed all the righteous YHWH had sent, even so the unrighteous will kill all whom Jesus will send. The reference to Abel and Zechariah indicate the killing will continue.

The scribes and Pharisees of Jesus' day are complicit with the murderers of the past. The Zechariah Jesus mentions appears to be the prophet murdered in 2 Chronicles 24:20–21. In the Hebrew Bible Genesis is the first book and 2 Chronicles is the last book. Thus, Abel and Zechariah are the "first and last" of the righteous to be murdered in the Old Testament. The murders of Abel and Zechariah are a form of merism, a figure of speech where the mention of a first and last incorporates all in between. An example: I searched "high and low" means I searched everywhere. Verse 36 seems to mean that all the past guilt will be laid on the generation that rejects Jesus. Since the lesser is incorporated by reference to the greater, and the greater is Jesus, then his death is the culmination of the nation's rejection of God's messengers and message.

Jerusalem was the city where God chose to place his name and was known in the Psalms as the city of the great king, who is God. Of all places on the earth, the people in this city should have

---

[1] Morris, *Matthew*, 587.

recognized their privilege and opportunity in the Person of Jesus. Yet, they rejected him. Jesus characterizes the city by its past deeds. We see should see in this characterization the entire nation, not just the city. YHWH placed his name in the city, and in its temple dedicated to him, but it was the nation itself that he made his own people, and in whom he had placed his name, and whom he gathered together in love.

The nation had turned against God's every effort to bring and keep them close to himself. Now Jesus, the One who could save them, is rejected by them. Just as they have rejected all God's servants in the past, even so they will reject the Son.

As the God who loved them and chose them out of all the nations on the earth, Jesus would have gathered his covenant people to himself as their Savior. They were not willing, and God leaves their nation desolate. Individuals can be saved, but the nation has lost its covenant relationship with YHWH. A New Covenant will be formed and a new people, the New Testament church, will be saved. Yet, as later passages show us, in the Gospels and the Epistles, there will be a gathering of national ethnic Israel under the New Covenant.

This is Jesus' last message to the crowds, his last effort to save all Israel in this first advent. Yet, all is not lost. There is coming a day when national ethnic Israel will recognize Jesus as their savior, v. 39. The final words are from Psalm 118:26, a psalm of trust, faith, and salvation in the Lord.

Matthew Twenty-Four

Translation Matthew 24:1–3

1 And Jesus having gone out was going away from the temple, and his disciples came near to point out to him the buildings of the temple. 2 Now he answering said to them, "Do you not see all these? Truly I say to you, there will be none left here, stone upon stone, which will not be thrown down." 3 Now as he was sitting upon the Mount of Olives, the disciples came near to him privately, saying, "Tell us, when these things will be; and what is the sign of your coming; and the completion of the age?"

EXPOSITION

True to his word in 23:39, Jesus leaves the temple area. He crosses the Kidron Valley to the Mount of Olives. As he is leaving the temple, his disciples direct his attention to the magnificent buildings. This particular version of the temple, known as Herod's temple to historians, had been in progress for forty-six years (John 2:20), and construction would continue for another thirty-six years. Josephus stated that Herod began the temple in the eighteenth year of his reign, which Josephus related to the visit of Augustus to Syria in spring or summer 20 BC; thus the reconstruction of the temple began in late 20 or early 19 BC. The sanctuary and inner courts were completed late 18 or early 17 BC, but the outer courts were not completed until AD 62. The temple mount was, by all accounts, a beautiful complex.

Jesus said it would be destroyed, and it was, at the conclusion of the AD 70 war with Rome. All that was left was part of one retaining wall supporting the temple mount. Today it is known as the western wall or the Wailing Wall, a name given to it by gentiles. For many years after the Jewish wars with Rome, Jews were forbidden to enter Palestine, except one time a year, to visit the ruins of Jerusalem. Gentiles hearing the Jews weeping at the wall gave it its name.

What follows in Matthew 24 and 25 are several prophetic announcements and explanations. The disciples didn't understand then (cf. Acts 1:6) and many do not understand now.

The very nature of any prophetic message does not require a complete understanding by the recipient. For example, in Psalm 22, David wrote what Christians now understand to be a hymn about the suffering of messiah. However, from David's point of view, his psalm was a hymn about his own suffering, using poetic imagery. The eunuch's comment (Acts 8:32–34) about Isaiah 53 (the same subject as Psalm 22), reflects the Jews' misunderstanding of these passages. Neither Isaiah, nor his immediate audience, nor readers in generations to come, fully understood the language, signs, and symbols of the prophecy. Jesus was the embodiment of messianic prophecies studied for centuries, yet even those who came to accept him as the promised messiah did not, at the time, grasp the necessity of his death and resurrection. A full and complete understanding of any prophecy waits for those who will experience the prophecy.

This is not to say some degree of understanding must wait until all the prophesied events are in progress or fulfilled. By comparing Scripture with Scripture one will find a suitable understanding of any prophecy, guided as always by the divine illumination and sovereign will of the Holy Spirit. We need not restrict the explanation of these prophecies in Matthew 24 and 25 to what the disciples and first century believers may have understood. Jesus gave these prophecies for his saints in every generation until his return.

Those parts that continue to remain unknown or uncertain will be understood by those living in the moment of fulfillment, as was Psalm 22 and Isaiah 53. However, every reader may understand enough for their faith and faithful living. Prophecy contains sufficient information to allow the interpreter to find an objective meaning and the significance of the text. In relation to these particular prophecies in Matthew 24, 25 more than enough can be understood to form an interpretation of the events leading up to and following the second advent of Christ, and an application for every believer from the first advent to the second.

My particular view of Scripture is from a dispensational perspective, which affects how I view "eschatology," the study of prophecies about last things. A comprehensive view of dispensationalism is beyond the scope of this commentary. My understanding of prophecy from a dispensational point of view is in my book, *Dispensational Eschatology*. An explanation of dispensationalism is in Ryrie's *Dispensationalism*.

> Dispensationalism views the world as a household run by God. In His household-world God is dispensing or

administering its affairs according to His own will and in various stages of revelation in the passage of time. These various stages mark off the distinguishable different economies in the outworking of His total purpose, and these different economies constitute the dispensations.[1]

As an example, one can easily see God managed his interaction with the world from Moses to Christ differently than he now does in the age between the two advents of Christ. The time from Moses to Christ, and the time from Christ's first to second advent, are different economies or dispensations in God's management of his household-world. The same is true if we view God's management of the world from Adam to Noah, or Noah to Abraham, or Abraham to Moses.

This is not to say there were different ways of salvation during the different economies/dispensations. Again, Ryrie:

The basis of salvation in every age is the death of Christ; the *requirement* for salvation in every age is faith; the *object* of faith in every age is God; the *content* of faith changes in the various dispensations.[2]

The content of saving faith under the Law, for example, was to bring the required sacrifice with faith in God's testimony that confession and repentance of sins and the death of the animal (as a substitute for the sinner) would result in forgiveness. The sinner's faith in God's testimony, accepted by God's grace, was saving. The death of the substitute was efficient for forgiveness because God by grace imputed Christ's merit to the believer's faith in offering the sacrifice with faith, repentance, and confession. Christ's merit was available because from eternity past God decreed that only Christ's merit would save sinners, Ephesians 1:4. Although Christ's death for sins was yet-future, God has from eternity past to eternity yet-future applied the result of his decree concerning Christ because what he has decreed is certain, Romans 4:17, God calls the things not yet existing into being.

The content of saving faith during this present New Testament church dispensation is faith in Christ alone, Ephesians 2:8–9, for he is the only propitiation (complete satisfaction) for sin, Romans 3:25;

---

[1] Ryrie, *Dispensationalism*, 29.
[2] Ibid., 115 (emphasis Ryrie).

1 John 2:2, and the only Savior, Acts 4:12. Salvation in the New Testament dispensation is through faith in God's testimony that dependence on the propitiation made by Christ to satisfy God for the crime of sin will result in forgiveness of the penalty of sin and receipt of eternal life.

There are three essential beliefs in dispensationalism.

> The essence of dispensationalism, then, is the distinction between Israel and the church. This grows out of the dispensationalist's consistent employment of normal or plain or historical-grammatical interpretation, and it reflects an understanding of the basic purpose of God in all his dealings with mankind as that of glorifying Himself through salvation and other purposes as well.[1]

Or, more simply, 1) A dispensationalist keeps Israel and the church distinct in the purpose, plans, and processes of God; 2) a dispensationalist uses a system of interpretation that understands scripture in the plain and normal sense of language and words; and 3) a dispensationalist understands the underlying purpose of God in the world is the glory of God, which he achieves through many means, including eternal salvation (the glory of his love) and eternal judgment (the glory of his holiness).

In a non-dispensational interpretation, the prophecies of chapters 24 and 25 are considered to have been, or are being, fulfilled in one way or another during the time between Christ's ascension to his second advent. The non-dispensational view generally sees the New Testament church as a new Israel assuming all the promises given to Old Testament Israel, in the same way the butterfly is a new phase of the caterpillar, which is to say, that in the non-dispensational view "the Church is really the *continuation* of Israel."[2] In the dispensational view, God has a distinct program for national ethnic Israel and the Church, although there are points where the two programs are similar or overlap.

My understanding of eschatology conforms to dispensational theology. God has separate eschatological programs for different people groups: the fallen angels; the peoples from Adam to Moses, national ethnic Israel, the New Testament church, unsaved

---

[1] Ibid., 41.
[2] Waldron, *Manifesto*, 7.

gentiles, Tribulation believers, and people living during the Davidic-Messianic kingdom of Christ on the earth. The prophecies in Matthew 24, 25 find their fulfillment in national ethnic Israel and the unsaved world during the Tribulation period and second advent. (The Tribulation is a period of about seven years during which Antichrist rules the world, God brings judgments upon the peoples of the world for their rejection of Christ, but many believe on Christ and are saved. The Tribulation period ends at Christ's second advent.)

Returning to the gospels, Mark and Luke more clearly indicate the disciples are admiring the buildings. I can imagine a different vocal emphasis from Jesus than from the disciples. The disciples said, "Do you *see* these things?" Jesus said "Do *you* see these things?" In direct response to their admiration of the temple he predicts its complete destruction.

One might draw one or more moral lessons here, but the plainest lesson takes into account the Jews' rejection and murder of Jesus. What seems magnificent to men is worthless to God without faith and obedience toward God. The temple God looks for is his active presence in the souls of his people.

The disciples were undoubtedly astonished. However, what Jesus said may have led them to believe the messianic reign would soon begin. Ezekiel 40 ff. describes a new city and temple built for Messiah's reign. If the current temple was to be destroyed, does that mean Jesus is about to bring about the end of the age and inaugurate his reign? Their questions are thus prophetically connected. When they reached the Mount of Olives, which was across the Kidron Valley opposite the city and temple, they asked Jesus to explain. Jesus sat down, the position of a teacher.

I believe the disciples thought they had asked one question with two intimately connected parts. They had, in their thoughts and theology, connected Jesus' statement about the temple with the messianic reign. They believed he was the Christ. Jesus had repeatedly told them he would be killed, a statement they had accepted but not understood because it did not fit into their messianic theology. He had repeatedly told them he would be raised the third day, a statement they did not comprehend—they believed in one general resurrection (e.g. Daniel 12:2; cf. John 11:23–24) prior to Messiah's Davidic Kingdom. Jesus had entered Jerusalem according to messianic prophecy. Now he was telling them the temple would be destroyed.

They knew from Zechariah 14 and other Old Testament passages that the world would worship the Lord in Jerusalem in the new age. From Ezekiel 40ff they knew that a new temple would be built for the messianic reign. How can all these things, some of them seemingly contradictory, be true? What is the prophetic order in which these things will come to pass? The disciples are more focused on Messiah's Davidic Kingdom than ever before. So, they are asking, "Tell us when all these things will come to pass; what will be the sign that this age has ended and your reign begins."

Many commentators acknowledge two questions by the disciples, but I find they have asked three questions:

When will these things be?
What will be the sign of your coming?
What will be the sign of the end of the age?

To understand Jesus' answers to these questions, we must understand the context in which they were asked and answered. The immediate subject was the temple, the essential component of Judaism, which would be present during Messiah's Davidic Kingdom, Ezekiel 40–48. Who was Jesus? The Messiah. What was the occasion? A prediction that Judaism would be destroyed. Who were the questioners? Jewish men looking for the Jewish' Messiah's Davidic Kingdom and believing Jesus was the Messiah of that Kingdom. What were the men expecting? Jesus the Messiah to judge his enemies, cleanse Israel, make the people ready, and bring the Davidic Messianic Kingdom into existence—soon.

The answers Jesus gave are not about the New Testament church. These Israeli men were concerned with Israel. Israeli men were asking the Israeli Messiah about the Israeli Kingdom. Jesus answered them as Israelis concerned with Israel. Every sign in Jesus' end-times discourse in Matthew (and Mark and Luke) concerns Israel, and every sign (except Luke 21:20–24, a prophecy of the AD 70 destruction of Jerusalem and Israel) concerns the Tribulation period.

The "end of the age" in the disciple's theology, and that of Jesus' also, see v. 14, was the end of "the times of the gentiles" followed by the reign of David's son, the Messiah/Christ, on the earth. The "times of the gentiles" is the rule of the gentiles over the earth in general and over Israel in particular, see Luke 21:24. The

Matthew Twenty-four

times of the gentiles began with the captivity of Israel by the Babylonian empire, and ends at Christ's second advent.

Jesus' answers to their questions arcs over the New Testament church age to the Israel of the future as Messiah's advent approaches. Many commentators believe the answers to the disciples' questions are interwoven throughout the discourse, so that it is not possible to clearly distinguish which answers belong to which questions. This is view is understandable because some of the characteristics that define the New Testament church age are similar to the characteristics of the times at the end of the church age. However, in the eschatological discourses in the Synoptic gospels (Matthew 24, 25; Mark 13; Luke 21) Jesus gives prophecy about national ethnic Israel, not the New Testament church.

Jesus does not directly address the New Testament church anywhere in the synoptic Gospels prior to his resurrection. This includes passages such as the Sermon on the Mount. In that sermon things such as the ethics of the kingdom and the reign of the King over his kingdom are applicable to the church, because the New Testament church will be part of the messianic kingdom with national ethnic Israel. Many other parts of the Synoptics are likewise applicable. However, the New Testament church is the mystery form of the kingdom, which is not revealed, except in parables (Matthew 13), until after the resurrection, and does not begin until the day of Pentecost, Acts 2.

In the Synoptic gospels Jesus addresses 1) the Jewish people for whom he is the messianic king, 2) the nation of Israel which is his messianic kingdom, and 3) in this eschatological discourse the relationship that nation and people bear to the Tribulation period and the second advent. This discourse is about Israel, not the church.

Where does Christ address the New Testament church? In the gospel of John, Jesus addresses the characteristics of the New Testament church age and his coming to remove the church from the world at the end of this present age. In John's Gospel Jesus speaks of tribulation the church will endure during the present age. In the Synoptics Jesus speaks about national ethnic Israel during the Tribulation period. Verses such as Matthew 24:4–14 (and their parallels in Mark and Luke) have an historical application to the New Testament church age, but these verses primarily concern Israel during the Tribulation. The events in Matthew 24:15–51 begin after

Matthew Twenty-four

the New Testament church has been removed from the world (the rapture).

The Olivet discourse may be divided into four parts.

Vv. 4–14, the character of Tribulation
Vv. 15–28, the great Tribulation period
Vv. 29–31, the signs of Messiah's second advent.
Vv. 32–51, the signs and character of the end of the age.

The AD 70 destruction of the temple is revealed in Luke 21:20–24, but not in Matthew. Historically, when Christians saw the Roman armies began to mass against Jerusalem in AD 70, they took it as the sign the abomination had come, Matthew 24:15 (cf. Daniel 9:27), and fled Jerusalem. However, that event was not the abomination of desolation.

Translation Matthew 24:4–14

4 And answering Jesus said to them, "Beware lest anyone misleads you. 5 For many will come in my name, saying, 'I am the Christ,' and they will mislead many. 6 Now you will hear of wars and rumors of wars. See that you are not alarmed, for it is necessary to take place; but not yet is the end. 7 For nation will rise against nation, and kingdom against kingdom. And there will be famines and pestilences and earthquakes in various places. 8 But all these are the beginning of sorrows. 9 Then they will deliver you to tribulation, and will kill you, and you will be hated by all the nations, on account of my name. 10 And then many will take offense, and they will betray one another, and will hate one another; 11 and many false prophets will arise, and will mislead many. 12 And because lawlessness is to be multiplied, the love of many will grow cold. 13 But the one having endured to the end, he will be saved. 14 And this good news of the kingdom will be proclaimed in all the world for a testimony to all the nations; and then the end will come.

TRANSLATION NOTE

In v. 7 the words "and pestilences" are not in some manuscripts, and are considered by some as imported from Luke 21:11.

EXPOSITION

There is no denying that the things described in vv. 4–14—wars and famines and pestilences and earthquakes—have been seen in the world repeatedly since Jesus gave this discourse, and will continue throughout the New Testament church dispensation, from the present to the rapture of the church. However, a similarity between an historical event and a prophecy is not necessarily the fulfillment of the prophecy. Though wars and natural events have occurred for the past (almost) 2,000 years, other, related, prophesied events have not occurred. Until those other events occur, the world will continue to experience wars and famines and pestilences and earthquakes, and it will not, yet, be time for the Tribulation.

Jesus' eschatological prophecies in the Synoptic Gospels may easily be applied to the character of the present age, the New Testament church age, because there have been, and will continue to be, wars and famines and pestilences and earthquakes. But as I have discussed extensively in other publications (e.g., *Dispensational Eschatology, John's Epistles; Antichrist*) the New Testament church age is the last time before the end times. The "end times" (a phrase not used in Scripture) are the Day of the Lord prophesied in the Old Testament. The end times begin with the rise of Antichrist to power through a covenant he makes, and there will be wars and famines and pestilences and earthquakes, Revelation 6:1–7, unlike any preceding period of time in the world, "such as has not been from the beginning of the world until now, no, nor may be" (Matthew 24:21). But until the Antichrist comes to power (Daniel 7:8, 20; 9:27, the time is not the end times, but the last time, i.e., the New Testament church age.

The end times are the Tribulation and second advent. The last time (1 John 2:18; 1 Peter 1:5, 20; Jude 18) is the present church age. The second advent of Christ has been imminent from the ascension, Acts 1:11, and the so-called "signs of the times" (wars and famines and pestilences and earthquakes) have been in evidence since the ascension.

From the time of Christ's ascension the world has seen, and the church has suffered, wars, and famines, and diseases, and earthquakes, and persecution, and tribulation. The world has persecuted Christians. Christian has betrayed Christian. False prophets have claimed to be Christ, or that the end is near, or here. False prophets have proclaimed false gospels and created false religions and have mislead many. Lawlessness has multiplied.

Because of these things many have abandoned their faith, and

Matthew Twenty-four

the love of many toward Christ has grown cold, i.e., they have followed the values and ways of the world. These are the things that have characterized the world and the church in church age. Nor is today different from the past. Martin Luther in AD 1532 thought Christ's advent was near when he wrote, *The Signs of Christ's Coming and the Last Days*. In 1843 people left jobs and houses and lands and friends to gather in fields and on hills for the return of Christ, and were disappointed. Today many continue to look for signs.

Why do cultural-political-social-generational-national-regional-tribal unrest and violence continue if it is not time for the end times? Because Satan does not know when the Tribulation begins; he does not know when Christ will return. Satan keeps the world in readiness with wars and rumors of wars, nation rising against nation, kingdom against kingdom, people against people, and famines, and pestilences in various places because he does not know the time of the end, but he wants to be ready. He sends his many antichrists to claim they will bring peace, so when the time of the end does come he and the world are prepared for his peacemaker, the Antichrist, who does bring peace, for a little while. These things—wars and rumors of wars, nation rising against nation, kingdom against kingdom, people against people, and famines, and pestilences, and antichrists—must come to pass during the New Testament church age, but the time of the end, i.e., the Tribulation, the Antichrist, and Christ's return, is not yet. Only God—not the world, not Satan, not the church—only God knows when it is time for the end times, Acts 1:7.

The religious, historical and cultural context of Matthew 24 requires we see the apostles not as leaders of the New Testament church, but as Israelis looking for the Davidic Kingdom in Jesus the messiah, and interpret Matthew 24 relevant to national ethnic Israel and Messiah's Kingdom. At this point in their history the apostles were looking for the kingdom, not the church, and Jesus answers them accordingly.

Let us now look at Matthew 24:4–14 in outline, so we can see how the prophecies here coordinate with the Revelation. Before beginning, I want to again emphasize that these prophecies of the end times refer to national ethnic Israel, not the New Testament church.

The events of 24:4–13 describe the beginning of the

Tribulation period, specifically Revelation 6:1–8. There Antichrist initiates his kingdom (Daniel 2:40–43; 7:7–8, 20, Daniel 9:27 describe this time period) and God begins to bring judgment to the unsaved.

Matthew 24:13, "But the one having endured to the end, he will be saved," is not a conditional statement but a statement of fact. The believer's salvation—whether the New Testament Christian or the Tribulation believer—is secured by the merit of Christ, not the believer's works. In the prophetic Tribulation context "the end" is the second advent. The "end" Jesus prophesies is not the end of the New Testament church age that precedes the Tribulation. It is not the Tribulation period that immediately precedes the second advent. "The end" is when the kingdom is realized on the earth, therefore "the end" is the return of the king to destroy his enemies and inaugurate his kingdom rule on the earth, Revelation 19:11–20:6.

The consummating purpose of the second advent is for God to take up his great power and reign, Revelation 11:17. The reign of God is the Messianic Kingdom of Jesus the Christ visible and active on earth. Therefore, to "endure to the end" in the context of "this gospel of the kingdom" means the Tribulation believers are to endure even unto death, for most, or to the second advent and into the Kingdom, for some. "This gospel of the kingdom," Revelation 11:17, is the king returning to take up his great power and reign.

Matthew 24:14 reflects two passages in Revelation: the good news of the coming kingdom and the eternal good news (the good news of salvation).

> Revelation 11:17, saying, "We give thanks to you, Lord, the one being God Almighty, and who was, that you have taken your great power and have begun to reign.
>
> Revelation 14:6–7, And I saw another messenger, flying in mid-heaven, having the everlasting good news to proclaim to the earth dwellers, and to every nation, and tribe, and language, and people. 7 He was saying in a loud voice, "Fear God, and give him glory, because the hour of his judgment has come, and worship the one having made heaven, and the earth, and sea, and springs of waters."

The prophecy of Matthew 24:14, "this good news of the kingdom will be proclaimed in all the world for a testimony to all the nations," is not fulfilled by the New Testament church. The church has, over the centuries, proclaimed the Gospel of Salvation worldwide. But the prophetic fulfillment is in the verses above, Revelation 14:6–7, when there are so few believers left alive (after persecution and martyrdom) to preach the word, that God in mercy sends an angel to proclaim the simplest form of the good news of salvation, during the last half of the Tribulation. Then the end will come, i.e., then it will be time for Christ's return, Armageddon, and the Messianic Kingdom.

Revelation 14:6–7 is a particular form of the good news of salvation designed for the Tribulation believers. The means of salvation is the same: faith in God; the propitiation made by Christ. The content of faith has been simplified: "Fear God and give him glory, because the hour of his judgment has come. Worship the Maker of heaven and earth, the sea and springs of water." This is the good news that will be preached "in all the world as a witness to all the nations before the end comes."

As the moment of the second advent draws near, God in his mercy has simplified the message of salvation to its most basic component: I am coming to judge you earth dwellers; turn from idolatry and worship me. Thus, the timing of the message within the chronology of the Tribulation is of importance. The beast has secured his authority over mankind. He is making war against the saints and overcoming them (Revelation 13:7); the living remnant of believers is diminishing. The voice of God's witness through human believers is being silenced. Millions are turning in fear to the beast. Then, from an earth-dweller's point of reference, the very heavens cry out with an eternal message of salvation: "Fear God and give glory to him."

To fear God requires self-humiliation and self-surrender to him. To give God the glory is an idiom of repentance. The means of this proclamation is the work of angels, a voice that cannot be silenced (the first and only time angels preach the good news). The subject is salvation. The timing is the coming return of the Lord Jesus and the judgments that accompany and immediately follow his return (Revelation 19:11–20; Matthew 25:31–46; Ezekiel 20:33–38). The recipients are those who dwell on the earth, i.e., those being led, duped, or coerced into worshiping the beast. The purpose is the mercy of God in saving souls.

In viewing this simple message of salvation, one should look to the larger picture. During the Great Tribulation God has many witnesses of his grace and mercy: the 144,000 (Revelation 71–8); those saved by the ministry of the 144,000 (Revelation 7:9–17; the two witnesses (Revelation 11:1–14); the angelic preaching (Revelation 14:6–7). The Tribulation may be the greatest period of evangelism and salvation in human history, Revelation 7:9. Surely God is merciful!

The content of the gospel may change, but the message is always the same, "fear God and give him the glory," compare Zechariah 14:16; Isaiah 2:2, 3; Micah 4:1, 2. One should not suppose a contradiction between the gospel that Paul, or Peter, or James preached, and this eternal gospel. The first duty of the creature has always been to "fear [reverence and awe] God and give the glory to him." The outward presentation of that duty is the message of salvation, because to accomplish the duty one must turn from sin to God in faith. As previously discussed above, the content of the "good news" message has varied according to the several economies of God's grace toward mankind from Adam to Christ. In this New Testament age of grace and church, the content is Jesus Christ crucified, buried, and resurrected. In the Tribulation period I have no doubt that the 144,000 will be preaching Jesus crucified, resurrected, ascended, and shortly arriving at his second advent; and souls will be saved.

I realize most readers have been taught to relate Matthew 24:14 solely to the New Testament church. However, this verse does not define the commission or mission of the church. The church's commission and mission are defined in Matthew 29:18–20; Mark 16:16–15; Luke 24:44–49; John 20:31; 21:22; Acts 1:8. The character of the New Testament church age reflects the coming events of the end times because during these last times the world is being kept in readiness for the end times.

Translation Matthew 24:15–22

15 "Therefore when you shall see the 'abomination of desolation' spoken of by Daniel the prophet, standing in the holy place,' the one reading let him understand. 16 Then those in Judea let them flee to the mountains. 17 The one on the housetop, let him not come down to take anything out of his house. 18 And the one in the field, let him not return back to take his garment. 19 But woe to those pregnant, and to those nursing infants, in those days! 20

Matthew Twenty-four

Now, pray that your flight might not be in winter, or on a Sabbath. 21 For then there will be great tribulation, such as has not been from the beginning of the world until now, no, nor may be. 22 And if those days had not been shortened, there would not have been anybody saved, but because of the elect, those days will be shortened."

TRANSLATION NOTE

In v. 22 the English past tense, "if those days had not been shortened" and "there would not have been anybody saved," is a result of translating the Greek aorist tense into English. The aorist presents an event as a whole, complete (but not necessarily completed) event without regard to time. In God's plan for these yet-future days, the days have been shortened so some believers survive to enter the kingdom.

EXPOSITION

Beginning in v. 15 Jesus transitions from describing the character of the Tribulation period to describing actual events occurring during the Tribulation. The "abomination of desolation" is the first of these events, a prophecy given at Daniel 9:27.

The abomination of desolation is an event that occurs at the mid-point of the Tribulation period, at which the Antichrist of the first half of the Tribulation becomes the beast of the last half of the Tribulation: same person, different name and character. Neither Jesus nor the Revelation nor other New Testament writings say much about the rise of Antichrist to world dominance during the first half of the Tribulation. I have previously listed the most relevant of these verses: Daniel 2:41–43; 7:8, 20; 9:27; Revelation 6:1–2. To this list may be added Revelation 13:1–2; 17:1–12.

Beginning at 24:15 Jesus talks about that time of the Tribulation known as the Great Tribulation, which is the last half of the Tribulation, after the Antichrist becomes the beast, 2 Thessalonians 2:3–4, Revelation 13:3–4. The abomination of desolation is described at Daniel 9:27.

> He will prevail in a covenant with many for one seven, but in half a seven sacrifice and offering will cease and on a corner [of the temple] will be the detestable idol which makes desolate, until the full end determined be poured out on the desolator. (JDQT)

I have explained this prophecy in depth in my commentary on Daniel and my book *Antichrist*. Without going into the explanation, a "seven" in this prophecy is 2,520 days, "half a seven" is 1,260 days. The 2,520 days is the length of the Tribulation period (nominally seven years), which is divided into two periods of 1,260 days each. The abomination of desolation occurs at the end of the first 1,260 days.

The person "he" in Daniel 9:27 is "the coming prince" in Daniel 9:26, who is the Antichrist in 1 John 2:18, the man of sin, son of perdition, and lawless one in 2 Thessalonians 2:3, 8, and the "beast" in Revelation 11, 13–17; 19–20. The Antichrist's act of desolation, Daniel 9:27, or as Jesus calls it, abomination of desolation, is explained at 2 Thessalonians 2:4,

> the one [the man of sin, son of perdition, lawless one] opposing and exalting himself above every (so-called) god or object of worship—so as to sit down in the temple of God, showing himself that he is God.

Which is why Jesus says the abomination of desolation will be standing in the holy place (in the temple), the place where "sacrifice and offering" take place Daniel 9:27. The Antichrist's act of abomination will take place at the "half a seven," i.e., the mid-point of the Tribulation, 1,260 days after the covenant that begins the Tribulation.

The abomination of desolation is both the man and his act in the temple. He goes to a rebuilt temple, pretends to be God, and demands everyone in the world worship him. The word "antichrist" describes his character. He is opposed to Christ and supplants Christ in the view of the world. After his pseudo-resurrection, Revelation 13:3, he commits his abominable act, 2 Thessalonians 2:4, and becomes the "beast" who rules the world and persecutes believers. The title "beast" names the man and describes the violence and brutality of his kingdom. In the fullness of his apostasy the unholy trinity of the beast, the false prophet, and the dragon (Satan), lead mankind into abominable idolatry.

Jesus describes those days in the most intense manner. He is prophetically addressing those persons, national ethnic Israel, who will be living during the Tribulation, who will be in Jerusalem when the event occurs. Jesus tells them, no matter where you might be when the act takes place, run away. Don't stop or return to grab anything. Take your life and flee. Pray that certain conditions do not prevail which would make your flight more difficult. The flight spoken of in vv. 16–20 most likely corresponds to Revelation 12:13–17. (See my commentary on the Revelation, *The Epistle of Jesus to the Church*).

We know the time is the Tribulation period because Jesus says the troubles will be greater than any that have ever occurred and an event of that magnitude will never occur again. That is also how we know the Tribulation has not occurred to this date. The terrible events that have occurred thus far in the history of the world have not been of the magnitude Jesus describes. Moreover, the events that have occurred in the history of the world have repeatedly occurred. The Tribulation has not yet taken place.

The coming days of the Tribulation are so terrible, that if God's plan had not shortened those yet-future days, no one would survive. The fact the duration has already been shortened in the plan of God is expressed in the aorist tense, indicating a complete act: the days have already been shortened. This is possible because the Tribulation is an event already planned and prepared on God's prophetic calendar, waiting for the proper day and time to begin. God has shortened the days so some believers survive to enter into Messiah's Kingdom.

Translation Matthew 24:23–28

23 "Then if anyone says to you, 'Look, here is the Christ,' or 'Here,' don't believe. 24 For false christs will rise and false prophets, and will give great signs, and wonders, so as to mislead, if possible, even the elect. 25 Look, I have foretold it to you. 26 If therefore they say to you, 'Look, he is in the wilderness,' do not go; 'Look, he is in the inner rooms,' do not believe. 27 For just as the lightning comes from the east and shines as far as the west, so will be the coming of the son of man. 28 For wherever the carcass might be, there the vultures will be gathered."

EXPOSITION

No one living today, or tomorrow, or at any time in the future until after the Tribulation begins, can know the date—year or month or week or day—when Christ will return. If they say they know, "Don't believe." Believers *during* the Tribulation are to look for the sign of Christ's return appearing in the sky (Revelation 11:15–19; 19:11–16). The sign is caused by Christ's return. So when the sign is seen, and not before, then there will be no doubt as to when

Christ is returning to reign over the earth. Therefore all who read or hear Christ's words during this New Testament church age cannot know. And all those enduring the trials of the great Tribulation should not be deceived by those claiming to be the messiah, for when the time for his appearing has come, the signs in the sky will make that appearing unmistakable.

Now, a word needs to be said about the duration of the Tribulation relevant to Christ's coming. According to Daniel 9:27 (coordinate with Revelation 6:2; Daniel 7:8, 20), the Tribulation begins with a covenant that is supposed to last one seven, which is 2,520 days. Because the context of the prophecy is Daniel's people, national ethnic Israel (9:24), one assumes it is a covenant that brings peace to the Middle East. So, someone knowledgeable could understand from the date the covenant is made that Christ is returning in 2,520 sunset-to-sunset days.

Again according to Daniel 9:27, with Revelation 13:3, and 2 Thessalonians 2:4, that covenant will be broken when the man of sin stands in the temple declaring himself to be God. Because Daniel 9:27 states the covenant is broken in the middle of the seven, then a knowledgeable person could count 1,260 sunset-to-sunset days to Christ's return from the date the Antichrist declares himself to be God.

These facts are all the more reason for believers *not* to be deceived by false Christs and seemingly miraculous signs and wonders. Even for these knowledgeable persons, what confirms the arrival of the second advent are the signs Christ's advent causes when it occurs.

So let me state again, *no person today*, during this New Testament church age, can know when Christ is returning. The three events that foretell when Christ is returning are Daniel 9:27a, the covenant that begins the Tribulation, Daniel 9:27b, the broken covenant in the middle of the Tribulation, and Revelation 11:15–19; 19:11–16 the sign in the sky caused by Christ returning.

Verses 23–28 are the Antichrist-beast and false prophet deceiving the world. Verse 24 refers to the Antichrist and the false prophet, Revelation 13. Verse 27 looks to Revelation 11:15–19; 16:17. Verse 28 corresponds to Revelation 14:17–20. In v. 28 the Greek word translated "vultures" means either eagles or vultures, because both are carrion eaters; the former as an act of opportunity, the latter as a career. The saying is proverbial in nature. When the messiah returns he will gather all his enemies into one place for destruction, Revelation 19:17–18.

Translation Matthew 24:29–31

29 "Now immediately during the tribulation of those days, the sun will be darkened, and the moon will not give its light, and the stars will fall from the sky, and the powers of the heavens will be shaken. 30 And then will appear the sign of the son of man in the heaven, and then all the tribes of the earth will mourn, and they will see the son of man coming on the clouds of heaven with power and great glory. 31 And he will send his angels with a great trumpet call, and they will gather his elect from the four winds, from the ends of the heavens to the ends of them."

TRANSLATION NOTE

In v. 29 the word I have translated "during" is *meta*, which is translated "after" by other versions. The word means "mid, amid, in the midst, with, among, implying accompaniment."[1] When used with the accusative case ("tribulation" is in the accusative case) it "strictly implies motion toward the middle or into the midst of something." The idea is one thing accompanies another thing, thus, the things happening to the sun, moon, etc., accompany—are part of—the Tribulation. Other translations view *meta* as indicating succession in time (thus, "after") because of the preceding "immediately."

EXPOSITION

Verses 29–30 correspond to the sixth seal and the seventh bowl, Revelation 6:12–17; 16:18–21. Verse 30 corresponds to Revelation 14:14–16, 17–20; 16:17–21; 19:11–21. Verse 31 relates to several Old Testament prophecies of the gathering of the Jews to the land of Israel for the Davidic Messianic kingdom, e.g., Zechariah 8:7–8; Ezekiel 20:33–38.

This is how Jesus answered the disciples' questions:

Question One: "When will these things be?"

Answer: "When you see these events happening, that is when these things will be."

Question Two: "What will be the sign of your coming?"

---

[1] Zodhiates, *WSDNT*, s. v. "3326."

Answer: "My coming will be as unmistakable as the lightening."

Question Three: "What will be the sign of the end of the age?"

Answer: "When my sign appears in heaven it marks the end of the age."

Obviously Jesus did not give sufficient information—no information at all—to justify the continual date-setting and constant watching for signs-of-the-times which some members of the New Testament church have engaged in for almost 2,000 years.

Translation Matthew 24:32–35

32 "Now learn the parable from the fig tree: when its branch is already become tender and it puts forth the leaves, you know that the summer is near. 33 And so you, when you see all these things, know that it is near, at the doors. 34 Truly I say to you, that this generation may by no means have passed away until all these things may have taken place. 35 The heaven and the earth will pass away, but my words by no means may pass away."

EXPOSITION

Verses 32–33 are plain enough: believers during the Tribulation are to look for the coming of the messiah. They are to gauge the timing of his coming by events in the world, the events Jesus has just described. Jesus is again answering the questions in general terms: when you see these things happening—events occurring during the tribulation—then my coming and the end of the age is near.

Though some would apply this to the church, there are no signs for the coming of Christ to take his New Testament church out of the world; there are no signs for the rapture. That coming is imminent: occurring at any time without any preceding signs. All the signs Jesus has revealed come after the church has been taken out of the world.

The New Testament church age believer is to wait in constant expectation for Jesus to deliver the church from the wrath to come, 1 Thessalonians 1:10; Revelation 3:10. These signs in Matthew indicate the wrath of God has arrived, so believers living during that period of wrath, the Tribulation, are to look for Jesus who is coming to bring God's wrath to its conclusion, Revelation 14:17–19; 19:11–

21.

"This generation," v. 34, refers to the generation alive when "all these things take place." Obviously the generation of the people of the disciples he is speaking to died before Christ returned. The same is true in modern times; many generations have passed away. Some believe "this generation" refers to the Israel that became a nation in 1948. These people have to keep extending the duration of a generation, because sixty-eight years have passed, to date. The beginning of the generation Christ speaks of is the generation alive when all those things he is speaking of begin, which is the Tribulation period. Verse 35 is Jesus' confirmation that these things he has prophesied are truth and will come to pass. Jesus himself is the confirmation of every word of God.

Translation Matthew 24:36–39

36 "But about that day and hour no one knows, not even the angels of the heavens, nor the son, except Father only. 37 For as were the days of Noah, so will be the coming of the son of man. 38 For as they were in those days, before the flood, eating and drinking, marrying and giving in marriage, until that day Noah entered into the ark, 39 and they knew not until the flood came and took all away; and so will the coming of the son of man."

TRANSLATION NOTE

In v. 36, the phrase "nor the son," is not in the majority of the witnesses of Matthew, including the later Byzantine text [KJV/NKJV text]. On the other hand, the best representatives of the Alexandrian and the Western types of texts [NIV, NASB, HCSB] contain the phrase.[1]

The probability of omission due to doctrinal considerations is more likely than the addition of the phrase by importing it from Mark 13:32.

EXPOSITION

No one can know when the tribulation begins or when Christ will return, until the Tribulation begins. Not even the son of God knew at the time the prophecy was given. During his earthly ministry the God the Son incarnate limited his divine omniscience

---

[1] Metzger, *Textual*, 51–52.

to those things revealed to him by the Holy Spirit, whether it was the thoughts of men, or the end-times calendar, because he chose to live his life as a Holy Spirit-filled man. If these things were not revealed to the Son when he was incarnate on the earth, why do some people think the Holy Spirit will reveal it to them?

At vv. 37–39 Jesus said no one can know. He was referring to the Noahic Flood. Someone may say there were signs of impending judgment because Noah was building the Ark. The Ark was not a sign of judgment but of salvation. In these verses Jesus plainly states life continued as normal until the day Noah entered the ark. We don't know how long after the Ark was completed until God commanded Noah to enter; and after he entered seven days passed before the flood began. Noah didn't know when the flood would begin. The people who would die in the flood "did not know until the flood came." So also will be the coming of the son of man. If we view Noah entering the Ark as analogous to the rapture, then Noah didn't know when to leave the earth—enter the Ark—until God called him up into the Ark. No one, not Noah, not anyone, except God, knew if the flood was near or when the flood would begin. So too the rapture and the Tribulation.

The fact that God the Son in his incarnation did not know during his time on earth when the Tribulation and the second advent would occur is not a limitation of his deity, but a function of the Christ in his prophetic office during his first advent. Pragmatically, if Jesus had known the day and hour, but did not tell us, then the New Testament church would have launched itself on an endless search to discover knowledge of that day and hour somewhere in all the words Jesus spoke during his first advent. As it is, even though Jesus said no one except the Father knew, compare Acts 1:7, men have still tried to assign a day and hour to these events. Naturally Jesus after his ascension knows, because the self-imposed limitations of his earthly ministry are removed.

In vv. 37–39 Jesus says life will be unassumingly normal before these events begin. The world at large will not be looking for or expecting in any sense a messiah, let alone the messiah, Jesus the Christ. When God begins his judgments, and allows the Antichrist to rise to power, then in the ensuing wars, famines, disease, and lawlessness men will begin to look for a savior, and accept the Antichrist as filling that position. In the interim, few will know and fewer will care that Christ is returning to reign. Judgment will overtake all those who do not enter the ark of redemption which is faith in Jesus the Christ.

Translation Matthew 24:40–44

40 "Then two will be in the field: one is taken and one is left; 41 two grinding at the mill: one is taken and one is left. 42 Therefore keep watch, because you do not know on what day your Lord is coming. 43 But know this, that if the householder had known in what watch of the night the thief comes, he would have watched, and not have allowed his house to be broken into. 44 And on account of this, you be ready, for the son of man comes in that hour you do not expect."

EXPOSITION

This is a simple description of the suddenness of judgment, and a warning to be prepared by having faith in Jesus the coming Messiah, because the unsaved do not know when Jesus is coming. In vv. 40–41 the one taken is taken in judgment, not salvation. The context of vv. 42–44 is the example set by the unbelievers in Noah's day: they did not know until judgment came. How do we know one is taken in judgment? Because the other is left. What comes after the Lord's return? The Davidic Messianic kingdom. The one left is left for the kingdom. Notice also that vv. 42–44 come on the heels of the judgment stated in vv. 40–41.

Translation Matthew 24:45–51

45 "Who then is the faithful servant, and wise, whom the master has set over his household, to give to them food in season? 46 Blessed that servant, whom the master having come, will find doing thus. 47 Truly I say to you, that he will set him over all his possessions. 48 But if that evil servant should say in his heart, 'My master delays,' 49 and should begin to beat his fellow servants, and to eat and drink with the drunkards, 50 the master of that servant will come in a day in which he does not expect, and in an hour which he is not aware, 51 and will scourge him and will appoint him a place with the hypocrites; there shall be the weeping and the gnashing of teeth."

TRANSLATION NOTE

In v. 51 the word I have translated "scourge" is *dichotoméō*, literally, "to cut in two or asunder."[1] A metaphorical meaning is required, because after the unfaithful servant has been *dichotoméō*, he/she is appointed a place with the hypocrites. The figurative meaning of the word is "scourging." The unfaithful servant will be judged and punished. The punishment is eternity in the place of weeping and gnashing teeth: ultimately the lake of fire.

EXPOSITION

Let us not be confused by the sound of words. Believers are used to hearing the word "servant" in the context of a Christians serving Jesus. But let us remember Jesus is prophetically addressing national ethnic Israel during the Tribulation. The "servant" is a representation of the people of the nation. The faithful servant is the saved servant who obeys the Lord through worship, service, obedience, and fellowship, always prepared for whenever Christ should appear. The unfaithful servant reveals by his actions that he is the unsaved person. The exhortation is for all to become faithful servants. The person who is unfaithful will be taken in eternal judgment. There is an application for believers in any time: be a faithful servant; and for unbelievers: believe and be saved.

---

[1] Zodhiates, *WSDNT*, s. v. "1371."

Matthew Twenty-Five

Translation Matthew 25:1–13

1 "Then the kingdom of the heavens will be like ten virgins, who having taken their torches, went out to meet the bridegroom. 2 Now five of them were foolish, and five wise. 3 For the foolish, having taken their torches, did not take oil with them, 4 but the wise took oil in the vessels with their torches. 5 Now the bridegroom delaying, they all became sleepy and slept. 6 And at the middle of the night there was an outcry: 'Look, the bridegroom, go out to meet him.' 7 Then all those virgins arose, and trimmed their torches. 8 But the foolish said to the wise, 'Give us from your oil, for our torches are going out.' 9 Now the wise answered, saying, 'No, lest it might not even be enough for us and you; go rather to those selling, and buy for yourselves.' 10 Now while going to buy, the bridegroom came, and those ready went in with him to the wedding feast; and the door was shut. 11 But afterward the other virgins also come, saying, 'Sir, sir, open to us.' 12 But answering he said, 'Truly, I say to you, I do not know you.' 13 Therefore watch, for you neither know the day nor the hour" [in which the son of man comes.]

TRANSLATION NOTE

In vv. 1, 3–4, 7–8 the word which most translate "lamp" but I have translated "torches" is *lampás*, "a torch, lamp, lantern." In New Testament times a lamp was a shallow bowl filled with oil in which a wick was floated; sometimes the bowl was covered. A torch was a long stick or metal staff with flammable material in one end. The torches in the story were probably a metal staff with a brass bowl on one end. Rags, oil, and pitch (an oily resin) were placed into the bowl and set afire.[1] A brass vessel of oil was carried to feed the flame as might be required. The *lampás* in the parable was used in an outdoor procession. Torch is the proper translation.

In v. 13, the longer ending formed by the clause in brackets is supported by some manuscripts, not supported by many more. The clause may have been added from 24:44 to provide a similar ending to a story with the same exhortation. The presence or absence of the clause does not materially affect the meaning. The shorter

---

[1] Freeman, *Manners*, s. v. "708."

ending does require the reader to reflect on previous warnings.

EXPOSITION

This is not an allegory but a parable. This means the point of the story is not in the details but in the conclusion. The bridegroom represents the returning messiah. The ten girls represent people who are viewed as members of the kingdom, but only five are genuine members. The defining moment of the story is when the bridegroom, the messiah, physically returns. The point of the story is when the bridegroom denies knowing the foolish girls.

This and the following parable are about national ethnic Israel during the Tribulation, not the New Testament church. The church is not waiting for the Messiah's Kingdom on the earth, but for their Savior to return for them, John 14:2-3, to take the church out of the world. Some interpret the foolish virgins as the church in the Tribulation. This is not possible: in the parable the messiah does not recognize some of the people, but every member of the New Testament church is recognized by the Lord, John 10:27. Nor is the oil representative of the Holy Spirit, who indwells every church member. One cannot go out and buy more Holy Spirit. The oil is simply a true-to-life detail: oil was used in torches.

The point of the ten girls parable is the same as the previous parable: national ethnic Israel during the Tribulation is to maintain readiness for Messiah's advent. The wise girls are the same kind of representation as the faithful servant; the ten foolish girls are the same kind of representation as the unfaithful servant.

Little is known about the details of first century marriage ceremonies and celebrations. What little is known tells us the bridegroom went to his betrothed's house and married her. The ten girls are waiting for his return. On his return the girls will go out with their torches and be part of the procession to light the way to welcome the bride to her new home. These are the normal and expected details of a wedding, not allegories to be filled in with imagination. More simply, the bride is part of the cart that is carrying the story. Simpler still: the church is not the bride

The word translated "virgins" means a young unmarried girl, therefore a virgin. In the cultural setting of the story the ten girls are to be the attendants of the bride. Married women were not attendants of the bride. Neither their age, nor their unmarried condition, nor their position as attendants is significant to the point of the story. These are conditions that are normal to the culture and therefore must be a part of the story if the story is to be a suitable medium to communicate the message. The fact that there are two groups of five each is not spiritually or prophetically significant, but is simply a convenient division to make the point: some of national ethnic Israel will be waiting and prepared when their messiah comes to set up his Davidic Messianic kingdom; some will not be prepared. I stress again that the New Testament church is not waiting for the messiah to come but for their Savior to return at the rapture. The church is not waiting for the Davidic Messianic kingdom but is already living with the king when they return with him from heaven at his second advent, immediately after which he inaugurates his Messianic kingdom.

The bridegroom is delayed; the ten girls sleep. We should remember that the culture had no accurate way to tell the time, so punctuality was not a virtue of the culture. This means the unpreparedness of the five foolish girls was inexcusable. Jesus is setting up the condition for the point of the parable. This was a dawn to dusk culture, therefore it would be natural for these girls to fall asleep as the night wore on. Since the point is preparedness, then there must be a plot point in the story that causes the oil in the torch to burn off, requiring more oil to be supplied. That plot point is that while they waited they fell asleep and their torches continued burning. In an era with no way to light the darkness except a flame, it was normal to keep a lamp or torch burning throughout the night.

Sometime during the night the alert is sounded: the bridegroom comes. The five wise girls pour more oil onto their torches. The five foolish have no extra oil. The foolish ask for oil from the wise, but the five wise girls have just enough oil for their own needs. Remember, the lesson here is preparedness. Preparedness cannot be shared, one either is, or is not, prepared.

Even though it is the middle of the might (not necessarily midnight) the five foolish are told to go and but some oil. For this to be true to the culture it must have been possible to wake up the oil merchant in order to buy oil to meet some urgent condition. This would take time, emphasizing the point that being prepared means to always be prepared. When messiah returns there will be no time to become prepared. Each person must be personally prepared for his return before he returns, waiting for his return in an always prepared condition until he returns. Succinctly put, being saved is the necessary preparedness for Messiah's return; when he returns, it will be too late to be saved. (Judgment as to who will enter the Davidic Messianic kingdom is preparatory to inaugurating the kingdom. See comments concerning Israel at vv. 31–46, below.)

The five wise girls meet the wedding party, attend to the bride, light the way to the house, and enter into the house to participate in the celebration. Much later the foolish five return, believing themselves to now be prepared; but they come after the door is shut and are refused entry. They were invited, but since they were not prepared and waiting the Messiah's response is, "I do not know you."

We miss the point if we think the bridegroom does not know them because they were not present when he arrived. Here is where we must apply the spiritual point of the story. He does not know them because only those who are prepared for the Davidic Messianic kingdom (saved) are the true members of that kingdom. He knows who the foolish are, but he does not know them in a salvific way. He does not acknowledge their right to the kingdom because they were never part of the kingdom. If they had been genuine members of the kingdom they would have been prepared (saved) for his coming.

The spiritual point of the story is that those who are saved during the Tribulation will be actively waiting for messiah's advent. Those who are not saved are not actively waiting. The point of the story cannot be carried beyond the biblical call to be saved. Those unprepared can become prepared by believing on messiah before he comes; after his arrival it will be too late. This spiritual point of the story applies eschatologically to every member of national ethnic Israel in the Tribulation: believe, be saved, be waiting in readiness for messiah's return. For the New Testament church, waiting for the rapture, a similar point is made in many places, none so plain as 1 John 3:3, every Christian actively waiting for Christ's promised return for his church keeps himself in readiness.

Translation Matthew 25:14–30

14 "For it is exactly like a man going on a journey. He called his own servants and delivered to them his possessions. 15 And to one indeed he gave five talents, but to one two, and to one one, to each according to his own ability; and he left the region immediately. 16

Having gone, he who having received the five talents, traded with them, and made five more. 17 Likewise, he with the two gained two more. 18 But he having received one, having went away dug into the ground, and hid his master's money.

19 Now after much time comes the master of those servants, and settled accounts with them. 20 And having come, he who having received the five talents, brought to him five other talents, saying, 'Sir, you delivered to me five talents; look, I have gained five more talents.' 21 His master said to him, 'Well done, good and faithful servant; you were faithful over a few things, I will set you over many things. Enter into the joy of your master.' 22 Now also having come, he with the two talents said, 'Master, you delivered to me two talents. Look, I have gained two more talents.' 23 His master said to him, 'Well done, good and faithful servant; you were faithful over a few things, I will set you over many things. Enter into the joy of your master.' 24 Now also having come, the one having received the one talent said, 'Master, I knew you, that you are a hard man, reaping where you did not sow, and gathering from where you did not scatter. 25 And I having been afraid, having gone away, I hid your talent in the ground. Look, you have what is yours.' 26 But answering, his master said, to him, 'Wicked and lazy servant. You knew that I reap where I sowed not, and gather from where I scatter not. 27 Therefore you ought to put my money with the bankers, and I having come, I should have received my own with interest. 28 Therefore take the talent from him, and give it to him having the ten talents. 29 For to everyone having will be given, and he will have abundance; but the one not having, even that which he has will be taken from him. 30 And the useless servant, cast out into the outer darkness.' There will be the weeping and the gnashing of teeth."

EXPOSITION

Verse 14 makes more sense when connected to v. 13, "Therefore watch, for you neither know the day nor the hour" 14 For it is exactly like a man going on a journey. He called his own servants and delivered to them his possessions," etc. So Messiah's Davidic Messianic Kingdom, in relation to being prepared for its coming, is exactly like a man who, going on a journey, did this and that, and the point of the story is, etc. This parable is about preparedness for the coming kingdom from a different point of view than the previous story.

Members of the coming Davidic Messianic kingdom show they are prepared for messiah's coming by working in and for the kingdom (thus the context of preparedness is the Tribulation period immediately prior to the second advent). This is a law of spiritual life. Those with spiritual life will produce spiritual fruit. Those who do not produce spiritual fruit will lose all that they have.

There are two ways of understanding v. 30. One, as referring to the believer who has not prepared for the coming of messiah by producing good works. He is saved, but he did nothing with his salvation for the good of the kingdom. Since he produced no spiritual fruit, the one talent he had will be taken away, and he will suffer intense regret and sorrow over the loss. Or, two, the person who did not improve on his one talent was never saved, demonstrated by the fact that he did not produce spiritual fruit. He was invited into the kingdom by receiving one talent, but he never responded to the invitation. Therefore he is rejected and suffers unending sorrow and regret.

Which view to take of v. 30 depends on which people group the interpreter applies the verse. If the parable applies eschatologically to national ethnic Israel, then it is a parable like the preceding. The good and faithful servants represent those during the Tribulation who believe in messiah and his soon appearing. Thus they are working to bring others into the kingdom (and other good works). The useless servant represents those of national ethnic Israel who are not saved during the Tribulation.

If the interpreter chooses to apply the parable to the New Testament church during the Spiritual kingdom existing between the advents, then the good and faithful servants are those Christians working to bring others into the Spiritual kingdom (and other good works). The useless servant is the unsaved person who looks like a Christian, but is not, and therefore his end is eternal punishment.

Translation Matthew 25:31–46

31 "But when the son of man comes in his glory, and all the angels with him, then he will sit upon the throne of his glory. 32 And all the nations will be gathered before him, and he will separate them from one another, as the shepherd separates the sheep from the goats. 33 And indeed he will set the sheep on his right hand, but the goats on the left."

34 "Then the King will say to those on his right hand, 'Come, those blessed of my Father, inherit the kingdom prepared for you from the foundation of the world. 35 For I hungered, and you gave me to eat; I thirsted, and you gave me to drink; I was a stranger, and you took me in; 36 naked, and you clothed me; I was sick, and you visited me; I was in prison, and you came to me.'"

37 "Then the righteous will answer him, saying, 'Lord, when saw we you hungering and fed you? Or thirsting and give you to drink? 38 Now when saw we you a stranger, and take you in? Or naked and clothed you? 39 Now when saw we you sick, or in prison, and come to you?' 40 And the King answering said to them, 'Truly I say to you, inasmuch as you did it to one of the least of these my brothers, you did it to me.'"

41 "And then he will say to those on the left, 'Depart from me, you cursed, into the eternal fire prepared for the devil and his angels. 42 For I hungered, and you gave me nothing to eat; I was thirsted, and you gave me nothing to drink; 43 I was a stranger, and you did not take me in; naked, and you did not clothe me; sick, and in prison, and you did not visit me.'"

44 "And then they will answer, saying, 'Lord, when saw we you hungering, or thirsting, or a stranger, or naked, or sick, or in prison, and did not minister to you?' 45 Then he will answer them, saying, 'Truly I say to you, inasmuch as you did not do it to one of the least of these, neither did you to me.' 46 And these will go away into eternal punishment, but the righteous into eternal life.'"

EXPOSITION

This is not a parable. Jesus is telling his listeners and readers what will occur when he returns as Israel's messiah to set up his Messianic Kingdom. The sheep are the ones who are saved, prepared, working, and waiting. The goats thought they were prepared, working, and waiting, but they substituted activity for a saving relationship with the messiah.

Contrary to the previous verses, this prophecy is about the "nations": the living gentiles at messiah's advent at the end of the Tribulation. The messiah will sit on his throne of glory to judge these gentiles. The criteria used for judgment is how the gentiles treated messiah's brothers: members of national ethnic Israel during the Tribulation. The result of the judgment of the sheep is that they enter into Messiah's Kingdom.

Jesus is not suggesting a works-based salvation. The fact messiah divided the gentiles into two groups *before* the judgment was proclaimed indicates each person has already been identified as saved or unsaved. Their works are listed so as to reveal their prior salvation. The reward for the sheep is not salvation—they were previously saved—but entering into Messiah's Kingdom, v. 34.

This is similar to the judgment of national ethnic Israel immediately after messiah's second advent, Ezekiel 20:33–38. The issue is who will enter into the Messianic Kingdom. Only those who have been saved—the ones who did not receive the mark of the beast (Revelation 14:11) during the Tribulation—will enter Messiah's Kingdom. Their works reveal their prior salvation.

The gentiles that care for national ethnic Israel during the Tribulation do so because they are saved, and thus are able to recognize saved Israelis as brothers. They will not treat every Israeli as a brother because 1) the relationship "brother" is not physical but spiritual; 2) the unsaved are aligned with the Antichrist and persecute the saved. Those being persecuted during the Tribulation are saved Hebrews and gentiles—those who deny the Antichrist, do not receive his mark, and believe on Jesus the soon-to-come messiah.

Some deny the prophetic nature of the passage and allegorize the brethren as the poor and oppressed of the world. This view makes good works the cause of entry into the kingdom. However, faith in the Savior is always the qualification for entry into the kingdom, regardless of the time or age. Some see a national entry into the kingdom, but salvation and judgment are always individual, not national.

The Old Testament tells us Messiah's Kingdom is for the Hebrews, the physical brethren of the Lord, both those who are saved during the Tribulation and the greater number saved at his coming (e.g., Zechariah 12–14; Romans 11:25–27). The Old Testament tells us that gentiles will be added to the kingdom (Acts 15:16–17; Amos 9:11–12).

The goats are identified as those gentiles who did not care for the Lord's brethren, national ethnic Israel. Their lack of prior salvation is revealed by their works, or rather their lack of acceptable works. Jesus and his saved people are a spiritual unity: what is done to his saved people is done to him. The unsaved did not do good works toward national ethnic Israel, and therefore not toward Jesus.

In v. 46 it seems as if the goats, the unsaved, immediately go to the Lake of Fire. However, this verse is forward looking to their final end. They go to hades to await the Great White Throne judgment of Revelation 20:11–15, at the end of Messiah's Kingdom.

Matthew Twenty-Six

Translation Matthew 26:1–5

1 And so it was when Jesus had finished all these words, he said to his disciples, 2 "You know that after two days the Passover comes, and the son of man is handed over to be crucified." 3 Then the chief priests and the elders of the people were gathered in the courtyard of the high priest, who is called Caiaphas, 4 and consulted together in order that they might take hold of Jesus by trickery and kill him; 5 but they said, "Not during the feast, that there not be a riot among the people."

EXPOSITION

What does Jesus mean by "after two days the Passover comes?" The Jewish day in Jesus' time extended from sunset-to-sunset (not midnight-to-midnight). Although this has been disputed, Mark 1:21–32 tells us the Sabbath began at sunset and ended the following sunset; and if the Sabbath, so too the other days of the week. The Passover celebration also tells us the Jewish day ran from sunset-to-sunset. Passover day was Nisan 14. The Passover was celebrated, i.e., the lamb was eaten, "between the evenings," Exodus 12:6, i.e., at twilight, just before the sunset that ended the day of Nisan 14. The Passover meal began as the sun was setting on Nisan 14, the sun set occurred, the day became Nisan 15, and the Passover meal was concluded.

The day Jesus said these words is Wednesday. The two days until Passover were Wednesday through Thursday. When Jesus speaks of Passover, he doesn't mean Passover day, but the Passover celebration at the end of Thursday as the sun was setting. The timing is, the daylight hours on Wednesday (as we do today, part of a day was reckoned as a day), then sun sat and the day became Thursday, and then sunrise and sunset Thursday: two days.

In the context of AD 33, the year Jesus was crucified, the Olivet discourse was given on day 4 of the week (Wednesday). As the sun set on day 4 (Wednesday), the day of the week changed to day 5 (Thursday). After sunrise on day 5 (Thursday), the disciples prepared for the Passover (26:17). As the sun was setting on day 5 (Thursday) the Passover meal was eaten. When the sun set on day 5 (Thursday), the day of the week changed to day 6 (Friday).

Matthew Twenty-seven

Jesus was arrested the night of day 6 (Friday), his trials by Jewish leaders were held between midnight and sunrise day 6 (Friday), his trial before Pilate was held after sunrise day 6 (Friday), he was crucified day 6 (Friday) afternoon, died, and was buried day 6 (Friday) just before the sunset that began day 7 (Saturday/Sabbath). So he was in the tomb day 6 (Friday), day 7 (Saturday/Sabbath), and rose sometime in the early morning hours of day 1 (Sunday).

The Jews had names for the days of the week from the time of the Babylonian captivity, but the Bible uses the old names: day 1, 2, 3, 4, 5, 6, Sabbath. In relation to modern times, day 1 corresponds to Saturday night sunset to Sunday night sunset, day 2 corresponds to Sunday night sunset to Monday night sunset, etc.

The day of the week on which Nisan 14 would occur was determined by the day of the week on which Nisan 1 occurred. This, of course, sounds obvious to the reader. However, the Jews used a 354-day lunar calendar versus the modern 365.25-day solar calendar. The Jews knew the solar calendar, but used the lunar calendar, as did most ancient cultures from the earliest days of civilization. Not until Julius Caesar did the Roman Empire begin to use the 365.25-day solar calendar, but the Jews continued to celebrate their religious holidays using the lunar calendar. Using a lunar calendar required the Jews to use the phases of the moon to determine when a new month began.

The day that began a Jewish month was the first day the waxing crescent moon was seen after a new moon. A new moon is when the moon is not visible; it is not visible for approximately three days. The first day of a new month was established by watching for the first sliver of the crescent of the waxing moon after the new moon. When the waxing moon crescent was sighted, that was the first day of the new month.

Today we know a lunar month is 29.5 solar days. To the ancients a lunar cycle varied from 28 to 29 days. Today, modern astronomical calculation can determine the new moon for any given month and year in the past. However, the ancient peoples were not able to make those calculations. The actual sighting of the waxing crescent moon, which determined the first day of the new month, might vary from the modern astronomical calculation by one to three days; for example, if the sky was overcast, or the azimuth of the moon caused it to be too low on the horizon to be seen on the first day. The Jews (all ancient peoples) also realized the lunar calendar and the seasons of the year did not synchronize, so intercalary days, and at times an intercalary month, were added from year to year to keep the months and the seasons synchronized.

The practical result of the sunset-to-sunset reckoning, the beginning of a new lunar month, and the possibility of an intercalary day or month, is that modern astronomical calculations cannot exactly determine what modern day the crucifixion (and thus the Passover) took place. To determine these days, one must consult the scriptures, which say the day Jesus was crucified was the day of preparation, i.e., it was day 6, the day when one prepared for the Sabbath. Knowing this information, the year is easy to determine with astronomical calculations: AD 33. In AD 33 Nisan 14/Passover was day 5/Thursday, which means the crucifixion took place on day 6/Friday. Jesus was crucified Friday afternoon in modern terms, died, and was buried before the sun set and the day became Sabbath. (To see the above discussion in much greater detail please read my commentary, *John 13–21*, appendix, "Reconciling John 18:28.")

The plot to kill Jesus was set in motion by Caiaphas. The "elders of the people" are the members of the ruling council, the Sanhedrin. The meeting at Caiaphas's house was not a legal meeting; as indeed it could not be, for none could be condemned to death except by an official trial at an official, legal, meeting. They did not want to kill Jesus during the Feast of Unleavened Bread, which was the seven days (Nisan 15–21) following the Nisan 14 Passover. If they waited until after the feast, then many pilgrims, including those from Galilee, would leave the city, and Jesus could be killed with little notice or protest. But God had other plans.

Translation Matthew 26:6–13

6 Now Jesus having been in Bethany, in the house of Simon the leper, 7 a woman came to him, having an alabaster vessel of very expensive fragrant oil, and poured it on his head as he was reclining. 8 But having seen, the disciples became indignant, saying, "For what purpose this waste? 9 For this could have been sold for much, and have been given to the poor." 10 But knowing this Jesus said to them, "Why do you cause trouble to the woman? For she did to me a beautiful work. 11 For the poor you always have with

you; but me you have not always. 12 For this woman in pouring this fragrant oil on my body, she did it for my burial. 13 Truly I say to you, wherever this good news may be proclaimed in all the world, that which this woman did will be spoken of for a memorial of her." 14 Then one of the twelve, who is called Judas Iscariot, having gone to the chief priests, 15 said, "What are you willing to give me, and I will deliver him to you?" Now they weighed out to him thirty pieces of silver. 16 And from that time he sought an opportunity that he might deliver him.

EXPOSITION

In John 6:71; 13:26, Judas Iscariot is identified as the son of Simon. The person here identified as Simon the leper, whom Jesus had healed, may be the father of Judas Iscariot.

This particular meal is recorded at John 12:1–8. This is not the Passover meal (John 13). Because John dates it as "six days before the Passover," it was the meal occurring immediately after the sunset that ended the Sabbath day. In modern terminology it was Saturday night just after sunset. The Jews would have thought of it as the beginning of day 1. Notice that this day is four days prior to 26:2. Matthew is looking back at an event that happened earlier than 26:2. This is a post-Sabbath meal used to celebrate Jesus' return to Bethany.

At this meal Mary of Bethany anoints Jesus with costly fragrant oil. Mark says it was spikenard. "Nard" was an oily perfume. The prefix "spike" refers to the shape of the plant from which the oil was obtained. The plant was native to northern India and a favorite perfume in antiquity. Some oils from similar plants in other countries were also called spikenard.

The best spikenard was imported from India in sealed alabaster boxes, to be opened only on special occasions. Nard oil was very expensive. Thus, the indignation of the disciples, who thought only of the money that might be gained from its sale, ostensibly to give to the poor.

Jesus responds that there will always be poor people, but he was departing. Priorities matter. At that time and place Jesus was the priority. Out of all the disciples, Mary of Bethany is noted as having understood Jesus' repeated references to his death. Because she was not at the cross or the tomb, which would be unusual for someone who loved Jesus as much as she demonstrates here, I believe she understood not only Jesus' crucifixion but also his resurrection. This is supported by v. 12. Mary of Bethany anoints Jesus beforehand in anticipation of his burial, which assumes she believed he was going to die. Her devotion and her spiritual perception are memorialized in the Gospels of Matthew, Mark, and John.

John 12:4–5 singles out Judas Iscariot as the one making the complaint Matthew records in v. 9. John 12:6 says Judas made this complaint because he was a thief and he held the money bag on behalf of the group. The spikenard, said Judas (John 12:5) could have been sold for 300 denarii; 400 day's wages at 12 *as* for a day's labor. In modern terms, the spikenard was worth $26,400 ($8.25 per hour, eight hours per day, 400 days). If it had been sold, Judas could have stolen a lot of money from the money bag. The implication is that simple greed motivated Judas.

That Judas was motivated by greed is supported by Matthew 26:15. Matthew and Mark note that Judas went to the chief priests after the anointing incident. Interestingly, Matthew does not here make a connection with the thirty pieces of silver in Zechariah 11:12. Exodus 21:32 states that thirty shekels of silver was the price paid when an ox gored the slave of another person. Jesus is valued by Judas as a non-person, an asset, property.

The amount paid to Judas to betray Jesus was thirty pieces of silver weighed out according to the temple *shekel*. The coins were either Greek silver *tetradrachma* or Tyrian silver *stater*. In modern terms the silver in the coins was worth about $225.00. Judas would have thought of the coins as worth about 20 denarii. When Judas received the money is not stated, but he had it when he went to the chief priests after Jesus was condemned to crucifixion. Regardless of when, from the time Judas made the bargain he sought an opportunity to get Jesus away from the crowds so he might turn him over to the chief priests.

Translation Matthew 26:17–19

17 Now on the first of Unleavened Bread, the disciples came to Jesus, saying, "Where would you like us to prepare for you to eat the Passover?" 18 Now he said, "Go into the city unto a certain man, and say to him, 'The Teacher says, "My time is near. With you I will keep the Passover with my disciples." ' " 19 And the disciples did as Jesus directed them, and prepared the Passover.

EXPOSITION

In v. 17 the text literally reads, "Now on the first of the unleavened." The reference is to the day that the Jews of Jesus' time considered the first day of the Feast of Unleavened Bread. That day was not the first day of the Feast Unleavened Bread, which was Nisan 15, but was Passover day, Nisan 14.

Because all leaven was removed from the house on Nisan 14 for both Passover day and the Nisan 15–21 Feast of Unleavened Bread that immediately followed Passover, the Passover day had come to be known by the Jews as the first day of the Feast of Unleavened Bread. The whole eight days, Nisan 14–21, had come to be known both as Passover and as the Feast of Unleavened Bread. The two designations had become synonyms and were used interchangeably. Josephus used "Feast of Unleavened Bread" and "Passover" as synonyms, and refers to the Passover-Feast of Unleavened Bread festival period as the Passover (all references *Antiquities of the Jews*, except as noted).

> 14.2.1. This happened at the time when the feast of unleavened bread was celebrated, which we call the Passover.
>
> 14.2.2. While the priests and Aristobulus were besieged, it happened that the feast called the Passover was come, at which it is our custom to offer a great number of sacrifices to God . . . they required them to pay a thousand drachma for each head of cattle." [Since only lambs are sacrificed on Nisan 14, the cattle referred to must be for the festal offerings during Nisan 15–21.]
>
> 17.9.3. Now, upon the approach of that feast of unleavened bread . . . which feast is called the Passover.
>
> 18.2.2. As the Jews were celebrating the feast of unleavened bread, which we call the Passover.
>
> 18.4.3. It was the time of that festival which is called the Passover.
>
> 20.5.3. When that feast which is called the Passover was at hand, at which time our custom is to use unleavened bread.
>
> *Wars of the Jews*, 2.1.3. At the feast of unleavened bread, which was not at hand, and is by the Jews called the Passover.

For further discussion and other historical references see the appendix in my commentary *John 13–21*.

Returning to 26:17, the disciples must buy all their herbs, and a lamb, and their wine, and other necessary things before noon on Nisan 14, Passover day. Work stopped at noon on Passover day in Jerusalem, according to m. *Pesahim*, 4.1, 4.6, meaning all the businesses and animal sellers closed by the noon hour. So either the night prior or after sunrise, Jesus' disciples asked him where he wanted to eat the Passover that evening.

There seems to be a contradiction between the Synoptics and John's gospel, 18:28 concerning the timing of the Passover celebration.

> Then they led Jesus from Caiaphas to the Praetorium, and it was early morning. But they themselves did not go into the Praetorium, lest they should be defiled, but that they might eat the passover.

If Jesus ate the Passover meal with his disciples before his arrest, then how could the priests refer to eating the Passover after his arrest? According to the instructions in Exodus and Leviticus, everyone was to eat the Passover at the same time: just before sunset on Nisan 14.

Above I explained that the entire Nisan 14–21, Passover-Feast of Unleavened Breed was called Passover. I have discussed this issue thoroughly in my commentary *John 13–21*, in the appendix "Reconciling John 18:28." In brief, the passover referred to in John 18:28, which the priests would eat, was not the Nisan 14 Passover celebration when the lamb was eaten, but the morning sacrifices the priests made each day during the Feast of Unleavened Bread.

> Leviticus 23:5–8, On the fourteenth day of the first month at twilight is the Lord's Passover. And on the fifteenth day of the same month is the Feast of Unleavened Bread to the Lord; seven days you must eat unleavened bread. On the first day [Nisan 14] you shall have a holy convocation; you shall do no customary work on it. But you shall offer an offering made by fire to the Lord for seven days [Nisan 15–21]. The seventh day [Nisan 21] shall be a holy convocation; you shall do no customary work on it.

Animal sacrifices were to be made every day for the seven days of the Nisan 15–21 Feast of Unleavened Bread. These sacrifices (which were in addition to the normal daily sacrifices) were two bulls, one ram, seven lambs, and a kid of the goats, which were intended as a feast for the priests on every one of those days.[1] If they entered the Praetorium, the priests believed they would be defiled and not be able to eat these sacrifices.

So, the priests in John 18:28 had eaten the Passover lamb in their homes at twilight on Nisan 14th, just as Exodus 12:1–13 commands. Then, after sunrise on Nisan 15th, about 9:00 a.m., they had to make additional sacrifices in the temple, just as Leviticus 23:5–8 commands. But they were at the Praetorium about 6:00 a.m., before the time for those sacrifices. They must be ceremonially clean to eat the festival sacrifices. Therefore they would not enter the Praetorium. The Leviticus 23:5–8 festival sacrifices are the "passover" the priests were referring to in John 18:28. There is no conflict between John and the Synoptics regarding the timing for eating the Nisan 14 Passover lamb.

Jesus instructs his disciples on where to prepare the Passover, which is at the house of a "certain man," *deína*, "a person one does not know or does not wish to name."[2] The message Jesus gives the disciples refers to Jesus as *ho didáskalos*. The word *ho* is the definite article "the." The word *didáskalos* may be translated instructor, master, or teacher.[3] If the unnamed man was a disciple, then *ho didáskalos* is better translated "the Master." Jesus may have told the disciples the man's name, but he might simply have given them the man's address, knowing the disciples would deliver the message to the head of the house. Of several versions, only the KJV and the Bible in Basic English translate "the Master." All others consulted (NKJV, HCSB, NIV, ASV, ESV, NLT, YLT) translate "the Teacher." By using *ho didáskalos* Jesus avoids any messianic implications, allowing him and his disciples to celebrate the Passover meal in peace and quiet.

As to why this unnamed man would accommodate Jesus, there are several possibilities. The man might have accommodated any *ho didáskalos*, such as a famous scribe or Pharisee. Perhaps Jesus had a previous arrangement; perhaps not. Many believed in Jesus—as prophet, perhaps messiah, certainly a teacher of righteousness—

---

[1] Josephus, *Antiquities*, 3.10.5.
[2] Zodhiates, *WSDNT*, s. v. "1170."
[3] Ibid., s. v. "1320."

and would have willingly opened their home for his use at Passover. Here is a place where one must trust that the Holy Spirit had prepared this man for his task.

Translation Matthew 26:20–25

20 Now evening having come, he reclined with the twelve disciples. 21 And as they were eating, he said, "Truly I say to you, that one of you will betray me." 22 And being exceedingly sorrowful, each one began to say to him, "Master, it isn't me, is it?" 23 And answering he said, "The person having dipped the hand in the dish with me, he will betray me. 24 Indeed, the son of man goes just as it has been written concerning him; but woe to that man by whom the son of man is betrayed. Better would it be for him if that man had not been born." 25 But Judas answering (who was betraying him), said, "It isn't me, is it, Rabbi?" He says to him, "You have said."

EXPOSITION

As the sun was setting on Nisan 14, Jesus and his disciples ate the Passover. The passing day ended with an evening and the new day began with an evening, so the Passover meal was eaten "between the evenings." This is the same Passover meal we see in Mark 14, Luke 22, and John 13.

Jesus and his disciples are reclining at the table, with their couches perpendicular to the table. Each is resting on his left elbow, eating with his right hand. At any meal small bowls with some kind of gravy or sauce was provided for flavoring a piece of meat or bread; hence v. 23. The fellowship at this particular meal meant one would dip a morsel into the dish and feed the morsel to the close friend on his right or left. John was on Jesus' right, John 13:23–25. Judas was on his left, John 13:26. Peter was across the table from him, John 13:24. Jesus and Judas were sharing a set of dipping bowls.

When Jesus stated one of them would betray him, the disciples questioned, "not I is it Master?" which I have rendered more naturally, "Master, it isn't me, is it?" Others translate, "Surely not I?" or "Is it I?" Though not clearly communicated in some translations, the question anticipated a "No" answer.[1]

---

[1] Robertson, *Word Pictures*, 1:208.

Because Judas wanted to appear as innocent as the others, he also asked the question. Jesus' answer, "You have said," is idiomatic for "You have stated the fact." Jesus' reply to Judas is not heard by the others because Jesus is leaning back into Judas, who is on his left, speaking just enough for Judas to hear—a private conversation. Jesus is giving Judas an opportunity to confess and repent. There is an important application here: when giving a gospel message, remember that the accusation of sin and the opportunity for repentance need not be public.

Before his private conversation with Judas, Jesus had given a public answer to the group: "The person having dipped the hand in the dish with me, he will betray me." John reports in his Gospel that this very general answer does not satisfy Peter. Peter urges John to ask, "Who is the betrayer?" John, on Jesus' right, leans back onto Jesus' chest and asks the question. Jesus replies to John, "He it is to whom I will dip the morsel and I will give." Judas asks his question, Jesus replies, Jesus gives Judas the morsel, Satan enters Judas, and Judas leaves the Passover supper. John doesn't hear the quiet conversation between Jesus and Judas, but he does see the result, and is able to draw the conclusion the betrayer is Judas.

Matthew could not have heard the conversation of John with Jesus and Jesus with Judas. Naturally at the time he is writing he knows what had happened. But Matthew writes his gospel using an in-the-moment perspective, so that the reader has an in-the-moment experience of what Matthew and others experienced in the moment. In-the-moment Matthew ignored Judas leaving (see why at John 13:27–29). As he is writing about this moment in his gospel, Matthew keeps his gospel focused on Jesus.

Translation Matthew 26:26–30

26 Now as they were eating, Jesus having taken bread, and having blessed it, broke it, and having given it to the disciples, said, "Take, eat; this is my body." 27 And having taken a cup, and having given thanks, he gave it to them, saying, "Drink from it, all of you. 28 For this is my blood, of the covenant, being poured out for many, for forgiveness of sins. 29 But I say to you, I will not drink, from this moment, of this the fruit of the vine, until the day when I drink it anew with you, in my Father's kingdom." 30 And having sung a hymn, they went out to the Mount of Olives.

TRANSLATION NOTE

At v. 28 Christ's blood is poured out for *áphesis* of sins. This Greek word can be translated "remission" or "forgiveness." I translated *áphesis* as "forgiveness," versus "remission" because remission is the result of forgiveness: the penalty due sins has been remitted because the sins have been forgiven. This view is reinforced by the word translated "sins," which is *hamartía*.[1] *Hamartía* in the plural form, as it is here, refers to each act of sinning. For example, that is how the plural form is used at 1 John 1:9, "If we continue to confess our sins," that is, if we continue to confess and repent of each act of sinning (see my commentary *John's Epistles*). So here, Jesus is saying that his blood (his propitiating death) causes every single act of sinning to be forgiven. If forgiven, as is the case, then the penalty is remitted; it is not enforced.

EXPOSITION

This is Matthew's version of the institution of the memorial of Jesus' death, v. 28, and hope of his return, v. 29.

The Passover meal was completed, with its several cups of grape juice. Jesus then took a large piece of unleavened bread, and the common cup used for the Passover, refiled the cup, and used the bread and cup to create a new ceremony for the church he would establish through his apostles. They all ate from one piece of bread and they all drank from one cup, passed from one to another until all had eaten and drank.

Here I want pause and discuss the contents of the cup. Jesus speaks of the contents as "the fruit of the vine." In New Testament times this was an idiom meaning unfermented grape juice. The liquid in the cup came from the same liquid used at the ritual of the Passover meal. That liquid had to be unleavened. An alcoholic liquid would contain leaven, which the Jews knew. The liquid in the Passover cup was unfermented grape juice. The confusion comes because the Greek language had one word for both fermented and unfermented juice: *oínos*, which translated is "wine."

The Mishnah (m.) is clear that fermented grain (used to make beer) and fermented juice was to be removed from the house prior to the Passover. At m. *Pesahim* 1.1 beer and vinegar were to be removed as containing leaven, made from fermented grain m.

---

[1] Zodhiates, *WSDNT*, s. v. "266."

Pesahim 3.1. Four cups of *oínos* were drunk at the Passover meal. Instructions at m. *Pesahim* 10.4 indicate the *oínos* was mixed, which means diluted with water (Babylonian Talmud, *Pesahim*, 108b), making the alcohol content 1%–2% (undiluted alcoholic wine is 12%–14% alcohol). One could not say benediction over the *oínos* until water was added, *Berakoth*, 7.5. In *Terumoth* 2.6 a heave offering may be given from unboiled *oínos*, which indicates the Jews boiled juice to prevent fermentation.

In ancient times there were four methods of keeping juice from fermenting.

> Boil off the excess liquid turning the juice into syrup. The juice would not ferment when water was added later.
>
> Remove the naturally occurring yeast by filtration.
>
> Allow the yeast to settle to the bottom of the container, cap to exclude air, and keep below 50F (e.g., in a deep well, or a river).
>
> Fumigate the juice with sulfur.

But let us assume, for a moment, that the juice was fermented (but at Passover it could not be), and thus alcoholic. The ancient custom was to dilute fermented juice with water in a 3:1 ration; three parts water to one part juice. The dilution ration could be as much as 10:1. This was the custom for drinking *oínos* at any time, for any use. The ancient world disapproved of drunkenness.

Finally, the liquid in the cup is symbolic of Jesus as the Christian's Passover, 1 Corinthians 5:7. It would be incredible if Christ used something containing leaven, a consistent symbol of sin in the Old Testament, in a memorial designed to "proclaim the Lord's death [thus the eternal life his death gives to believers] until he comes," 1 Corinthians 11:26.

Returning to the passage, the bread is symbolic of Jesus' body, broken by death on the cross. Bread in the ancient world was symbolic of life. Each believer shares that eternal life which Christ gives in response to saving faith.

The contents of the cup represent Jesus' blood, shed for the remission of sins. The life is in the blood, according to Leviticus 17:11; it is the blood that makes atonement for the soul according to the same verse. The covenant that forgives sins and remits the penalty is made in the blood of the redeemer. "Blood" in contexts referring to forgiveness of sins, remittance of the penalty of sin, eternal life, the cross, etc., is symbolic of death. It is the death of the Redeemer that propitiated God.

This passage has been used to teach the doctrines of transubstantiation and consubstantiation. Transubstantiation teaches the bread and juice have been magically transformed by a priest into the real body and real blood of Jesus; the appearance of bread and juice are "accidents." Consubstantiation teaches the bread and juice are magically transformed by a priest such that the real body and real blood of Jesus coexists in and with the real bread and real juice.

The words used to substantiate these doctrines are "Take, eat; this is my body" and "Drink from it [the cup] . . . for this [drink? cup?] is my blood." Obviously as Jesus' stood there, his real physical body with its real physical blood could not be at the same time be the bread and cup/juice (transubstantiation), or be present in and with the bread and cup/juice (consubstantiation) as the bread and cup were being passed around. Jesus himself says the liquid in the cup is juice (fruit-of-the-vine), not blood, so the reference to blood is symbolic: the juice symbolizes his blood, i.e., the juice symbolizes his death to propitiate God for our sins.

The words are "Take, eat; this is my body" and "Drink from it [the cup] . . . for this is my blood" are figurative, and were so understood by the early church. Certainly Paul, 1 Corinthians 11:17–26, understood the bread, cup, and juice as literal bread, cup, and juice. Otherwise we must make the ridiculous conclusion that Paul thought the cup itself was the covenant of salvation as he quotes Christ saying, "This cup is the new covenant in my blood." Moreover, the purpose of the bread and cup are not a supposedly saving religious ritual (the mass) but a memorial of Christ's death until his return, 1 Corinthians 11:26; Luke 22:19.

What Jesus is saying is that the new covenant of salvation is made in his death. Blood is a symbol of death, and in Jesus' case a symbol of his propitiation for sin. This is how the Writer of Hebrews understood it, 8:7–13; 916–22; 10:5–10, 16–18. As did Paul, Romans 3:25; and Peter, Acts 2:36; 1 Peter 1:11; 2:24; 3:18; and John, 1 John 2:2.

In v. 29 Jesus may be saying he will not participate in this ritual until he reigns in his Davidic Messianic kingdom, but more probably he is saying he is looking forward to drinking it anew with them in his Davidic Messianic kingdom. We all too often forget that the

"Communion" the cup symbolizes is fellowship with Jesus in his death and resurrection. The hymn they sung would be portions of Psalms 114–118, or 115–118.

Translation Matthew 26:31–35

31 Then Jesus says to them, "You all will fall away because of me during this night, for it has been written: 'I will strike the shepherd, and the sheep of the flock will be scattered.' 32 But after I have been raised, I will go before you into Galilee." 33 Now Peter answering said to him, "If all will fall away because of you, I will never fall away." 34 Jesus said to him, "Truly I say to you that this night, before the rooster crowing, you will deny me three times." 35 Peter says to him, "Even if it is necessary for me to die with you, I will never no never deny you." In like manner also said all the disciples.

EXPOSITION

In v. 31 Jesus refers to Zechariah 13:7. Zechariah's context is the Day of the Lord (Tribulation) and second advent. Jesus makes an application of this scripture to his first advent. All the disciples abandoned Jesus when he was arrested. Peter and John followed, but did not come to his defense.

In v. 32 Jesus implies his death and subsequent resurrection by saying "after I have been raised." He tells the disciples that after he has been raised he will meet them in Galilee. Jesus did first meet with the disciples in the upper room, John 20:19, 26; Luke 24:36; Mark 16:14. Afterward he met with them in Galilee, Matthew 28:16; John 21:1.

In vv. 33 Peter boldly declares his allegiance and courage, as do they all (v. 35). Jesus predicts Peter's denial, even down to the time it will occur. "Apparently it was usual for roosters in Palestine to crow about 12:30 a.m., 1:30 a.m., and 2:30 a.m., prompting the Romans to give the term "cockcrow" to the watch between midnight and roughly 3:00 a.m."[1]

Translation Matthew 26:36–46

36 Then Jesus comes with them to a place called Gethsemane, and he says to the disciples, "Sit here while I go over there and

---

[1] Carson, *John*, 487.

pray." 37 And having taken with him Peter and the two sons of Zebedee, he began to be sorrowful and deeply distressed. 38 Then he says to them, "My soul is very sorrowful, even to death. Remain here and watch with me." 39 And having gone forward a little, he fell upon his face, and praying says, "My Father, if it is possible, let this cup pass from me. Nevertheless, not as I will, but as You." 40 And he comes to the disciples and finds them sleeping, and says to Peter, "So, were you not able to watch one hour with me? 41 Watch and pray, so that you do not enter into temptation. The spirit indeed is willing, but the flesh is weak." 42 Again for a second time having gone away, he prayed, saying, "My Father, if this is not possible to pass, unless I drink it, Your will be done." 43 And having come again, he finds them sleeping, for their eyes were indeed heavy. 44 And having left them again, having gone away, he prayed for the third time, having said again the same thing. 45 Then he comes to the disciples and says to them, "Sleep for the time remaining, and take your rest. Look, the hour has drawn near, and the son of man is betrayed into the hands of sinners. 46 Rise; let us go. Look, he who is betraying me has drawn near."

TRANSLATION NOTE

At v. 45 the phrase *katheudete to loipón kai anapauesthe* (grammatical forms) is very literally translated, "sleep the henceforth and rest oneself." The phrase is susceptible to two interpretations, but has only one plausible translation. The NKJV, HCSB, NIV and others interpret the phrase as a question, "Are you still sleeping and resting?" They do this because such an interpretation seems to fit the immediacy of the next sentence, "Look, the hour has drawn near," etc. However, the word *loipón* means "remaining," and with the definite article (*to*) is "used of time meaning henceforth, hence forward."[1] The proper translation is as Hagner has it, "Sleep for the time that remains."[2] This means the next sentence, "Look, the hour has drawn near," etc., is not said immediately, but some period of time, more or less, later. The verse should have been divided thusly: "45 Then he comes to the disciples and says to them, "Sleep for the time remaining, and take your rest." 46 "Look, the hour has drawn near, and the son of man

---

[1] Zodhiates, *WSDNT*, s. v. "3064."
[2] Hagner, *Matthew 14–28*, 779.

is betrayed into the hands of sinners."

EXPOSITION

The disciples and Jesus come to Gethsemane, which was a grove of olive trees on the west slope of the Mount of Olives (facing Jerusalem). Jesus may have frequently come to Gethsemane, because we see that Judas, who had left the company earlier, was able to lead the temple police to the location to arrest Jesus.

In Gethsemane Jesus prays. He withdraws a little ways off from the main group of disciples, taking with him his inner circle of friends, Peter, James, and John. The others may have been able to hear some of what was said, and see a little in the moonlight. The phase of the moon is always full the night of Nisan 15.

The subject of the prayer was the impending crucifixion. Jesus was not afraid of physical death. The physical sufferings did not deter him because he had come to be crucified. His prayer, I believe, was twofold. One, to not die as he endured the physical sufferings which were to come: "the flesh is weak." Two, strength for the spiritual sufferings he would experience: "The spirit indeed is willing." There is another possibility. When Jesus said the words in v. 41 he was speaking to Peter, whose courage would shortly be tested.

Jesus became the sin-bearer when the judicial guilt of sin was imputed to him. During that time he suffered the wrath of God due the crime of sin, was therefore separated from his fellowship with God. He thus experienced a temporary spiritual death. Death, whether physical or spiritual, is separation: the soul separates from the body in physical death; the soul is separated from God in spiritual death.

Jesus was fully human, and his desire to avoid loss of fellowship with his Father was a normal human desire. But he was (and is) the God-man, empowered by the Holy Spirit to carry out his salvific mission in full, and therefore his desire to do the will of God overrode all other desires. Verse 41 might be seen as the perfect expression of these conflicting desires. Luke tells us an angel strengthened Jesus as a result of his prayer.

Looking again at v. 41, this is a warning to Peter (see v. 40). Peter is the one facing temptation. Peter is the one whose spirit is willing "to die with you," but his flesh is weak, "will deny [Jesus] three times."

Verses 42–44 express the harmony Jesus had between flesh and spirit as a result of his prayers. He was always in the state of obedience to the Father's will, "And the One having sent me is with me. The Father has not left me alone, because I always do the things pleasing to him," John 8:29. The Father's will was that Jesus become sin for us, i.e., to suffer the penalty due our crime of sin, 2 Corinthians 5:21, in our place and on our behalf.

The apostles slept because they were sleepy. The time was late at night in a culture that normally rose and set with the sun. They slept because they did not grasp the importance of the moment. They slept because the Holy Spirit gave them rest to prepare them for coming events. They slept because this path belonged to Jesus alone. Verses 45, 46 show Jesus going out to fulfill the Father's will, just as he had prayed.

Translation Matthew 26:47–50

47 And as he is still speaking, look, Judas, one of the twelve, came, and with him a great crowd with swords and clubs, from the chief priests and elders of the people. 48 Now the one betraying him gave them a sign, saying, "Whomever that I may kiss, he it is; seize him." 49 And immediately having come to Jesus, he said, "Greetings, Rabbi." and kissed him. 50 But Jesus said to him, "Friend, for what are you come?" Then having come to him, they laid hands on Jesus and seized him.

EXPOSITION

John says Judas arrived with the company of men (*speíra*, a band, troop, company[1]) and their officers (*hupērétēs*, a subordinate official[2]). Though these words properly refer to Roman soldiers, the more likely scenario is the company and officers sent to capture Jesus were wholly composed of Levites working in the temple, with the officers in charge of the company distinguished by the word *hupērétēs*. John used *speíra* to indicate a large number of temple police—a number grossly out of proportion to their task—not Roman soldiers. Knowing they had eleven men to subdue in order to arrest Jesus, the priests and Pharisees probably sent about twice, perhaps three times, that number.

---

[1] Zodhiates, *WSDNT*, s. v. "4686."

[2] Ibid., s. v. "5257."

John also mentions a *chilíarchos*, translated "captain."¹ In the context of the Roman army the *chilíarchos* was a military officer commanding a thousand men. In the context of the temple a *chilíarchos* commanded the entire police force. Here the context requires the *chilíarchos* to be the person in charge of the company (*speíra*) of men and their officers (*hupērétēs*).

Some believe Roman soldiers accompanied the temple police. But we must ask, how likely is it that Jewish officials entered a gentile building on the first day of the Feast of Unleavened Bread (cf. John 18:28) to ask for a company of Roman soldiers? How likely is it that Roman military leaders would respond to a request for military assistance from Jews to arrest one Jew, especially without notification of—if not explicit approval from—the Roman Procurator? These Roman soldiers did not know who Jesus was (Pilate didn't), and therefore had no knowledge of broken laws or disturbances of the peace which might have legally required them to accompany a band of temple police—whom they would have despised as amateurs and Jews. These soldiers had seen the crowds gather for the Triumphal Entry and made no move to disperse them. They had seen the Jews gather in large numbers in and around the temple and had left them alone. Having earlier left the crowds alone, they had no knowledge as to whom the crowds had come to hear and see. The temple police, not Roman soldiers, accompanied Judas.

Judas identifies Jesus to the others with the familiar greeting of a friend. Verse 50 could be a statement or a question. I view it as a question to force Judas to consider his motives as well as his actions, thus an opportunity for repentance.² This was not the last chance Judas had to repent (he could have repented instead of hanging himself), but he always failed his chances.

Translation Matthew 26:51–56

51 And look, one of those with Jesus, having stretched out his hand, drew his sword, and having struck the servant of the high priest, cut off his ear. 52 Then says Jesus to him, "Return your sword to its place; for all having taken the sword, by the sword will perish.

---

[1] Ibid., s. v. "5506."

[2] Compare Morris, *Matthew*, 674; France, *Matthew*, NICNT, 1012. Carson, *Matthew*, 547.

Matthew Twenty-seven

53 Or think you that I am not able to call upon my Father, and he will provide to me right now more than twelve legions of angels? 54 How then should the Scriptures be fulfilled, that it must be thus?" 55 In that hour Jesus said to the crowds, "Are you come out as against a robber with swords and clubs to seize me? Every day in the temple I was teaching, and you did not seize me. 56 But this is come to pass, that the scriptures of the prophets might be fulfilled." Then the disciples, all having forsaken him, fled.

EXPOSITION

John 18:10 tells us that it was Peter who cut off the ear. Luke tells us Jesus healed the ear. Luke is the one who tell us, 22:36, that Jesus had counseled his disciples to prepare for his departure by taking a money bag, traveling bag, and a sword.

Using the sword was inappropriate in this place, for Jesus must be arrested, tried, condemned, and crucified, v. 54. The words in v. 52 are recorded only by Matthew. The Christian way is not to attack but to defend. Those who use violence to achieve their ends will find that violence is the response of those they have attacked. Jesus had resources with which to defend himself, but chose to allow events to unfold as they would in the hands of sinful men, according to the will of God, Acts 2:23.

Jesus says he could call for twelve legions of angels. The comparison is probably to the Roman army. At this period of time, a Roman legion was about 5,500 foot and mounted soldiers. Twelve legions of angels would be about 66,000 angels. Perhaps the number twelve was chosen to mean a legion to protect each disciple. Certainly heaven could supply enough angels to protect Jesus as might be necessary, Psalm 91:11–12.

Jesus chastises the crowd in v. 55. The secretive arrest was unjust and unlawful. Implied is the question, "For what crime am I being arrested?" His behavior was well-known, and the fact he had not been arrested openly indicated he had committed no crimes. However, v. 56, prophecy must be fulfilled (Isaiah 53:12?); probably not any specific prophecy, but the general intent of prophecy regarding the propitiation to be made by the Redeemer. The disciples saw they could not help, and were in danger of arrest themselves, so their courage left them, and they ran away.

Translation Matthew 26:57–61

Matthew Twenty-seven

57 Now those persons having seized Jesus led him away to Caiaphas the high priest, where the scribes and the elders were assembled. 58 But Peter followed him from afar, even to the courtyard of the high priest. And having entered within, he sat with the temple police to see the outcome. 59 Now the chief priests and the whole council sought false testimony against Jesus, so that they might put him to death, 60 but they found none, many having come forward as false witnesses. But at last two having come forward 61 said, "This man said, 'I am able to destroy the temple of God and in three days to rebuild it.'"

EXPOSITION

Jesus is brought first to the house of Caiaphas. This is another indication the arresting officers were temple police, not Roman soldiers, for Roman soldiers would have taken Jesus to their garrison, the Fortress of Antonio.

Matthew tells us Peter came into the courtyard of the house with the temple police, without telling us how he got past the guard at the gate. This was a bold move by Peter, who had just fled from these very police at Gethsemane. But there were many police, so he may have thought not all had seen him, or would recognize him. John tells us (in his gospel) he helped Peter gain entry.

The time is probably just after midnight. We see the arrest and trial of Jesus is a coordinated effort, for the high priest has his cronies with him. Under Jewish and Roman law this is an illegal trial, a meeting of the leaders to pre-determine the outcome of the official trial, which could only be held after sunrise.

False witnesses testified many contradictory things, but finally two agreed on something Jesus had said, or what they thought he had said, which is found only in John 2:19. The crime intended by the accusation in v. 61 is uncertain, but probably blasphemy. The temple was viewed as God's house, therefore a threat against the temple could be construed as blasphemy.

Translation Matthew 26:62–64

62 And having stood up, the high priest said to him, "Answer you nothing? What do these witness against you?" 63 But Jesus was silent. And the high priest said to him, "I adjure you by the living God, that you tell us if you are the Christ, the Son of God." 64 Jesus says to him, "You have said. Moreover, I say to you, from now you

will see the son of man sitting at the right hand of the Power, and coming in the clouds of heaven."

EXPOSITION

One sees the frustration of the high priest in v. 62. He wants to condemn Jesus to death, but he has no capital crime with which to convict Jesus. He may have believed that at this point anything Jesus might say in response to the accusations would help him manufacture a capital crime.

Jesus recognizes that the testimony is not only false but does not specify a crime, so he says nothing. This must have puzzled and frustrated all present, because most accused would try and refute every charge. Jesus, however, was knowingly there to be condemned, however unjustly, to fulfill the Father's will by his redeeming death. The proceedings were therefore irrelevant, both as to any crime they might accuse him of doing, and as to the outcome, which had been prophesied by the prophets and was planned in advance by Caiaphas and his crew.

Caiaphas, however, needed legal justification in order to sentence Jesus to death, and present the case to Pilate for Jesus to be executed. We see in v. 63 that Caiaphas obviously knew that Jesus had performed miracles and that many people believed him to be the Christ. The question Caiaphas asks understands the terms "Christ" and "Son of God" as indicating a relationship with God. But it is doubtful that Caiaphas used these terms in the same sense that Christians understand them today. His question is meant to have Jesus testify against himself. The question Caiaphas asks, although not in these words, is whether or not Jesus will testify under oath that he himself is the Christ, the Son of God. Jesus answers the question because 1) Caiaphas has asked in his official capacity as high priest, 2) the question is about Jesus' messianic claims, and 3) Caiaphas has called on Jesus to tell the truth with God as his witness.

Jesus' reply, "You have said," is an idiom meaning "You have stated the fact." Jesus does not directly answer the question "are you the Christ," because these people didn't understand the biblical testimony about the Christ during his first advent. Jesus answers that he is equal with God. If they had understood who the Christ was, then they would have accepted his answer.

They didn't understand the phrase "Son of God" in the context of "the Christ." All believers are "sons of God," but only one, the one who is the Christ, is the only begotten Son of God, John 3:18. Let us not misunderstand. The term "Son of God" does not refer to the God-man's essential deity nature. God the Son is eternally generated by the God the Father (and the Holy Spirit eternally generated by the Father and the Son). The term "Son of God" is used forty-six times in the New Testament and forty-five times refers to the Christ, who is God the Son in his incarnation with Jesus of Nazareth (in Luke 3:38 it refers to Adam).

Jesus gave testimony that allowed the high priest to declare the sentence of condemnation. To sit on the throne of God ("at the right hand of the power") is to be equal with God. To come on the clouds of heaven is to command the angelic armies of heaven, which is authority possessed only by deity.

Translation Matthew 26:65–68

65 Then the high priest tears his clothes, saying, "He has blasphemed! Why have we any more need of witnesses? Look, now you have heard the blasphemy! 66 What do you think?" Now answering they said, "He is deserving of death." 67 Then they spit in his face, and struck him. Others slapped him, 68 saying, "Prophesy to us, Christ, who is he having hit you?"

EXPOSITION

Caiaphas instantly understood that Jesus was claiming to be the equal of deity. For any other human being this would be blasphemy; to Caiaphas Jesus is just another human being. On the basis of Jesus' testimony Caiaphas asks for a verdict and judgment. Jesus is pronounced guilty of blasphemy and sentenced to death.

The actions in vv. 67–68 are illegal in any legal system, but fulfill prophecy, Micah 5:1, "They will strike the judge of Israel with a rod on the cheek," and Isaiah 50:6, "I gave my back to those who struck me, and my cheeks to those who plucked out the beard; I did not hide my face from shame and spitting." These actions fully indicate the hatred Jesus inspires in sinful human beings.

Translation Matthew 26:69–75

69 Now Peter was sitting outside in the courtyard, and a serving girl came to him, saying, "You also were with Jesus the Galilean." 70 But he denied before all, saying, "I know not what you say." 71 Now having gone out to the gateway, another female saw him, and

says to those there, "This person was with Jesus of Nazareth." 72 And again he denied, with an oath, "I know not the man." 73 After a little while, those also standing close by, having come to him, said to Peter, "Surely you also are one of them, for even your speech gives you away." 74 Then he began to curse and to swear, "I know not the man!" And immediately a rooster crowed. 75 And Peter remembered the word of Jesus, having said, "Before the rooster crowing, you will deny me"; and having gone out, wept bitterly.

EXPOSITION

It is helpful to compare Luke's account, 22:31–34.

"Simon, Simon, look, Satan asked to sift all of you like wheat. 32 But I prayed for you all, that your faith might not fail. And you, when you have turned back, strengthen your brethren." 33 Then Peter said to him, "Master, I am ready with you to go both to prison and to death." 34 And he said, "I tell you Peter, the rooster will not crow today, until three times you will deny knowing me."

Some manuscripts of Mark 14:30, 68, 72 indicate Peter was to deny Jesus in two separate events before the rooster crowed twice. Some don't. I see no reason to doubt those manuscripts reporting two cock crowings. The texts are included in most translations and modern reproductions of the Greek texts.[1]

Carson wrote, "Apparently it was usual for roosters in Palestine to crow about 12:30 a.m., 1:30 a.m., and 2:30 a.m., prompting the Romans to give the term "cockcrow" to the watch between midnight and roughly 3:00 a.m."[2] Bruce wrote, "Cockcrow was the third of the four Roman night-watches, halfway between midnight and dawn; cf. Mark 13:35."[3] Godet wrote, "The cock-crowing of which Jesus speaks [in John 13:38] is that which properly bore this name; the second, that which precedes the break of day, about three o'clock in the morning (Mark 13:35). In the prediction of the denial in Mark (14:30) allusion is also made to the first, the one at midnight."[4]

So in Matthew's account the timing is "before the rooster

---

[1] Metzger, *Textual*, 96, 97.
[2] Carson, *John*, 487.
[3] Bruce, *John*, 295.
[4] Godet, *John*, 267.

crowing." In Mark's account the timing is between the first and second night-watch. In John's account the denial is before the second night-watch occurs. The accounts, then, harmonize, with Mark's account giving the greater detail.

If we compare the four accounts of the denials, we discover two series of denials at two separate times. the first series of denials was at the house of Annas for former high priest, father-in-law of Caiphas the current high priest. The second series of denials was at the house of Caiphas the current high priest.

Appendix: Harmonizing Peter's Denials

The four gospel accounts of Peter's denials of Christ don't quite fit into one narrative of three denials. Below is a table showing the characteristics and differences in the report of Peter's denials.

First Set of Denials	Second Set of Denials		
John 18:12–27	Matthew 26:57–75	Mark 15:66–72	Luke 22:54–62
At Annas's house	At Caiaphas house	High Priest, priests elders, scribes.	High Priest's house
Warming Fire Servant girl Servants, officers	Servant girl Others 2nd servant girl	Warming fire Servant girl Temple police	Warming fire Servant girl Others
First question, asked by servant girl/doorkeeper: Are you one of his disciples?	Statement by servant girl: You were with Jesus the Galilean.	Statement by servant girl: You were with Jesus the Nazarene.	Statement by servant girl: This man was with him.
Second question asked by servants and officers: Are you one of his disciples?	Statement by another female: This person was with Jesus.	Statement by another female: He is one of them.	Statement by another: You are also one of them.
Third question asked kinsman of man whom Peter had cut off his ear: Did I not see you in the garden with him?	Statement by others: You are one of them your speech gives you away.	Statement by others: You are one of them you are a Galilean.	Statement by another: You are one of them, he too is a Galilean
Rooster crows	Rooster crows	Rooster crows twice	Rooster crows
Jesus Sent to Caiaphas	Morning comes, Jesus sent to Pilate	Morning comes, Jesus sent to Pilate	Morning, at Sanhedrin, then to Pilate.

When compared side-by-side, one is able to see there were two sets of three denials each by Peter.

Peter is recognized visually as one who companied with Jesus,

Matthew Twenty-seven

and by his Galilean accent. Peter curses and swears—takes an oath—that he is not with Jesus of Nazareth. IN a sense, Peter's crime is similar to that committed by Judas; both men betray Jesus. Peter remembers what Jesus had said. HE is struck with remorse that leads to confession and repentance, Luke 22:32; 1 Corinthians 15:5, and Peter's presence after the resurrection.

[Note: the table is an appendix from my book, *Four Voices, One Testimony*, a narrative gospel harmony.]

Matthew Twenty-Seven

Translation Matthew 27:1-10

1 Now morning having come, all the chief priests and elders of the people took counsel against Jesus, so that they might put him to death. 2 And having bound him, they led him away and delivered him to Pilate the Procurator. 3 Then Judas (the one having delivered him), having seen that he was condemned, having regretted his actions, returned the thirty pieces of silver to the chief priests and elders, 4 saying, "I sinned, having delivered innocent blood." And they said, "What is that to us? You will see to it." 5 And having cast the pieces of silver into the temple, he left; and having gone away, hanged himself.

6 But the chief priests having taken the pieces of silver said, "It is not lawful to put them into the treasury, since it is the price of blood." 7 And having taken counsel, they bought with them the potter's field, for a burial place for foreigners. 8 Therefore that field was called "Field of Blood" to this day. 9 Then was fulfilled that having been spoken by Jeremiah the prophet, saying, "And they took the thirty pieces of silver, the value of him having been priced, whom they set a price on by the sons of Israel priced, 10 and they gave them for the potter's field, as the Lord directed me."

TRANSLATION NOTE

In v. 2 the word I have translated "procurator" and which all other versions translate "governor" is *hēgemōn*, "leader, chief, head."[1] When not used of a military official, this word is a general term for the Roman administrative offices of prefect, proconsul, legate, or procurator. In relation to the region of Judea, the English "governor" is not a proper translation. Judea was part of the Syrian province, which was an Imperial province, i.e., it was under the direct control of the Emperor (as versus a Senatorial province under the direct control of the Roman Senate). The Emperor appointed persons to the office of legate to govern Imperial provinces. For example, in Luke 2:2, Quirinius was *hēgemōn* over the Syrian province when Jesus was born: Legate Quirinius administered the

---

[1] Zodhiates, *WSDNT*, s. v. "2232."

military and foreign policy of the Syria province while Legate Varus ran the government.[1]

Judea was a smaller administrative region within the Syrian province. An official of lesser rank than legate was appointed over Judea. This lesser official was known as a procurator. "Procurator" was a general term for various officials of Equestrian rank (a Roman social and political status). A procurator handled financial matters, but could also act as magistrate, tax collector, and manager for government construction projects. A procurator could also be an agent working directly for the Emperor. In AD 33 Syria was an Imperial province under Emperor Tiberius (ruled AD 14–37), governed by the Imperial Legate Flaccus. The lesser official who administrated the Judean region of the Syrian province was the procurator Pontius Pilate.

EXPOSITION

In vv. 1–2 the reference to "all" the chief priests and elders of the people refers to the Sanhedrin. All the members need not have been present at the Roman trial (e.g., Nicodemus, John 7:50–54; 19:39), just those working with Caiaphas to have Jesus executed. The Sanhedrin had to take Jesus to Procurator Pilate because the Roman government reserved execution of criminals to itself.

Judas apparently never thought beyond the money until Jesus was condemned to death. Did he think Jesus would be tried and dismissed as a crackpot; or perhaps scourged and set free, or imprisoned? It would seem that Judas did not think Jesus would be condemned, and now that he was condemned, Judas regretted his actions. The word *metamélomai* in the aorist passive (as it is here) means "changing one's mind or purpose after having done something regrettable."[2] The action falls short of repentance, indicating only dread of the consequences of one's actions.

The priests did not care, they had achieved their goals. Matthew tells story of Judas to its conclusion before continuing with the story of Jesus. Judas took out his guilt on himself by condemning himself to death. The priests used the money to buy a field in which to bury foreigners. The prophecy fulfilled was Zechariah 11:13.

---

[1] Ramsay, *Was Christ*, 243–244.

[2] Zodhiates, *WSDNT*, s. v. "3338."

Matthew says the buying the field was a fulfillment of a prophecy by Jeremiah, not Zechariah. Two solutions have been proposed. One, Matthew was making a composite out of Zechariah 11:13 plus Jeremiah 18:2–3; 19:1–13; 32:6–15. Because Jeremiah was the more prominent prophet, Matthew attributed the saying to Jeremiah. Or, two, the book of Jeremiah was the first book in the scroll of the prophets, so Matthew may have been referring to the scroll, not the specific prophet.

In the Zechariah passage, Israel is getting rid of the shepherd they do not want, which was the Lord, Zechariah 11:12, 13,

> Then I said to them, "If it is agreeable to you, give me my wages; and if not, refrain." So they weighed out for my wages thirty pieces of silver. And the Lord said to me, "Throw it to the potter"—that princely price they set on me. So I took the thirty pieces of silver and threw them into the house of the Lord for the potter. (NKJV)

In Matthew's view, Judas selling Jesus for thirty pieces of silver was the religious leaders of Jesus' day fulfilling a prophecy to rid themselves of the Shepherd of Israel. Buying a potter's field (a field in which to bury foreigners) with that blood money was a suitable fulfillment.

Translation Matthew 27:11–18

11 Now Jesus stood before the Procurator, and the Procurator questioned him, saying, "Are you the King of the Jews?" Now Jesus said, "You say." 12 And in his being accused by the chief priests and elders, he answered nothing. 13 Then Pilate says to him, "Hear you not how many things they witness against you?" 14 And he did not answer him, not even to one word, so as to greatly amaze the Procurator. 15 Now at the feast the Procurator was accustomed to release to the crowd one prisoner, whomever they wished. 16 Now they had then a notorious prisoner called Barabbas. 17 They therefore having been gathered together, Pilate said to them, "Whom will you that I release to you? Barabbas, or Jesus who is called Christ?" 18 For he knew that they delivered him through envy.

EXPOSITION

Matthew's account is very brief, the minimum needed to understand that Jesus will be condemned to die. In this scene Jesus admits to being king of the Jews. As explained before, "You say" is an idiom meaning "You have stated the fact." Jesus does not respond to the Jews' accusations. To respond would be to admit their plausibility and to argue against his crucifixion. He chose to do neither.

A compilation of every gospel account of the Roman trial indicates Pilate tried to free Jesus by offering to free Jesus or Barabbas, and then by having Jesus flogged (scourged). When these attempts failed he condemned Jesus to death, which required a second flogging.

Pilate imagines this innocent man called Christ will be freed in lieu of the notorious prisoner Barabbas, a robber, John 18:40, and a rebel and murderer, Mark 15:7; Luke 23:18. Pilate's custom of releasing a prisoner occurred only during the Passover. The word "envy" in v. 18 may mean Pilate suspected the religious leaders were jealous that Jesus was popular and they were not. This presupposes some knowledge of Jesus by Pilate, which does not seem likely from the gospel accounts. However, Pilate could have deduced from the charges that the religious leaders felt Jesus somehow threatened their authority and they were therefore acting in "religio-political self-interest"[1] to rid themselves of someone whose claims threatened their status and authority.

Pilate almost certainly did not understand the term *christós*, Christ, as the Sanhedrin applied the word to Jesus in the indictment for execution. In prior Greek and Roman literature the word meant to anoint in the sense of rubbing or smearing some kind of ointment on an object or person.[2] *Christós* refers to a person only in the LXX and New Testament. The way Pilate uses the word, "Jesus who is called Christ," indicates he did not understand. He was simply repeating what the chief priests and elders had said. In his mind he was thinking, "Why are they calling this person 'anointed?' "

Translation Matthew 27:19–23

19 Now as he was sitting on the Judgment Seat, his wife sent to him, saying, "Have nothing to do with that righteous man, for many things I suffered today in a dream on account of him." 20 But the chief priests and the elders persuaded the crowds that they should ask for Barabbas; but Jesus execute. 21 Now the Procurator

---

[1] France, *Matthew*, NICNT, 1049.
[2] Bromiley, *TDNT*, 9:493–495.

answering said to them, "Which do you want of the two I might release to you?" Now they said, "Barabbas." 22 Pilate says to them, "What then should I do with Jesus who is called Christ?" They all say, "Let him be crucified." 23 But he said, "For what evil did he commit?" But all the more they cried out, saying, "Let him be crucified."

EXPOSITION

Only Matthew relates the message from Pilate's wife. It was unheard that a wife should interrupt official business, therefore the matter must be important; dreams were considered significant portents of the future. John doesn't report the wife's message, but he does reveal Pilate's response, John 19:1–3. In v. 26 Matthew condenses the release of Barabbas, the first flogging, the condemnation, and the second flogging.

The religious leaders led the crowd to demand Barabbas be freed. When Pilate asks the crowd about "Jesus who is called Christ" they demand Jesus be crucified. Pilate recognizes the priests are using the word *christós* as a title or term that has significance to the assembled crowd, and that is why he uses it here, to present the choice in as stark terms as possible. Shall I release a murderer, or this one whom you call Christ? This attempt fails, so he tries another approach, asking what evil Jesus might have committed that would condemn him to death by crucifixion. Barabbas had committed capital crimes worthy of crucifixion. "What about this Jesus?" he asks the crowd. The response is the same, "Let him be crucified."

Translation Matthew 27:24–26

24 Now Pilate having seen that it availed nothing, but rather an uproar is rising, having taken water, he washed his hands before the crowd, saying, "I am innocent of the blood of this. You will take care for yourselves." 25 And answering all the people said, "His blood be on us, and on our children." 26 Then he released to them Barabbas; now having flogged Jesus, he delivered him that he might be crucified.

EXPOSITION

Although Pilate had many duties, he would be swiftly removed from his job for failure to collect taxes and keep the peace. The Romans hated conflict in conquered territories because conflict interrupted taxes and cost a lot of money to resolve. The peace was at stake here, because "an uproar is rising." However, keeping the peace was not reason enough to condemn Jesus to death. The matter could have been handled with a *fustigatio* kind of flogging (see below), which Pilate first tried. So why does Matthew report Pilate was condemned to keep the peace?

Matthew severely condenses the account, and below I will describe the trial in more detail. Matthew keeps his focus on Jesus. He ignores (or doesn't know) the material John presents (see below). Matthew gives us the beginning, 27:11–18, and the end, 27:24–26, of the trial. In Matthew's view the Jews are responsible for Jesus' death and the Roman government is the instrument of his death. From Matthew's perspective, v. 26, when the crowd could not be appeased Pilate condemned Jesus.

In washing his hands Pilate symbolically denies any involvement in the process to have Jesus murdered. Hand washing was a Jewish custom. Pilate's meaning is unmistakable. He declares himself innocent and tells the crowd to see to the execution themselves.

But the crowd can't execute Jesus, because that was a Roman function. Pilate knows this. It is another attempt by Pilate to free Jesus and keep himself clear of any wrongdoing. Jesus had not committed a violation of Roman law.

But the chief priests offer Pilate a real crime that he could write into the official record, and to which he must respond (a crime Matthew doesn't relate to the reader). John 19:12 tells us the official crime was treason, "[the] Jews cried out, saying, 'If this man you release, you are not a Friend of Caesar. Anyone making himself a king speaks against Caesar.' " Jesus had admitted as much to Pilate, Matthew 27:11.

Like to or not, Pilate must now act; but he forces the Jews to accept responsibility for the crime of executing an innocent person: "His blood be on us, and on our children." John tells us Pilate makes the Jews deny King Jesus and claim a worldly king as their only king (John 19:15). This is deeply ironic, for Jewish opposition to Rome was in part motivated by the belief that God was Israel's one and only king.

Verse 26 is very condensed, and I will expand it with the other Gospel accounts. First, Pilate releases Barabbas. Then Pilate tries having Jesus flogged in order to satisfy the crowd. Luke 23:22 and John 19:1–3 report this first flogging.

> Now a third time he said to them, "For what evil did this man commit? I found no cause of death in him. Therefore, having chastised him, I will release him." (Luke 23:22)
>
> Pilate therefore then took Jesus, and had him flogged. 2 And the soldiers, having twisted together a crown of thorns, put it on his head, and put around him a purple robe. 3 And they came up to him and said, "Hail King of the Jews!" And they hit him with the palm of their hands. (John 19:1–3)

After the first flogging Pilate returns with Jesus to the crowd, John 19:4–6.

> And Pilate again went out and says to them, "Behold, I bring him out to you in order that you might know that I find no guilt in him." 5 Jesus therefore went out wearing the thorny crown and the purple robe; and he says to them, "Behold the man." 6 Therefore when the chief priests and the officers saw him, they cried out, saying, "Crucify! Crucify!" Pilate says to them, "Take him yourselves and crucify. For I find in him no guilt."

The crowd still wants Jesus crucified, but Pilate continues to try and gain his release, John 19:7–11.

> The Jews answered him, "We have a Law, and according to the Law he ought to die, because he made himself Son of God."
>
> 8 Therefore when Pilate heard this word he was more afraid. 9 And he went into the Praetorium again and says to Jesus, "From where are you?" But Jesus did not give him an answer. 10 Therefore Pilate says to him, "Speak you not to me? Do you not know that I have authority to release you, and I have authority to crucify you?" 11 Jesus answered him, "You would have no authority over me at all, if it were not given to you from above. Because of this, the one having delivered me to you has greater sin."

But the crowd threatens Pilate, and he orders Jesus' crucifixion, John 19:12–16.

> From that time Pilate sought to release him; but Jews cried out, saying, "If this man you release, you are not a Friend of Caesar. Anyone making himself a king speaks against Caesar."
>
> 13 Pilate, therefore, having heard these words, brought out

Matthew Twenty-seven

Jesus, and sat down upon the judgment seat, at a place called Stone Pavement, but in Aramaic, Gabbatha. 14 Now it was the preparation of the Passover; it was about noon; and he says to the Jews, "Behold your king." 15 They cried out, therefore, "Away with him, crucify him!" Pilate says to them, "Should I crucify your king?" The chief priests answered, "No king we have, except Caesar." 16 Therefore he then delivered him to them that he might be crucified. (John 19:13–16)

By Roman law and custom, an order of condemnation to death by crucifixion required the kind of flogging designed to hasten the victim's death, Mark 16:16–19; Matthew 27:31.

The Romans used different forms of corporal punishment, depending on who the person was and what he had done. A freedman (a slave who had been given his freedom or had bought his freedom) was beaten with rods of birch or elm bound together in a bundle.[1] Slaves and non-Romans were flogged (also known as scourging). Flogging was performed using a whip made out of leather straps or knotted cords (rope) often weighted with pieces of metal or bone. Flogging was used in four circumstances.[2]

Simple flogging: torture during questioning of a prisoner

Fustigatio: punishment

Flagellatio: punishment

Verberatio: execution or as preparation for crucifixion

The "*fustigatio* was a less severe beating meted out for relatively light offences, [think misdemeanor] . . . the *flagellatio* was a brutal flogging administered to criminals whose offences were more serious," [think felony].[3] The *verberatio*[4] was used as capital punishment for people sentenced to death by flogging, or as preparation for crucifixion . . . the *verberatio* could be so severe that bones and organs could be exposed.[5]

The gospel accounts, being written in Greek, do not use the Latin words *fustigatio, flagellatio,* or *verberatio.* Matthew and Mark

---

[1] Bromiley, *ISBE,* s. v. "Scourge."

[2] Ibid.

[3] Carson, *John,* 597.

[4] Ibid.

[5] Bromiley, *ISBE,* s. v. "Scourge."

use *phragellóō*, to scourge with a whip.[1] Luke uses *paideúō*, to instruct by chastisement.[2] John uses *mastigóō*, to whip, scourge.[3] A lictor in Rome, or a skilled and practiced soldier in the provinces, could deliver a painful flogging without inflicting permanent or fatal damage to the victim. Those condemned to die by flogging were whipped by a team of executioners until the condemned person died.

The first flogging of Jesus was the *fustigatio* kind of flogging, ordered by Pilate in an attempt to secure Jesus' release. John describes it with the word *mastigóō;* Luke describes it as *paideúō*. The second flogging is described by Matthew and Mark as *phragellóō*, which is the *verberatio* kind of flogging used as preparation for crucifixion. The gospel records do not report how many lashes Jesus received. The flogging left Jesus alive, but inflicted injuries that contributed to his death.

Translation Matthew 27:27–32

27 Then the soldiers of the Procurator, having taken Jesus with them to the Praetorium, gathered before him all the company. 28 And having stripped him, they put on him a scarlet robe. 29 And having twisted together a crown of thorns, they put it on his head, and a reed in his right hand; and having bowed the knees before him, they mocked him, saying, "Hail, King of the Jews." 30 And having spit upon him, they took the reed and struck him on his head. 31 And when they had mocked him, they took the robe off him, and they on him his clothes, and led him away to crucify him. 32 Now going out, they found a man of Cyrene, named Simon. They compelled him that he might carry his cross.

EXPOSITION

Matthew reports the flogging required for the condemned, using the Greek *phragellóō*, for the Latin *verberatio*. Jesus lived in a brutal time, when a person's worth was valued by his social status. A condemned man had no status, and therefore had less than human worth. This treatment was normal and expected; it was a way to brutalize the victim to hasten his death.

---

[1] Zodhiates, *WSDNT*, s. v. "5417. *phragellóō*."
[2] Ibid., s. v. "3811."
[3] Ibid., s. v. "3146."

Matthew Twenty-seven

Matthew uses a word that means a cohort of soldiers, which was about 400–500 men. This may have been the number of soldiers garrisoned in Jerusalem for the feast (extra soldiers were brought in for the feasts). However, in relation to Jesus' brutalization, the number of soldiers hitting and mocking him was probably far less. No one could survive 400–500 soldiers hitting them. Many soldiers would be outside the Praetorium on duty in the city during the feast. Some who worked the night watch would be sleeping. Others would have duty that prevented them from being present.

The brutalization was not out of malice or sadism. This was the job. Every soldier had participated in the crucifixion process at one time or another. The soldiers present were those responsible to carry out the crucifixion, those who would provide crowd control on the march to the site and during the crucifixion, and those within the Praetorium not on duty who decided to participate in yet another brutalization of yet another condemned criminal.

To the soldiers and their superiors, and to the mass of common people, this was expected treatment of a condemned man. Jesus' crime was treason against the Roman Empire by claiming to be a king in competition with Caesar. Therefore, they made their brutalization fit the crime. Because he had claimed to be a king, he was mocked as a pretend king. The crown of plaited thorns was part of this mockery. They hurt him, mocked him, degraded him, and then led him away to be crucified.

As to Simon of Cyrene, Jesus probably collapsed at the gate exiting the city, and there the Romans made Simon of Cyrene carry the cross, because he just happened to be entering the city at that time. Matthew simply reports the fact.

Crucifixion seems to have been invented by the Persians as impalement on a stake, sometimes as a means of execution (e.g., Esther 7:10), and sometimes to display the dead body of the condemned executed by other means. The Greeks and Romans refined the method as a means of executing the worst criminals.

The Romans had the condemned carried his cross: "The malefactor who is to be crucified carries his cross on his own body" (Plutarch, AD 45–120, *On the Delay of the Divine Justice*, section 25).

Almost certainly Jesus did not bear both pieces of the cross.

The word the Four Gospels use for cross is *staurós*,[1] a stake, which in Roman times came with a cross-piece, hence a cross, not the modern meaning of "stake." A cross consisted of two or three pieces. The heavier upright, the *stipes*, was permanently fixed in the ground at the crucifixion site. The cross-piece, on which to nail the hands and tie the upper arms, was called the *patibulum*. Then there was a small cross piece used to nail the legs to the *stipes* through the victim's heels. Some crosses also had a peg or seat on which the condemned could rest, in order to prolong life—to make the victim die from dehydration instead of asphyxiation. Without the peg the condemned must lift up with his arms and push upwards with his feet in order to breathe—causing excruciating pain—until too exhausted to do so, at which time he died from asphyxiation (this is why the soldiers broke the legs of the two thieves). The three crosses at this execution did not have a peg or seat.

The history of Roman execution by crucifixion tells us that Jesus almost certainly carried only the cross piece, i.e., the *patibulum*. The upright piece, the *stipes*, was left in place at Golgotha, a constant reminder of Roman occupation and Roman laws.

Translation Matthew 27:33-37

33 And having come to a place called Golgotha, which is called, place of a skull, 34 they gave him wine mingled with gall to drink; and having tasted, he was not willing to drink it. 35 Now having crucified him, they divided his clothing, casting lots; that might be fulfilled that which was spoken by the prophet: "They divided my clothing among themselves, and for my clothing they cast a lot." 36 Sitting down, they kept watch over him there. 37 And they put up over his head the accusation written of him: This Is Jesus The King Of The Jews.

EXPOSITION

Wine mingled with gall was fruit juice (in this case probably fermented, but as always diluted with water) mingled with something that made it bitter. Some suggest it was simply sour wine, i.e., vinegar, but more likely it was juice with some

---

[1] Zodhiates, *WSDNT*, s. v. "4716."

frankincense in it so as to dull the senses (this appears to have been a Jewish custom).[1] Jesus refused to drink after tasting. The inference is that he refused to dull his senses.

Casting a lot (or, lots) meant to throw the dice (or die), sometimes a form of gambling, but usually used to determine the will of the gods, e.g., Jonah 1:7. Here in Matthew the soldiers were not gambling they were deciding who would get which piece of clothing. We might think of casting lots as similar, i.e., with the same intent, to drawing straws. From ancient times the dice were shaped and looked similar to modern versions. Sometimes the dice were stones or pebbles painted or colored. When the die were thrown, if two dark sides landed up, the usual interpretation was no. If two light sides landed up, that was yes. A light and a dark side meant throw again.

The place of crucifixion was the usual place the Romans executed criminals at Jerusalem, by the side of a well-traveled road into the city, probably the busy road going north into Samaria (only the most "orthodox" Pharisees, scribes, and Sadducees refused to travel through Samaria), Galilee, and Damascus. Death by crucifixion was reserved for the worst criminals. Jesus qualified because of his claim to be king of the Jews.

Upon arrival at the crucifixion site the condemned was fastened to the *patibulum*, the cross piece, probably by both nails and ropes. The arms were stretched out and a nail hammered through each wrist into the *patibulum*; the wrist was considered part of the hand. Ropes were used to secure the arms on the *patibulum*. Once the condemned was fastened to the *patibulum*, it was lifted up and fastened to the upright piece. The upright piece was already fixed in the ground, left there between executions. There was no excruciating drop into a hole (as in some movies), which might have torn the nails out of the victim's wrists.

The assembled cross was not very tall. The victim's feet when attached to the *stipes* were a foot or so off the ground. To attach the feet the legs were twisted and bent at the knees and a nail passed through both heels into the *stipes*. The victim's body sagged on the cross, preventing the diaphragm from contracting, requiring the victim to push up with his legs and pull up with his arms in order to breathe. Each time the victim lifted to take a breath, the nails

---

[1] Morris, *Matthew*, 715.

would grind against the nerves in wrists and feet causing excruciating pain.

The Roman soldiers regularly performed crucifixions, so they had made the process easy and efficient. They nailed and tied the condemned to the cross piece, lifted the cross piece and fastened it to the upright piece, nailed the heels, and then sat down or stood around and waited for the condemned to die.

The place of execution was known as "Of the Skull." No reason is given for the name. It may be because it was a place of death; it may be that the place had some resemblance to a skull. There is no biblical evidence that it was a hill. A place of crucifixion by the side of a well-traveled road would have served Roman purposes as well a high place that could be seen from the city wall or gate. Two crucifixion sites are proposed, both near the city and both near the road to Samaria as it enters/leaves the city.

The traditional crucifixion site was identified in the days of Emperor Constantine (AD 272–337) as north of the first wall and west of the second wall (thus west of the temple) near the Gennath Gate (Josephus mentions this gate, *Wars*, 5.4.2), where the old road to Samaria left the city.

As to the second (and more likely) site, in 1842 the German theologian Otto Thenius published a proposal for a site north of the Damascus Gate, on a rocky hill which resembled a skull. Several others proposed the same site in 1850 and 1872. In 1882 General Charles Gordon was visiting friends in Jerusalem and, knowing the previous proposals, verified for himself a hill to the north of the second wall in which caves formed two eye sockets, a feature which is visible today. Gordon's proposal received more attention than those of Thenius and others. Gordon suggested the location of this hill on the north side of the city agreed with a typological reading of Leviticus 1:11 (animal sacrifices were to be killed on the north side of the altar). Gordon wrote,

> The morning after my arrival at Jerusalem I went to the Skull Hill, and felt convinced that it must be north of the Altar. Leviticus 1:11 says that the victims are to be slain on the side of the Altar northwards; if a particular direction was given by God about where the types [he means those animals whose sacrifice illustrated Christ's person and work] were to be slain, it is a sure deduction that the prototype [i.e., the antitype, Christ] would be slain in some position as

to the Altar: this the Skull Hill fulfills. . . . The Latin Holy Sepulchre (*sic*) is west of the Altar, and therefore, unless the types are wrong, it should never have been taken as the site.[1]

A garden tomb was found around the backside of the hill in 1867 (the date this tomb was made is much debated). The hill with skull-like features is known as Gordon's Calvary and today is accepted by many as the genuine site of the crucifixion. Gordon's Calvary is located north of the temple, north of the Fortress of Antonia, north of the second north city wall, and nearby is another road which, in Jesus day, exited Jerusalem to Samaria and Damascus through the upper gate. (The road from Samaria splits as it nears the city, with each leg entering a different gate. The two gates were separated by a residential area, which was surrounded by the second wall.)

Locating the site of the crucifixion at Gordon's Calvary north of the city and north of the temple fits one of the Old Testament types of Christ. A "type" is a divinely purposed illustration of some biblical truth. For example, the Baptist said, "Behold God's Lamb, he who takes away the sin of the world!" The Old Testament lamb sacrificed for sin was a type—a divinely purposed illustration—of the Person and work of Jesus the Christ. So too all the sacrifices were types of the Person and work of Christ.

At Leviticus 1:11 the whole burnt offering was to be killed on the north side of the altar. The whole burnt offering symbolized a person's wholehearted dedication to YHWH, and thus typified Jesus' complete submission to the Father's will. Other offerings are described as being killed at the door of the Tabernacle (e.g., Leviticus 3:2; 4:4), making a strong argument that all the offerings were killed on the north side of the altar.

When Jesus was crucified, the temple, and thus the altar, was in the location proposed today by archaeological discoveries: on the north side of the city. The location of the temple makes Gordon's Calvary the likely crucifixion site. The traditional site is west of the temple. The Fortress of Antonia was also on the north side of the city, north of, and sharing a supporting wall with, the temple. The Fortress was the permanent garrison for Roman soldiers stationed

---

[1] Charles George Gordon, *Eden and Golgotha*, in *Palestine Exploration Fund Quarterly Statement*, (London, 1885), pp. 79–81.

at Jerusalem, making the entire company available to Pilate to maintain control of the crowd assembled for Jesus' trial, and to carry out the execution without delay. I believe Pilate was at the Fortress of Antonia when he judged Jesus (not Herod's Palace, which was on the far west wall of the city). Today a bus station is located at the foot of the hill known as Gordon's Calvary.

Pilate, as was the custom, posted the crime on the cross above the victim. Other gospels tell us the notice was written in the three languages of the day, Latin, Greek, and Hebrew. Crucifixion victims were nailed nude to the cross, but the Romans allowed crucified Jews a loin cloth, in deference to their religious sensibilities. The executioners were entitled to the victim's clothes. They cast lots for the outer robe because it was woven in one piece, making it an expensive piece of clothing. Then, they sat and waited for him to die. They were there to prevent any rescue, and to keep the crowd from further brutalizing the victim. Crucifixion was the legal penalty for a crime, no audience participation allowed.

Death through crucifixion came either from physical stress and blood loss or from asphyxiation. If not seated on a peg (to prolong the suffering) the victim ultimately lost the necessary physical strength to push up and take a breath. To hasten death the victim's legs could be broken so he could not push up to take a breath. The legs were broken in this particular crucifixion because the Sabbath was at sundown. The Jews' treaty with the Romans stated crucified victims would not be left on the cross during the Sabbath.

Translation Matthew 27:38–44

38 Then two robbers are crucified with him, one at the right hand, and another at the left. 39 Now those passing by blasphemed him, wagging their heads 40 and saying, "The one destroying the temple and building it in three days, save yourself. If you are Son of God, also come down from the cross." 41 In the same manner also the chief priests, mocking with the scribes and elders, said, 42 "He saved others; he is not able to save himself. He is King of Israel; let him come down now from the cross, and we will believe in him. 43 He trusted on God; let Him deliver now if He wants him. For he said, 'I am Son of God.' " 44 Now also in the same manner the robbers, those having been crucified with him, reviled him.

EXPOSITION

Two thieves were crucified at the same time as Jesus. Jesus

was placed in the middle position of the trio. Isaiah 53:9, 12, he made his grave with the wicked . . . he was numbered with the transgressors.

Matthew shows the complete rejection of messiah by his people. They mock his words. They say they will believe if he can free himself from the cross. Since he cannot, in their view the one who claimed he came from God has been forsaken by God. They remember his words, they simply cannot believe in them or in him. They rejected a crucified Savior, in the same way they will reject a resurrected Savior.

Everyone knew him: the common person, the civil and religious leaders, and even the two thieves, who also reviled him. Matthew keeps his focus on Jesus and does not mention the repentant thief.

Translation Matthew 27:45–49

45 Now from the sixth hour darkness was over all the land, until the ninth hour. 46 Now about the ninth hour Jesus cried out with a loud voice, saying, "Eli, Eli, lama sabachthani?" that is, "My God, my God, why have You forsaken me?" 47 Now some of those who were standing there, having heard, said, "This man calls Elijah." 48 And immediately one of them having run and having taken a sponge, having filled it with vinegar and having put it on a reed, gave him to drink. 49 But the rest said, "Let be; let us see whether Elijah comes to save him."

EXPOSITION

The sixth hour was about noon and the ninth was about three p.m. This was a supernaturally caused darkness. At about the ninth hour Jesus cried out to God. This cry of God forsaking his Son tells us Jesus had been the sin-bearer, suffering the wrath of God for the sin of the world.

Before the sixth hour Jesus had asked the Father to forgive his executioners. He had saved the repentant thief. He had given his mother into the protective care of his disciple John (who took her away before the darkness began, John 19:27). Then, beginning about noon (Matthew 27:45), darkness covered the whole land for three hours. God was transacting business with the God-man. The Trinity had imputed the guilt of sin to Jesus the Christ. He was suffering the undiluted wrath of God against the sins of all human kind from Adam to the last yet-future sinner. God covered the moment in darkness, to give his Son dignity in his sufferings, and to reveal the spiritual darkness of the moment when the Creator suffered for his sinful creature.

Because Jesus suffered for the judicial guilt of sin, not the moral defilement of sin, the Trinity did not separate from God the Son—an impossibility since they are the same essence. What took place was God separating from fellowship with the God-man. Isaiah 59:2, "Your sins have separated you from your God; your sins have hidden your God from you so that he will not hear you." The hours of darkness were when Christ suffered a temporary, but altogether genuine, spiritual death: separation from God because he "became sin for us."

His entire life Jesus had experienced fellowship with God, an unbroken and intimate communion. When he imputed man's sins to himself, that intimate communion the God-man had always experienced with the Father and the Spirit was forsaken for three hours. That was the moment he dreaded, the moment he prayed about in the Garden of Gethsemane, that it might pass from him; but he submitted to God's will for the sake of sinners. Jesus the Christ took on the debt of sin; God turned his back to his son; Jesus suffered the spiritual death of separation from God.

John tells us that after the cry to God, Jesus said, "I thirst." John also tells us there was a vessel with vinegar sitting nearby (probably for the soldiers). In response to the cry of thirst, someone gave Jesus some vinegar to drink. Vinegar diluted with water was a common drink of poor people or laborers. Jesus was thirsty. His exsanguination and dehydration were very real. The *verberatio* would have left him with severe blood loss. He almost certainly had not had anything to drink since his arrest about fifteen hours earlier. Bleeding on the cross, and exposure to the elements, with his muscles working hard to take every breath, left him very thirsty; painfully so. He received the vinegar, but many wanted him to continue suffering so he would continue crying out, because they thought he had cried out to Elijah.

We can forgive Matthew for not including the cry "I thirst." The only disciples near enough to hear the words "I thirst," were the apostle John and some women, John 19:28, standing at the edge of the crowd, watching, Luke 23:49. The other apostles must have been further away, so they heard only what was shouted, and knew only what they saw. Matthew and Mark (Peter was Mark's source according to Papias, *Fragments*, VI[1]) heard the cry out to God, and several persons speaking about Elijah, and saw the drink of vinegar. We also see in v. 50 that Matthew (Mark also, 15:37) heard Jesus make a loud cry and saw him die. Luke, based upon his interviewed sources, records Jesus' next to last words, Luke 23:49, but only John was close enough to hear the final words, John 19:30.

Translation Matthew 27:50–54

50 Now Jesus again having cried out with a loud voice, yielded up his spirit. 51 Then, look, the veil of the temple was torn from top to bottom, into two; and the earth was shaken, and the rocks were split, 52 and the tombs were opened, and many bodies of the saints having fallen asleep arose, 53 and having gone out of the tombs after his resurrection, they entered into the holy city and appeared to many. 54 Now the centurion and those with him keeping guard over Jesus, having seen the earthquake and the things taking place, greatly feared, saying, "Truly this was God's son."

EXPOSITION

Luke 23:46 tells us the loud cry was ""Father, into your hands I commit my spirit." John 19:30 tells us after the loud cry Jesus gave the cry of victory, "It is finished!" Then Jesus died. Scripture states the death of Jesus in the plainest terms. Matthew 27:50, Jesus yielded up his spirit. Mark 15:37, Jesus breathed his last. Luke 23:46, Jesus breathed his last. John 19:30, Jesus gave up his spirit.

During his last moments of physical life on the cross, we can see that the sin-debt had been fully paid. Earlier he had cried out that God had forsaken him. Now he said "Father," Luke 23:46. This word from their familial and filial relationship indicated the spiritual penalty had been paid and his fellowship with God had been restored. He said, "Father, into your hands I commit [entrust] my spirit," knowing that he would be received in heaven. Jesus had died spiritually—separated from fellowship with God—during those three hours of darkness, fully satisfying the spiritual penalty for sin. Fellowship had been restored. Now he died physically, fully satisfying the physical penalty for sin.

Someone might question whether Jesus died from the physical stress of the crucifixion, or deliberately and voluntarily died to pay

---

[1] Roberts, *ANF*, 1:154.

the penalty for sin. Jesus is the offering and the offeror: in the Old Testament type the offeror killed the sin offering, Leviticus 4:4, 24, 29, 33. John 19:30 answers the question. "Jesus said, 'It is finished.' Then bowing his head he gave up his spirit." Jesus held up his head during the crucifixion, until the payment of the penalty was completed. He declared his work was finished, then he deliberately and purposefully separated his soul from his body: he voluntarily caused his physical death (the offeror killed the sacrifice).

The word translated "it is finished," is *teléō*, "to complete something, not merely to end it, but to bring it to perfection or its destined goal."[1] Before he died physically Jesus cried out, "*Tetelestai*," the perfect tense of the verb *teléō*, indicating the action of the verb was brought to completion. It was his cry of victory at having completed the propitiation for sin, both the spiritual death now past, and the physical death about to come.[2]

And then he yielded up his spirit. With the physical and spiritual penalties of sin paid in full, with every necessary Scripture fulfilled, he caused his soul to separate from his body, and went to his Father, taking the saved thief with him (Luke 23:43).

The veil in the temple, said to have been a hand's breadth in width, was torn in two from top to bottom. The reason God tore the veil was because Jesus had paid for sin that separated man from God, which the veil symbolized. The way into God's presence is now through Jesus alone (Hebrews 10:20). Through Jesus alone the believer can boldly enter into God's presence.

There was an earthquake, often a symbol of judgment, in this instance symbolizing judgment on Israel for crucifying their messiah. Many graves are opened and some people were resurrected after Jesus' resurrection. Nothing is said as to what later happened to them; perhaps they went to heaven when Jesus ascended.

The centurion heard Jesus' cry of victory, witnessed the earthquake, and testified that Jesus was God's son. He (and his men with him) would have heard that claim from the crowd in v. 43. As a Roman he would have thought of the living emperor as a son of the gods, and the dead emperors as deities to be worshiped.

---

[1] Zodhiates, *WSDNT*, s. v. "5055."
[2] Quiggle, *Incarnate*, 153.

So, this is not a cry of saving faith, but a gentile recognizing that the man whom they crucified was a man worthy of religious affection. The "truly" means the centurion, and those with him, spoke with the sincerity of conviction. This man whom they had just executed was, in their view, not just another man. They saw in him some manifestation of deity and they were greatly afraid. Matthew gives this gentile testimony concerning Jesus with a view to the evangelization of gentiles that was happening as he wrote his Gospel circa AD 58–60.

Translation Matthew 27:55–56

55 Now there were many women from afar off, looking on, who followed Jesus from Galilee, ministering to him, 56 among whom was Mary Magdalene, and Mary the mother of James and Joses, and the mother of the sons of Zebedee.

Translation note

In v. 56 the name "Joses" in the Byzantine manuscripts is "Joseph" in the Western manuscripts. Mark has "Joses," at 15:40. I decided to follow Mark and the Byzantine manuscripts.

Some commentators believe James and Joses in Matthew 27:56 were the half-brothers of Jesus, Matthew 13:55, making Mary the mother of James and Joses to be Jesus' mother. But the person "James" in v. 56 is in Mark 15:40 named James the Less, or in some manuscripts, James the Younger. This designation would be used to distinguish this James from a James who was more prominent in early Christian circles.

We know of three "James" in early Christianity. First in importance was James the apostle, He would be distinguished as an apostle, as the brother of John the apostle, and as the son of Zebedee. The next "James" in importance was James the Lord's half-brother. He would be distinguished by his physical relationship with Jesus, as the leader of the Jerusalem Council, Acts 15:13, as the author of the epistle of James, and in as the pastor of the Jerusalem church. That means James the Less/Younger of Matthew 27:56 and Mark 15:40 was not the apostle James or the half-brother James, but another James. This means the Joses and James and Mary of Matthew 27:56 are not the mother and brothers of Jesus. See below for a possible identification.

EXPOSITION

Matthew says nothing about the apostles at the cross. He can't, because he and they were on the fringes of the crowd. The only apostle at the cross was John, with Jesus' mother, his mother's sister, Mary [the wife] of Clopas, and Mary Magdalene. Matthew saw the women from a distance. Why didn't he report John and Jesus' mother at the cross? Because John had taken her to his house in Jerusalem after the clothing was divided, which was before the sixth hour, John 19:27 (John returned at the ninth hour, 19:28–30).

Luke's account speaks of the women who had followed Jesus, so there may have been more women present at the foot of the cross than the women mentioned by Matthew. Others are mentioned in the other Gospels. Using the complete list, the mother of Zebedee's sons is Salome, who was the sister of Mary the mother of Jesus. This fact would account for Jesus placing his mother into John's care, John 19:27, because Mary the mother of John was Jesus' aunt, making John his mother's nephew and Jesus' cousin. Jesus' brothers did not at this time believe in him as the messiah, making it unlikely Jesus would commit his mother to the care of the next eldest son, James.

In Matthew, Mark and John there are three women other than Jesus' mother, giving rise to the assumption that these accounts identify the same three women. The women at the cross, excluding Jesus' mother (John's account), are defined in the following table.

Matthew's Account	Mark's Account	John's Account
Mary Magdalene	Mary Magdalene	Mary Magdalene
Mary mother of James and Joses	Mary mother of James the Younger, and Joses	Mary wife of Clopas
Mother of Zebedee's Sons	Salome	His mother's sister

It would be natural for Mary and her sister to be at Passover together. The identification of one of the women as Mary the mother of James the Less/Younger and Joses in both Matthew and Mark make it likely Mary wife of Clopas in John is Mary the mother of James the Less/Younger and Joses. Why don't Matthew and Mark mention Mary Jesus' mother? Because John took her to his house before the hours of darkness began.

Translation Matthew 27:57–61

57 Now evening having come, a rich man came from Arimathea, named Joseph, who also himself was discipled to Jesus. 58 He having gone to Pilate asked for the body of Jesus. Then Pilate commanded it be given. 59 And having taken the body, Joseph wrapped it in clean linen cloth, 60 and placed it in his new tomb, which he had cut in the rock; and having rolled a large stone to the door of the tomb, went away. 61 Now there was Mary Magdalene and the other Mary, sitting opposite the tomb.

EXPOSITION

Joseph of Arimathea was a member of the Sanhedrin, Luke 23:50; it is likely Nicodemus was also a member,[1] John 3:1; 7:45–52. Joseph and Nicodemus must have been at the crucifixion site waiting for Jesus to die in order for the embalming and burial to fit into the limited time they had to do these things. They would have watched as the soldier pierced Jesus' side, proving he was dead, John 19:34. They must have agreed that Joseph would get permission to take the body, while Nicodemus went and bought the embalming myrrh and aloes.

The Romans would have left the bodies on their crosses for several days to be eaten by birds and wild animals, as a warning to insurrectionists and murderers. But it was 3:00 p.m. Friday afternoon and the Sabbath would begin in just a few hours. The Roman treaty with the Jews required the dead crucified on a Friday be removed before sunset so they would not be hanging there during the Sabbath. The Roman soldiers broke the legs of the thieves so they would die and could be removed before the Sabbath began.

That it was Friday gave Joseph of Arimathea and Nicodemus a reason to claim the body. The Romans might throw the bodies into the garbage dump in the Valley of Hinnom, or the Jews might throw the bodies into a common grave for criminals[2] (one or the other is what happened to the bodies of the two thieves).

The Jews would not have cared what happened to Jesus' body. Who would dare to claim the body of a thief, murderer, or rebel,

---

[1] Quiggle, *John 1–12*, 81.
[2] Josephus, *Antiquities*, 4.8.6.

thereby declaring themselves friends of thieves, murderers, and rebels? But Joseph did. Pilate may have known Joseph from the Sanhedrin. Allowing Joseph to take Jesus' body and give it a proper Jewish burial may have been a way for Pilate to humiliate the Jews and reiterate his judgment that Jesus was an innocent man whom the Jews had coerced Pilate to crucify.

By the time Jesus' body was removed from the cross, Joseph and Nicodemus had about two hours to prepare his body and place him into the tomb before sunset came and Sabbath began. Assuming Jesus died at 3:00 p.m., and sunset was 6:00 p.m., we can estimate the activities between death and burial.

Immediately after Jesus died, Joseph walked to Pilate's location (most likely the Fortress of Antonio), waited to be granted an audience with Pilate, and then asked Pilate for the body. Pilate sent a servant to bring the centurion in charge, to verify Jesus was dead, Mark 15:42–45. So that servant had to walk to the crucifixion site, explain to the centurion, who would have placed the next raking soldier in charge, and then walked with the servant to Pilate's location. Then Joseph would have walked back to the crucifixion site with the Centurion. All the walking and time spent with Pilate may have taken up to an hour. When Joseph and the centurion arrived back at Golgotha, the centurion would have had his soldiers take Jesus' body down from the cross and place it on the ground. Did Joseph have servants, or fellow disciples, to help carry the dead body to the tomb site? The apostles John may have been the helper, and Nicodemus may have returned from shopping for spices.

While Joseph was doing his task, Nicodemus went to the marketplace and bought the spices and carried them to the tomb site. The spices weighed about seventy-five pounds, John 19:39, so Nicodemus was helped by his household servants or his disciples. (The Greek text of John 19:39 reads "one hundred *litras*." The *litra* was a Roman measurement of weight equal to about twelve ounces,[1] thus, 100 *litras* X 12 ounces = 1200 ounces / 16 ounces = 75 pounds.) How did John know the weight of spices purchased by Nicodemus? There is nothing in the gospels that prevents John from helping Joseph and Nicodemus prepare the body for entombment. Later, we find that John knew where the tomb was

---

[1] Zodhiates, *WSDNT*, s. v. "3046."

and led Peter to it, John 20:4.

Buying spices and returning with them to Golgotha probably took about the same amount of time it took for Joseph to get the body. The marketplace was a further walk from the crucifixion site than Pilate's office,[1] but Nicodemus only walked there and back, versus the three trips by Joseph, the servant, and the centurion.

How did Nicodemus know where to take the spices? Either he met Joseph at Golgotha or by prior arrangement he knew where Joseph would take the body. Getting the body and buying the spices and taking the body to the nearby tomb would have taken about an hour: they walked everywhere and the wheels of government and commerce move slowly in any century. So they had about two hours to wash, redress, embalm and wrap, and then entomb the body. They hurried to do all these things, because it was the Preparation (John 19:31) and Sabbath drew near (Luke 23:54).

The fact that Nicodemus could buy spices speaks to the issue of the day on which Jesus was crucified, i.e., was it on Thursday, Nisan 14, Passover day, or on Friday, Nisan 15, the first day of the feast of Unleavened Bread?

In Jerusalem, according to m. *Pesahim*, 4.1, 4.6, work stopped at noon on Passover day. Nicodemus, however, bought burial spices the day Jesus died. He could have bought them before Jesus was crucified. More likely he bought the spices after Jesus' death at the ninth hour, and John's account naturally reads that way. Until he and Joseph together arranged to declare themselves disciples of Jesus by giving the body a respectful burial, Nicodemus was still a secret disciple. Buying the spices, embalming the body, and entombing Jesus outed both him and Joseph as disciples of Jesus.

Therefore, it is reasonable to suppose Nicodemus bought the spices while Joseph of Arimathea secured the body from Pilate, i.e., after the ninth hour/3:00 p.m. If Nicodemus did buy the spices after Jesus died, then the day of the crucifixion was not Passover day, for on Nisan 14 the shops in Jerusalem closed at noon. Jesus was not crucified on Passover day.

Embalming also speaks to the issue of Jesus' death, i.e., he did not faint on the cross and revive in the tomb. Jesus' dead body was

---

[1] Holman Quick Source Bible Atlas, 336–337.

wrapped in strips of linen cloth (*othónion*[1]) coated with myrrh, aloes, spices, and aromatic gums, Matthew 27:59; Mark 15:46; Luke 23:53; John 19:39–40. He wasn't wrapped in a shroud. Jesus was wrapped in strips of linen cloth "as is customary among the Jews, to prepare for burial." (The separate cloth on his head, 20:7, also indicates he was not wrapped in a shroud.) Matthew 27:59; Mark 15:46, and Luke 23:53 use the word *sindṓn*,[2] a sheet or wrapping of linen, to describe the burial cloth. Is there a contradiction between John and the Synoptics? No. Mark's source was Peter, who saw the finished product in the tomb, John 20:5, which, stuck together by the dried myrrh, would have the appearance of a linen sheet. Matthew's source could have been Mark's Gospel, or he may have paid a visit to the tomb at a later time. Luke's source depends on which eyewitness—Mary Magdalene, John, Peter, or someone else who had looked into the tomb—he had interviewed for his gospel.

The Holy Spirit guided each Gospel writer to write accurately what he had observed, or what he had discovered through those who had observed the empty tomb. That perspective supports the assumption that John helped Nicodemus and Joseph embalm Jesus, see John 20:5–7 where John again uses *othónion*. John knew from first-hand, eyewitness, on-the-scene experience how Jesus' body had been prepared for burial; he had been there when the body was wrapped in strips of linen cloth.

Myrrh was an exuded gum from a tree which could be dried to a solid resin and, among other uses, was used for embalming. The body was wrapped in multiple layers of linen strips of cloth. Each layer was coated with the myrrh, aloes, and spices. As these dried the cloth was hardened by the dried resin of the myrrh. No one so embalmed could have wriggled out of the hardened cloths, compare John 11:44. Washing the body and then embalming the body with layer upon layer of linen strips and myrrh and aloes and spices, would have taken an hour or more.

The seventy-five pounds of myrrh and aloes was according to custom (John 19:39). "Nicodemus's vast provision of spices is not in the least 'ludicrous.' It is the culturally recognized way of

---

[1] Zodhiates, *WSDNT*, s. v. "3608."
[2] Ibid., s. v. "4616."

appropriately honoring a very imminent person."[1] Josephus said the funeral procession of Herod the Great included "five hundred of his domestics [i.e., household servants] carrying spices."[2]

Rolling a large rock over the opening of the tomb was a normal procedure to keep out animals and robbers. At least two of the women saw the entire process, Mary Magdalene and the other Mary. The other Mary was probably the wife of Clopas, mother of James the Younger and Joses.

Translation Matthew 27:62–66

62 Now the next day, which is after the preparation, the chief priests and the Pharisees were gathered together before Pilate, 63 saying, "Sir, we have remembered how that deceiver said while living, 'After three days I arise.' 64 Command therefore the tomb to be secured until the third day, lest having come his disciples steal him away, and say to the people, 'He is risen from the dead'; and the last deception will be worse than the first." 65 Pilate said to them, "You have a guard; go make it as secure as you know how." 66 Now having gone they made the tomb secure, having sealed the stone, with the guard.

EXPOSITION

The Day of Preparation was the day before the Sabbath. Since the Sabbath was always a Saturday, the Day of Preparation was Friday. Jesus was buried before sundown Friday. This was also a holy day because it was a Sabbath occurring during the Feast of Unleavened Bread. All this means that the priests went to see Pilate on the Sabbath day. Their scruples about the Sabbath and about gentiles were easily set aside.

Jesus' enemies seemed to have remembered more of his words than his disciples. They asked Pilate to help them make the tomb secure. Pilate gave them a small band of soldiers. To seal the tomb means a blob of wax was put between the covering stone and the rock face and a seal impressed into the hot wax. The soldiers remained to make sure the disciples did not fake a resurrection.

---

[1] Bauckham, *Testimony*, 165–166.

[2] Josephus, *Antiquities*, 17.8.3.

Matthew Twenty-Eight

Translation Matthew 28:1

1 Now after Sabbath, it being dawn toward the first day of the week, came Mary Magdalene and the other Mary to see the tomb.

EXPOSITION

There appear to be two pre-resurrection visits and one post-resurrection visit to the tomb by Mary Magdalene and the Other Mary.

Visit number 1, on Friday evening, Matthew 27:61, before sunset Mary Magdalene and the Other Mary see where Jesus was entombed.

Visit number 2, Matthew 28:1, the Greek text uses a word meaning as the day after the Sabbath began to draw near. This would be our Saturday after sunset, but for the Jews this sunset was the beginning of the first day of the week, our Sunday. Mary Magdalene and the Other Mary apparently came to the tomb after sunset Saturday and left.

Visit number 3, Mary Magdalene and the Other Mary returned Sunday morning.

The problem with understanding Matthew is that his account is extremely compressed. B. F. Westcott provides a chronology that reconciles all the resurrection day visits reported by the Four Gospels.[1]

Just before sunset Friday evening

Mary Magdalene and the Other Mary see where Jesus is entombed (Matthew 27:61).

Just Before 6 p.m. Saturday

Mary Magdalene & Mary the mother of James go to view the sepulcher (Matt 28:1).

After 6 p.m. Saturday

The purchase of spices by Mary Magdalene, Mary the mother of James, and Salome, (Mark 16:1)

Very Early on Sunday

---

[1] Westcott, *John*, 288.

The resurrection, followed by the earthquake, the descent of the angel, the opening of the tomb (Matthew 28:2–4).

5 a.m.

Mary Magdalene, Salome, and Mary mother of James and Joses, probably with others, start for the sepulcher in the twilight of early dawn. Mary Magdalene goes before the others, and returns at once to Peter and John (John 20:1ff)

5:30 a.m.

Mary Magdalene's companions reach the sepulcher when the sun had risen (Mark 16:2). A vision of an angel. Message to the disciples (Matt 28:5ff; Mark 16:5ff)

6 a.m.

Another party, among whom is Joanna, come a little later, but still in the early morning (Luke 24:1ff) A vision of "two young men." Words of comfort and instruction (Luke 24:4ff)

6:30 a.m.

The visit of Peter & John (John 20:3–10). A vision of two angels to Mary Magdalene (John 20:11–13). About the same time the company of women carry their tidings to the apostles (Luke 24:10ff)

7 a.m.

The Lord reveals himself to Mary Magdalene (John 20:14–18; Mark 16:9). Not long after he reveals himself, as it appears, to the company of women who are returning to the sepulcher. Charge to the brethren to go to Galilee (Matt 28:9ff).

4–6 p.m. (approximate)

The appearance to the two disciples on the way to Emmaus (Luke 24:13ff; Mark 16:12).

After 4 p.m.

An appearance to Peter (Luke 24:34; 1 Corinthians 15:5).

8 p.m.

An appearance to the eleven and others (Luke 24:36ff; Mark 16:14; John 20:19ff).

This chronology seems to satisfy all objections made to the various post-resurrection visits to the tomb. The visit Matthew reports in v. 1 is on Sunday morning, the first day of the week.

Translation Matthew 28:2–4

2 And look, there was a great earthquake; for an angel of the Lord having descended out of heaven, and having come, rolled back the stone, and was sitting upon it. 3 Now his appearance was as lightning, and his clothing white as snow. 4 Now from the fear of him, those keeping guard trembled with fear, and became as dead.

EXPOSITION

The earthquake was apparently the result of the angel coming to the tomb and rolling away the stone. The angel allowed some of his glory as an unfallen spirit being to shine out into our material world. The soldiers have a typical reaction when faced with heavenly glory. The stone is rolled away so believers can see in; Jesus has already resurrected and is not within the tomb.

Falling down in worship or fear was often a reaction to the presence of a heavenly person. However, fainting ("became as dead") was a not a typical reaction, compare Exodus 3:5; Joshua 5:14.

Using Daniel as an example, we find that the human reaction to heaven's glory appears to vary with the heavenly visitor. In one instance Daniel did faint when he saw an angel face to face, 10:9, but another time he did not, 9:21. One thinks of Balaam, a carnal prophet who, in Numbers 22:31, bowed down to the Angel of the Lord in fear, but did not faint. Gideon did not recognize his visitor as divine until after the encounter, and then his reaction was fear. Samson's parents had a similar experience.

The reaction of a human being to an appearance of an angel or of Deity is determined partly by the "amount" of glory (essential glory in Deity, added or reflected glory in angels) that the person experiences, and partly by the person's spiritual nature (saved, unsaved) and spiritual maturity. When Christ appeared in the upper room after his resurrection the disciples were afraid, but no one fainted (Luke 24:37; compare v. 5). Neither did Paul in Acts 9.

Thinking upon the appearances of angels and Deity throughout Scripture, the soldiers' reaction is duplicated only in Revelation 1:10 when John saw the exalted Christ. So, while the reaction of the soldiers is not typical, it does fit into the range of reactions that vary with the "amount" heavenly glory revealed. Their fainting speaks to the intensity of the glory and authority that radiated from the presence of the angel.

Translation Matthew 28:5–10

5 Now answering the angel said to the women, "Fear not; for I know that Jesus, the one having been crucified, you seek. 6 He is not here, for he is risen, as he said. Come, see the place where he was lying. 7 And having gone quickly, say to his disciples, that he is risen from the dead; and look, he goes before you into Galilee; there you will see him. Look, I have told you." 8 And having gone out quickly from the tomb, with fear and great joy, they ran to tell his disciples. 9 Now as they were going to tell his disciples, also look, Jesus met them, saying, "Rejoice!" Now having come to him, they took hold of his feet and worshiped to him. 10 Then Jesus says to them, "Fear not. Go tell my brethren that they go into Galilee, and there they will see me."

EXPOSITION

The women must have experienced a different "amount" of glory radiating from the angel. It seems apparent the soldiers were supposed to be incapacitated by the angel and the women to have a lesser experience that left them capable of hearing the angel's message. That message is the resurrection and to go and tell the disciples that Jesus will meet them in Galilee, (26:32). The women immediately left to tell the disciples.

In Matthew's Gospel Jesus reveals himself to the women, bringing a message of joy and a reminder of their mission to inform the apostles. Now they can say that they have seen the risen Lord. They "took hold of his feet and *proskunéō* (bow, worship) him." This is stated as two separate acts, i.e., since they must bow to the ground in order to touch his feet, it seems *proskunéō* here indicates worship.

Touching his feet reveals that the resurrected Jesus had a genuinely physical body. This is in agreement with all else the Bible says about resurrection. Resurrected believers will have a glorified and transformed physical body. Resurrected unbelievers will have a sin-corrupted physical body.

Jesus repeats the command for his disciples to go to Galilee. Matthew does not include the appearance in the upper room. By not showing Jesus convincing his disciples he has resurrected, Matthew keeps the focus on Jesus. In Galilee, the disciples will receive their commission and authority to continue the message of the Spiritual kingdom until the King returns.

Translation Matthew 28:11–15

11 Now they were going, look, some of the guard having gone into the city reported to the chief priests all things that happened. 12 And having been gathered together with the elders, and having taken counsel, they gave to the soldiers much money, 13 saying, "Say that 'His disciples having come at night stole him, we being asleep.' 14 And if this may be heard by the Procurator, we will persuade him, and keep you out of trouble." 15 Now having taken the money, they did as they were instructed. And this saying is spread abroad among the Jews until this day.

EXPOSITION

"Now they were going" refers to the women Jesus sent with a message to his disciples. The soldiers, however, went to the priests, not to Pilate, because Pilate had placed them under the authority of the priests. The soldiers were also trying to avoid the penalty for failing in their duty. The fact the priests promised to protect the soldiers from punishment indicates some form of military punishment was due for allowing the body to be gone from the tomb. The true explanation would not have been believed by their military superiors.

Matthew states the false report was spread abroad among the Jews until "this day." Matthew means when he wrote his Gospel, so the false report was still the unbeliever's current explanation for the resurrection some thirty-five years afterward.

Translation Matthew 28:16–20

16 Now the eleven disciples went into Galilee, to the mountain where Jesus directed them. 17 And having seen him they worshiped; but some doubted. 18 And having come to them, Jesus spoke to them, saying, "All authority in heaven and on earth has been given to me. 19 Having gone therefore, disciple all the peoples, baptizing them in the name of the Father and of the Son and of the Holy Spirit, 20 teaching them to observe all things whatever I commanded you. And look, I am with you all the days, until the completion of the age."

TRANSLATION NOTE

At v. 20 the Byzantine group of manuscripts ends the verse with *amén*, "amen." The older Western texts do not. If the word was originally present, there is no reason for eliminating it. Its presence in the Byzantine texts reflects liturgical usage of the passage. Jesus often used *amēn* at the beginning of a sentence, in the sense of "truly." But at the end of a sentence *amēn* means "so be it." Jesus never used *amēn* at the end of a sentence (for 6:13 see comments there). Therefore it is unlikely Jesus ended his instructions here with "so be it."

EXPOSITION

Although we have the command from Jesus for the disciples to meet him in Galilee after his resurrection, 26:32, we do not know the location. Matthew ignores the Judean appearances and the Ascension from the Mount of Olives. His concern is with the commission to preach the gospel. When the eleven apostles saw Jesus some worshiped and some doubted. Considering that this meeting is not their first with the resurrected Jesus, doubt seems unwarranted. Some versions translate this word as "hesitated" versus "doubted. The question remains. What was the cause of their hesitation? Unless there were other disciples present besides the apostles, the matter of hesitation or doubt seems unsolvable. Perhaps their hesitation was not about whether or not this was Jesus, but about whether or not they should worship him. Perhaps they had doubts about the next step in their mission. Regardless, Jesus answers by giving them a mission and the authority to carry out that mission.

Jesus begins by announcing that he has full and complete authority over heaven and earth. He then uses that authority to give the disciples their mission, v. 19–20. I want to labor over this mission as there is widespread misunderstanding. The Christian mission is:

Disciple all peoples

Baptize all those discipled

Teach all those discipled to "observe all things whatever I [Jesus] commanded you [the disciples/apostles then present]"

The first thing to notice, in contrast to almost every version, is that the first command is not "make disciples." The Greek text is not *poiēma mathētés*, make disciples, in the sense of producing, as one might make a chair or grow grain. The text is simply *mathētés*, to disciple. The word is in the aorist tense: teach a person to follow.

In this context *mathētés* means, "teach a person to follow Christ's commandments." By implication the commandments incorporate Christ's doctrine.

The reason Christ did not say *poiēma mathētés* is because he knows the human tendency to try and do God's job. He knew his followers would misunderstand *poiēma mathētés* as "go, save people, and make them disciples," which is exactly how the command is misused today. We disguise this tendency to do God's job: go and get people saved; go and be a soul-winner; go and evangelize and people will be saved.

The hard fact is, only Christ saves sinners; his followers do not. A saved person becomes a disciple by being saved, because the Holy Spirit makes sinner's followers of Jesus through salvation and regeneration. The Christian's task is to instruct the newly saved disciple how to be a follower of Jesus, i.e., how to live the Christian life through obedience to Jesus' commandments and doctrine.

The command is not to make disciples, but to disciple every person Christ saves. Those who are already discipled are in turn to disciple those whom Christ has saved. When this is understood—when we truly believe only Christ saves, when we truly believe Christ sends us the ones he has saved in order to be discipled by us—then we will properly understand the command "*mathētés* all the peoples" as "teach all those whom Christ has saved to be disciples." Viewed as a command to individual believers, the command means "disciple those saved persons Christ sends to you to be discipled by you."

Understanding that Christ alone saves, and Christ commands his people to disciple those he has saved, we may now add in other scriptures that are implicit in the command "disciple all the peoples." Part of the discipling process is evangelization, for through salvation a person begins his/her life-journey as a follower of Christ. The apostles "did not stop preaching and teaching Jesus is the Christ"; the Christians (scattered by the persecution launched by Saul) "went everywhere preaching the word [that Jesus is the Christ]"; God was "pleased through the foolishness of the message preached to save those who believed"; Christ "added to the church daily those who were being saved." The command to disciple all peoples is a command to initiate the discipleship process through evangelization, a process continued when Christ is pleased to save a sinner.

Matthew Twenty-eight

The word I have translated "peoples" is *éthnos*, "a multitude, people, race, belonging and living together." To the Jews—all those hearing Matthew 28:19-20 were Jews—the word meant all the non-Jews, called by them "gentiles." Yet, the disciples did not at first preach to the *éthnos*. Guided by Acts 1:8, they began evangelizing and discipling Jews, not gentiles.

Limiting the Gospel of Salvation to Hebrews became a mindset, which was not broken when God scattered them through persecution (Acts 8:1). About three years after the ascension, the disciples brought the Gospel of Salvation to the Samaritans (Acts 8:5). A little later God brought the Gospel of Salvation to a proselyte, Acts 8:26ff.

Seven to ten years after the ascension, Christ used Peter to bring the Gospel of Salvation to gentiles who were God-fearers, acceptable to those Jews still wanting to limit the message to Hebrews. Not until Paul, thirteen to fifteen years after the ascension, Acts 13, did the Gospel begin to go to "all the peoples." Undoubtedly God had his reasons for the slow progression of the Gospel to all the peoples. Today the Gospel continues to go to all the peoples.

What does the command "disciple all the peoples" mean to the individual Christian. I think we err today when the command is broadly applied to the individual Christian as though he/she is to go into all the world. Such foolishness lays a grievous burden on the individual. Certainly the apostles did not interpret the command in that way. Most of them remained in Jerusalem for many years. None of them individually went to "all the peoples," less to "all the world." Even if we limit "all the peoples" to its historical context, the Greco-Roman Empire, all the apostles failed this commandment, including Paul, if the command is to go to "all the world."

Let us forever eliminate the word "world" from the command, because it is not in the text. Christ never says to his saved people, "Evangelize the world." (Matthew 24:14 is eschatological, and the word translated "world," is *oikouménē*, the inhabited earth, corresponding to the *éthnos* of 28:19, and is accomplished at Revelation 14:6-7.) No one person can evangelize all peoples, even by proxy through supporting others (e.g., missionaries). A little common sense tells us the "peoples" whom a disciple is to disciple must be this or that person to whom Christ—the one who does the saving—sends to evangelize and disciple. The global term "all the

Matthew Twenty-eight

peoples" is limited by what the individual can do personally, under the guidance and with the empowerment of the Holy Spirit.

The intent of the command is "evangelize and disciple those people within the sphere of your influence." To this, considering the whole testimony of Scripture, we can surely add, "as the Holy Spirit gives you opportunity." Not every person the Christian passes on the street, meets in the marketplace, works or plays alongside, can be evangelized by him/her. Neither Jesus, nor his apostles, made an effort to give the Gospel of Salvation to "all the peoples."

Acts 3 is an example. As Peter and John were going to the temple at the hour of prayer, they passed by scores of people. They deliberately passed by the others and gave the Gospel message to one. Why? Because that was the way the Holy Spirit guided them. Then, through the testimony of that one, the Spirit gave them opportunity to give the Gospel to many. But every day the twelve passed by many peoples without giving the Gospel message. If I am to save people through evangelism, then I am guilty of letting many thousands continue to a Christ-less eternity through both inaction and inability. But I am not the Savior; I am not the Holy Spirit. Christ saves; the Holy Spirit guides Christ's saved people into evangelism.

There are petitions to make and questions to ask, daily, before going out into the world, which only the Holy Spirit can answer. "Please give me today opportunities to evangelize, and reveal those opportunities to me"; "Please give me the grace and power and words necessary to evangelize"; "Tell me who You want to give the Gospel of Salvation message today, through me." And, if you have some particular person in mind, ask, "Do I have your permission to evangelize this person?"

If, as is the case, Christ is the Savior, and the Holy Spirit is the Person who reveals the truth and convicts the soul and gives God's gift of grace-faith-salvation (Ephesians 2:8–9), then what presumption to assume everyone or some one must be evangelized by *you*. The command to disciple all the peoples is general, the application is specific. Paul wanted to bring the Gospel of Salvation into Asia (Minor), Acts 16. The Holy Spirit said "No, go to Macedonia." The Spirit had other plans for Asia (see 1 Peter 1:1). Paul wisely obeyed the Spirit. So should each Christian obey the Holy Spirit in fulfilling the command to "disciple all the peoples."

The second part of Christ's commandment is "Baptize all those discipled." Baptism is an essential step in discipleship, because it is a step of obedience. Setting aside other arguments about baptism (how it is to be performed and what it means), Christ states clearly that every believer is to be baptized. If, as is the case, every believer is to obey Christ, then baptism is not optional. As is the case with every commandment, obedience brings blessing and assurance. A person cannot be a follower of Jesus Christ—a disciple—without being obedient to him.

Jesus says believers are to be baptized "in the name of." That is to say, not in the names, plural, of the Father, Son, and Spirit, but in the name of the Father and the Son and the Spirit. God is one God, not three gods. Christ's choice of the singular is deliberate: there is one God who is three personal subsistences in the one substance/essence deity. This fact at once eliminates the practice (by some) of baptizing a person three times: once for the Father, once for the Son, once for the Spirit. There is one name and therefore one baptism. The word *baptízō* means to immerse.[1] There is to be one immersion in the Name of the Father and the Son and the Holy Spirit. Baptism is not to be repeated.

Baptism is not the condition for entry into the church. The New Testament church is not a building. The New Testament church is the body of Christ: one living organism composed of individual members vitally united with Christ through salvation and the indwelling Holy Spirit. One enters the church through salvation, not baptism.

Baptism is not an act of salvation, but an act of obedience to the command of Christ. In the order of Christ's commands, "disciple" comes before "baptize." The meaning is that those persons to be baptized are already disciples. One becomes a disciple through salvation. Discipleship is improved through teaching—the third command. Baptism is an act of obedience by a disciple, not a sinner seeking salvation.

Baptism is also not the means for entry into a local church. Some churches require a previously baptized believer to be baptized again in order to become a member of their particular local church. Baptism is one-time act of obedience, No person in the New Testament was baptized more than once. The baptism Christ commands symbolizes spiritual death and spiritual resurrection. The

---

[1] Zodhiates, *WSDNT*, s. v. "907."

believer is dead to sin through faith in Christ, thus buried with him in that spiritual death—immersed in the water—and raised with Christ to new spiritual life—he/she is raised out of the water. Romans 6:4–5, describe the symbolic meaning of water baptism by describing the spiritual realities of saving faith in Christ: dead to sin and alive to God, v. 10.

Although baptism is not a scriptural requirement for membership in a local church, many churches define their membership as composed of baptized believers. That is because the members of a local church should be in fellowship with Christ. Fellowship requires obedience; baptism is a step of obedience. I offer three working definitions of a local church, one of which incorporates prior baptism as a requirement.

> A local church is an organism composed of individuals joined together so that each can make vital contributions to the work and welfare of the whole body.

> A local church is a company or community of persons who strive to please God in celebrating his worship

> A local church is a body of baptized believers, joined together upon a credible profession of saved by grace through faith in Christ the only Savior, regularly meeting together under the leadership of elders and deacons, participating together in a common purpose to worship God, to propagate the Gospel locally and worldwide, to make disciples, to observe the ordinances of baptism and the Lord's supper, to present a common witness of faith and doctrine centered on the word of God, and to encourage one another in the daily practice of the principles, precepts, and values of God as expressed in his Word.

The first is by me. The second is by John Owen, in his work, *Biblical Theology*, page 144. The third is by me, with some parts taken from a number of sources.

Christ final command was to teach disciples. "Teaching them to observe all things whatever I commanded you." The word "commanded" is in the aorist tense. The aorist is, in a sense, the tense of something that has already happened. The action, in this case the action is "whatever I commanded," is viewed as complete. Christ's commandments to his church are complete. Nothing more need be added. Let us be cautious here, because one of Christ's commandments was John 16:12–15.

> "Many things I still have to say to you; but you are not able to bear them now. But when he, the Spirit of Truth, comes, he will teach you in all the truth; for he will not speak from himself, but whatever he will hear he will speak; and he will speak to you coming things. He will glorify me, because he will take and declare to you out of that which is mine. All things, whatever the Father has, are mine; on account of this I said that out of that which is mine he will take and declare to you."

So in John 16:12–15 Christ told his saved people to listen to his apostles, because he would communicate more information and more commands through them after his resurrection. But this command does not extend beyond what was written in the New Testament. Christ does not continue to give commandments. Some denominations teach Christ continues to issue new commands through the church, or church councils. Jude sums up the biblical view: the faith which was delivered once for all to the saints (Jude 3).

Those who are saved—whether newly saved or saved a long time—need to be taught how to follow Christ. A disciple is by definition a follower: following Christ's commands, living by God's values, principles, and applicable precepts (rules, commands).

When a person is saved, they have experience living according to the world's values. The Holy Spirit does not wash away that knowledge, because the Christians must continue to live in the world. But he/she is to live in the world according to God's values, principles, and rules, so as to glorify God and evangelize sinners. The Spirit does not overwhelm the newly saved with all-at-once understanding of God's ways. He teaches a little here and a little there, allowing time to practice and master one thing before adding another. How does the Spirit teach? Through his Word; through those whom he has previously taught. Let us not misunderstand. No believer is perfect; all are learning to live to God. But those longer in the faith have more practice and understanding of how Christ wants his people to live in the world. Hence the command to teach.

In the final promise, v. 20, Jesus tells the apostles, disciples, and every other believer, that he is always with each and every believer, all the way to the end. The gospels do not look beyond the second advent, so the "completion of the age," means Jesus is always with each and every believer from the time he made this statement until his return at the end of this present New Testament church age. This does not mean Jesus is not with his people when this age ends, just that the gospel accounts do not look beyond the second advent to the next stage of the kingdom, messiah reigning on earth. Matthew does not speak of the ascension, just as John does not, so he can emphasize the continuing presence of Jesus with his people. Other scriptures tell us (just as John 17:24 tells us) that the New Testament believer will always be wherever Christ is, which means Christ will be with us always.

Appendix: Who Knew Jesus Was Deity?

This essay was first published in James D. Quiggle, *Biblical Essays IV* (Amazon/KDP, 2020, 269–290), lightly edited to the present purpose.

Introduction

One of the issues in biblical interpretation is the relationship of the Old Testament revelation to the New Testament revelation. This article examines one aspect of that issue. Specifically, the tendency to interpret the Old Testament revelation with information available only in the New Testament revelation.

The question this article asks and will answer is this. Did the apostles, and others, know, from the day they met Jesus, up to the day they met with Jesus after his resurrection, did they know Jesus was God incarnate? The purpose of this article is to show from Scripture they did not know—that no one—the apostles, his disciples, those Jesus healed, those opposing Jesus, and the fallen angels—no one believed Jesus of Nazareth was God incarnate during the time of his earthly ministry, whether or not they believed him to be the Messiah.

The reason most believers today do believe the apostles believed Jesus the Christ was God the Son incarnate, is due to the traditions of Reformed theology, particularly preaching traditions based on English translations. Traditions are wonderful servants but terrible masters. They become terrible masters when "God's word is made of no effect on account of your tradition," Matthew 15:6.

Let me pause for a moment and assure the reader I believe Jesus the Christ was and is God the Son incarnate in Jesus of Nazareth. At the moment the human being Jesus was conceived in Mariam's womb, God the Son joined himself to that newly conceived and still rudimentary human body and human soul. From that moment both the human being and the deity were inseparably the God-man.

The Christocentric hermeneutic used by Reformed theology is to blame for the belief the apostles and other disciples supposedly knew (during the time of his earthly ministry) Jesus was God incarnate. The Christocentric hermeneutic is used to interpret the Old Testament revelation by the New Testament revelation. In the Christocentric hermeneutic the Old Testament revelation is not

Appendix: Who Knew Jesus Was Deity

allowed to speak for itself; original authorial intent is made subordinate to New Testament revelation. But as Vlach has said,

> The primary meaning of any Bible passage is found in that passage. The New Testament does not reinterpret or transcend Old Testament passages in a way that overrides or cancels the original authorial intent of the Old Testament writers. [Vlach, 31].

The issue, then, is the proper use and application of the grammatical-historic (literal) hermeneutic Literal hermeneutic.

Old Testament Revelation

Let us, then, begin with what the Hebrews of Jesus' time knew about the Messiah. The first necessary action is to set aside all we know about the deity of Jesus Christ from the New Testament revelation. That revelation was not available when Jesus walked the earth. The New Testament revelation can play only a limited part in answering the question, "Did the apostles know Jesus was God incarnate?" Our only sources of information are the Old Testament revelation, and what is recorded in the four gospels as spoken by angels, Jesus, the apostles, other disciples, those healed, and the enemies of Jesus. We may not use any explanatory comments the gospel writers may have made, only what was spoken, because that alone reveals what everyone thought and knew.

The Hebrew word *māshîah*, transliterated in the English "messiah," means "anointed" to an office or function. (The equivalent Greek word is *christós*.) The word *māshîah* occurs thirty-nine times in the Old Testament. However, only three times in those thirty-nine occurrences does *māshîah* refer to the person who would be Jesus the Messiah. Those three times are Psalm 2:2, Daniel 9:25, 26.

We may immediately dismiss Daniel 9:25, 26 from this discussion. The words "messiah the prince" in 9:25 do not communicate any revelation the messiah will be God incarnate. Daniel 9:26, messiah cut off" is understandable only through the New Testament revelation, and also does not communicate any revelation the messiah will be God incarnate. Those scriptures are never directly referenced in the gospels. The Jews did not connect Daniel 9:25 to the Triumphal Entry (to which it almost certainly refers, Luke 19:42), and the apostles did not connect 9:26, "Messiah cut off," to Jesus' several declarations of his impending

Appendix: Who Knew Jesus Was Deity

crucifixion (cf. Matthew 16:21–23). No one in gospel times connected Jesus with Daniel 9:25–26.

Psalm 2

The key Old Testament scripture for understanding how the Hebrews understood the person and office of Messiah is Psalm 2 (LXX). I have highlighted the key words.

> 1 Wherefore did the heathen rage, and the nations imagine vain things? 2 The kings of the earth stood up, and the rulers gathered themselves together, against the Lord, and against his *Christ*, saying,
>
> 3 Let us break through their bonds, and cast away their yoke from us. 4 He that dwells in the heavens shall laugh them to scorn, and the Lord shall mock them. 5 Then shall he speak to them in his anger, and trouble them in his fury. 6 But I have been made king by him on Sion his holy mountain,
>
> 7 declaring the ordinance of the Lord: the Lord said to me, *Thou art my Son, to-day have I begotten thee.*
>
> 8 Ask of me, and I will give thee the heathen *for* thine inheritance, and the ends of the earth *for* thy possession. 9 Thou shalt rule them with a rod of iron; thou shalt dash them in pieces as a potter's vessel. 10 Now therefore understand, ye kings: be instructed, all ye that judge the earth. 11 Serve the Lord with fear, and rejoice in him with trembling. 12 Accept correction, lest at any time the Lord be angry, and ye should perish from the righteous way: whensoever his wrath shall be suddenly kindled, blessed are all they that trust in him.

In 2:2, Brenton has translated the Hebrew word *māshîah* as "Christ," a transliteration of the corresponding Greek word *christós*, versus the genuine translation of *māshîah* which is "anointed."

This is the psalm of Messiah the King, not Messiah the Redeemer of souls from sin. YHWH would anoint a man to conquer and rule the gentiles. Without the New Testament revelation, that is what the Psalm says. A man would be anointed, 2:2, by YHWH to hold the offices or functions of king, 2:6, be YHWH's son, 2:7, conquer the rulers of the earth, 2:9, and rule as YHWH"s representative, 2:10–12.

What the Hebrews of Jesus' life and times expecting? The

Messiah-King of Psalm 2.

> The older Messianic hope virtually moves within the boundary of the then present circumstances of the world, and is nothing else than the hope of a better future for the *nation*. That the nation should be morally purified from all bad elements, that it should exist unmolested and respected in the midst of the Gentile world, whilst its enemies were either destroyed or forced to acknowledge the nation and its God, that it should be governed by a just, wise, and powerful king of the house of David, and that therefore internal justice, peace and happiness would prevail, nay that all natural evils would be abolished and a state of unclouded prosperity would appear—this may be said to have formed the foundation of the future hope among the older prophets. [Schurer, *A History*, Division 2, 2:129–130. Emphasis Schurer.]

A Messiah-Redeemer was not expected.

Jesus called himself "son of God," Matthew 26:63–64. The fallen angels called Jesus "son of God," Matthew 8:29. The angel Gabriel named him "son of God," Luke 1:35. Satan challenged him to prove he was "son of God," Luke 4:2, 9. Nathaniel said Jesus was the "son of God," John 1:29. What did that title mean to those persons?

When Jesus and the angel Gabriel used the term it referred to the incarnate person Jesus the Christ. When Nathaniel used the term he meant Jesus of Nazareth was the promised Messiah of 2 Samuel 7:13, 16; Psalm 2. At John 19:7 The priests who had brought Jesus to Pilate for crucifixion said, "We have a Law, and according to the Law he ought to die, because he made himself Son of God." Pilate would have thought the Jews meant a demigod. That is why he was troubled. The Jews had allowed Jesus to claim he was "the Christ, the son of God, Matthew 26:63, that did not bother them. But they specifically denied Jesus of Nazareth was God, Matthew 26:64–65, and for that claim by Jesus he needed to die.

What about when others used the term?

Every Bible-believing Hebrew believed he or she was a son of YHWH, Hosea 11:1. Every believer is a "son of God," Genesis 6:2, Job 1:6; 38:7; Romans 8:14; Gal 3:26.

Appendix: Who Knew Jesus Was Deity

The biblical "sons of" is a description of character. The biblical terms "offspring of" "sons of," or "daughters of," are, when speaking metaphorically, those persons whose characteristics are like the person of whom they are a "offspring of," "son of," or "daughter of."

When used symbolically neither "sons of" nor "daughters of" is a gender specific term. The term "sons of" means a person possesses the characteristics of the person or thing he or she is a "son of." The "sons of rebellion," at 2 Samuel 23:6 were the rebellious. The "sons of the prophets," 2 Kings 2:3, were those men who were faithful to God and preached his Word. The sons of fools, and the sons of vile men, Job 30:8, were fools and vile.

The term "sons of God" (Hebrew: *benê 'ĕlōhîm;* Greek: *huiós theós*) is used in Genesis 6:2, 4; Job 1:6; 2:1; 38:7; Matthew 5:9; Luke 20:36; Romans 8:14, 19; Galatians 3:26. In every use it refers to persons who are like God because they are in a faith-based relationship with God. No fallen angel and no unsaved human being are ever characterized as a son of God. [Quiggle, *Dictionary.*]

The Hebrews hearing Jesus in general had no issue with being identified as "sons of God." For example, no Hebrew objected to this saying by Jesus, "Blessed the peacemakers, because they will be called sons of God," Matthew 5:9. Compare Matthew 5:45, "So that you may be sons of your father in the heavens." Those in the resurrection—which every devout Hebrew expected to achieve—were "sons of God," Luke 20:36. So also Jesus was accepted when he said he was the son of God. Today, through the New Testament revelation, we know "son of God" means "God the Son incarnate in Jesus of Nazareth. The phrase in the New Testament revelation always refers to the incarnate person. But those in gospel times *did not* have the New Testament revelation.

Do not be misled by translations. Every Bible version capitalizes "son" when referring to Jesus the Christ. In the mouth of Jesus such capitalization may be appropriate because he knew who he was (but did Jesus speak of himself in terms of English grammar; did he speak of himself in capital words?). In the mouth of his enemies it is highly inappropriate. In the mouth of disciples and apostles and others following him it is an assumption not born of Scripture.

In the absence of New Testament revelation, Psalm 2 meant

to its Hebrew readers that the Messiah would be a devout Hebrew (devout because he would be a son of God), anointed by YHWH to conquer the gentiles and rule over them. In the absence of New Testament revelation, Psalm 2:7 does not teach an incarnation of God in human flesh, but a consequence of God anointing a human being to be messiah-king and God's son.

Nor could the Hebrews imagine or accept God becoming incarnate. The idea was repulsive, being too similar to the pagan concept of demigod: a human being as the offspring of one of the male gods and a human female, such as Hercules (1264 BC) or Perseus (700 BC). (Psalm 2 was written ca. 1000 BC.) No right thinking Hebrew would commit such blasphemy. Every time Jesus declared himself to be God he was accused of blasphemy.

Isaiah 9:6

Someone will say, "Surely Isaiah 9:6 taught the Hebrews the Messiah was God incarnate?" And so it would seem, "his name will be ... mighty God ... everlasting father." The first thing to note is the word *māshîah* occurs only once in Isaiah, at 45:1, where it refers to the Persian king Cyrus. There is a reference made to King David at 9:7. The child to be born will sit on David's throne, "even forever." What did this mean to Isaiah and subsequent Hebrew readers? One thing it mean is a child to be born would be the messianic-king (as the *Targum Isaiah* states [Beale, *Commentary*]), thereby confirming 2 Samuel 7:13, 16 and Psalm 2. Second, this would be a human child, again confirming both 2 Samuel and Psalm 2. At this point it is difficult to see how any Hebrew would believe this child would be God-in-the-flesh, God incarnate. That was a pagan belief.

Again, we cannot allow ourselves to be misled by a translation. The only word in 9:6 that needs to be capitalized is *'êl*, the most basic Hebrew word for God or god. For certain, this verse, seen apart from the New Testament revelation, does not teach the Messiah will be YHWH incarnate. However, in a later chapter, Isaiah uses the same words, mighty God (*'êl*) to refer to YHWH. So Isaiah 9:6, in conjunction with other scriptures, does teach the messiah-king is God; the child to be born must in some way be God—a way not yet disclosed; Isaiah 7:14 had no obvious connection with Psalm 2:2, 7. (See Matthew 1:23–23; Luke 1:31–33, the angel Gabriel did not make that connection of Isaiah 7:14 with 9:6 or Psalm 2.)

Appendix: Who Knew Jesus Was Deity

What use did the people in gospel times make of Isaiah 9:6? Nothing. Not an angel, not Jesus, not his mother or Joseph, not his disciples or apostles, not his enemies. Nothing. Isaiah 9:6 is not quoted, not referred to, not alluded to in the four gospels [Beale, *Commentary*, index]. Let us remember Isaiah has said he is quoting God, 8:11, writing direct revelation word for word, "YHWH spoke thus to me." So even Isaiah might not have understood; there is no indication one way or the other. What is certain is no one during Jesus' time on earth applied Isaiah 9:6 to messianic prophecy or to Jesus. With the application of New Testament revelation we can see it; but without that New Testament revelation no Hebrew understood Isaiah 9:6 to mean Jesus of Nazareth was deity incarnate.

New Testament Revelation in the Four Gospels

What do the four gospels say about the beliefs of the Hebrew people concerning Jesus? What were they told, what did they understand, what did they believe? Space limitations permit examination of only a few scriptures, but the principle remains the same in every relevant Scripture.

Matthew's Gospel

Let us begin at Matthew 1:23

> Matthew 1:23, Behold, the virgin shall be with child, and bear a son, and they shall call his name Immanuel, which is translated, "God with us."

The Hebrew words *immānū 'ēl* occur at Isaiah 7:14; 8:8, 10. The Greek equivalent, *emmanouēl*, occurs at Matthew 1:23.

The angel makes sure Joseph knew what the Greek word *emmanouēl* meant: God with us. The angel quotes from Isaiah 7:14 (ESV), "Therefore the Lord himself will give you a sign. Behold, the virgin shall conceive and bear a son, and shall call his name Immanuel [*immānū 'ēl*]."

Again, subtracting all subsequent New Testament revelation from our interpretation—because not yet written—we must look only at the uses Joseph knew. Did *emmanouēl* indicate to Joseph that this child born of a (the Hebrew word) '*almâ* (a young unmarried girl—thus, a virgin) would be God-in-the-flesh? No. As New Testament believers, having the benefit of all the New Testament revelation, we interpret "God with us" as "God

Appendix: Who Knew Jesus Was Deity

incarnate." But *emmanouḗl* means "God with us," not God incarnate. What *immānū 'ēl* / *emmanouḗl* meant to Joseph and every other Israeli is God would be with Israel, without specifying how God would be with Israel.

A plain example is Isaiah 8:10 (LXX), "And whatsoever counsel ye shall take, the Lord shall bring it to nought; and whatsoever word ye shall speak, it shall not stand among you: for God [*'ēl*] is with us [*immānū*]." In Isaiah 8:10 YHWH is Immanuel, "with us" to help us. No more than that can be known from the name, *emmanouḗl*, in Matthew 1:23, within the historical context and the scriptures given up to that time, the Old Testament revelation. Jesus born of Mariam would be God with us as the Messiah of God, Psalm 2:2, not as YHWH incarnate.

Earlier prophecies might have shown Isaiah this "Immanuel" will be of the Davidic line, thus heir to the Davidic-Messianic throne (2 Samuel 7:13, 16; Psalm 2). Isaiah 8:8 refers to "your land, Immanuel." Isaiah and others probably made the connection between Immanuel and the coming messiah who was to be the heir of David. But, again, this is not the understanding of an incarnation. Nothing in the promise of an heir to David, as interpreted without adding in the New Testament revelation, indicates any one of those many heirs of David will be God incarnate.

For example, how could David's house and throne and kingdom be "established forever?" Answer: through the natural generation of offspring continuing the Davidic line and inheriting the kingdom and throne. When we subtract the New Testament revelation from the interpretation of Nathan's prophecy, as we must, then another reasonable interpretation immediately presents itself. I know I am repeating, but the point of view must be remembered: the people in gospel times *did not have* the New Testament revelation by which to interpret or apply the Old Testament revelation.

That last statement unavoidably requires us to take small side path away from the main discussion. At 2 Samuel 7:13, 16, the prophet says David's rule (his "throne) will be established "forever." Within the Old Testament context, without adding in New Testament revelation, what the Davidic covenant meant to David and his fellow Hebrews, was just this: as long as there is a kingdom of Israel, so there will be a descendant of David on the throne.

Luke 1:32, 41; 2:11

Appendix: Who Knew Jesus Was Deity

Although there are more verses to consider in Matthew's Gospel, the angel's conversation with Joseph calls to mind Gabriel's months earlier (about three months, Luke 1:56) conversation with Mariam of Nazareth. The pertinent verse is Luke 1:32, "He will be great and will be called 'son of the Most High.' And the Lord God will give him the throne of David, his father." Neither Mariam then, nor Luke later, could hear a capital letter in the angel's voice, except the reverence given to "Most High" and "Lord God," which were recognized titles of YHWH. Mariam would not have thought of a capital "Son" of the Most High, because a human being as God was blasphemous.

Everything in the angel's announcement conforms to 2 Samuel 7:13, 16; Psalm 2:2, 7. Indeed, it conforms to Isaiah 7:14, although Mariam was not told of that connection, as Joseph was later. Nor in any recorded words of Mariam throughout the four gospels do we see her making a connection with Isaiah 7:14. Nothing Mariam says in the four gospels indicates she thought of her son Jesus as God incarnate. Nothing in Mariam's song to Elizabeth infers or implies or alludes to an incarnation. No recorded word of Mariam in the four gospels infers or implies or alludes to an incarnation.

Nor is an incarnation to be found Elizabeth's comment. Through the Holy Spirit Elizabeth recognized Mariam as the mother of the messiah-king, not of God incarnate. Because that is what Elizabeth knew—that her son would be the Messiah's herald, Luke 1:17. Nor did the shepherds know the Messiah was God incarnate. The angel told them the *māshîah* prophesied in Micah 5:2 had come to Bethlehem just as prophesied (and to their barn, as prophesied, Micah 4:8).

Matthew 4, the Temptation of Jesus

Did the fallen angels know Jesus the Christ was God incarnate? If they did, then those human beings they influenced against Jesus might know the same from them. But the fallen angels did not know.

One proof they did not know is the actions of their leader, Satan. In his third temptation Satan said to Jesus, Matthew 4:9, "These things [the kingdoms of the world and their glory], to you I will give all, if falling down you will worship me." If Satan had understood Jesus Christ was God the Son incarnate, he would not have made the offer. Satan knew God is "Holy, Holy, Holy," Isaiah

Appendix: Who Knew Jesus Was Deity

6:3, or as the later revelation of James 1:13 states, "God cannot be tempted by evil." God who created will never worship one of his creation.

Why, then, did Satan say, Matthew 4:3, "If you are the son of God," as though assuming Jesus' deity? I will show this statement by Satan did not refer to Jesus' deity. Satan was demanding Jesus prove God was right when God had said, "This is my son," at Jesus' baptism. We will see this by examining two issues. First, what does the "if" mean? Then, what does the term "son of God" mean?

The "if" in the phrase, "if you are the son of God," performs a certain grammatical function (in the Koine Greek dialect in which the New Testament was written) known as a condition of the first class. This is a "simple conditional assumption with emphasis on the reality of the assumption (not of what is being assumed); the condition is considered a real case" [Morris, 73, n. 11]. Satan is stating a condition that was presented as reality (God had said, "This is my son"), but Satan is questioning whether the condition is factual by demanding Jesus furnish proof that God was right. Satan could be viewed as saying, "I assume as true that you are the son of God, so prove it by commanding these stones to become bread." Or, he could be viewed as saying, "In view of the fact that you are the son of God, command these stones to become bread." Satan's "if" meant, "Prove what God said about you is true. Prove you are a son of God."

(Side issue: why did Satan ask Jesus to "command" the stones to become bread, if he did not believe Jesus was God? Because Satan doesn't know much more than anyone else. Because Satan also reads commentaries and listens to preachers and Bible teachers. The Rabbis taught that the Messiah, as a prophet like Moses, Deuteronomy 18:15, would give them bread like Moses—their belief, John 6:31.)

Satan said, "if you are the son of God." The term "son of" in Scripture, when not used of literal physical descent, indicates a person has the characteristics of the person or thing of which he (or she) is a "son of." Sons of men are sinners, Psalm 4:2; 58:1–2. Sons of the sorceress are offspring of the adulterer and the harlot, Isaiah 57:3. The sons of the prophets (1 and 2 Kings) were preachers and keepers of God's Word, like the prophets. Adam was a son of God, Luke 3:38, a human being in a faith-based relationship with God. The phrase "sons of God" in the Old

Testament identified human beings (Genesis 6:2, 4; Job 1:6; 2:1) and holy angels (Job 38:7). The completed revelation of scripture (Matthew 5:9; Luke 20:36; Romans 8:14, 19; Galatians 3:26) supports the earlier revelation. The "sons of God" are holy angels and human believers who are in a faith-based relationship with God. No fallen angel and no unsaved human being is ever identified as one of the sons of God. The sons of God possess the moral character of God, obey God's commandments, and glorify God in their words and deeds.

Satan tried to accomplish with Jesus what he did with Eve: he used God's words to suggest rebellion against God. Could this "son of God" prove he was a son of God? Jesus did, but not the way Satan proposed. Satan's temptations provided Jesus son of God the opportunity to act independent of God's will. Adam son of God self-originated sin when tempted to act independent of God's will (Genesis 2:17; 3:6). Will Jesus seek his own way, like Adam, or will he honor God?

Put another way, the claim Jesus was a "son of" God was to be tested. Because Satan did not understand Jesus was God the Son incarnate, he presented temptations that would test the faith of a wholly human son of God. Jesus chose to endure the trial through the natural limitations of his humanity, because as a genuine human being, the baptismal designation "This is my son" defined the character of his humanity, not his deity.

Satan did understand Jesus was the Christ. This was part of his motive for tempting Jesus. He had heard this Jesus would be given "the throne of his father David," Luke 1:32, and had heard this Jesus was "Christ the Lord," Luke 2:11. (The fallen angels are one-third, Revelation 12:4a, of an innumerable host, Revelation 5:11—thus present in sufficient numbers to know what is happening on the earth in both spirit and material domains.) Satan's understanding of the Christ was the same as the religious leaders: the Christ would be a human being, much like themselves, who had been specifically anointed (*māshîah*), Psalm 2:2, to be king, 2:6, be God's son, 2:7, to conquer the rulers of the earth, 2:9, and rule as God's representative, 2:10–12.

We must, therefore, wash away our presuppositions and interpretive traditions to place ourselves within the progressive revelation of biblical knowledge at that time, which was Genesis through Malachi. At this time in history, Satan did not use the term "son of God" to identify Jesus as the God-man (no one did). To Satan, Jesus was a human being in a faith-based relationship with God who had been *māshîah*, anointed, Psalm 2:2, by God, to fulfill the coming king and kingdom prophecy of 2 Samuel 7:13, 16; Psalm 2. To Satan, Jesus of Nazareth was just another human being in a long-line of "sons of God" that he would defile, just as he had defiled the first son of God, Adam.

Like their leader, the fallen angels knew Jesus was the Christ, but did not know Jesus was God the Son incarnate.

> The divinity of Christ, or his identity with a divine person, does not seem to have been known to the spirit [Mark 1:24], but only that the man whom he addressed was one, to use his own expressions, whom the Father had sanctified and sent into the world (John 10:36), i.e., chosen and commissioned for an extraordinary service. [Alexander, 22].

Why then did the fallen angels call Jesus, "the holy one of God"; "son of the Most High God"; "son of God"? These titles came from what they had heard: the angel Gabriel's announcement to Mariam that this Jesus was "son of the Highest," Luke 1:32, the "holy one" and "son of God," Luke 1:35.

Conclusion. The fallen angels believed Jesus of Nazareth was the Christ, but none of them understood Jesus the Christ was God the Son incarnate.

Mark 1:23–25

Jesus' first encounter with an angel inhabiting a human being.

> And shortly [after he had begun teaching] there came into their synagogue a man with an unclean spirit. And he cried out, saying, "What do you have to do with us, Jesus of Nazareth? Are you come to destroy us? I know who you are, the holy one of God."

The confrontation Mark reports here was the first such confrontation in Jesus' ministry, and it was the only time such a confrontation was initiated by a fallen angel. The angel who was cast out was undoubtedly surprised God had delegated this authority to a human being. The others, being warned by their comrade's experience, avoided Jesus as much as possible. In other such confrontations recorded in the New Testament, the fallen angels had not sought out Jesus but met him due to varied circumstances. See Mark 5:2, 8; 7:25, 30; 9:18, 25; Matthew 9:32–

Appendix: Who Knew Jesus Was Deity

33; 12:22. The same is true during Jesus' preaching and healing tours, e.g., Luke 6:18. After this first encounter they knew he would cast them out.

The fallen angel asked, "Are you come to destroy us?" The angel wasn't questioning Jesus' origin, but purpose. If my analysis, above, is correct, then this purpose question must be seen in the light of the prophesied duties or works of the Messiah-Christ. One of those duties is expressed at Isaiah 61:1 (LXX), "the Spirit of the Lord is upon me ... to proclaim liberty to the captives ...." Jesus had quoted this verse at Nazareth a month or two earlier, Luke 4:18, "The Spirit of the Lord is upon me, because of which he has anointed me to ... proclaim deliverance to captives ...." The fallen angel's question was about himself and others like himself who were inhabiting human souls. Did "to destroy us" fit into the mission Isaiah had prophesied, and which Jesus had announced at Nazareth? Yes. Casting out demons wasn't all that prophecy meant, but casting them out was included.

The word translated "destroy" is *apóllumi*, to destroy, perish, deprive. Understanding *apóllumi* depends on how one views the fallen angels' understanding of Jesus.

If one believes the fallen angel in Mark 1:23–25 understood Jesus was God the Son incarnate, then *apóllumi* refers to eternal imprisonment in the lake of fire, Matthew 25:41, which verse was not yet spoken, but the demons knew from the beginning (of their original sin) that the "everlasting fire was prepared for the devil and his angels." The fallen angels are intelligent but have no grace or spiritual perception for understanding scripture. First Corinthians 2:14, the natural person does not understand spiritual matters, applies to them as it does to any unsaved human soul. They did not understand two advents, so they could have wondered—if they understood Jesus was God incarnate—whether the time had come for their eternal imprisonment.

If one believes, as I and others do, that the fallen angels did not understand Jesus was God the Son incarnate—their leader Satan did not—then *apóllumi* refers to some other kind of loss. The most reasonable interpretation is fear of imprisonment in the abyss for the crime of habitation of a human being, Luke 8:31, "And they were begging him, that he would not command them to go away into the abyss."

The fallen angel, Mark 1:23–25, came on behalf of his

comrades (the plural "us" in his questions) to find out who this Jesus was, and what this Jesus, "Christ," would do. He found out. Jesus cast into the abyss all fallen angels with whom he came into contact who were inhabiting a human being, thereby fulfilling (at least toward these particular angels) the messianic prophecy of Isaiah 61:1; Luke 4:18.

Because Jesus did cast out every angel he met inhabiting a human soul, we may assume a law against habitation, and the punishment imprisonment in the abyss, there to join the large number of fallen angels already imprisoned, Jude 6, 2 Peter 2:4; Revelation 9:1–3. I believe every fallen angel Jesus cast out of a human being went into the abyss, per Luke 8:31. They knew the power to cast them into the abyss was from God. They may or may not have known, until that first confrontation, the Old Testament revelation gave the Messiah the authority to cast them out. The fallen angels, like their leader Satan, did not know Jesus of Nazareth was God-in-the-flesh.

Matthew 11:3, The Baptist Doubts

Did John the Baptist know his relative Jesus of Nazareth was God incarnate? Some think so from failure to consider all of John's testimony. When Jesus came to be baptized, on seeing him, the Baptist said, Matthew 3:14, "I have need to be baptized by you, and you come to me?" It would seem he knew. But the Baptist also testified, John 1:31, "I knew him not." He knew his relative Jesus. They had known each other for almost 35 years (their births ca. 5 BC to Jesus baptism late AD 29). They had seen each other every year at the three mandatory feasts, and probably at other times also, as the families visited one another over the years. The Baptist knew Jesus to be a righteous man. The Baptist was preaching the Messiah was coming, but he did not know who the Messiah would be, until he saw "the Spirit descending and abiding on him," John 1:33. No testimony of the Baptist states or implies he knew the Messiah would also be God incarnate.

If John Baptist knew Jesus was God incarnate, then why did he doubt he had baptized the right man? If you know the Messiah is God incarnate, then there is no doubt. John was informed by Old Testament revelation, neither more nor less. He knew the Messiah was coming to be king. He had not seen that expectation fulfilled. He did not understand Messiah as Redeemer of men from their sins.

Jesus, Mathew 11:5, gave him the signs of Messiah the Redeemer, Isaiah 35:5–6; 61:1, which scriptures the Baptist knew. Jesus told him to have faith, 11:6.

Matthew 14:33

At Matthew 14:22–33, we have the incident when Jesus and Peter walk on water. When Peter and Jesus got into the boat, those in the boat, "bowed to him, saying, "Truly you are God's son." The issue here is not the Greek text, but the English translation. The common English translation says, they "worshiped him." Naturally, the reader assumes those in the boat believed Jesus the Christ was God incarnate. But the word English versions translate "worship" is *proskunéō,* to "do obeisance, show respect, fall or prostrate before, literally to throw a kiss in token of respect of homage" [Zodhiates, 4352]. To translate *proskunéō* as worship assumes what is not evident: that the apostles/disciples believed the man who had just walked on water was God-in-the-flesh.

Let us think clearly. If the twelve believed God was literally in their presence in the person of Jesus of Nazareth, then they would not have been able to function as his companions. They would have fallen flat on their faces and remained prostrate before him in reverent awe. They would have feared for their lives, because God had said to Moses, "Thou shalt not be able to see my face; for no man shall see my face, and live," Exodus 33:20 (LXX). They were in awe of him, but not the worshiping, "you are God," kind of awe. No prophet had ever done what Jesus had just done. So they had continued to ask themselves, "Who is this man?" Here they come to a conclusion.

What, then, did they mean when they said, "Truly you are God's son"? Three meanings are available.

> One, they understood he was God incarnate in Jesus of Nazareth. This is unlikely. They were completely discouraged following the crucifixion, e.g., Luke 24:21, "But we were hoping it is he who is about to redeem Israel." Not redemption from sin but national redemption from the oppressive gentiles. They didn't understand he would resurrect, and didn't believe when they were told he had resurrected. The Holy Spirit withheld spiritual perception of Jesus as deity incarnate until after the ascension, compare Matthew 28:17 with Acts 3:33.

Two, they could have been declaring him a true son of God. The Hebrews believed they were sons of God. If this was the disciples' meaning, then they were giving respect to a prophet who had shown that he truly was a son of God, i.e., one to whom God had given great authority and power.

Three, they bowed to him and called him, "God's son" in the sense of Psalm 2:7, "declaring the ordinance of the Lord: the Lord said to me, 'Thou art my Son, to-day have I begotten thee.'" If this was the case, it was a moment when they began to believe Jesus was the Messiah-king—not merely a prophet in the Old Testament mold, but the deliverer and king promised by the prophets.

My view is that they saw him through the lens of options two and three.

Matthew 16:16, Peter Confesses Jesus is the Christ

Peter states Jesus, "is the Christ (of God, Luke 9:20), the son of the living God." Jesus says this understanding, that "Jesus of Nazareth was the Christ of God," was given to Peter by, "my Father who is in heaven." How did Peter know about the Christ of God? From schooling at the village synagogue, which every boy attended in his home village. From a lifetime of hearing about the Messiah when he attended the synagogue on Sabbath, what Peter knew about the Christ of God was what the Scriptures said and what the Rabbis taught. Everything Peter confessed fits into Psalm 2.

Peter: You are the Christ of God. Psalm 2:2, YHWH and his *māshîah*.

Peter: son of the living God. Psalm 2:7, You are my son, today I have begotten you.

Peter did not think of the Messiah as God incarnate. If he had he would have confessed, "You are God the Christ." If we doubt, and some will, let us look to the sequel, 16:22. Peter rebuked the Christ for revealing the Christ must die. If you believe the person in front of you is God incarnate, you do not correct him. You worship. You politely ask for an explanation of the thing you do not understand.

Matthew 26:63–64

The Bible scholars did not believe the Messiah was God incarnate.

Appendix: Who Knew Jesus Was Deity

And the high priest said to him, "I adjure you by the living God, that you tell us if you are the Christ, the son of God." Jesus says to him, "You have said. Moreover, I say to you, from now you will see the son of man sitting at the right hand of the Power, and coming in the clouds of heaven."

Caiaphas needed legal justification in order to sentence Jesus to death and present the case to Pilate for Jesus to be executed. We see in 26:63 that Caiaphas obviously knew Jesus had performed miracles and that many people believed him to be the Christ. The question Caiaphas asks understands the terms "Christ" and "son of God" as indicating a relationship with God. But it is doubtful that Caiaphas used these terms in the same sense that Christians understand them today. Caiaphas was not a believer; he was not seeking faith in Jesus the Messiah.

The question Caiaphas asks, although not in these words, is whether or not Jesus will testify under oath that he himself is the Christ, the son of God. Jesus answers the question because 1) Caiaphas has asked in his official capacity as high priest, 2) the question is about Jesus' messianic claims, and 3) Caiaphas has called on Jesus to tell the truth with God as his witness.

Jesus' reply, "You have said," is an idiom meaning "You have stated the fact." This reply, in itself, was not sufficient to condemn Jesus to death. And Jesus knew this. The Christ was perceived by all as a man anointed by God to be king of Israel. We see this was the way the Sanhedrin understood the Christ by their accusation before Pilate—the accusation that caused Pilate to condemn Jesus.

> John 19:12, but Jews cried out, saying, "If this man you release, you are not a Friend of Caesar. Anyone making himself a king speaks against Caesar."

The accusation that made Pilate condemn Jesus was the claim he was a king. They had previously tried to get Jesus condemned for blasphemy, but that failed,

> John 19:7, The Jews answered Pilate, "We have a law, and according to the law he ought to die, because he made himself Son of God."

Notice here I capitalized the word "son." How had Jesus made himself, "Son of God." Not when Jesus had agreed with the high priest, Matthew 26:63–64a, that he was, as the high priest had stated, "the Christ, the son of God." No one got excited over that claim. Claiming that Psalm 2 applied to you was not blasphemy.

The blasphemy was the next thing Jesus said. "I say to you, from now you will see the son of man sitting at the right hand of the Power, and coming in the clouds of heaven." To sit on the throne of God ("at the right hand of the Power") is to be equal with God. To come on the clouds of heaven is to command the angelic armies of heaven, which is authority possessed only by deity.

> Matthew 26:65–68, Then the high priest tears his clothes, saying, "He has blasphemed! Why have we any more need of witnesses? Look, now you have heard the blasphemy! What do you think?" Now answering they said, "He is deserving of death." Then they spit in his face, and struck him. Others slapped him, saying, "Prophesy to us, Christ, who is he having hit you?"

Obviously, they did not believe his claim to deity. No knowledgeable Hebrew believed a man could also be God. That was paganism, that was blasphemy.

After the Crucifixion and Resurrection

Did the apostles/disciples grasp Jesus was God incarnate after the crucifixion? Not until Jesus appeared to them. In the days between the crucifixion and resurrection the apostles and disciples went into hiding, not expecting Jesus would resurrect, John 20:19. What about when the empty tomb was reported by the women? No, their words seemed like idle tales, Luke 24:11. How about when Peter and John saw the empty tomb. No, Peter was amazed at what happened, Luke 24:12, and John believed a miracle had happened, but "they did not yet understand the Scripture, that Jesus must rise out from the dead," John 20:9.

Late on the resurrection day, about 8:00 p.m. [Westcott, 288], Jesus appeared to ten apostles, and others, Judas being dead and Thomas being absent, John 20:19. Did they then believe? They "rejoiced, having seen the Lord," but there is no positive indication they believed he was God incarnate. Eight days later Jesus again appeared to his apostles, and this time Thomas was present, John 20:26. Thomas sees Jesus and declares him to be, "My Lord and my God." All the events of the preceding three years suddenly added up for him to faith in Jesus the Christ as his God. Did the other apostles came to this same belief then, or perhaps eight days earlier? There is no positive indication they did, no indication they did not.

The same is true in John 21, when Jesus appeared to some of them at the lake in Galilee. Thomas was there, and Peter, John and James, and two who are not identified, so we know there was at least one person there, Thomas, who believed Jesus was God incarnate. Many days later Jesus appeared to the eleven in Galilee, at "the mountain which Jesus directed them. And having seen him, they worshiped; but some doubted," Matthew 28:16–17. Believing the man in front of you is deity is a difficult thing to grasp, even if he has resurrected from the dead.

At Matthew 28:19, prior to the ascension, Jesus gives the Trinitarian statement, but we do not have any comments about or from those who were present. Nor do we see any comments about or from the apostles and disciples at the ascension, as recorded in Mark 16:15–20; Luke 24:47–43; Acts 1:4–11.

At the Ascension, and on the Day of Pentecost

Did the apostles believe Jesus was deity at the ascension? Matthew's statement at 28:17 probably still applies, "they worshiped, but some doubted." They asked the Messiah about the kingdom, Acts 1:6, which supports the view some believed he was the Messiah, and some doubted he was God incarnate. But on the day of Pentecost, they were given understanding. Acts 2:33, "Therefore [the Christ] being exalted to the right hand of God." Acts 2:34, "God has made this Jesus, whom, you crucified, both Lord and Christ." Peter makes the same claim Jesus did at his trial, "you will see the son of man sitting at the right hand of the Power," Matthew 26:64. The Holy Spirit had come in power and given them understanding.

Jesus the Christ is the God-man

I have addressed selected scriptures to show that during Jesus' earthly ministry, the apostles did not understand this man, Jesus of Nazareth, whom they came to believe was the Christ, was also God incarnate. I have shown that the fallen angels did not realize Jesus the Christ was God the Son incarnate. Nor his family, nor his enemies.

We must be clear their disbelief was not because Jesus was reluctant or hesitant to reveal his deity (see below). But why did they not believe? There were those who naturally lacked the spiritual perception, 1 Corinthians 2:14, to comprehend God could

Appendix: Who Knew Jesus Was Deity

and did become incarnate, because they lacked faith in Jesus as the Messiah. In those who did have faith Jesus was the Messiah, the Holy Spirit withheld their understanding of Jesus as the God-man.

I believe the Holy Spirit withheld understanding so Jesus the Christ could interact with his apostles and disciples as a normal human being. There is a holy fear when you believe God is standing in front of you, e.g., John 21:12. Although Jesus the Christ is clearly the God-man, and gave clear and sufficient evidence he was the God-man, it is just as clear he lived his life in complete dependence upon and submission to God as a Spirit-filled man. His life set the pattern for every believer. Believers are not to ask, "What would Jesus do?" because no believer has the same mission, nor the spiritual empowerment (every spiritual gift) that Jesus was given, to do what Jesus did. The believer is to walk with Jesus daily, in that same attitude of submission to and dependence upon God that characterized Jesus' life on the earth.

Jesus did reveal his deity. In every miracle Jesus revealed his deity; but they believed God had given great power and authority to a prophet, who might be (and some came to believe) was the Messiah.

In John 5, Jesus reveals his deity.

John 5:17, My Father is working up to the present moment, and I am working.

The Hebrew scholars had asked themselves, "If God keeps the universe running on the Sabbath, is God violating the Sabbath day by working on the Sabbath?" No. The Jews rationalized their law by recognizing the entire universe as God's domain. Therefore, in working on the Sabbath God did not break their Sabbath rules; but for anyone else work on the Sabbath was a religious and civil violation. Thus the enormity of Jesus' declaration: if Jesus had the authority to work when the Father worked, then Jesus was equal to the Father. But the Hebrews rejected Jesus' claim, "because he not only was breaking the Sabbath, but also he called God his own father, making himself equal with God."

Jesus claimed to be increate. John 5:26, "For as the Father has life in himself, so also to the Son he gave life, to have in himself." Only God is eternal (without beginning or ending), and only God has life-in-himself (self-existent, Exodus 3:14, "I exist because I exist"). The Father has granted the Son to have life-in-himself. Does this mean there was a time when the Son did not have life-in-himself, but now the Father has given him life-in-himself? Or perhaps Jesus meant that his incarnate self was granted life-in-himself by the Father. No. John clearly states that God the Son always had life-in-himself, John 1:4, "in him was life." When Jesus the Christ made this claim at John 5:26 he was claiming deity.

Jesus claimed, John 10:30, "I and my Father are one." The word translated "one" is the neuter *hen* not the masculine *heis*. Jesus and his Father are not one person, as the masculine would imply (else Jesus could not pray to the Father, or act in obedience to the Father, or be able to say, "I and my Father."). What is asserted is not identity but unity. Because of their essential deity unity they are one in the action of preserving the sheep. The neuter *hen* might lead some to believe the Father and Son are only one in purpose and action, a union of persons, not a unity of persons. But the Jews understood Jesus to be saying he and the Father were a unity of essence, 10:33, "You, being a man, make yourself God." They didn't believe him, but they understood his claim.

Application of this Doctrine

The views expressed in this appendix honor the scriptures as the accurate, authentic, and therefore credible record of all that was said and done—in a word, inspiration. One applies the inspiration of the Scripture by understanding the words in the plain and normal sense of their meaning—the Literal hermeneutic. Using the analyses methods of the Literal hermeneutic one arrives at an accurate interpretation—the historical-cultural, contextual, lexical-syntactical, theological, literary, and doctrinal analysis of the Scripture.

By properly using the Literal hermeneutic, performing all the required analysis, the interpreter avoids two errors. The first is the one mentioned at the beginning of this article: preaching Reformed traditions. The Reformed traditional interpretations that "discover" (meaning "insert") Christ into every Old Testament Scripture bleeds over into the New Testament interpretation that "discovers" the apostles and disciples knew the Christ was God incarnate. The conflict that view sets up is unbearable. If, as proposed, the apostles knew Jesus was God incarnate, then why did Peter rebuke the God-man for announcing his death? Why did Judas betray the

Appendix: Who Knew Jesus Was Deity

God-man? Why did all but John abandon the God-man at the crucifixion? Why did the eleven hide in fear after the crucifixion? Why did "some doubt," after the resurrection, Matthew 27:17? We come away believing the apostles were faithless men, not true to their convictions, and thereby justify our own lack of faith.

Better is the view expressed in this appendix.. When we see the apostles as men of faith beset with the weaknesses that trouble every believer, our faith is encouraged and strengthened. They persevered. So too every believer is able to persevere.

The second error is even more pernicious: adding to the gospel of salvation. The gospel of salvation is simple volitional faith in God's testimony concerning ourselves as sinners and the risen Christ as Savior. Nothing else is required. But some want to add to the gospel, by making belief in Christ as deity necessary to saving faith. The apostles were saved without understanding Christ was deity.

We see their salvation in the spiritual perception given to them by the Holy Spirit. One sample should suffice, John 6:68–69, spoken by Peter after the feeding of the 5,000. Jesus had forced a crisis of faith. He had accused those who sought him after that event of seeking not him, but what he could give him—prizing the gift more than the giver. Some of those following Christ responded to this crisis negatively, they "turned back and no longer walked with him." Jesus asked the twelve, "Do you also desire to go away?" Peter gave the response of a saved man, "Master, to whom will we go? You have the words of eternal life. And we have believed and have known that you are the holy one of God." Not, "you are the holy God," but, "you are the holy one of God," exactly as the Scripture testifies: the *māshîah*, the *christós*, is the son of the living God, Psalm 2:7.

Conclusion

How one interprets Scripture is critical. The Literal hermeneutic requires a complete consistency in the interpretation of Old Testament and New Testament revelation: the primary meaning of a passage is in that passage. We dare not impose the knowledge given in the New Testament revelation onto the understanding of the Old Testament peoples. We dare not "reinterpret or transcend Old Testament passages in a way that overrides or cancels the original authorial intent of the Old Testament writers" [Vlach, 31].

Appendix: Who Knew Jesus Was Deity

To even suggest the Old Testament peoples had the knowledge available only in the New Testament revelation is to teach extra-biblical revelation in Old Testament times—the four gospels are Old Testament times, a form of Old Testament historical narrative. Surely we want to avoid the Reformed hermeneutical error of putting New Testament revelation into the minds of the Old Testament peoples.

During the time of Jesus' earthly ministry, the apostles did not understand Jesus was God incarnate. Their daily interactions with him argue against that understanding. A simple example. In the last few months of their third year with him (between January–March, AD 32), Jesus will go to the tomb of Lazarus. Philip will say to his fellow disciples, "Let us also go, that we might die with him." Even after almost three years, after watching all the miracles, hearing all the discourses, they still did not believe Jesus was God incarnate. That would be paganism, that would be blasphemy—under the Law of Moses that would be idolatry, giving the invisible God a material image—and therefore the thought was never entertained. The Holy Spirit withheld their understanding, as suitable to the mission of the Christ. And even today, we avoid idolatry by understanding Jesus the Christ is the God-man, and so we worship the God-man, not the man.

The apostles interacted with Jesus as a man, not as the almighty God YHWH. The man born blind and healed by Jesus expresses the understanding of all who believed Jesus was the Christ. John 9:33 (highlighting added), "If this *man* were not *from God*, he would not be able to do anything." In their understanding Jesus was a man sent from God, not a man who was God.

Sources

Alexander, Joseph Addison. *The Gospel According to Matthew.* 1860. Reprinted, Grand Rapids, MI: Baker Book House, 1980.

Bauckham, Richard. *Jesus and the Eyewitnesses, The Gospels as Eyewitness Testimony.* Grand Rapids, MI: Eerdmans Publishing, 2006.

———. *The Testimony of the Beloved Disciple.* Grand Rapids, MI: Baker Academic, 2007.

Bock, Darrell, L. *Jesus According to Scripture.* Grand Rapids, MI: Baker Academic, 2002.

———. *Jesus in Context.* Grand Rapids, MI: Baker Academic, 2005.

Bromiley, G. W., ed. *International Standard Bible Encyclopedia.* 4 vols. Rev. Grand Rapids, MI: Eerdmans Publishing, 1988.

———. Translator and Editor. *Theological Dictionary of the New Testament.* 10 vol. 1935. Reprinted, Grand Rapids, MI: Eerdmans Publishing, 1964.

Brown, Colin, ed. *The New International Dictionary of New Testament Theology.* Grand Rapids, MI: Zondervan, 1982.

Bullinger, E. W. *Number in Scripture.* 1894. Reprinted, Grand Rapids, MI: Kregel Publications, 1967.

Bruce, F. F. *The Gospel of John.* Grand Rapids, MI: Eerdmans Publishing, 1983.

Calvin, John. *Calvin's Commentaries.* Grand Rapids, MI: Baker Book House, 1996.

Carson, D. A., *Matthew.* The Expositor's Bible Commentary. Edited by Frank E. Gaebelein. Vol. 8. Grand Rapids, MI: Zondervan, 1984.

———. *The Gospel According to John.* The Pillar New Testament Commentary. Grand Rapids, MI: Eerdmans Publishing, 1991.

Chemnitz, Martin. *The Two Natures of Christ.* 1578. Reprinted, St. Louis, MO: Concordia Publishing House, 1971.

Cheney, Johnston M. *The Life of Christ in Stereo, the Four Gospels Combined as One.* Portland, OR: Western Baptist Seminary Press, 1969.

Sources

Chill, Abraham. *The Mitzvot, The Commandments and their Rationale.* Jerusalem: Keter Books, 1990.

Cox, Steven L., and Kendall H. Beasley. *Harmony of the Gospels.* Nashville, TN: Holman Bible Publishers, 2007.

Danby, Herbert. *The Mishnah.* Oxford, England: Oxford University Press, 1933.

Daniel, Orville E. *A Harmony of the Four Gospels.* 2nd ed. Grand Rapids, MI: Baker Academic, 1996.

Davis, John J. *Biblical Numerology.* Grand Rapids, MI: Baker Books, 1968.

Edersheim, Alfred. *The Temple, its Ministry and Services.* 1874. Reprinted, Hendrickson Publishers, Peabody, MA: 1994.

France, R. T. *The Gospel According to Matthew, an Introduction and Commentary.* Tyndale New Testament Commentary. Vol. 1. Grand Rapids, MI: Eerdmans Publishing, 1985.

———. *The Gospel of Matthew.* New International Commentary on the New Testament. Grand Rapids, MI: Eerdmans Publishing, 2007.

Freeman, James M. *Manners and Customs of the Bible.* Reprinted. Plainfield, NJ: Logos International, 1972.

Godet, Frederick Louis. *Commentary on the Gospel of John.* 2 vols. 1893. Reprinted, Grand Rapids, MI: Zondervan, n. d.

Hagner, Donald A. *Matthew 1–13.* Word Biblical Commentary, vol. 33a. Dallas, TX: Word Books, 1993.

———. *Matthew 14–28.* Word Biblical Commentary, vol. 33b. Dallas, TX: Word Books, 1995.

Harris, R. Laird; Gleason L. Archer, Jr.; and Bruce K. Waltke. *Theological Wordbook of the Old Testament.* 2 vols. Chicago, IL: Moody Press, 1980.

Hendrickson, William. *Exposition of the Gospel According to Matthew.* New Testament Commentary. Grand Rapids, MI: Baker Book House, 1973.

Hollingsworth, David R. and James D. Quiggle. *Old Testament and New Testament Chronology.* CreateSpace, 2015.

Holman Quick Source Bible Atlas. Nashville, TN: Holman Bible Publishers, 2005.

Josephus, Flavius. *The Works of Flavius Josephus.* Translated by

William Whiston. Philadelphia, PA: Porter and Coates, n. d.

Meeks, Wayne A. *The Moral World of the First Christians*. Philadelphia, PA: The Westminster Press, 1986.

Metzger, Bruce M. *A Textual Commentary on the Greek New Testament*. 2nd ed. Deutsche Bibelgesellschaft, D–Stuttgart, 1994.

Morris, Leon. *The Gospel According to Matthew*. The New International Commentary on the New Testament. Grand Rapids, MI: Eerdmans Publishing, 1992.

Moulton, J. H. and G. Milligan. *Vocabulary of the Greek Testament*. 1930. Reprinted, Peabody, MA: Hendrickson, 1997.

Pentecost, J. Dwight. *The Words and Works of Jesus Christ*. Grand Rapids, MI: Zondervan, 1981.

Quiggle, James D. *A Private Commentary on the Bible: 1 Peter*. CreateSpace, 2012.

———. *A Private Commentary on the Bible: Daniel*. CreateSpace, 2014.

———. *A Private Commentary on the Bible: Ephesians*. CreateSpace, 2012.

———. *A Private Commentary on the Bible: James*. CreateSpace, 2013.

———. *A Private Commentary on the Bible: John 1–12*. CreateSpace, 2014.

———. *A Private Commentary on the Bible: John 13–21*. CreateSpace, 2015.

———. *A Private Commentary on the Bible: John's Epistles*. CreateSpace, 2016.

———. *Antichrist, His Genealogy, Kingdom, and Religion*. CreateSpace, 2011.

———. *God Became Incarnate*. CreateSpace, 2014.

Ramsay, Sir William M. *Was Christ Born in Bethlehem?*. 1898. Reprinted James Family Publishing, Minneapolis MN: 1978.

Roberts, Alexander and James Donaldson. *Ante-Nicene Fathers*. Vol 1. *The Apostolic Fathers, Justin Martyr, Irenaeus*. 1885, Reprinted Peabody, MA: Hendrickson, 1994.

———. *Ante-Nicene Fathers*. Vol 5. *Hyppolytus, Cyprian, Caius, Novatian, Appendix*. 1885, Reprinted Peabody, MA:

Hendrickson, 1994.

Robertson, A. T. *Matthew, Mark.* Word Pictures in the New Testament. Vol. 1. Nashville, TN: Broadman Press, 1932.

Ryrie, Charles C. *Dispensationalism.* Chicago, IL: Moody Press, 1995.

Schaff, Philip, and Henry Wace. *Nicene and Post-Nicene Fathers, Second Series.* Vol. 1. *Eusebius: Church History, Life of Constantine the Great, and Oration in Praise of Constantine.* 1890. Reprinted, Peabody, MA: Hendrickson, 1999.

Strong, James. *The Exhaustive Concordance of the Bible.* McLean, VA: Macdonald Publishing Co., n. d.

Trench, Richard C. *Notes on the Parables of Our Lord.* Old Tappen, NJ: Fleming H. Revell, 1953.

Waldron, *MacArthur's Millennial Manifesto, A Friendly Response.* Owensburg, KY: Reformed Baptist Academic Press, 2008.

Westcott, B. F. *The Gospel According to John.* 1881. Reprinted, Grand Rapids, MI: Eerdmans Publishing, 1978.

Wight, Fred H. *Manners and Customs of Bible Lands.* Chicago, IL: Moody Press, 1953, reprinted 1980.

Wilson, William. *Wilson's Old Testament Word Studies.* Mclean, VA: Macdonald Publishing Co., n. d.

Zodhiates, Spiros. *The Complete Word Study Dictionary New Testament.* Rev. Chattanooga, TN: AMG Publishers, 1993.

www.ingramcontent.com/pod-product-compliance
Lightning Source LLC
Chambersburg PA
CBHW050518100526

44581CB00001B/23